Leisure in Different Worlds

Vol. 2

Leisure in Industrial and Post-industrial Societies

Edited by Mike Collins

LSA Publication No. 49

First published in 1996 by
Leisure Studies Association

A catalogue record for this book is available from the British Library.

ISBN: 0 906337 53 4

Layout design and typesetting by Myrene L. McFee
Reproduction by University of Brighton
Binding by Kensett Ltd., Hove (UK)

Contents

Leisure in Industrial and Post-Industrial Societies: Editor's Introduction

Mike Collins

Loughborough University, UK

This is the second of three themed volumes which have been developed from work originally presented at the Leisure Studies Association's third International Conference — "Leisure in Different Worlds", held in Loughborough in July 1993. Volume 1 (edited by Ian Henry) is *Modernity, Postmodernity and Lifestyles* (LSA Publication No. 48 [1995]: ISBN 0 906337 52 6); Volume 3 (edited by Guy Jackson) is *Leisure, Tourism and the Environment* (LSA Publication No. 50 [ISBN 0 906337 xx x [forthcoming in 1996]). Other work originating from the conference has been published in the Association's Journal *Leisure Studies*, Vol. 13, No. 3.

The conference sought to reveal the variety of forms, practices, structures and organisation of leisure in different parts of our contemporary world and over recent history, and that is what the wide-ranging papers in this volume represent.

I Leisure in Industrial Societies

Part I of this volume examines leisure in the industrial phase of human society. Britain led Europe into the machine and factory manufacturing age, and is arguably also leading the world into the post industrial phase. **Booth** shows how the very wealthy Lowther family in 19th century Cumbria enjoyed their sport, especially horse racing and hunting but exercised both patronage and hegemony over that of the villagers (in fell running and wrestling) while encouraging and participating in bourgeois (e.g. cricket) and social activities. **Jarvie**'s account of the life of John Murdoch, draper, excise officer, councillor and shinty player in southern Scotland, on the other hand, is one of radical criticism, resistance and attempts to reform the control of landlords and monied interests over ordinary people's lives.

In countries where primary and manufacturing industry is still dominant, there are influences analogous to those western Europe has passed through, and of contemporary, transnational, post-industrial trends. **Nassis** shows how strong an influence party politics after the military dictatorship has on central and local government leisure policies in Greece, with an increasing reliance on sponsorship and commercial provision; more recently Kontovas (1995) has shown how the most embryo of sports management professions is strengthening this tendency because most of those with any management training have gained that in the USA. Also in Greece, **Papadimitriou and Taylor** analyse the perceptions of six groups — scientific counsellors, national coaches and team members, international officials, Federation board members, and paid officials — on what makes for an effective national sports federation.

Sadar describes how the struggle to change from a communist command economy has reduced the participation in holidays, increased TV watching and sustained interest in gardening, but had not, by 1993, cut the participation in sport and its support, as widely reported by Krawcyk (1996 forthcoming) for Eastern Europe generally. **Grobler** shows how sport was a vehicle for anti-apartheid groups and political factions as well as a beneficiary of apartheid's abolition, and yet until very recently sport for black schools and communities was systematically underfunded, and the unwillingness of experienced white sports administrators to open up opportunities for blacks has lead to their widespread replacement in organisations, but with black people who have consequently little experience.

Myotin demonstrates that many of the features of young women's sport in Western societies are reproduced in Brazil; female stereotypes and lack of time are associated with not playing; health and body image concerns are linked with much activity; and the fact that volleyball is more popular than either keep-fit or swimming can be linked to TV coverage.

Japan is in many ways compressing a century and a half of social and economic change into a few decades. In the first of two papers on leisure in postwar Japan, **Uchiumi** shows how for a long time sport was available only to the affluent; the 1962 Olympics proved a spur to a Sports Act and a reconstituted Bureau for Physical Education. Nevertheless, apart from a few years in the 1980s, government investment in facilities and programmes for Sport for All has lagged behind desire to take part. Thus, the private sector plays a major role, and is expected to grow from 5% of facilities in 1989 to 24% in 2000AD. **Ozaki** describes the growth of commercial sport to US$52bn in 1991-92, especially in the form of 10 pin bowling alleys, tennis courts, golf ranges and courses; as in many countries, there was a slump after the oil price shocks, but another boom is occurring, in fitness centres. One feature of post-industrial society that Japan has not yet faced is leisure for the growing numbers of older people; from having 11 workers to every pensioner in the 1960s, like most of the OECD nations, Japan will have fewer than 3 in 2020 (Ermisch, 1989).

The two final papers in Part I show sport as a vehicle for helping change and itself being changed in the process. The Commonwealth provides a world forum for small republics, and a stage for some of the larger to take a world lead e.g. for Canada in anti-doping and anti-apartheid actions and lobbying. **Houlihan**'s paper clearly shows how, while sport has played its part in keeping the Commonwealth alive as a meaningful grouping, the nature of the Commonwealth Games is being transformed. It had been hoped that, compared with the Olympics, "the Games will be very different, free from both the excessive stimulus and babel of the international stadium. They should be merrier and less stern", but they have been, as a global event, prey to the same pressures of TV and sponsorship as the Olympics and World championships, albeit less fiercely. At the same time, as the Communist bloc has exploded and sunk, the Commonwealth adapts to face the 21st century.

Gratton argues that the internationalisation — indeed the globalisation of leisure service companies — is a special case, because leisure meets stimulation-seeking needs rather than basic ones, which are not therefore so limited by a saturation level as manufactured products. He illustrates two sorts of growth. The first is fuelled by the development of a worldwide demand for a product which started nationally; he exemplifies this by Nike which now sells 90 million pairs of shoes for a turnover of US$3.5bn. The second is a diversification across leisure products to reduce the risks of roller coaster rises and falls in demand, and his examples are Rank Xerox and Disney.

II Leisure in Post-industrial Societies

In part II we have 10 papers that examine current trends and pressures in the highly structured British leisure system at a time of marked political engineering, 4 from other countries and 2 concerned with studying contemporary leisure.

The British leisure system had highly developed public, voluntary and commercial sectors (Collins, 1990), but a series of Conservative governments have set about restraining if not drastically reducing the public sector and subjecting it to forms of management and operation taken, often with little thought or tailoring, from private sector manufacturing and financial services, and encouraging the growth of the second and third sectors. This has altered the structures and policies of public agencies, especially local authorities, and changed their relations with voluntary and commercial providers.

Theodoraki and Henry use techniques pioneered by Canadian researchers to classify the structures of 45 UK Governing Bodies of Sport. They discover six clusters, four of which are variants of Mintzberg's simple structures. Although the requirements of accountability for Sports Council grant in aid has led to some formalisation of procedures and application of specialist skills, it has not lead to such *dirigiste* planning methods and organisation as was demanded by Sport Canada. Interestingly, women feature more in the upper ranks of simple organisations where volunteers have a greater say, than in more complex structures where a stronger role is played by professionals and where more women appear amongst 'the rank and file' grades. **Taylor** examines how customers and information brokers used the information services of a national consortium of UK sports information providers, who offer many services freely or cheaply. Many users were poorly informed about what was available or how to access it, and so many of them did not take the optimum time needed to perform complex searches. The subsidy was therefore partly ineffective. He concludes that some improvement in reducing overlaps and search costs was needed, but also that promotion targeted at certain users or brokers is needed to increase use; charging for what was now cheap or free would be resisted unless such improvements were undertaken.

Long looks for signs of devolution in UK leisure services but the Regional Tourist Boards are more advice and consultancy agencies than branches of the ETB; the Regional Arts Associations have had some small growth of autonomy in distributing local grants from the Arts Council; since the White Paper *Sport: Raising the Game* (DNH, 1995), the Regional offices of the Sports Council were ordered not to go on servicing the Regional Councils for Sport and Recreation through which it had had much influence on local government policy and spending. In 1991 Dearlove and Saunders had said that the future for regional government was to either properly democratise it or to privatise it, and Long concludes, under Conservative rule the latter seems far more likely.

A clutch of papers look at the challenges facing local authorities when the philosophy has been ideologically or practically to 'roll back the state'. **Ravenscroft and Tolley** examine how they have reacted to the requirement to put their leisure management out to competitive tendering; some comply with the authority of the market, others pragmatically accept CCT as inevitable, while using various tactics to control the process. This has worked out in a political economy where a minority of New Right authorities are pro private contractors or management buy-outs, and a majority of Centre-Left authorities which support the Direct Service Organisations. Nevertheless, the process has only very marginally increased competition, and most operations are effectively public monopolies.

Abrams argues that this imposed change has only occasionally been internalised, most often resisted, with traditional hierarchical structures and bureaucratic procedures re-emerging in half-hidden ways.

The partner of CCT has been to emphasise quality of product and service to customers and citizens. **Stabler** looks at theoretical ways to operationalise this idea, and practically suggests wider use of customer satisfaction surveys using rating or ranking methods, or even expert (Delphi) panels to assess scenarios, and to assess willingness to pay through Contingent Valuation or Hedonic Pricing techniques. **Lentell** is of the opinion that the work of the watchdog on public spending, the Audit Commission, has been neglected in the way it seeks to get professional managers to comply with improving efficiency and effectiveness, but the weak, partial and mechanistic nature of the Performance Indicators it has chosen are not appropriate to public services of the plastic nature of leisure, and not representing the customer's real interests in having a fulfilling experience at a price that is reasonable.

The other two British papers are of a different nature, and investigate particular aspects. **Tsuchiya** examines four of a growing number of projects that unashamedly use leisure as part of a portfolio of activities to help young offenders to change their behaviour and attitudes to society and to crime; even though evaluations are unsatisfactory and partial, he argues the data suggests that such schemes are at least as effective in reducing recidivism as custodial care, and certainly much cheaper. **Whannel** paints a picture of how the peculiar economics of television allows Channel 4 to bring American football, Australian Rules Football, Sumo wrestling and Italian league football into British homes cheaper than it can broadcast domestic minority sports. Nevertheless, this channel has carefully educated an audience in "exotic' imports. Yet satellite-carried sport, dominated by the buying power of American TV networks and the Murdoch media conglomerate, may (as shown by the Sky deal in November 1995 for Football League soccer) mean that live sport becomes very much the prerogative of 'narrow- cast' subscription audiences.

Turning to other parts of the world, **Bammel and Burrus Bammel** argue that volunteering has grown to be essential even to government, and become a vital part of lifestyle. Using a sample of their Park and Recreation major students who undertook a 10 week, 30 hour placement, they show how it had proved a worthwhile effort for almost all of them, and for some, even a life-changing one. **Parker**, using a sample of older Australians, shows how five of the six characteristics of 'serious leisure' identified by Stebbins (1992) — effort, perseverance, tangible benefits and developing an identity — are associated with the values of middle class people. He contends, however that it is not necessary to have the potential for a 'career' in terms of skill levels leading almost to professionalism; enjoyment is sufficient reward.

Te Kloeze analyses in considerable detail the Dutch literature on leisure and the family, showing how a wider variety of styles is developing, with some emancipation for women, some more independent activity for children, partly beguiled by what commerce offers them, but still a substantial legacy for most families of traditional homemaking and caring roles.

Kikulis, Slack and Hinings take di Maggio's and Zucker's earlier ideas about how organisations adapt to an institutional environment and pressure from powerful (in this case Canadian federal government) interests. They show how, despite adapting to an 'approved' organisational structure and appointing professionals within voluntary structures, the national sports bodies resisted ceding organisational control to these professionals, retaining the amateur culture from which they were born, while acceding to the federal plan to focus on developing excellence. Interestingly, since that time and the review of its support for sport after the shock of the Dubin inquiry into Michael Johnson's doping, the government has decided it could only afford to focus on a smaller 'core' of sports; but after a new party came to power, the policy is to support Sport for All more strongly and to make efforts to redress inequalities associated with gender, ethnic group and income. The British sports minister visited Canada during his policy review in 1994 and took away the ideas for focus sports and concentrating on excellence, combined them with copying a central national Sports Institute from Australia (just as that country was developing more accessible state and city centres of excellence), and enacted these ideas in a White Paper, *Sport: Raising the Game*, just as Canada and Australia were moving towards established British ways of regarding the sports development continuum!

The last two contributions look more widely at studying leisure in post-industrial societies. **Aitchison** looks at positivistic, humanistic and structuralist approaches in studies of sport and recreation, leisure and tourism, and contends that all three types should be used in extending beyond the present stage of collating data from single-nation studies. **Veal and Cushman** show how the more recent generation of national leisure surveys have begun to obtain more valid and reliable responses, to seek qualitative answers, and to demonstrate a consistency of findings that encourages more confidence in their findings. They also look more than hitherto at home-based leisure and at new forms like leisure shopping.

Conclusion

These 26 papers by 32 authors — 23 male and 9 female, 19 British citizens or workers and 13 from other places — show something of the variety of issues and styles facing leisure researchers; another conference with the same objective in 2003 or 2013 will, despite trends of globalisation, also demonstrate geographically and culturally specific innovations, adaptations and resistances to sameness or subservience, for leisure is as plastic and as diverse as humanity and its creativity; hence its fascination and its challenge as a field of study. As it continues to grow in importance in more of the lives of citizens of Lifeboat Earth, however, the paraphernalia of structures and procedures, both public and private, are sure to grow, and to interest more of the scientific disciplines, including some which are only just becoming aware of leisure as a fruitful field of study — e.g. political science and organisational studies.

References

Dearlove, J. and Saunders, P. (1991) *An introduction to British politics.* Cambridge: Polity Press.

Department of National Heritage (1995) *Sport: Raising the game.* London: The Department.

Ermisch, J. (1989) *Fewer babies, longer lives.* York: Joseph Rowntree Foundation.

Kontovas, E. (1995) *Is there a Sports Management Profession in Greece?.* Unpublished MSc dissertation. Loughborough: The University.

Krawcyk, Z.(1996 forthcoming) 'Images of Sport in Eastern Europe', in proceedings of *Images of Sport in the World* conference. Cologne: German Federal Sports Institute.

Stebbins, R. (1992) *Amateurs, professionals, and serious leisure.* Montreal: McGill University Press.

I.

Leisure in Industrial Societies, Past and Present

Autonomous Sport or Politico-Economic Tool? The Case of the Lowther Family in Cumbria 1807–1908

Bernard F. Booth

University of Ottawa, Ontario, Canada

Introduction

While there has been a great deal of scholarly work written on rational recreation as a means of controlling the working classes, there has been little published on the role of leisure in the North-West of England as a means of social control (Bailey, 1978; Marshall and Walton, 1981; Murfin, 1990). Various arguments have been advanced by scholars on the value of hegemony theory as a means of assessing the process of social control (Gruneau, 1983). Hegemony theory is viewed as a process whereby accommodation is achieved between two opposing parties. Alliances are formed in order to overcome obstacles and achieve what some scholars have referred to as "common sense" solutions (Hargreaves, 1986). This paper examines the correspondence and sporting records of the Lowther Collection housed at the Cumbrian Record Office in Carlisle in order to assess whether sport was simply an autonomous activity that provided fun for the rich, or whether it was perceived as having political and social value. Hegemonic theory is used to assess the role of gentry sport — the kind of alliances formed, levels of accommodation between commoners' sport and gentry control, for example. One important question to be answered is, to what extent was the meaning of popular leisure transformed in nineteenth century Cumbria?

The correspondence of five earls is studied over the period 1807–1908. The period is divided as follows: First Earl 1807–44; Second Earl 1844–72; Third Earl 1872–76; Fourth Earl 1876–82; Fifth Earl 1882–1944. The records of the last Earl, with exception of a few letters and the horse-registers, have yet to be examined.

The periods under study are interesting, because they almost parallel the periods examined by leisure historians. The first period is one of social dislocation and reform credited with heralding the *raison d'etre* for rational recreation. The middle classes were afraid of the Chartists and so they were determined to control the leisure of the working classes. Hence the period coincides with the Lowthers taking an active part in developing the Jockey Club as an exclusive social club while maintaining apparently easy relationships with rural Cumbria.

The period of the Second Earl coincides with the beginnings of the rational recreation movement and seems to illustrate the Lowthers' promotion of middle class values in certain sports but their bias for field sports is apparent. Sport as a business is clearly evident in this second period and it continues to be so throughout the period under study. However, the fun of sport is clearly evident, and becomes very apparent in the case of the Fifth Earl whose business interests in racing help to cover his debts.

From a hegemonic perspective the paper will try to show that the Lowthers were active in the development of sport as an autonomous institution for their own benefit but that sport did not remain an autonomous unit since it had spin-offs into the politics of social reform, into the politics of rural deference and, finally, into the accommodation of gentry to populist sports via rational recreation.

1807–1844

The First Earl was the Lord Lieutenant of the county and its largest landowner with power to select nine Members of Parliament, at least until the 1832 Reform Act. He approved appointments to livings in Church of England parishes situated on his land. Only the Duke of Devonshire was wealthier. The Lonsdale estate provided an income of over £100,000 a year which was a very considerable sum for that period. A large part of Lowther income ultimately came from the Port of Whitehaven, from the Hodbarrow mines at Millom and from other mining properties along the west coast of Cumbria. He was educated at one of the older Public Schools and Trinity College, Cambridge. Letters of the First Earl demonstrate a wide social circle of friends and acquaintances in the foreign service, the armed forces, British Conservative politics and the University of Cambridge. I saw no letters to the clergy among this collection.

The sporting focal point of the correspondence was horse-racing and allied interests, in particular, the development of Newmarket and the Jockey Club, which underwent a great deal of restructuring during this first period in order to cater to the demands for social exclusivity by its membership. Interestingly, the development of social exclusivism dates, in the correspondence, from as early as 1807. Lowther Castle, the home of the Lowthers, was thought to have been built circa 1807 and it was described in the correspondence as "the nerve centre of Cumbria; a kind of neo-medieval shoulder padding against damn radicalism"[1]. The correspondence on Newmarket, the headquarters of the Jockey Club, carries on in the same vein. In 1830 plans were drawn up for club rooms at Newmarket which were designated "the nerve centre of racing". The plans show a billiard room, a card room and a dining room[2]. Much of the correspondence on Newmarket and the Jockey Club deals with questions of protocol and, in particular, about gambling. A series of letters with Lord Wharncliffe pursues the question of nullifying a bet[3].

The social context of this period is vexing with respect to sharpening its meaning. Leisure historians have examined the meaning behind the social change of this period marked by the Luddite riots and followed by the appearance of Chartism with its sinister implications for reform. The 1832 Reform Bill, added to the gospel of the social reformers of the day, notably Cobbett and Chadwick, served notice on the power brokers of the day that change was imminent. The correspondence illustrates that the Lowthers had no doubts about the evils of damn radicalism. Consequently, the development of the Newmarket premises and Jockey Club rules in order to standardise racing, when placed within the context of what was termed "damn radicalism", appears to have been a systematic attempt to exercise hegemony not only within the autonomous context of racing but, through powerful social networking, within the wider realm of politics.

Prior to 1839, the date when cockfighting was outlawed, gentry and commoners attended carnival occasions together. One Furness diarist of 1813 describes how gentry and commoners attended a county cockfighting main in Ulverston[4]. Later reports, after the outlawing of this blood sport, illustrate that the sport continued, and continues even today, although without the easy mingling of earlier times. Wrestling illustrates some indication of the growth of commoner hegemony during this first period. It appears that wrestling benefited indirectly from the Enclosure acts of 1774 and 1801 initially, and later in 1836 and 1845 because the Acts had the effect of localising farming and making it more scientific, particularly with reference to sheep farming (Ward, 1985). Better quality sheep created a market for sheep and a need for young people to work on the farms. Consequently, seasonal hiring fairs at places like Ulverston developed. It was at these fairs that populist competitive sports are thought to have emerged. Wrestling competition was probably a by-product of these fairs.

I have been told how it was considered necessary for school leavers in the Ulverston area to work on a farm in order to relieve family overcrowding. Good relations existed between the Lowthers and their tenant farmers.

Usually the individual who was granted land to farm was known and approved by the gentry concerned. Hence, wrestling, a farming sport, was not perceived as being a threat to the hegemony of the gentry who provided prize money and food. Gradually the sheep fairs were replaced by small race meetings with wrestling matches initially continuing as a side-show. Gradually, however, wrestling grew in popularity to the extent that it was being reported in the press as more popular than racing. However, it should be noted that the gentry homes in Cumbria, notably at Greystoke, home of the Howards, Melmerby and Langwathby, and Lowther had held competitions in wrestling, although with a few exceptions, the gentry did not compete against commoners (Murfin, 1990, p107).

The hegemonic significance of wrestling was that it was able to develop a folklore of its own that the socially distant sport of horse-racing could not. The commoners, through wrestling, were able to celebrate themselves through their own local village heroes. Wrestling was not dependent upon gentry patronage to the extent that local horse-racing was, and by 1843 it had emerged as a populist sport in its own right at the Ulverston Flan sports.

What was significant about this first period was that social reform was in the air and the gentry, personified in the Lowthers, were taking steps to enhance their own hegemony over the sport of horse-racing while continuing to mix, at local race meetings, with commoners. Scientific progress in farming, aided by the Enclosure Acts, while depriving many of the commoners of land usage, did create a demand for farm-workers which in turn helped to develop local sports. Wrestling, in particular, by 1843 was assuming its own hegemony, to which the gentry ultimately accommodated through their patronage of the Grasmere Sports. In contradistinction to the Lowthers' practice with the Jockey Club, the year 1823 provides evidence of the emergence of business acumen directed at the Yorkshire *nouveau riche*. Whereas Lowther's work with the Jockey Club focused entirely on the interests of his own social class, his game record book indicates that he was beginning to lease land on his estate for week-end shooting to Yorkshire woollen merchants (see **Table 1**).

1844–1872

Correspondence illustrates a more business-based approach to sport coupled with a foray into the domain of popular sport. While the First Earl had begun to keep records of game shot and horses bought, it is the Second Earl whose correspondence illustrates a greater commitment to new sporting organisations.

Table 1 Lowther Estate: game killed up to November in 1823

	By Gentlemen	By Keepers
Grouse	715	95
Partridge	315	219
Pheasant	93	20
Hares	130	95
Snipe	9	48
Rabbits	4	38

Source: Lowther game Book L6/1: Game Shooting, C.R.O., Cumbria.

However, a secondary common theme running through the correspondence is one of concern for the benefits of the Enclosure Acts. The earliest correspondence dates from the mid-1850s when he states his interest in punishing poachers. A later letter signifies his determination to enclose, "without interference from the commoners"[5]. The explanation is that this measure would promote the shooting of game and the sport of hare-coursing. One letter from a John Gill of Brampton requests 60-100 hares from the Earl for coursing. The Earl complies[6]. In 1836 a letter from the First Earl had proposed a gold cup for hare-coursing[7]. The Enclosure Acts undoubtedly would have increased the profitability of hare-coursing by protecting the formerly wild game which could now be sold to coursing clubs. By 1863 the Earl had agreed to greyhound racing on Knipe-Scar[8] and by 1869 he had instituted a system for game management at Lowther Park[9]. While the Earl does appear to be accommodating popular interest in coursing and trailing much of his correspondence does concern the policing of the Enclosure Acts[10].

The sport of wrestling continued to develop at Ulverston without any evidence of gentry patronage. There are no references in the correspondence to the rise of Flan Sports while reference is made to the Grasmere Sports. The Flan Sports appear to have been founded circa 1843 by its municipality. The town of Ulverston was mentioned in the Fleming diaries for organising county cockfighting mains between Lancashire and Cumberland. Consequently there was a tradition of competitive sport pre-dating Flan. Hence, it is not surprising that by 1845 Ulverston was still attracting large numbers of spectators without gentry patronage. Wrestling and other events were publicised in *Bell's Life* and the Lowther correspondence provides proof that they did subscribe to *Bell's Life*[11]. Consequently it seems likely that they would be aware of the great popularity of the Flan Sports.

The Lowther correspondence is sometimes addressed from Carlton Place in London and at other times from the Lowther estate, indicating perhaps that the management of the estates is left to others. For example, the Hon. William Lowther appears to be managing the estate while his uncle resides in London. The Earl appears to have health problems as many of his letters continually describe his respiratory troubles. During this period some cricket was being introduced into Cumbria. It was a largely middle class affair imported by the products of public schools. There is no evidence of works teams beginning until the 1870s. Hence, while Lonsdale was generous enough to grant land by the Eden for the formation of the Whitehaven Cricket Club it may not indicate any great drive for hegemony. At this time prior to the industrialising of Cumbria it was common for the gentry to play cricket with the villagers. An example would be the Cavendishes who frequently played with the Cartmel villagers.

1872–1876

The Third Earl was named Henry Lowther and was educated at Westminster and Trinity, Cambridge. In 1847 he became the Conservative Member of Parliament for West Cumberland where he remained until 1872. He appears to have been a large man described as rather ferocious in looks but not unkind. His stated primary interests were hunting and horse-riding. He owned the Cottesmore hounds at Melton Mowbray in Leicestershire from 1870 to 1876 when he died in Whitehaven Castle.

The letters of the Third Earl are concerned largely with requests for donations, requests for sport patronage by clubs and associations and for shooting rights. Some of the correspondence deals with legal argument over rights to land adjoining Lake Windermere. Other correspondence concerns a dispute over mineral rights illustrating the growing value of land as a source of income from tourism and industrialisation. The majority of the correspondence, however, concerns horse-racing, horse breeding and hunting.

It is interesting to note who the recipients of Lowther donations were. Field sport associations were usually funded but the Kendal Cricket Club, founded in the 1850s, was unsuccessful on the basis that "they ought to be self-supporting by now". A donation for £50 was made to the new public school, St. Bees, while the trustees of the Wesleyan Methodist Sabbath school were refused land for a school because "the tendency of these chapel people is decidedly radical[12]. A request from the committee of the Kendal Industrial and Fine Arts Exhibition composed of members of the Working Men's Club received a donation because the Earl was "deeply impressed with the sense of the utility and importance of such exhibitions"[13]. The Earl appears to have been selective in his funding policy on the basis of the perceived threat or merit of the organisation concerned. The Wesleyans were perceived as a radical threat, whereas the workingmen's exhibition was not. The cricket club had been in existence for 20 years and consequently being a middle class organisation was thought neither to need patronage nor to pose a threat.

There is no doubt regarding the Earl's support for the hunt. He donated three guineas to the Carlisle Otter Hounds and recommended that the subscription be increased to five guineas. This organisation had a tradesman's history, having been founded by a butcher and a miller. As subscription packs of otterhounds were formed, the Earl usually became an honorary member. Interestingly, these packs tended to be urban in composition rather than rural and to be largely working class. It appears therefore that the Earl had no objections to the respectable working class participating in hunting activities which had been by tradition a gentry prerogative.

Lonsdale support for wrestling at the Grasmere Sports dates from 1873 when he was petitioned to become president of the games (Vamplew, 1988). The Lonsdales remained patrons of the Grasmere Sports through the period of this study. The Grasmere Sports developed through gentry support after being established at a public house. With the advent of gentry patronage it became a place 'to see and to be seen'. Winning wrestlers were presented to visiting dignitaries and in some cases received the tenancy of a public house on gentry land. In contrast, by 1885 the Ulverston Flan Sports, when Grasmere was at its peak, had become extinct. Interestingly, Grasmere, as the Flan Sports previously had done, was awarding cash prizes for fell racing, hound trailing and wrestling. All of these activities had their roots in rural sport. They were now receiving full gentry recognition. Perhaps it can be argued that Grasmere Sports represented a minimum level of accommodation between gentry and commoner. The gentry had another opportunity to demonstrate their social position by accommodating and perhaps even forming an alliance with populist sport with cash prizes.

1876–1882

The Fourth Earl does not merit discussion as he died at aged about 25, and apart from some interest in yachting, demonstrated no interest in sport.

1882–1908

The Fifth Earl died in 1944 but his records, largely the horse registers, only go as far as 1908. He became known as a great sportsman possessing great riding prowess. He was a man who described himself as "loving to be in at the kill" of the hunt. He is reputed never to miss the opportunity for a challenge. For example, legend has it that he competed with a professional long distance walker on a 100 mile walk along the Great North Road. He was also a great traveller. There are stories of his exploits in Wyoming, USA.

The horse registers document the money spent on the purchase of horses or realised from offering them. Prize money rose significantly between 1802 and 1910 and the demand for thoroughbred horses also rose[14]. Between 1880 and 1910 the Lonsdale estate made a profit of over £63,000. This seems to be a significant profit when the estimate for the average prize money during that period of time ranged from £132 to £16[15]. Horse breeding and selling appeared therefore to be a more lucrative business than the actual winning of races (see **Table 2**).

Horse-racing itself appears to have been more for fun than for profit. The Lowther correspondence indicates a friendly rivalry with other gentry. One letter illustrates the fun of racing horses from their own stable at small races where the prizes would also be small. A letter to the Duke of Rutland, the winner of the Queen's Plate at Chester, made reference to its being "a bay colt raised at Lowther", and further, "I hope it will win me some more little races"[16] . The same correspondence made fond references to a mare named Marmite and her foal, presumably as a good prospect. The introduction of new Jockey Club rules from 1882 corresponded with evidence of increased business interests of the Fifth Earl with respect to horse-racing and breeding. The new rules required the enclosure of all horse-racing courses and the charging of an entrance fee which was to be used to increase the prize money. Consequently an incentive was created for improving of horse breeding. The introduction of enclosed courses led to the demise of the smaller race-courses in Cumbria. Carlisle was enclosed in 1884. Cartmel continued to this day but as a point-to-point race, usually at Whitsuntide. Consequently it can be argued that the Lowthers have exercised their hegemony over the sport of racing and gained financially from it.

The correspondence shows that the new money the Fifth Earl obtained from horse breeding helped to offset his losses when the Millom Hodbarrow mines failed at the turn of the century. He was able to sell a considerable number of his stable to help to cover his debts. Proof that the Earl was influential in changing the character of racing to benefit the interests of the rich and powerful is particularly evident when the rulings of the Jockey club after 1870 are further considered (Vanplew, 1988). Prize money was increased to 300 guineas a day from 1877, and new rules were introduced to prevent cheating whereby horses had been withdrawn just prior to a race. The railways organised excursions to the races which benefited Carlisle and Cartmel but also bigger races further afield, namely at Ascot and Sandown. Horse-racing had become a sport controlled by the rich with the skilled working man willing to spend his wages to participate as a gambler.

Table 2: The Lonsdale Estate: Horse Purchases and Sales 1890–1908

	Spent in Purchase	(including)		Gained in Sale
Year	£			£
1908	3,039			
1907	19,472			6,980
1096	4,811			1,417
1905	9,267			5,230
1904	4,545	(gift to Lady Girard)		1,292
1903	6,568			1,690
1902	2,510			1,190
1901	7,569			3,699
1900	3,200			1,841
1899	4,520			3,777
1898	9,615			4,935
1897	9,418	(gift to Mr. E. T. Moore)		5,840
1896	9,028			5,268
1895	5,198	(gift to Lady Girard)		2,943
1894	6,752	(gift to Lowther for breeding)		3,142
1893	14,508	(gift to Mrs. Robinson)		5,800
1892	4,401	(2 gifts to Churchill, 1 to Lowther)		2,355
1891	3,849	(gift to Lowther)		3,795
1890	4,485	(gift to R. S. Hays)		1,428
Total	•£132,892		Total	••£63,030
		•••Difference: £ 69,772		

error —•adds to 132,755; error—••adds to 63,022; error—•••

Source: D/Lons/L61 Horse Register July 1877–January 1908. C. R. O., Cumbria.

Notes:

a. The Register lists the name of the horse, the dates bought and sold, name of persons from whom purchased and to whom sold, with price and details of pedigree.

b. Between 1890 and 1908, 803 horses were accounted for; the average length of time a horse was kept before being sold was three years.

The accommodation of gentry power to populist sport has been discussed already in this paper with reference to Flan Sports and Grasmere Sports. It should be noted that from 1885, about a decade after the Earl's agreeing to be president of the Grasmere Sports, it became a scene of gentry display allied with populist sport. The press chronicled which gentry were

Table 3: Partial list of gentry present at Grasmere Sports, 1885–1907

Year	Gentry
1907	Hon. Earl of Lowther; Earl of Lonsdale
1906	Earl of Lonsdale
1903	Col. Bagot MP; W. J. Wilson
1899	Lady Evelyn Cavendish; Vistor C. W. Cavendish
1895	Lady Muncaster; S. H. Le Fleming
1894	Lady Henry Bentinck
1891	Canon Rawnsley; Lady Muncaster; Lord Muncaster
1885	Countess of Lonsdale; Earl of Lonsdale

Source: A History of Grasmere Sports, C. R. O., Cumbria.

Notes:
This list is far from complete — but it does show the interest consistently displayed by the Lowther family and local gentry for the games. The Grasmere Sports in the 1880s and 1890s served as a focal point for social gatherings; distinguished people from London and from abroad were brought to Grasmere to enjoy the games.

present while commenting upon the jollity of the day. A new tradition was begun, whereby winning wrestlers would be introduced to the gentry. A prize was awarded for the most attractive wrestling costume. While there had been a tradition in Cumbria of the victorious wrestler wearing a belt of victory the idea of wearing a costume was novel. **Table 3** illustrates some of the gentry who attended the Grasmere sports, between 1885 and 1907.

Control of urban working class recreation during this period came about through gentry membership of governing boards. An example would be the Board of Guardians which administered public assistance to the needy. It should be pointed out here that the Lowthers had demonstrated concern for the welfare of their own tenants. Several letters mention charitable acts such as the provision of extra coal during extremely cold weather. On other occasions blankets had been made available to the poor. Therefore it seems logical that the gentry would be involved in helping to administer public assistance in the growing urban community. With respect to sport there are many accounts not only in the Lowther correspondence but also in that the Cavendishes and the Bagots of works outings or dinners.

Much populist sport took place under conditions controlled by the gentry. One example to illustrate this point is their utilisation of the Ground Game Act of 1880 which was designed for "the better protection of occupiers of land". Under this act the landed gentry were protected to pursue the sport of winged game shooting while their tenant farmers were restricted to shooting hares and rabbits. Consequently shooting as a sport was denied by the act to those who did not possess land. However, by sponsoring quasi-military groups such as the Volunteers, the gentry were able to provide the urban working class with opportunities to engage in the sport of shooting. The gentry maintained their hegemony by maintaining control of the land. At the same time they formed an alliance with the people of urban middle class who became the officers of the Volunteer movement. The middle class accommodated the interests of urban working class youth who wanted to shoot and who were prepared to conform to the demands of the military to do so.

Summary and conclusions

The correspondence of the five Earls of Lonsdale was examined to learn whether sport was treated as a purely autonomous phenomenon or whether it helped to serve other political and social needs. The period 1807–1908 was selected because it was a period when leisure and sport became rationalised and utilitarian. The middle classes, primarily through the Muscular Christianity ethic and rational recreation movement, tried to control the working classes by influencing the norms governing their leisure. In short, the working class was to become respectable through civilised management of its leisure time and thereby not pose a threat to the propertied classes. Whether or not the middle classes were successful in this endeavour is still being debated, and more ethnographic studies will help to clarify this issue. What this paper has tried to do that has not been attempted before has been to examine a region of England that was largely rural during this period from a gentry perspective. Urbanisation in the Furness region only dates from the late 1860s. Consequently any ethnographic study of Cumbria with any interest in power relations in sport and leisure would need to study the gentry rather than the urban middle classes. A study of the Lowther correspondence made this possible.

The Lowthers did enjoy sport, from their perspective, as an autonomous unit. Their letters testify to the great joy that hunting and riding gave to most of them. At the same time they did demonstrate a perception that social reform posed a social threat. Their work with the Jockey Club has proven to be a means of combating radicalism. The letters of the First Earl illustrate his recognition of the need for what we would today call social networking. Therefore, the sport of horse-racing with its Newmarket club served to unite this very prestigious group in its Conservative ideology.

It is interesting that the First Earl, in addition to resisting radicalism, also saw the value of leasing his land for week-end shooting to gentlemen woollen merchants from Yorkshire. Whether he did this purely to raise funds for his estate or to encourage an albeit distant alliance with an emerging upper middle class is not clear from his letters. What is clear is that the Earl was astute enough to realise that he and his peers could not live within a vacuum without planning to protect their status and power. Their letters illustrate that sport did serve a partial utilitarian function in this respect.

The Second Earl demonstrates a high level of accommodation to demands from both the middle class and the working class in meeting their demands to lease land in order to form sport clubs. It was hunting clubs, often in the form of Otter Hound Clubs that received the greatest support from Lowther. This is understandable, given the commitment of the Lowthers to hunting. Nevertheless an examination of Lowther sponsorship does indicate some bias on the basis of perceived radicalism. A further indication of the utilitarian value of sport may be seen in the Third Earl's acceptance of the presidency of Grasmere Sports. This decision corresponded with the embarkation of a new Lancashire monied class on property acquisition in the Lake District. Consequently a *nouveau riche* population may have been perceived as a potential social and economic threat to Lowther power. Certain letters pertaining to litigation hint at this. Possibly, the presidency of a very visible populist activity like the Grasmere Sports would have enabled the Lowther family to manifest their power symbolically. Arguably, they were seen to be supporting such popular sports as fell running, wrestling and hound trailing while extracting deference from the competitors and the press. Such a position allied to the increased and visible power of the later Lowther stable was a manifest form of increased hegemony.

In conclusion, the paper has argued that, while field sports by their very nature were extremely important to the enjoyment of the Lowther family, they seemed to have had the foresight to plan for greater hegemony both inside and outside these sports and other sports. By their accommodation to outside interests they demonstrated an awareness of the value of sport as an instrument of social and political control. The result has been that while commoners appear to have enjoyed pockets of local hegemony, they never achieved permanent control of their own sport. Hence, while no transformation of power in sport has occurred, instances of accommodation have.

Notes

1 W.D/P.D Acc 1640/3, CRO (Carlisle Record Office).

2 D/Lons/L1/2 129-138, 20 March, 1832, CRO.

3 D/Lons/L1/2, "Letter from Newmarket", 3 May, 1830, CRO.

4 The Fleming Diaries, 24 February, 1813, BRO (Barrow Record Office).

5 D/Lons/L1/2, 17 March, 1857, CRO.

6 D/Lons/L1/2, 17 October, 1836, CRO.

7 D/Lons/L1/2, 17 October, 1836, CRO.

8 D/Lons/L1/3, 486, CRO

9 Ibid. 543.

10. Several letters refer to quarrymen trespassing on his land on Sundays.

11 A subscription is made to *Bell's Life*.

12 D/Lons/L1/2, 26 November, 1874, CRO.

13 D/Lons/L1/3, 2 July, 1873, CRO.

14 D/Lons/L6/1, The Horse Registers, CRO.

15 D/Lons/L3, 9 May, 1875, CRO.

16 D/Lons/L3, 10 July, 1872, CRO.

References

Bailey, P. (1978) *Leisure and class in Victorian England*. London: Routledge and Kegan Paul.

Gruneau, R. (1983) *Class, sports and social development*. Massachusetts: University of Massachusetts Press.

Hale, R. A. (1991) 'Horse-Racing in Cumbria'. Unpublished undergraduate dissertation, University of Lancaster.

Hargreaves, J. (1986) *Sport, power and culture*. Cambridge: Polity Press.

Machell, H. (1911) *Some Records of the Annual Grasmere Sports*. Carlisle: Kendal Record Office.

Marshall, J. D. and Walton, J. K. (1981) *The Lake Counties from 1830 to the mid-twentieth century*. Manchester: Manchester University Press.

Murfin, L. (1990) *Popular leisure in the Lake Counties*. Manchester: Manchester University Press.

Rollinson, W. (1974) *Life and tradition in the Lake District*. London: JM Dent & Son.

Vamplew, W. (1988) *Pay up and play the game — professional sport in Britain 1875-1914*. Cambridge: University Press, pp. 100-115, and 183-203.

Ward, I. (1985) 'Lakeland Sport in the Nineteenth Century'. unpublished Ph.D thesis, University of Liverpool.

Land, Labour and Leisure in the Life and Politics of John Murdoch

Grant Jarvie

Heriot-Watt University, Edinburgh, UK

Introduction

Born illegitimate in industrial Lanarkshire, Keir Hardie typified, in his younger years, many of the attributes of the Scots working class. Politics and morality were indistinguishable and self-help and temperance were often two corner-stones of pre-modern socialist and liberal reforms. When Keir Hardie and some two dozen other like-minded individuals gathered in Glasgow, in May 1888, to form the Scottish Labour Party the man asked to preside at their meeting was John Murdoch (Stewart, 1921). A seasoned land reformer, nationalist and socialist, temperance zealot (a useful attribute for an excise-officer), and newspaper journalist (published *The Highlander Newspaper* from 1873-1882), Murdoch was also an enthusiast of Celtic sports.

By this time he was 70 years old and nearing the end of a political career which had included support for the Irish Land League, American Land League, English Land League, the Scottish Land Restoration League and the Scottish Labour Party. He became the Scottish Land Restoration League's first secretary and stood as it's parliamentary candidate for Partick in the 1885 general election (like all Land Restoration candidates he came bottom of the poll, another experience similar to that of Keir-Hardie who came last in the Mid-Lanarkshire by-election of April 1888). Yet Murdoch is perhaps best remembered as the catalyst who introduced the philosophy of the Irish Land League to Inverness and helped initiate a protest movement which led to the passing of the Crofters Act in 1886. He urged crofters to give evidence to the Napier Commission when it toured the Highlands in 1883 to enquire into the conditions of the crofters and cottars in the Highlands and Islands of Scotland.

Developing interests — shinty and land reform

Writing of his school days on Islay during the 1830s Murdoch recalls that, "coming home from school on the Saturday we had quite a field day at Traigh an Luig at shinty playing" (unpublished autobiography, Vol. 1: p. 69). He goes on, " my great delight was to play at this game and soon I became not only a good player but came to be recognised as such" (Murdoch, Vol. 1: p. 69). Contrasting the state of things in the 1890s with those early childhood days Murdoch tells us that, "Traigh an Luig is now silent under the feet of cattle and the small farms from which the keen shinty players of these days came are consolidated into larger farms" (Murdoch, Vol 1: p. 70). That Murdoch should talk of land policy and the development of shinty is no accident, for like many central figures in the land agitations of the latter half of the nineteenth century land politics, Gaelic affairs and shinty were often inextricably linked.

The following are but four illustrative examples. John Gunn Mackay, a founding member of both Skye Camanachd and the first Glasgow Skye shinty club, was one of the most forthright and effective of the Land League activists (Macdonald, 1992: pp. 12-13). He was born in 1849 in Lochalsh, where his Sutherland born father was a schoolmaster, and brought up in Skye, his mother being from Bracadale. He learned the draper's trade in Glasgow where he was sacked in 1881 for making a pro Irish Land League speech at a rally. Having set up business in Portree in 1885, in the appropriately named Gladstone Buildings, he immediately became embroiled in land politics, shinty and Gaelic affairs — being elected as Land League councillor for Portree on the then recently formed Inverness City Council.

Born in Strathglass in 1825, Archbald Chisolm was the founder of Strathglass shinty club and author of the first set of printed shinty rules in the Highlands (Hutchinson, 1989: p. 115). A practising Roman Catholic and committed Gaelic speaker, Archibald Chisolm expressed a great deal of sympathy with Highland radicals and land reformers of the nineteenth century (Hutchinson, 1989: p. 116). On a number of occasions he offered financial assistance to Murdoch's newspaper, *The Highlander.* Murdoch was often an honoured guest at Strathglass Highland Gala days, a position which was more often than not filled by his sworn enemies. In July 1881 Archibald Chisolm not only invited Murdoch to the Strathglass gathering but the prizes on the day consisted of six-month subscriptions to *The Highlander.* Like Murdoch, Archibald Chisolm disliked tobacco and strong drink and on more than one occasion warned the Strathglass shinty players that "Ach chan ionan fear air mhisg is fear an uisg" (the drunken man and the drinker of water are not alike).

One of the most prominent women in the land agitations of the late 1880s was the Skye bardess Mary Macpherson, more popularly known as Mairi Mhor nan Oran (Big Mary of the Songs). It is perhaps worth mentioning that Murdoch himself recalls that many an hour was spent on Islay being entertained by another bardess, Margaret MacLeora, who told tales of the kings of Lochlann (Norway), Ireland and Rome, but also upon getting a fresh pair of teeth went on to live to the age of 109 (Murdoch, Vol. 1 pp34-35). Mairi Mhor was born in 1821 in Skeabost where her father John Macdonald was a crofter. Through her songs and her poetry she took an active part in the Crofters cause during the 1880's, regularly appearing on Land League platforms throughout the Highlands (Macphail, 1989; Macdonald, 1992). Like John Gunn Mackay, Mairi Mhor also commented upon the relationship between Highland social and economic history and the development of shinty (cited in Macdonald 1992: p. 3) :

> Bho'n chaill sinn am fearann
> Gun chaill sinn an iomain
> S cha mhor gu bheil duin' ann tha eolach oirr
>
> [Since we lost our land
> We lost shinty as well
> And there are few men left who are skilful now].

Finally, there is John Murdoch himself born in 1818 in the parish of Ardclach, Nairnshire. His father John Murdoch senior combined the management of a series of crofts with employment on a number of highland estates, while his mother Mary Macpherson was the daughter of a sea captain and had had "far greater advantages in her training than he had had" (Murdoch, Vol. 1: p. 107). In 1827 the Murdoch family moved to Islay and such was the influence of the place on John Murdoch junior that he told the Napier Commission " I feel myself as if I were an Islay man" (cited in Hunter, 1986: p. 13). In his later life Murdoch was to become an associate of Michael Davitt, Henry George, Joseph Ashby, Patrick Ford (editor of the *New York Irish World)*, Keir Hardie, and many other land and labour agitators (Young, 1969).

By the time Murdoch had given evidence to the Napier Commission in 1883 he had : spoken out against organised religion; shown support for the ideas of Feargus O'Connor and other chartists; spoken out against Irish and Highland emigration; championed improved working conditions for excise officers; refused the opportunity to sit as a Parnellite MP in Tipperary in 1880, and come out in support of both the Gaelic Athletic Association and the Irish Land Act of 1881. While his attitudes towards workers' conditions, education, nationalism, and socialism might have been finely tuned by his experiences on the mainland after 1840, many of his fundamental beliefs concerning landlordism, labour, sport and social life were influenced by his experiences of community, authority, and people on the island of Islay.

The first part of Murdoch's unpublished autobiography contains numerous accounts of Islay people and events which influenced his political thinking. In particular, he reflects upon his relationship with Walter Fredrick Campbell and his son John Francis Campbell (The Campbells of Islay were descended from Daniel Campbell of Shawfield who bought Islay in 1726). John Murdoch senior came to Islay as one of Walter Fredrick Campbell's tenants. Under normal circumstances there would have been no question of there being anything but the most restricted of contact between the children of the laird and the sons and daughter of itinerant crofters or employees. This being a feature of Highland life that Murdoch always deplored. He wrote in 1853 (*Argyllshire Herald*, October, 1853):

> The landlord if born at all among his people, is carefully removed from the reach of their Celtic influences and educated so as have a language and mode of thinking quite foreign to the sphere into which he is destined to act the most important parts in the serious drama of life. One consequence is that not one landlord in a hundred is capable of communicating directly with the great bulk of the people. There is thus an impenetrable barrier between him and them.

Like much of the conventional wisdom on the Highland clearances, Murdoch's writings, at times, tend to be clouded by the portrayal of all lairds as bad, bourgeois and exploitative and all crofters as good, proletarian and exploited. Yet there were many individual cases of traditional landowners whose actions did not sit easily with the label of a uniform, exploitative class: one was Lachlan Macdonald of Skeabost, patron of Bernisdale shinty club and reputed to be the richest man on Skye during the 1880s, who took a pro-crofters stance during the land agitations of this period. According to Murdoch the Islay landowner seemed to be another exception since he insisted on his son being brought up as a gaelic speaker — a fact which in Murdoch's opinion made Walter Fredrick Campbell a better person than almost any other Highland landowner of the time.

Some have suggested that Walter Fredrick Campbell's regard for Gaelic and the insistance that his son learned as much from the working culture of people in and around the estate provides a good deal of the explanation for Murdoch's consistent portrayal of Islay in the 1830s, 1840s and 1850s. This portrayal was of a place where traditional relations between landowner and crofter had not been completely severed by eviction, emigration and other manifestations of proprietorial oppression (Hunter, 1986: p. 14).

John Francis Campbell and John Murdoch both recall how much of their informal education and upbringing were left to the tradesmen, working women, and the piper (himself called John Campbell) around the estate (John Francis Campbell papers, National Library of Scotland, Adv 50/5/8/ f26). The most popular passtimes included stone throwing, shinty playing, leaping and running, swimming, cock fighting, singing and dancing. After the day's labour young men and women often gathered for a dance to the fiddle or the pipes or both. Work itself was often competitive. Murdoch recalls "the young women from different houses shouldered the spinning wheels, marched to some neighbour's house where they competed against each other to see who could spin the greatest quantity of linen" (Murdoch, Vol 1: p. 10). Songs often accompanied tasks such as spinning but also the pounding and waulking of the tweed cloth. Reading was also popular, since many of the island assembly schools contained movable libraries (Murdoch, Vol 1: p. 114).

Although Murdoch's writings rarely mention the role of dancing within Islay customs and community, other accounts of social life amongst crofting communities have recalled more vividly it's popularity. Mairi MacArthur's account of the crofting community on Iona between 1750 and 1914 records how popular dancing was both in the early and latter part of the nineteenth century. She writes (MacArthur, 1990: pp. 57-58):

> In 1807 Necker de Saussure rewarded the boatmen who had brought him to Iona with a dance in the evening, as dancing is the favourite amusement amongst Hebrideans of all ages.

The same writer also notes (MacArthur, 1990: pp. 167-168) :

> It was the main form of entertainment for young people. Marion MacArthur from Clachanach used to organise dances on the flat grassy field above Burnside cottage in the 1890s. Mary Ann MacLean born in 1884, remembered dancing on the Nunnery corner, a favourite meeting place for the young, and also on the Machair at Sithean and Culdamph.

The days spent loitering amongst people both in and out of work certainly had a profound effect on Murdoch, who described them as " humble but potent teachers of his" and as awakening within him " a fellow feeling for men and women of whatever degree in life" (Murdoch, Vol 1: p. 39). Their names are many, of whom the following are but a few; Donald Ross, the shoemaker, provided the lapstone for putting, Peter MacCuaig and Neil Shaw were amongst the leading ploughmen; Angus Macdougall often took the prize for tossing the caber; John Campbell was remarkable for his swiftness and indeed Dugald MacGregor, an older man, said of John's running "that he was not at full speed as long as one could see his feet and at his best his feet became invisible" (Murdoch, Vol. 1. p. 41); John Macphee was a fine fiddler, while Donald and Duncan Bell were two fine pipers who eventually had to leave the island after their father was evicted from the farm (Murdoch, Vol 1 p. 91). The great gathering place for district shinty matches in those early days. was Lag buidhe, although after Walter Fredrick Campbell had planted trees on Lag buidhe shinty matches moved to the Glebe (Murdoch, Vol 1: p. 23).

In 1847 Walter Fredrick Campbell fell bankrupt. By this time Murdoch had served as an exciseman in Scotland, Ulster and Lancashire. He had publicly expressed his views on such issues as organised religion, temperance (even critical of Islay's whisky trade), and landownership; been appalled by the conditions of the workers in Lancashire; had spoken out against the implementation of the Poor Law Amendment (Scotland) Act of 1845 — a law "which was used much more as a terror to keep the poor from applying for relief than as a means of ameliorating their condition" (Murdoch, Vol 1: pp. 16-17); been outspoken in his condemnation of bloodsports at a time when the Highlands were just beginning to open as a leisure playground for the southern aristocracy in particular; and had begun to write about the desirability and pragmatism of bringing land and labour issues together on the same political platform.

In an attempt to save Walter Fredrick Campbell, Murdoch tried to implement a smaller version of Feargus O'Connor's National Land Scheme in Ireland . Murdoch's plan was to set up a peasant proprietary on Islay with all debts paid and 20, 000 acres left to Walter Fredrick Campbell (*Argyllshire Herald*, May 1852). Of Islay's 140, 000 acres the remainder was to be divided into as many as 3, 000 holdings . Each of these would have about 28 acres of land, of which 12 would be arable and the rest rough pasture. Murdoch suggested that if crofts were sold to their occupiers at a rate of some £5 an acre then all the debts of the Islay estate could be cleared and crofters would own their own land (Hunter, 1986: p. 80).

During this time Murdoch's father had been killed in a shooting accident and the factor had evicted his mother and family from their small farm at Claggan. The famine years in the middle of the century, particularly between 1846 and 1852, added to the misery being experienced by many in the Highlands and Islands. If Islay and the mainland were anything like Skye then a dispirited, fever-ridden population had little reason to celebrate and even less energy for shinty (Macdonald, 1992: p. 3). Writing of these times the parish

Minister of Diurinish noted that all public gatherings whether for shinty playing, or throwing the putting stone or drinking and dancing, for marriages or funerals had been discontinued, and people lived very much apart (cited in Macdonald, 1992: p. 3).

Numerous factors might be mentioned for the temporary demise of shinty, but organized religion was certainly one that was perhaps uppermost in the mind of the Minister of Diurinish. Shinty, like most other popular pastimes, was temporarily assigned to the devil, perhaps because of its association with drinking and communal revelry (Macdonald, 1992: p. 4). This had not been the first time that organised religion, in alliance with the state, had clashed with popular culture. Indeed, Adam Smith suggested that public diversions would provide a useful check on the fanaticism and frenzies stirred up by popular religious sects (Hamish-Fraser & Morris, 1990: p. 237).

This view would have found some sympathy with Murdoch, since for him, organised religion spread discord and strife, divided people, and obscured rather than elucidated the central truths of religion. Churches had " become like betting shops competing for customers for themselves instead of being agents of Christ" (Murdoch, Vol 1. p. 33-35). In the 1870s he was to argue that "it was time for them to come out of their sectarian shells, time to recognise that their common beliefs were more important than their theological differences" (cited in Hunter, 1986: pp. 15-16). Indeed one of the strongest testaments to Murdoch's ability to cross the religious divide was in convincing the staunchly Presbyterian crofters of Skye to accept the staunchly Catholic Michael Davitt as their parliamentary candidate in 1886 (*Oban Times*, May, 1887).

Shinty, gaelic politics and Highland landlords

If Murdoch criticised organised religion for the fear it instilled within ordinary people, it was secondary to the wrath and condemnation that he saved for those responsible for implementing social and economic changes in the Highlands during the later stages of his life. For all the complex analysis that has been put forward concerning the Highland clearances (which were complex and uneven), Murdoch's political conviction over many issues was partly fueled by a sense of outrage at the state of fear under which many people lived — people such as Donald MacAskill who in 1884, at a land reform meeting in Dunvegan, Skye, openly admitted "I am ashamed to confess it now that I trembled more before the factor than I did before the Lord of Lords" (MacPhail, 1989: p. 1).

By 1873 Murdoch had retired as an excise officer and returned to Inverness where he launched his newspaper *The Highlander*. Like the Highland Societies, newspapers and journals interested in the crofters' cause multiplied during the 1880s, and so argues MacPhail (1989: p. 11), Murdoch's newspaper was the first to cater primarily for the interests of the people of the Highlands and Islands. The same writer commented that in an early edition of the newspaper Murdoch urged those who attended convivial reunions to devote more of their time to more practical ways of helping the good of the people (MacPhail, 1989: p. 21). By the end of the decade the Federation of Celtic Societies had been criticised as being too political with hardly a musical programme or soiree not including songs about the clearances.

Since shinty was not just a casual pursuit but an integral part of Highland culture and community, *The Highlander* regularly reported upon shinty events, controversies and personnel. In the 1870s organised shinty made considerable strides in Scotland with several of the early soccer sides, such as Vale of Leven being shinty clubs as well (Harvie, 1993). Shinty was supported by numerous land reforms and nationalists such as John Stuart Blackie, Michael Davitt and Captain Chisolm of Strathglass. A report of an event in Strathglass read (*The Highlander*, January 19, 1881):

> The festival of the Epiphany has always been a day of great solemnity and rejoicing for the Catholics of these glens.... After the celebration of mass, the congregation, men, women and children, headed by the local piper, marched to Cannich Bridge, where many more had assembled from the surrounding glens, in expectation of the match appointed to be played on that day by the Strathglass Shinty Club....

Shinty matches were reported from as far afield as London, Birmingham, Manchester, Glasgow and Edinburgh (*The Highlander*, January 6, 1876;June 1, 1878; April 18, 1879;). Several editions of the newspaper covered a debate between London and Glasgow shinty clubs on whether players should wear kilts or knickerbockers, the last word seemingly being left to Ronald Walker of Glasgow Camanachd who asserted (*The Highlander*, April 13, 1878; May 8 1878; May 18, 1878):

> Playing matches to doomsday won't decide which is the most suitable dress.... A Highlander is a Highlander, though shinty should be played in pantaloons. They are purely practical in the sense that they are light and hold their place when a player is upside down.

The paper provided a forum for debate and co-operation between Gaelic speakers and political and cultural nationalists in both Scotland and Ireland.

It served as a catalyst to the development of the Highland Land Law Reform Association by regularly reporting on the developments in Irish politics such as the Irish Land Bill. The issue of fixed tenure was a central clause of the Irish Land Act yet according to one Sir Frederick Heygate (*The Highlander*, 22nd June, 1878):

> ... fixity of tenure would be a curse upon Irish tenants.

The same article went on:

> It is perfectly amazing that so late in this world's history as 1878, such opinions should be entertained by gentlemen not wholly impervious to reason. Yet we may expect some member of the Land Committee to propose a report embodying the views of Sir Frederick Heygate. And what is more it may be carried, for the majority of the committee are Tories.

For Murdoch the plight of the Irish peasantry, which he saw as analogous to the problems of the crofting community in the Highlands, was the greatest condemnation of the Anglo-Irish Union of 1800 (*The Highlander*, 25 April, 1874). One of the lessons from Ireland for Murdoch and organisations such as the Highland Land League was that Irish and Highland questions only loomed high on Westminster's political agenda when respective groups began to organise outside the British political framework. The new departure in Irish politics of 1879 and the development of the Irish Land League was one of many factors which influenced the development of the Highland Land League. This organisation was established in 1883 to give a political dimension to the crofters' protest.

By 1884 sporting estates accounted for 1,975,209 acres of Scotland while by 1920 the total acreage under deer had grown to 3,432,385 acres (McConnochie, 1923: p. 49). Deer not only required tracts of land but also attacked crops on neighbouring lands. The development of deer forests for sporting consumption was greatest after about 1870. By the 1880s sporting rents had increased to such a level that social class barriers were reproduced and consolidated through the prohibitive cost of sport alone. For the crofter the immediate problem was that the deer literally ate into any living that could be made from the land. Since the sporting tenant, *nouveau* forms of land use and in many instances *nouveau* landowners all posed a threat to the livelihood of many crofters, it is not surprising that the destruction of deer forests and sporting estates along with a refusal to pay rent to the factor were but two of the most popular forms of protest used in the land agitations of this period. Protests over the development of sporting estates contributed to a number of popular demonstrations such as those on Bernera in 1874, Skye in 1876 and Pairc (Lewis) in 1887.

The Highlander reported on anti-landlord agitation and the actions of landlords themselves with the *cause celebre* being the sequence of incidents involving Captain William Fraser who bought the Kilimuir estate on Skye in 1855 for £85,000. Fraser saw himself as an improving "laird", and saw no reason why he should not extract a high rent from tacksmen, farmers, sportspeople, and tenants. Following a valuation of rents in 1876, Fraser promptly informed his tenants of rent increases which were double what they had been in 1855. On Sunday 13 October 1877 the two local rivers burst their banks and flooded Uig Lodge, the residence of Captain Fraser. Uig graveyard had also been devastated and several bodies washed into the lodge garden. Murdoch's own autobiography talks of coffins being deposited in the dining room of the lodge (Hunter, 1986: p. 157). This was too good an opportunity for *The Highlander* (30 March, 1878) to miss, given Fraser's treatment of the crofters. It reported (although Murdoch himself didn't sanction the report, he took responsibility for it) :

> Their lives [Kilmuir crofters] were bitter enough before but now their burdens are unbearable. This is the time for Captain Fraser to show his charity if he has any. The Lord has given him means, which he can turn to good or evil account, just as he pleases, but he must now bear in mind that there is One who is fearful in judgement and that an account must be rendered.

The laird sued the newspaper and although Murdoch, in this instance, managed to scramble together the fine, *The Highlander* was always struggling financially. It folded in 1881, by which time Murdoch was increasingly involved in Irish and Labour politics. Although he refused the opportunity to stand as a Parnellite MP because he believed that the real work was to be done outside politics, namely in agrarian agitation, in 1880 he shared a platform in Philadelphia with both Charles Stewart Parnell and John Dillon. Murdoch disliked Parnell although Highland Land League MPs were to have the support of the Parnellities in parliament. Newspaper reports make it clear that Murdoch was certainly more popular in Philadelphia, a point which seemed to annoy Parnell (Hunter, 1986, pp33-34). Murdoch's dislike may well have been based on the fact that while Parnell's commitment to Ireland was total, his interest in Scotland was nil. Indeed Parnell's opinion of the Scots is enshrined in his remark that "Scotland had long since ceased to be a nation" (Jarvie, 1993: p. 80).

It was different with Michael Davitt, with whom Murdoch toured the Highlands in 1887. Three years earlier they both had sought support among the industrial workers, in Scottish coalfields in particular, for land reform. Davitt's Highland speeches not only attacked the system of landownership in the Highlands but also their systematic development as a leisure playground for the southern aristocracy. Crofters, Davitt declared must organise and agitate until they had overthrown the whole fabric of the landlord system — "bad laws had to be broken before good laws could be made". This was music to the ears of the land-raiders but it is doubtful if Murdoch a die hard pacifist, Ghandi type figure, would have agreed whole-heartedly with Davitt on this issue. Unlike Parnell, Davitt had shown an interest in Scottish questions and Scottish home rule, and his thinking on land reform, nationalism and the role of sport in Celtic culture were similair to that of John Murdoch. Both had shown support for the Gaelic Athletic Association, formed in 1884.

Appraising John Murdoch

Only a year after touring the Highlands with Davitt, Murdoch was campaigning on behalf of Keir Hardie during the mid-Lanarkshire by-election of 1888 (result: J. W. Philips, Lib 3,847; W. R. Bousfield, Con 2,917; J. K. Hardie, Lab 617). By this time Murdoch was in his late 70s, and although he supported the land raids in Vatersay, Lewis and other islands in 1900 and toured the Southern counties of England with Joseph Ashby in 1891 on behalf of the English Land League, he was nearing the end of his political career. His final public speech was to a Highland Association meeting in Glasgow in 1901. By this time he and his wife had moved to Saltcoats, Ayrshire where he died in 1903 (Jan 29th) at the age of 85.

Socialists, land-reformers and Gaelic nationalists have at times all claimed John Murdoch as their own. Land raids, argued John Maclean, were the Highland equivalent of strikes and as such, they deserved the support of the working class . Some have suggested that the Highland Land League Reform Association, by acting as the party of the crofters, was the real precursor to any subsequent political parties which laid claim to independent parliamentary working class representation, a cause Murdoch was certainly sympathetic to. Others have argued that the Highland Land League was naturally aligned with the Liberal party in opposition to the landed party of the Tories. Murdoch's denounciations of British imperialism and international war are but two other factors which have led both nationalists and socialists to lay claim to his writings.

Of the original members of the Highland Land League, only G. B Clarke had any socialist convictions. Although Murdoch moved more to the left as he grew older, he is perhaps best described as a left wing radical rather than a class conscious socialist. He hesitated to use the word socialist himself, although he did hold true to some early Scottish Labour Party ideals, for example, support for trade unions, communal ownership of land, and temperance initiatives. Murdoch's Crofters Party was not a proletarian party, but more of a populist coalition. He certainly identified and worked with the struggles of ordinary people in the Highlands, viewed shinty as a vital aspect of Gaelic culture and was critical of the Highlands becoming a leisure playground for the southern aristocracy. As such Land, Labour and Leisure were perhaps three of the most important themes in the life and politics of John Murdoch.

It is perhaps misleading to compare the issue of Highland and Island land ownership in the late nineteenth century with developments in the late twentieth century. At a recent Scottish Labour Party Conference, Labour MP for the Western Isles, Calum Macdonald called for future potential estate owners to fulfil an environmental audit before being allowed to buy land (*Northern Times* 19th March, 1993). Murdoch might not have agreed with such an unproductive venture, especially if it meant landowners being paid large sums of government money for *not* utilising the land. However, he would undoubtedly have welcomed the recent developments which led to the Assynt Crofters proprietorship of the North Lochinver estate. The historic purchase of the 21,000 acre estate is seen by many as one of the most important developments in Highland land ownership since the days of the Land League. If nothing else, the events in Assynt have placed the possibility of transfer of ownership and control of land to local communities in the agenda for the 1990s (*Northern Times*, 19 March 1993). It also illustrates that the issue of who owns the land and what it is used for remains one of the most intensely felt political issues in many Highland and Island local communities.

Yet the past casts a long shadow over many local communities. The 1955 Crofters Act specifically states that "the crofter will permit the landlord or any person authorised by the landlord to enter upon the croft for the purpose of ... mining or taking minerals ... quarrying or taking stone". In the 1950s the concept of the super quarry or the coastal quarry had not arrived at townships such as Carnish on the island of Lewis. In the 1880s, when impoverished Lewis cottars sent a delegation to see Lady Matheson, widow of the drug baron who had cleared Carnish, to plead for access to land given over to sport, she retorted these lands were hers and local cottars had nothing to do with them. In the 1990s Lady Matheson has been replaced by Redland and MacIver Aggregates Ltd but the role of crofting law in protecting tenants against unwanted super-quarry developments remains as ineffectual as it was in 1955.

References

Hamish-Fraser, W. and Morris, R. J. (1990) *People and society in Scotland, Volume II, 1830–1914*, Edinburgh: John Donald, pp. 236–264.

Harvie, C. (1993) 'Sport and the Scottish State', in G. Jarvie and G. Walker (eds) *Ninety-minute patriots? Scottish sport in the making of the nation.* London: Leicester University Press, pp. 115–132.

Hunter, J. (1986) *For the people's cause: From the writings of John Murdoch.* Edinburgh: HMSO.

Hutchinson, R. (1989) *Camanachd: The story of shinty.* Edinburgh: Mainstream Publishing.

Jarvie, G. (1993) 'Sport, nationalism and cultural identity', in L. Allison (ed) *The changing politics of sport.* Manchester: Manchester University Press, pp. 58–80.

MacArthur, M. (1989) *Iona: The living memory of a crofting community, 1750-1914.* Edinburgh: Edinburgh University Press.

Macdonald, M. (1992) *Skye Camanachd: A century remembered.* Portree: Skye Camanachd.

MacPhail, I. (1989) *The crofters war.* Stornoway Acair.

McConnochie, A. (1923) *The deer and deer forests of Scotland.* London: Witherby.

Stewart, W. (1921) *J. Keir Hardie — a biography.* London: Independent Labour Party Publication Department.

Young, J. (1969) 'John Murdoch: A Scottish land and Labour pioneer', *Labour History Bulletin*, No xix: pp. 22–25.

An Analysis of Sports Policy in Greece (1980-92)

Pantellis P. Nassis

Loughborough University, UK

The aim of this paper is to explore the role of central government in sport, in Greece, to explain the nature of sports policy and also to identify key trends and/or changes in its direction. The focus of the analysis will be on the nature of sports policy in the 1980s and early 1990s. However, since the sports field has been recognised as an area of government intervention, an adequate analysis of sports policy must take a wider approach where political, economic and social developments will be considered as influential factors. For the purposes of this paper, it is useful to provide some information on the major political, economic and social developments in Greece since 1980.

Analysis of the above developments has been based on the review of literature (in Greek and English), while the picture of sports policy developments has been constructed from the findings on legislative measures, records of parliamentary debates, national accounts, policy documents, newspaper articles and so on. Furthermore, in an attempt to go beyond mere description, interviews with key individuals constituted an essential part of the research, to provide an in depth explanation of the relationship between political values and sports policy goals in Greece; the impact of the changing political and economic structure on policy goals and implementation; and the significance of national, local and transnational influences on sports policy.

Politics and sport in the 1980s

From 1981 to 1989 Greece experienced the first socialist government in its modern history led by PASOK (Panhellenic Socialist Movement). The reasons for PASOK's victory in the 1981 election cannot be traced to a single factor, but rather must be treated as the result of a number — the rise of the lower middle class, the increasing electoral appeal prompted by PASOK's 'catch all' programme, the promotion of the party's profile as a moderate socialist power, and the charismatic election campaign of the party's leadership (Clogg, 1986; Lyrintzis, 1990). During that period the socialist party attempted, with only partial success, to incorporate in its policies the different and in some cases contradictory interests of its supporters. What appeared to benefit the lower classes were the introduction of some basic welfare measures (i.e. expansion of national insurance and pension schemes, introduction of a National Health System), the rise of wages and the implementation of a programme of high public spending (Karambelias, 1989). Extensive government spending was met by public borrowing which resulted, in conjunction with the low productivity of the Greek economy and the global fiscal crisis, in the economic crisis of the Greek state in the later half of the 1980s (Kazakos, 1990).

During that period, PASOK, in its second term in office, introduced an economic programme known as "stabilisation", which included measures such as devaluation of drachmae, restrictions on wage increases and reduction of public expenditure (Spourdalakis, 1988). The popular dissatisfaction with PASOK's failure to bring about the change the socialists had proclaimed in 1981, the deep economic recession, and the financial and political scandals that shocked Greece and involved members of the administration, all led the right wing party of New Democracy to an independent majority in the April 1990 election that followed two coalition governments after June 1989. The new government declared its intention to pursue strict monetarist policies for the recovery of the Greek economy, and amongst others it enforced greater control on public spending, placed strong emphasis on the mechanisms of the free market, and required the privatisation of the companies "socialised" under PASOK.

The changing nature of the political and economic structure is likely to have affected the direction of sports policy. Before presenting the main findings of the research, it is necessary to give some principal information on how sports are organised in Greece. The smallest unit of organised sport is the sports club, which for its foundation and administration depends on private initiatives. The sports clubs are collectively represented by the sports federations that are the national governing bodies of sport (NGBs). Above these bodies stands the Ministry for Culture, which directs central funds and implements the government's plans for sport through an appointed Junior Minister and a governmental agency, the General Secretariat for Sport (GSS). The sports organisation is financed mainly from the national budget through grant to the GSS and from the revenues of football pools.

The Infrastructure of Sport

Sport as an area of government spending is a relatively unimportant area of state investment (just above 1% of the national budget). However, government grant to sport increased in real terms in the late 1970s and remained at a relatively high level throughout the 1980s (Figure 1). Since 1989 the amount of state subsidies to sport through the National Budget has gradually been reduced, and sport has been financed through the public investments programme and the revenues from the football pools.

Figure 1: GSS funds from investment and football pools in real terms (1977–91)

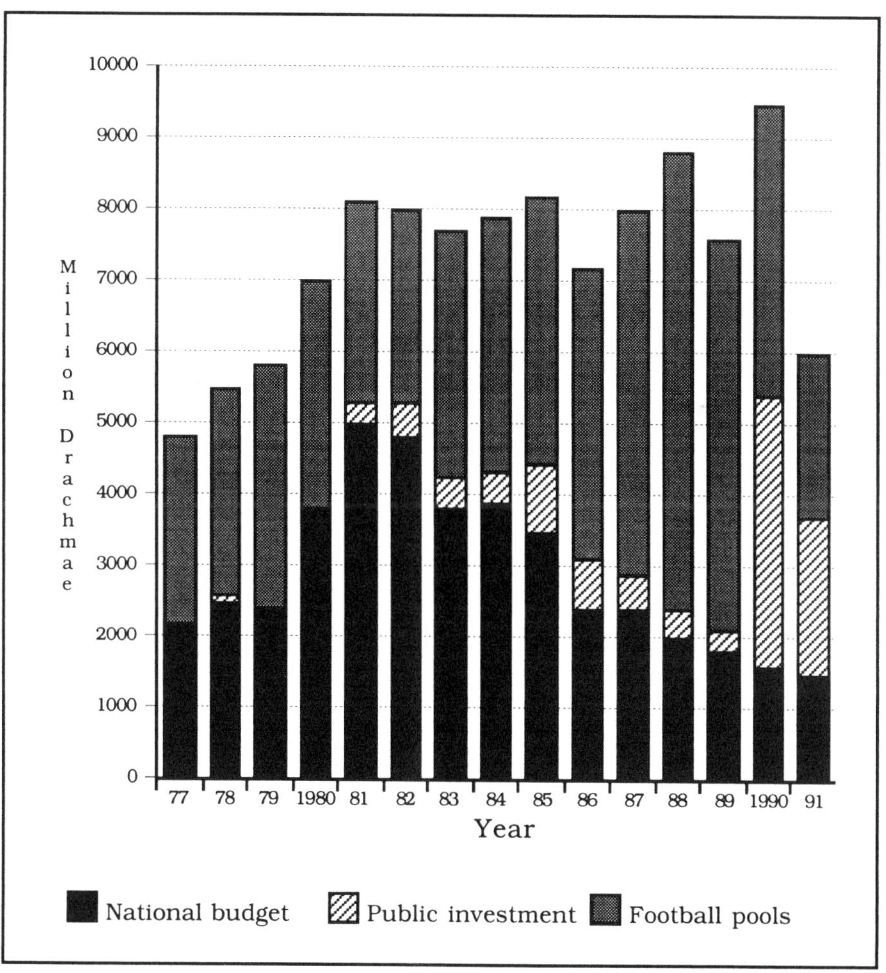

Source: Ministry of National Economy, Organisation of football pools 1977–91

The period of high spending for sport coincided with the PASOK administration (1981-89). However, high expenditure on sport after 1989 sustained by public investments was imposed by Greece's bid for the 1996 Olympic Games and hosting the 1991 Mediterranean Games. In the early period of its administration, PASOK intensified the programme of new sports facilities that started as early as the late 1970s and included finance for the building and maintenance of regional sports facilities, multi-purpose sports centres, indoor sports halls and outdoor swimming pools and also the construction of large scale facilities, concentrated near Athens, host for big international events. Expenditure for large scale facilities absorbed the great majority of GSS' budget from 1977 to 1981, especially for building the Olympic Stadium where the 1982 European Athletics Championship was held (Figure 2).

Figure 2: GSS capital expenditure as a percentage of its budget (1977–92)

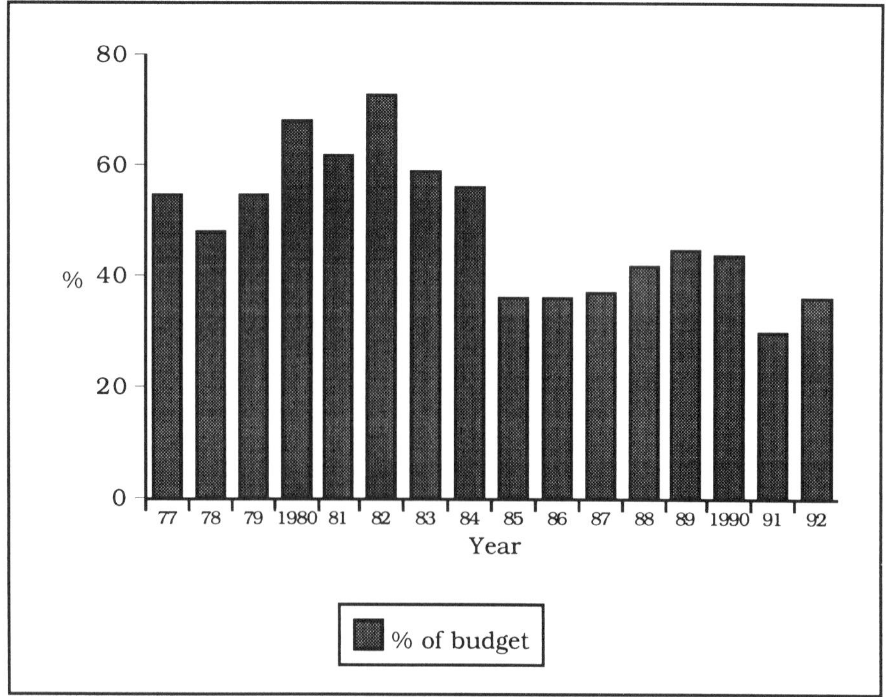

Source: Ministry of National Economy 1977-92

The "Sport for All" Campaign

Spending on the construction of small scale, regional facilities was one of the central aims of the strategy of the socialist party to make sport largely accessible to the public. According to this line of policy, local government was recognised as an essential partner of the central state by virtue of its ability to identify local needs for sports facilities and make efficient use of GSS funds which from 1983 introduced nation-wide "Sport for All" programmes. Local authorities undertook the responsibility for running these "Sport for All" programmes, such as "sport and women", "sport in childhood", "sport and the elderly", "sport and disabled children", and several others. The emphasis was clearly to broaden the base of participation and the aim of these programmes was "to change the relationship between citizens and sport... Sport is a right of citizenship that everyone should enjoy independently of gender and age". In the same report local government's role was regarded as essential to achieve the designated objectives. GSS suggested that every local authority should run the programmes, but adoption of the "Sport for All" message was optional (GSS, 1987).

However, after its initial introduction in the municipality of Athens, the "Sport for All" programme has been adopted by a gradually increasing number of local authorities. In an extensive analysis of local government's role as a provider of leisure during the 1980s, Papageorgiou (1989) pointed out that provision for leisure including arts and culture varied substantially between local authorities. According to her, a clear relationship seemed to exist between the priority given to leisure policy and the political affiliation of the council majority with the central (socialist) government.

There were also great differences between councils over issues such as the amount of funds granted by central government and how far sport policy was integrated into the municipal social programme. For instance, Papageorgiou also noted that socialist controlled councils tended to make quicker and fuller use of the opportunities provided by central government than those controlled by an opposition party. These themes were pursued in interviews with Junior Ministers and General Secretaries for Sport.

Further, the quality of local "Sport for All" services also varied according to the ability and willingness of local authorities to formulate a comprehensive policy for sport. The shortcomings have been many due to a number of reasons; the haphazard way central funds were distributed, the reluctance of local authorities to invest in facilities for sport and finally their dependence on GSS for securing special grants (Papageorgiou, 1993).

Although socially accepted, the programmes remained a campaign. The socialist government did nothing to safeguard these programmes by legislation (Nikitaras, 1990). The establishment by Presidential Decree (No. 77) of a new department within the GSS for the development of sport, as well as the accepting the need for regional committees to run more effectively the programmes for the prevention of sport violence articulated in the Preamble of the 1986 Act (Panagiotopoulos, 1990) have proved insufficient to ensure government's commitment to "Sport for All". The great reduction in the number of people participating in "Sport for All" events after 1989 (Figure 3) indicates that the importance of the programmes has faded.

The national governing bodies of sport

NGBs are voluntary associations primarily responsible for policy concerning the development of each particular sport, its competitiveness at home as well as abroad, the means of obtaining public and state support, its relationship

Figure 3 Participation in "Sport for All" Programmes (1983–90)

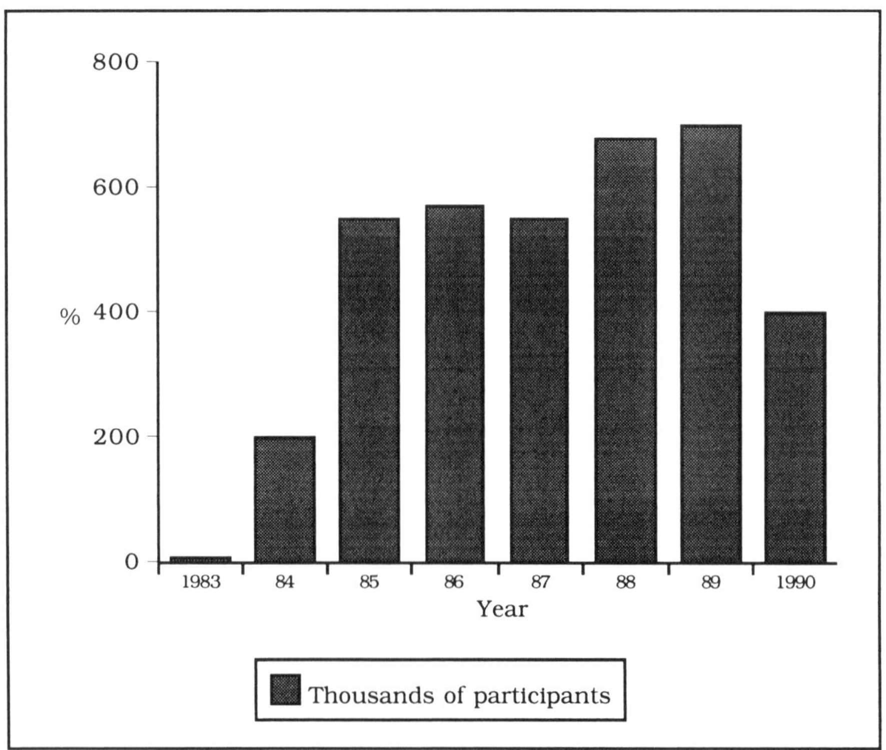

Source: GSS, Department of Sports Development, 1991

with the mass media and decisions about all those factors that can enhance its prestige. GSS' role is restricted to the supervision and funding of NGBs, and the latter is usually based on criteria such as the number of sports club-members, the international performance of individual clubs and/or the national teams, participation in or organising international tournaments, the level of expenditure for running the national and local leagues and development needs. However, it would be naive not to add to these the pressures exerted by most NGBs on government through political mechanisms or lobbying efforts.

Funding for competitive sport increased gradually between 1981 and 1987 both as a percentage of GSS total spending and in real terms, then reduced dramatically until 1990 and increased only as a percentage since then (Figure 4). Despite the increase of sports bodies' share of the GSS

Figure 4: GSS grant to governing bodies of sport and sports associations as a percentage of GSS budget (1977–92)

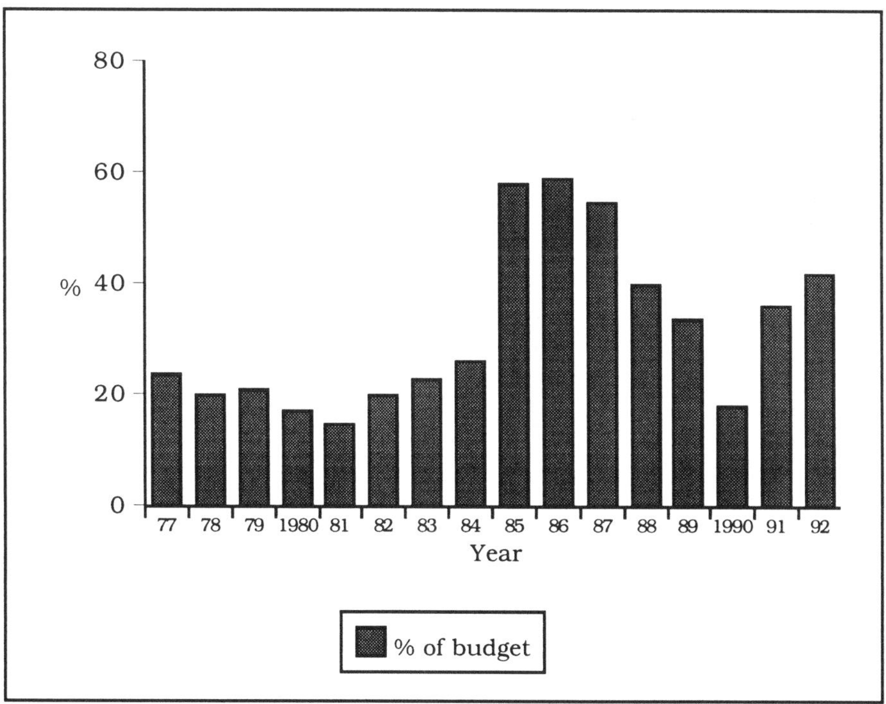

Source: Ministry of National Economy, 1974-92

Figure 5 GSS grant to Governing Bodies of Sport and Sports Associations in real terms (1977–91)

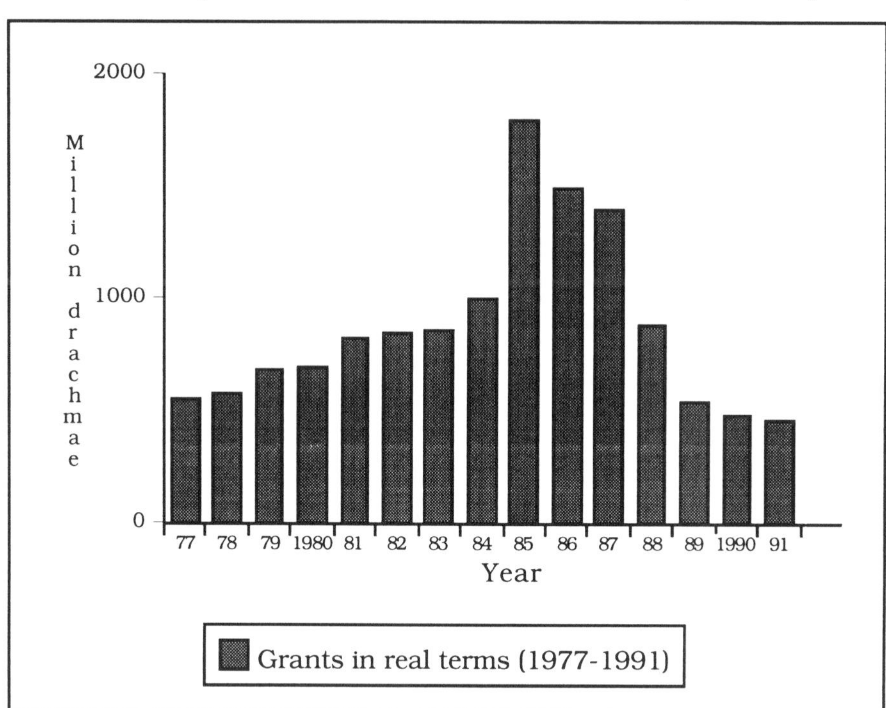

Source: Ministry of National Economy, 1974-92

budget, the grant has severely declined in real terms since 1987 as a result of government grant reduction (Figure 5).

The reduction of total GSS grants to NGBs since 1987 does not necessarily imply that all of them have faced a proportional reduction of funds; distribution varied considerably from 1988 to 1992. Unfortunately, lack of data for earlier years restricts drawing any safe conclusions. Nevertheless, a number of observations can be made. Figure 6 (opposite) presents data on subsidies to the governing bodies of basketball, athletics and gymnastics, and sailing for the period 1988-91 in real terms.

The most striking feature is that a major reduction of GSS subsidy has been suffered by the governing bodies of athletics, gymnastics and sailing after the 1988 Olympic Games in Seoul. Was the poor performance of athletics in the 1988 Seoul Games a sufficient reason for the continuous reduction of its subsidy? If so, a considerable increase for 1993 should

Figure 6 GSS's subsidies for basketball, athletics and sailing in real terms (1988–91)

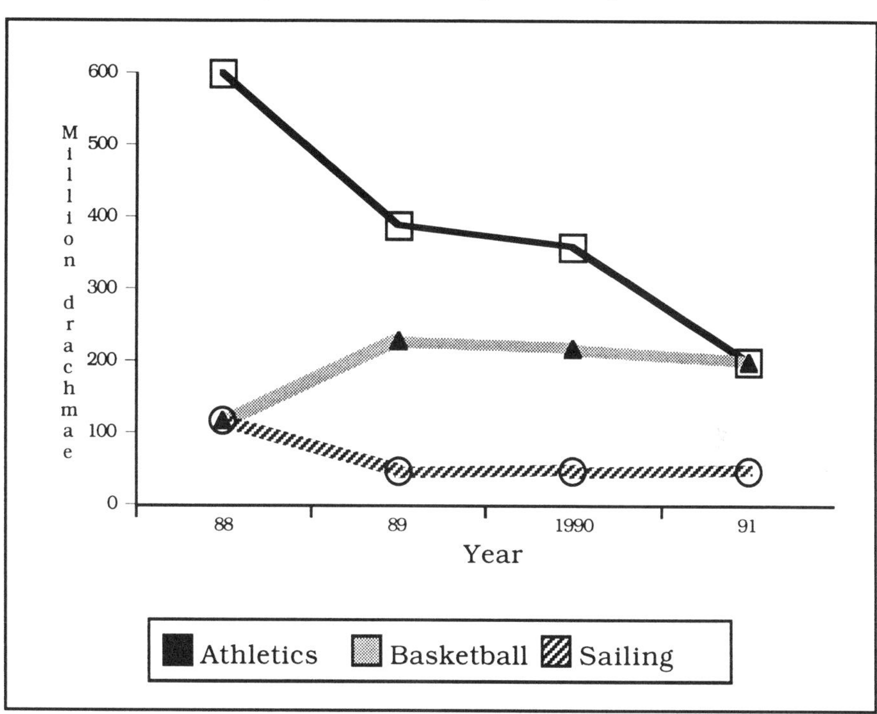

Source: GSS-Department of Competitive Sport, Organisation of football pools, 1988-91

be expected as a result of the most successful Greek appearance in the modern Olympiad by the national athletics team in Barcelona Games in 1992 (if success is to be measured according to the number of medals won). If this does happen, then reasons for the impetus of GSS decisions will have to be sought within spheres of decision-making other than sports performance.

In other words, political affiliation *or* conflict between the GSS and the NGBs could be the factor that dictated the funds allocated to the latter. The political sympathy when PASOK was in power and the conflict between the athletes' council and the GSS after 1989 was documented in a report the NGBs published in 1992; there is a clear reference to the close co-operation before 1989 and it is implied that the reason for the reduced received after 1989 was the political hostility between NGB and the present leadership of the GSS.

On the other hand, there is no doubt that reduction of funds allocated to the Sailing Association is due to administrative changes. The NGB of sailing has also been the channel through which the funds for the "Sport for All" programmes have been distributed. Diminishing government interest in the efficient operation of this programme and the introduction of "sport in childhood" into the national curriculum have resulted in the funds granted to sailing being substantially reduced since 1988.

The only one of these NGBs that has received increasing funds over the period under examination is that of basketball. Basketball absorbs one fifth of total NGB grant and its funds have been doubled in real terms since 1988. It is also remarkable that the major difference occurred between 1988 and 1989, immediately after the 1987 European Championship in Athens where Greece's national team won the gold medal.

What has been argued is that distribution of central funds to NGBs is a procedure open to multiple inputs and vulnerable to political criteria, as shown by the three case studies.

Basketball has attracted the new government's attention, not only as an area of substantial GSS spending, but also as one of the sports whose popularity and growing entrepreneurial prospects led to a sports law, which New Democracy advocated to encourage free market activity. This was brought about by the rapid expansion of business interests (mass media, advertising etc.), and the international success of individual clubs. The new Act has always been confronted with scepticism by the opposition because it failed to take into account the infrastructure of "Sport for All", and because the government's attempt to pass over the governing bodies for basketball and volleyball by appointing a committee of entrepreneurs to run the national leagues risks policies for the development of these sports being dictated by commercial interests.

Conclusion

In Greece, the relationship between state and sport is not a clear one. The state appears to play a role restricted to supervising and funding sport with all the formulation of sport policy taken over by the governing bodies of sport. On the other hand, there is enough evidence to suggest that state funding of sport implies some intervention. The way central funds are distributed in different areas of sports spending suggests a line of government policy for sport. For PASOK, the programmes for sports infrastructure and "Sport for All" enhanced the means for wider participation in sport. On the other hand, the abandonment of "Sport for All", the introduction of the new law for sport and the reliance of the sport office on funds from the football pools are indicators to argue that the interest of the New Democracy government is focused on those areas of sport that are able to bring money in and finance themselves through their own activities.

Bibliography

Clogg, R. (1986) *A short history of Modern Greece*. Cambridge: Cambridge University Press.

General Secretariat for Sport (1985) *Organisational and Economic Framework of "Sport for All" Programmes*. Athens: Department of Sports Development.

——— (1987) *Implementation of "Sport for All" Programmes*. Athens: Department of Sports Development.

Government Newspaper (1985) *Presidential Order, No. 77*, The General Secretariat for Sport, Art. 1 & 3. Athens: National Printing Office.

Karambelias, G. (1989) *State and society after the restoration of democracy (1974-1988)*. Athens: Exantas (in Greek).

Kazakos, P (1990) 'Financial policy and elections: State control of the economy in Greece: 1979-1989', in C. Lyrintzis and I. Nikolakopoulos (eds) *Elections and Parties in the 80s*. Athens: Themelio (in Greek).

Lyrintzis, C. (1990) 'Popularism: Meaning and practices', in C. Lyrintzis and I. Nikolakopoulos (eds) *Elections and Parties in the 80s*. Athens: Themelio (in Greek).

Nikitaras, N. (1990) *Sport for all*. Athens: Telethrion (in Greek).

Panagiotopoulos, D. P. (1990) *Sports code*. Sakoulas, Athens (in Greek).

Papageorgiou, F. (1989) 'Leisure and the quality of life in Athens', in P. Bramham *et al.* (eds) *Leisure and urban processes: Critical studies of leisure policy in Western European cities*. London: Routledge.

——— (1993) 'Leisure policy in Greece', in P. Bramham, I. Henry and H. van der Poel (eds) *Leisure policy in Europe*. Oxford: CAB International.

Spourdalakis, M. (1988) *The rise of the Greek Socialist Party*. London: Routledge.

Organisational Effectiveness of Greek National Sport Organisations: A Qualitative Methods Approach

Dimitra A. Papadimitriou and Peter Taylor
University of Sheffield, UK

Introduction and theoretical background

The national sport organisations (NSOs) of Greece are non-profit institutions which have been established to direct, promote and develop specific sports. Operating under the close supervision and funding support of the Secretary General of Sport (SGS) and the guidelines of the International Sport Federations, each organisation holds the entire responsibility of organising and managing the development of one sport, nation-wide. Therefore, for the prosperous development of sports it is imperative that these organisations demonstrate effective functioning in their organisational and technical affairs. This also will prepare them to face the increasingly competitive environment that appears internationally. In concordance with this, the concept of organisational effectiveness attains increasing interest in the context of NSOs and encourages further research on the topic.

In the literature it has been well documented that operationalising the concept of organisational effectiveness is not a straightforward matter, especially in a non-profit organisational setting (Kanter and Summers, 1987). A number of practical limitations led the authors, while advocating research on effectiveness, to abandon the 'goal' oriented definition (Georgopoulos and Tannenbaum, 1957; Price, 1968) of the term. As a result, fragmentation and disarray followed such attempts to generate applicable measures of the concept. Thus the question which remains unanswered is, how one measures the degree to which a non-profit organisation is doing well. Towards resolving this, theoretical discussions have focused on defining and identifying the dimensions associated with the term effectiveness.

Recently, organisation theorists have been approaching the definition of effectiveness from a political point of view. Connolly, Conlon and Deutsch (1980) introduced the 'multiple-constituency' view of the effectiveness concept which argues that different stakeholders in an organisation will support different effectiveness measures. This theoretical standpoint defines that an organisation is effective to the extent that it satisfies the demands imposed by various different groups. Thus, the organisation-related interests of the stakeholders should reflect upon the effectiveness definitions and measures.

In the relevant literature the term 'constituency' is used to imply a group of individuals who play an influential role on organisation's activities, have identified common interests they attempt to promote, and to an extent are irreplaceable claimants of organisational effectiveness (Miles, 1980; Mendelow, 1983).

Within this conceptual framework, there are a number of different interpretations which favour some groups in an organisation over others (Cameron, 1978; Scott, 1977). However, one of the primary questions remains to what extent these different groups can demonstrate consensus over the effectiveness dimensions. Another aspect to be examined is how far effectiveness measures of an organisation that derive from different stakeholders are in agreement.

In the organisational context of NSOs no research exists to illuminate the effectiveness concept from the multiple-constituency point of view. The isolated studies of Vail (1983) and Chelladurai (1991) are confined to comparing effectiveness measures produced by a few NSO-related constituency groups in response to statements predetermined statements by the researcher.

The aims of this paper are: (a) to discuss the major problems or dilemmas associated with assessing the organisational performance of NSOs; and (b) to present preliminary results of an empirical study that endeavours to define and explore the concept of organisational effectiveness in the context of the national sports organisations of Greece.

Specifically, the study investigates the conceptualisations of effectiveness of six influential constituent groups involved with the NSOs in Greece. These constituencies are NSO board members, paid administrative staff, national coaches, national team athletes, international officials, and scientific counsellors. All the groups examined play an influential role in the day-to-day well functioning of NSOs, and their responsibilities are irreplaceable.

This organisation-group dependency justifies them as claimants of organisational effectiveness.

Problems related to assessing organisational effectiveness in NSOs

Similar to many other non-profit organisational settings (such as education, religion and health institutions) there are some characteristics in NSOs that function as obstacles to assessing effectiveness.

First, NSOs are oriented towards providing services rather than producing tangible goods. They have been established to provide training opportunities and administrative support systems and services to talented athletes willing to compete internationally. In addition, they are responsible for organising competitions and initiating programmes that will broaden the mass participation of their sport. Both major areas of responsibility lead, by nature, to intangible outcomes and their quality measurement is surrounded with scepticism. As Kanter and Summers (1987) argue, when dealing with assessing non-profit oriented services, it is the social values that prevail over any financial standards. Also, the fact that each NSO holds a monopoly within the nation on providing these services renders the organisation to function in an environment of low perceived uncertainty in attracting recipients. Even more, the recipients of the services are not often asked for feedback or effectiveness judgements because they are not primary providers of resources for the organisation.

Second, the assessment of NSO effectiveness is compounded by defensiveness by any powerful constituent group, particularly when this assessment initiated by an external, unauthorised agency. When a long tradition has established these organisations as 'autonomous' and beyond the control of any formal and consistent performance assessment, such an attempt is expected to be unwelcome by the NSO community. The Board of Directors of these sport organisations view such assessment as national agency's or government's attempt to interfere with or control the direction and decision making of the organisations. The effectiveness and legitimacy of the NSOs, according to their Board members, cannot be subjected to scrutiny by anyone, because the provision of free sporting services by the state is declared clearly by the Democratic Constitution of Greece.

Third, one will have a difficult time to identify concrete objectives pursued by these organisations, by which we mean measurable goals communicated freely within the organisation and which direct the aggregate effort of the different groups involved.

In contrast, NSOs of Greece appear to have many informal goals which range from unit to unit or between different constituent groups. These goals very often are inconsistent with the principal mission of the organisation, and sometimes contradict the goals of other interest groups. A profound example of such goal is the systematic concern of the board members to take such actions or make such decisions that their re-election to the NSO board is ensured even when this conflicts with any systematic and well-thought attempt to develop the sport.

The complexity of this problem increases if we take into consideration that NSOs prefer to keep their goals unstated and/or to define them *post hoc* such that they justify their actions. This, as Kanter and Summers (1987) state, creates opportunities for internal politics, goal displacement and loose coupling between official and operative goals. In the same line of argument Chelladurai (1987) describes this problem in Canadian sport organisations as taking the form of incompatible goals being followed. For him, the pursuit of excellence and the promotion of mass participation differ considerably in nature, making it necessary to divide the assessment of the whole organisation's effectiveness into two separate procedures.

Finally, non-profit organisations including NSOs tend to avoid concern with keeping and processing numerical data of any kind or with trying to concentrate on becoming more efficient. This means providing the same services at lower cost, or optimising their labour costs. Rather their major concern is how they will attract more financial inputs to create more services. This makes them a difficult research target for anyone seeking for tangible evidence of organisational performance.

Summarising: all these problems — together with the absence of a concrete and systematic pressure for systems of controlling effectiveness — are to blame for the complete lack of such control mechanisms in the NSOs in Greece today. However, this by no means indicates that constituent groups are not interested in determining whether the organisations they are involved with are "doing well".

The problem of studying organisational effectiveness in organisations like NSOs lies in developing such systems of obtaining information relative to effectiveness that informs the interest groups about aspects of the organisational performance of interest to them (Kanter and Summers, 1987). Yet, these effectiveness indicators, according to Cameron (1978) should be comparable across organisations of similar type. Apparently, such dimensions are specific for each organisational setting and must be identified inductively by researching the relevant constituencies.

Methodology

To inductively generate effectiveness dimensions, sixty semi-structured interviews were conducted with individuals working in twenty NSOs in Greece.

These sixty interviews were equally divided among the six constituencies. An interview schedule of seven questions was developed, tested and used to help individuals articulate how they perceive "effectiveness". A few examples of questions are:

1. *As a participant in the operation of this sport organisation how do you understand the effectiveness of this organisation? How would you define an effective sport organisation?*
2. *According to your experience, which specific characteristics would an effective sport organisation possess?*
3. *Would you please think of another sport organisation within or outside the country that you perceive as more effective? Now, please identify some factors or characteristics that makes this organisation more effective?*

Each interview lasted from forty five minutes to two hours, and took place at the place of work of the interviewee. During the discussion, the interviewer made persistent attempts to keep the interest focused on aspects referring at the organisational level rather than on specific behaviours of individuals. Where this was unavoidable, the aggregates of individuals, such as athletes, national coaches etc., was the focal point of the discussion. All interviews were tape recorded and transcribed without any modifications.

Data analysis considerations and preliminary results

It is generally understood that analysing qualitative data is a process that involves personal activity and great discretion on the part of the researcher. However, some techniques have been proven workable by other researchers (Seidman, 1991; Jones, 1985) concerning different ways of viewing qualitative data and consequently how the data are coded into meaningful categories.

An inductive approach was favoured, since the purpose of this project was to examine conceptions of organisational effectiveness of individuals associated with NSOs without presupposing a theoretical framework. Therefore, two major categories emerged easily after preliminary examination of the data: these were of NSO Administrative and NSO Technical Effectiveness. These were chosen because they were broad enough to incorporate every possible NSO effectiveness dimension discussed in the interviews. Two other reasons for advocating these particular categories were the existence of a clear dividing line between them, and the modest constraints imposed upon future data analysis.

The data of this study are analysed and presented for each of the six groups separately, since we were interested in identifying commonalities about the effectiveness conceptions of each by identifying the most prevalent dimensions discussed during the interviews. For economy of space, each pattern is presented in a summary form with minimum explanatory comments.

Constituency 1: NSO scientific counsellors

The scientific counsellors form a relatively new and small group within NSOs with blurred responsibilities and job descriptions and were introduced in most cases after governmental initiative. They are paid employees with highly technical specialisation for each sport. Their major tasks include organising seminars, conferences, training camps, and competitions, co-ordinating the work of the national coaches, and collecting and evaluating performance results.

Working very closely with both the Board of Directors and the National teams, their conceptions of NSO effectiveness reflect significantly the administrative and technical aspects of NSOs.

For this constituency, an NSO is effective if it is administered by a flexible and adaptable board, is not engaged in long and senseless bureaucratic procedures to solve routine problems, and attains increasing performance results internationally. As a counsellor put it:

> "... the term of NSO effectiveness engages the precondition, the means and the procedure necessary to maximise the organisational performance in all sectors, competitive, administrative. That is to say finding out the courses of action that lead to the desirable end. Effectiveness is more a continual process than an end result, and every sport organisation should unceasingly struggle for improvement, because even if it is effective it can always become more effective."

Apparently the judgement of this constituency is not dominated by the number of medals obtained or the records shattered by the NSO's high performance athletes. Rather it is a much broader view which takes into account components of the internal well being of the NSO.

Regarding the administrative sector, therefore, such effectiveness components relate to the having an updated organisational rules and procedures manual that clearly distinguishes the areas of responsibility and skills required for every volunteer and paid staff. Goal consensus, effective performance at committee level, realisation of the planned programmes, information management, communication, resource autonomy and efficient resource allocation are some other elements highlighted by this group. All counsellors agreed explicitly that the principal objective of an NSO in Greece should be to support high performance sports, whereas for the mass participation level it should hold only a consultative role. In the words of another counsellor:

> "For me, the NSOs should be concerned about high performance athletes only, that is our focus group. The mass participation element of the sport is facilitated by a number of other vehicles, several sport clubs, municipal sport departments etc. However, this has not been explicitly stated by the federation leaders and major part of our scarce resources are allocated to this direction for a number of reasons."

Furthermore, there is no doubt that this constituency strongly associates NSO total effectiveness with Board effectiveness, and the availability of ample financial support. Concerning the technical effectiveness of NSOs, valuable components are the job autonomy of technical employees to develop and administer programmes concerned with the identification, selection and training of athletes; concerns for incentives, career opportunities, and promotion of athletes; and sport science support.

Constituency 2: National coaches

The occupation of national coach is a contract position of one or two years' term. The major area of responsibility of this constituent group is technical, confined to the daily training of the national team's athletes. It may be anticipated that their effectiveness notions will be directed to the technical side of NSOs. However, due to the fact that most of the examined NSOs in Greece are small, this group tends to be well-informed about administration too. The majority of the national coaches interviewed defined the NSO effectiveness in very tangible terms. As one of them put it:

> "Firstly, NSO effectiveness is the speed of the national team boat [this refers to the sport of rowing]..., there is no other way to convince that the federation is doing well..., even what the public is looking is medals. Secondly, it is the quality of support of the domestic side.., actually, these are the two sides of the same coin, but the high performance goals always prevail'.

For the administrative sector, this constituency underlines as essential to effectiveness the professionalism of the staff. That is to say, employees of NSOs, particularly the Executive Director and the Head National Coach, should be highly professionalised, with distinctive responsibilities and freedom of action in their areas. Then good co-operation between volunteers and paid staff, a functional internal structure, explicit planning and goal setting, competent work by committees, sufficient resources, and satisfactory wages are all proven contributing factors to effectiveness for this group. More specifically, this group underlines the advantages of clear operating plans in the NSOs with achievable and measurable objectives. Such written plans must be followed by the commitment of financial and human resources. In addition, this group believes that the major source of NSO ineffectiveness today is the Executive Boards and the way they operate. Here, consistent reference is made to the inability of the NSO Boards to handle the contemporary demands of the high performance sector, and to operate in an environment which requires very rapid and complex decision making procedures.

Concerning the technical side, this group grounded the NSOs' effectiveness on a complete technical and scientific team to care for the accurate detection of talented athletes and to monitor their development. Undoubtedly, all coaches view positively any athlete-oriented policies initiated by NSOs which will strengthen the self esteem of athletes and prevent the high turnover rates common currently in the Greek sport system. Finally, many coaches discussed the lack of well organised sport centres where the NSOs can have comfortable access.

Constituency 3: International officials

Officiating in Greece is a capacity with as yet undefined employment terms. However, for the subgroup of international officials (qualified by the International Federation of the sport) one can assert that their relations with the NSO are clearer. This is because their international involvements and progress depends completely on NSOs, whereas at the national level engagements are managed by the National Federation of Officials of the sport or various leagues of officials.

The effectiveness of an NSO for this group was a construct defined by a series of management oriented functions including good social and international relations, quality organised competitions, communication, expeditious information sharing, sport marketing, workable internal structuring and standing committee work . As the following excerpt illustrates:

> "The effective NSO is well known abroad, works hard at international relations, stands well competitively and develops and promotes competent officials initially."

Furthermore, this group more than any other underlined the necessity of independent officiating services because it concerns the long term survival of each sport, along with many social consequences. International officials call for professional operation of the NSOs' matters, which means managerial skills at the level of Board of Directors.

Constituency 4: National team athletes

This constituency is composed of athletes participating in international competitions. If the mission of NSOs is defined around high performance sport, competitive athletes and their needs are perceived to be the main focus of services development by the NSOs. In congruence with this group's understanding, the effectiveness of a NSO is based upon a strong athlete oriented support system. To put it in the words of one elite athlete:

> "NSOs are effective only if they are close to their athletes on a permanent basis. That is to say, that they, as organisations, are concerned and help their athletes overcome their problems and realise their performance objectives. We cannot say that a NSO is effective based only on the medals obtained or other sport performance distinctions because, sometimes, all these are the end result of personal initiatives and hard work on the part of the athlete and the coach. We should rather ask these athletes to express their satisfaction with the NSOs' support systems."

More specifically, high performance athletes indicated that a NSO cannot be perceived as effective if it fails to provide them with a smooth performance progression from entry to high performance level. This process incorporates programmes characterised by fair treatment and equal opportunities for all athletes, by moral support and adequate recognition. Other effectiveness-related dimensions supported by the national athletes were long-term planning and strategy, stability in policies, athletes' input to decision making, and development of competent coaches. In addition, financial support from the NSOs will make them able to meet the demands of hard training and competition schedules; they were unanimous that the most of them were unable to keep up training without reasonable subsidies or sponsorship for training expenses. Without this, elite athletes drop out at a very early age. The final administrative concern of the national team athletes was that the NSOs should care for their needs after their competitive careers.

Regarding the technical dimensions of effectiveness of NSOs, the elite athletes again underlined the sport science approach to training. In their perception, the current ineffectiveness of NSOs technically relates more to the noticeable lack of highly specialised employees including doctors, physiotherapists, and sport psychologists than to the lack of modern sports facilities. Finally, for them the scientific monitoring of their training with laboratory testing and reliable feedback is also an invaluable contributor to the technical effectiveness of NSOs.

Constituency 5: Board of Directors Members

National Sports Organisations in Greece rely considerably on volunteers for mapping out their courses of action. The Executive Committees — so called Boards of Directors — are elected by the General Assemblies of the NSO affiliate-clubs with the aim of undertaking the entire decision making process and overseeing every aspect of management. Therefore, the effectiveness conceptions of these individuals has more administrative than technical meaning. As one of the interviewees put it:

> "...the concept of effectiveness for the NSO implies to work seriously as an organisation on whatever you undertake..., and I mean on whatever you organise or you participate in; to conduct your organisational affairs with consistency and success; and to take part in all sport-related international meetings with meaningful suggestions."

Similar to the other groups, the NSO effectiveness profile of this group has a number of dimensions, major among which are good volunteer—paid staff relationships, competent professional administrative personnel, expeditious decision making by the Boards, good social relations, an efficient internal structure and the availability of financial resources.

Furthermore, this group raised repeatedly two major sources of ineffectiveness associated with the NSO-Government relationships. These are the dependency of these sport organisations on government, and the legislative chaos characterising their operations. Both concerns, according to the interviewees, have grown to major issues. Concerning the former, the Board members contend that often this dependency has been cultivated by the state through undiscussed sport policies or unexpected resources cuts. Furthermore, political interference in the constitution of the Boards by the ruling party is prevalent and sometimes very provocative. Regarding the latter issue, the interviewees highlighted that the present sport legislation is out- of-date and in several points inapplicable, while repeated amendments have produced immense complications for NSO functioning. Therefore, for a few board members being effective as a NSO means also achieving working harmoniously with the government.

Constituency 6: NSO paid administrative staff

Initially NSOs are formed and run by volunteers. However, as they grow, the demand for full-time occupation becomes strong. Today all Greek NSOs employ at least one worker, whereas a few of them reach fifty. These individuals assume the day-to-day operation of the organisations, permitting the volunteers to handle direction, development and decision making. At this point of development, the paid administrative staff forms a unique group and plays an important role in the effectiveness of the NSOs. As all the previous groups, the administrative staff have clear perceptions of what characterises an effective sport organisation. To put it in the words of one interviewee, "organisational effectiveness means to be able to do your assignments properly, smoothly and consistently at all levels".

This group implied that a number of administrative elements should appear in an effective sport organisation, namely: the development of a distinctive structure with horizontal and vertical differentiation, encouraged by a meaningful manual of rules and procedures. Other aspects included good working relationships between Board members and staff, Board coherence, good technology, formalisation of routine tasks, communication and information sharing, and leadership skills on the part of the Board members.

According to the experience of this group, the principal source of dysfunctionality in the NSOs of Greece today is the lack of professional occupations specialised in the sport administration. In addition, what must be clear for them is "who is accountable for what and to whom". The latter is ambiguous in the NSOs of Greece, most of which operate without an Executive Director.

Conclusions

It is easy to argue that this study serves pure research objectives, and neglects providing practitioners with easy-to-handle tools for assessing the organisational effectiveness of NSOs. However, when a new organisational context becomes a research target, the researcher should be sceptical as to what to adopt as a theoretical guide or instrument for data collection. This is because in organisational studies there are a number of parameters that can render a framework inapplicable, of which some are the nature of the services delivered, the developmental stage achieved (structure, age, culture, technology), and the environment. Following this line of thought, the NSOs of Greece constitute a new organisational context for research, necessitating careful and well designed investigations. This study forms the introductory steps of applying a multiple-constituency approach of effectiveness. The preliminary analysis of these data justifies the multidimensional nature of the effectiveness concept. This is to say that any reliable assessment on NSOs should use multiple measures which capture several organisational aspects. Despite doing so, the findings are blurred. For those NSOs investigated, and the six constituent groups, the results indicate that there is considerable overlap between their different conceptions of effectiveness. Most groups identifying sources of ineffectiveness manifested on these NSOs attribute the flawed performance to similar organisational defects. As a result, in disagreement with the main postulation of the theoretical framework, the personal interests of each constituent group do not dominate explicitly how they perceive the organisational effectiveness of the NSOs.

References

Cameron, K. C. (1978) 'Measuring organisational effectiveness in institutions of higher education', *Administrative Science Quarterly*, Vol. 23, No. 604: pp. 6–7.

Chelladurai, P. (1987) 'Multidimensionality and multiple perspectives of organisational effectiveness', *Journal of Sport Management*, Vol. 1: pp. 37–47.

——— (1991) 'Measuring of organisational effectiveness of Canadian NSOs', *Canadian Journal of Sport Science*, Vol. 16, No. 2: pp. 126–133.

Connolly, T., Conlon, E. J., and Deutsch, S. J. (1980) 'Organisational effectiveness: A multiple-constituency approach', *Academy of Management Review*, Vol. 5: pp. 211–217.

Georgopoulos, B. S., and Tannenbaum, S. A. (1957) 'The study of organisational effectiveness', *American Sociological Review*, Vol. 22: pp. 534–540.

Goodman, P. S., and Pennings, J. M. (1977) *New perspectives on organisational effectiveness*. San Francisco: Jossey-Bass.

Jones, S. (1985) 'The analysis of depth interviews', in R. Walker (ed) *Applied qualitative research*. London: Gower Publishing Company Ltd, pp. 56–69.

Kanter, M. R., and Summers, V. D. (1987) 'Doing well while doing good: Dilemmas of performance measurement in nonprofit organisations and the need for a multiple constituency approach', in W. W. Powell (ed) *The nonprofit sector: A research handbook*. New Haven and London: Yale University Press , pp. 154–166.

Mendelow, L. A. (1980) 'Setting corporate goals and measuring organisational effectiveness: A practical approach', *Long Range Planning*, Vol. 16, No. 1: pp. 70–76.

Miles, R. A. (1983) *Macro organisational behaviour*. Santa Monica, CA: Goodyear.

Price, J. L. (1968) *Organisational effectiveness: An inventory of propositions*. Homewood, III: Richard, D. Irwing Inc.

Scott, W. (1977) 'Effectiveness of organisational studies', in P. S. Goodman and J. M. Pennings (eds) *New perspectives on organisational effectiveness*. San Francisco: Jossey-Bass.

Seidman, E. I. (1991) *Interviewing as qualitative research: A guide for researchers in education and the social sciences*. New York: Teachers College Press.

Vail, S. E. (1985) *Organisational effectiveness in national sport governing bodies: A multiple models perspective*. Unpublished Doctoral Dissertation, University of Ottawa.

Changes in the Quality of Life in a Post-Socialist Society

Nevenka Černigoj Sadar
University of Ljubljana, Slovenija

On the road to independence

The changes in the political and economic systems in Slovenia began in the mid 1980s. Documents published by the League of Communists from 1986 to 1989 announcing the elimination of its power monopoly, its separation from the state and the introduction of a market economy did not stop a long-lasting and growing economic crisis. Several social movements, civil associations and groups criticised the leading party, and demanded political and economic changes.

In 1987 Slovenia was at the head of East European socialist countries in the democratisation movement. Articles about the Slovenian national program were published in *Nova revija*, No. 57, 1987. Some months later the so-called "Writer's Constitution" written by writers, lawyers and sociologists was published. In late spring and summer of 1988, tensions increased when three journalists of the weekly *Mladina* and a warrant officer were arrested and put on trial, charged with "attacks on the Yugoslav Army and making public certain military secrets". The Board for the Defence of Human Rights established at that time received massive support from the people.

In 1989 several groups and associations such as the Peace Movement, Amnesty International, Board for Defence of Human Rights, Helsinki Declaration Group, Association of Writers, Sociological Association, Commission for Equity and Peace, and others heightened people's awareness of the need for change. The same year the opposition political parties in Slovenia formed a coalition called Demos. The Slovenian National Assembly accepted amendments to the Constitution which enabled political and economic changes. In Spring 1990 the Demos coalition won the first free elections. At a referendum held in December 1990, 88.5% voted in favour of independence. The Slovenian Assembly adopted the Constitutional Charter for the Independence of Slovenia on June 25, 1991. The tensions with the Federal Yugoslav Government and the Yugoslav army reached a climax with open conflict breaking out on June 27, 1991. In the ten-day war the Slovenes resisted *en masse* and in a well-organised manner. In October, Slovenia took control of its own borders and introduced its own currency — the tolar. In January 1992 the EC recognised Slovenia as a new, independent state, and in May 1992 Slovenia became a member of the UN.

The economic situation

After winning independence, Slovenia lost most of its former Yugoslav market and subsequently many public enterprises are experiencing problems. There is a lack of capital to restructure production and to initiate a new economic cycle. The majority of workers are still employed in industry (45.1%) and in service sectors (39.9%) (Svetlik, 1992). GNP per capita fell during the 1980s; however it is still relatively high — US$ 5,463 in 1991 — compared to many East European countries (Svetlik, 1992: p. 11).

Although it was clear that the former (socialist) social contract was broken, the problem of unemployment did not surface immediately. The rate of unemployment was 2.6% in 1989, increasing to 4.9% in 1990 and then to 12.8% in 1992. In spring 1993 there were 120,000 unemployed, which creates not only financial problems but also considerable socio-psychological disturbance. Work ranks very high in the Slovenian value hierarchy — family is in first place followed by work. The results of a Quality of Life study in 1984 showed that only 18.1% of employed women and 19.9% of employed men would leave their jobs (even though their working conditions were quite exhausting) if they could have a decent standard of living without receiving salary (Cernigoj Sadar, 1987). The loosening of social bonds, a high level of insecurity compared to the times of lifelong employment of the active population, and rather ineffective coping with the drastic changes increased social pathology.

The process of privatisation of former socially owned firms has only just started, there are a lot of ambiguities and unresolved problems concerning the ownership transformation. The transformation of the legal system is quite slow and it does not sanction the illegitimate transformation of social property, and so a special parliamentary commission has been established to investigate such cases. After the first democratic elections much energy was invested in creating new political parties, transforming already established ones, and the fight for power among the parties which attracted attention away from the more urgent problems of social and economic modernisation.

Material standard of living

Despite the worsening of the economic situation, the fall in real wages (3.8% in 1986–1990) and the steps taken by the state towards withdrawing from the area of welfare service provision, the standard of living was not greatly affected until the beginning of 1991. This could be ascribed to inter-generational and family solidarity (about 11% of respondents with pre-school or school-age children reported regularly receiving some financial or material resources from their relatives), to the population's utilisation of their savings and to an increasing use of various types of informal economy. In 1991, 16% of respondents in the representative sample of population in Slovenia reported receiving regular additional resources from agricultural work (mostly amongst the older generation), and 6.2% from additional intellectual work (mostly among the young and middle-age generation).

The consumption of durable goods, electronic appliances and the leisure industry products increased. The young generation in particular is well equipped with cars and audio and video devices. Material standard of living and related material life style is highly dependent on educational level (Table 1 and Table 2 overleaf).

In the mid 1980s the objective and subjective indicators of material well-being showed that families with children were in a disadvantaged position at all family life stages. Therefore we wanted to know if there were accumulations of material deprivations in different life stages at the beginning of 1990s.

Seven groups were distinguished: the young; young with children; middle aged with children up to 5 years; middle aged with children aged from 6 to 15 years; and middle aged with children older than 15 years; old-aged over 55 having children at home; and old-aged having no children at home. These were analysed regarding their social position and material standard of living. The following dimensions were included in the discriminant analysis: education of — respondent, his/her mother, his/her father, place of permanent residence, infrastructure of the place of living, educational, health and cultural/recreational institution nearby, general housing standard, sq. meters per person in the household, household appliances, electronic devices (radio, TV, video, PC etc.), car, number of persons in the household with regular income, subjective evaluation of financial resources for everyday necessities (food, cloth and housing).

Groups in different family life stages are differentiated most by housing conditions, especially in the number of floor area per person. The older generation no longer living with their children have the best housing standard, while the younger generation with children have the worst. But the

Table 1 Ownership of material goods (cars and audio-visual equipment)

	Respondent or other household member has a car		One TV and at least one Hi-Fi, video or PC per household	
	1984	1991	1984	1991
	%	%	%	%
All respondents	54.2	76.5	17.8	48.5
Age groups:				
15-24 years	27.5	80.3	24.7	69.5
25-34 years	74.7	80.8	21.3	59.7
35-44 years	75.1	83.8	19.2	58.0
45-54 years	60.7	79.6	17.8	42.0
55-64 years	34.2	61.8	9.4	25.4
65-75 years	15.8	52.9	6.5	16.1
Educational level:				
Less than 8 years	28.2	38.9	4.3	21.1
Elementary school	40.7	61.7	12.1	33.6
Vocational school	69.9	79.7	17.7	48.6
Secondary school	74.0	90.5	30.8	62.2
High school, university	82.3	92.7	38.1	72.1

Source: Svetlik *et al.* (1991)

younger generations are not deprived in other dimensions of material standards: they are well supplied with electronic leisure equipment, and live in towns with relatively good infrastructure. Although the groups in different family life stages are differentiated at the material level of living, there is no accumulation of deprivation on a number of indicators simultaneously (Cernigoj Sadar, 1993). With the exception of housing conditions, the different generations had until the beginning of the 1990s roughly equal access to material well- being.

The consequences of the decrease of real income appeared only with a time lag, so there was no indication of a greater decrease in actual material

Table 2 Ownership of weekend cottage/flat

	1984	1991
	%	%
All respondents	4.3	10.7
Age groups:		
15-24	2.2	13.8
25-34	3.6	7.7
35-44	5.6	9.4
45-54	6.6	11.2
55-64	7.5	12.7
65-75	1.1	9.2
Educational level:		
Less than 8 years	2.6	10.5
Elementary school	3.1	4.4
Vocational school	4.6	9.3
Secondary school	6.4	15.7
High school, university	23.0	21.8

Source: Svetlik *et al.* (1991)

standard (housing conditions, consumer goods and access to welfare service provision) until the beginning of 1990s. However, comparing the living conditions at the beginning of 1991 with those in the middle of the 1980s, 46.5% of respondents evaluated them as worse. Dissatisfaction with living conditions rapidly increased in recent years. In 1992 more than 3/4 of respondents evaluated their living conditions as worse compared to five years ago. The subjective evaluations indicated fewer opportunities to resolve housing problems, to get a permanent job and also to have and bring up children (Klinar & Trampu, 1992: p. 1059) for the three groups of unemployed, those with low job positions and those who do not have Slovenian nationality.

Free time activities

Cultural life styles differentiate the population of Slovenia more than their material standard of living. Expenditure on education, culture and entertainment has fallen, reflected in a decreasing number of people attending institutions such as cinemas, theatres and museums. But the people of Slovenia have not become less active and creative in their free time (**Table 3** and **Table 4**).

Table 3 Involvement in creative activities

	ART CREATIVITY*		HOBBIES**	
	1984	1991	1984	1991
	%	%	%	%
All respondents	10.1	16.6	38.8	40.4
Men	13.4	18.8	20.8	21.9
Women	6.9	14.5	54.5	57.7
Age groups:				
15-24 years	24.2	36.8	46.3	44.5
25-34 years	10.4	21.4	40.1	47.8
35-44 years	9.1	11.1	39.0	34.6
45-54 years	6.1	11.1	32.2	44.7
55 -75 years	4.9	8.0	34.6	35.1
Educational level:				
Less than 8 years	2.2	5.3	26.9	32.4
Elementary school	7.2	9.7	36.4	38.4
Vocational school	10.7	12.0	37.2	34.6
Secondary school	16.1	24.6	46.9	45.7
High sch., university	22.3	33.3	51.2	50.9

Notes: * rarely or often play music instruments, write poems or prose, paint, artistic photography etc..

** rarely or often engage in art and crafts, collecting stamps and other hobbies

Source: Svetlik *et al.* (1991)

Most people have tried to keep up with their most popular leisure activities such as gardening, TV watching, excursions and socialising. Besides the positive trends in recreational and creative activities, there were also a number of negative trends. The percentage of those reading literature decreased especially among the younger population, and the percentage of people in representative samples who had no social contacts in their free time with either relatives or with friends increased from 1984 to 1991 by 5%.

Table 4 Taking part in sport, recreation and holidays (Slovenia or former Yugoslavia)

	Sport and Recreation		Holidays / Trips	
	1984	1991	1983	1990
	%	%	%	%
All respondents	59.7	65.3	54.4	37.8
Men	66.6	70.2	54.3	37.6
Women	52.9	60.6	54.4	38.0
Age groups:				
15-24 years	78.4	86.6	66.8	46.9
25-34 years	71.4	72.2	66.2	44.9
35-44 years	64.3	68.8	64.1	47.0
45-54 years	50.3	58.4	47.5	35.4
55-75 years	39.3	46.8	31.5	19.4
Educational level:				
Less than 8 years	29.5	31.6	29.1	15.8
Elementary school	46.2	44.5	41.2	21.6
Vocational school	71.4	68.7	60.7	36.1
Secondary school	81.1	84.0	78.2	53.5
High school, university	87.9	88.5	83.6	63.0

Source: Svetlik *et al.* (1991)

The greatest change is indicated by holidays. In 1983 more than half the population (54.4%) went on holidays (somewhere in Slovenia or the former Yugoslavia) while during the 1990s the number of holiday-makers decreased to 37.8% (Table 4). Although the leisure patterns have become very diversified in recent years, two old and dominant leisure patterns have remained. These are: physically passive and social leisure on the one hand, and gardening and hobbies on the other. Differences between gender, age and educational groups remain. The combination of female gender and low education leads to extremely negative consequences, especially for women manual workers.

Aspirations for education among those who have finished their formal education drastically increased, especially by women in all life stages. If at least part of these aspirations from 1991 are realised, there are possibilities of a cultural shift amongst women.

Since the middle of the 1970s, TV watching has been a very popular activity for all generations. Based on data from 3-day viewing diaries kept by 3rd, 5th and 7th year elementary grade classes in winter and spring 1989-1990, 35% to 50% (depending on season and class) were heavy TV viewers — more than 2.5 hours per day at the weekend (Novak, 1992: p. 63). Children's leisure changed from the 1970s to the 1990s: during the weekend they sleep longer, their leisure time is less active, and they read less literature. In spite of their better provision of leisure goods, children have a lower quality of life in their leisure time in the 1990s, which has negative consequences on their health.

New initiatives

The new welfare system, consisting of public, private, voluntary and informal sectors, is still in the formation phase and the new legal system is not yet adapted to it. The state withdrawing from the area of leisure services caused a reduction in programmes and staffing, and a tendency towards commercialization. On the other hand, organizations financed by state and voluntary organizations have became very active and innovative in seeking consumers.

To prevent a decrease in the quality of life, to monitor the situation, to enhance the positive legal changes and concrete actions, the Bureau of the Republic of Slovenia for Youth at the Ministry of Education and Sport (1991) and the Bureau for Women in the Government of the Republic of Slovenia (1992) were established. These bureaux collaborate with academic institutions, and the private and voluntary sectors in implementing concrete actions.

Let us mention some actions in the field of leisure. The theme of the second Children's Parliament in February 1992 was "Young People's Leisure", and some months later in June a public round table was held on the same theme. The participants at this round table were professionals and young people. They made an appeal for equal access of all children and young people to leisure activities and requested the support of government bodies to help maintain the already achieved quality of life in which leisure plays an important role. The organisers of this round table, The Alliance of Friends of Youth, published two booklets on leisure. The first contained professional articles on young people's leisure, while the second contained information about the programmes of leisure activities for young people in Slovenia. The Ministry of Education and Sport delegated the organisation of a project entitled "Sport for All" in 1992 to a private firm and tried later to evaluate its results.

In autumn 1992 the Slovenian Adult Education Centre set up a "Learning exchange" and 283 persons had responded to this project by the end of February 1993; there were no gender differences, most of them (85%) had secondary or higher education. The most popular fields of knowledge are languages, computer skills and software, mathematics and physics and art and crafts (Knific, 1993).

Besides the growing activity of state institutions there is a constant growth of self-help groups and voluntary organizations, some of which are partially supported by the state.

In recent years the interest in spiritual questions, 'new religions' (Krishna, Bahai, etc.), and bioenergy has increased rapidly among young people and also in the middle aged. In a special edition of the *Journal for Science Criticism* (May 1992), 19 New Age Groups in Slovenia presented themselves and a further 11 gave just their addresses. All these groups stress the quality of human relations and creativity. Meditation and methods of relaxation have become very popular in private and public leisure programmes.

The more the holistic planning of life course is endangered, the greater the degree of uncertainty facing people during the radical changes in society, the more they search for psychic and spiritual quality of life, but at the moment those who achieve this are exceptions. The transformation towards a market economy and the ownership transformation demands changes in our way of thinking, and this is more difficult to achieve than had been expected. The problem for individuals is the decreased social security which hinders their freedom of choice in increasing new outside options.

References

Černigoj Sadar, N. (1987) *Različne interpretacije položaja žensk v sistemu plačanega dela* (Different interpretations of the position of women in the system of paid formal work). Seminar about the position of women in Slovenian society. Center for Permanent Education at the Faculty for Sociology, Political Sciences and Journalism, University Ljubljana. Mimeo, 10pp.

—— (1993) *Kvaliteta življenja v različnih življenjskih obdobjih* (Quality of life in different life stages). *Družboslovne razprave*, FDV, IDV, Ljubljana. In print.

Happy New Age (1992) *Casopis za kritiko znano znanosti.* Stuentska Organizacija Univerze v Ljubljani.

Klinar, P., Trampuž, C. (1992) *O družbeni neenakosti in reščini v Sloveniji 1992* (Social inequality and poverty in Slovenia 1992). *Teorija in praksa*, XXIX, 11-12, 1055-1067.

Knific, M. (1993) *Statistika borze znanja* (Statistics of learning exchange). Slovene Adult Education Center, Ljubljana. Mimeo, 2pp.

Novak, H. (1992) *O prostem času slovenskih osnovnošolcev — koliko ga imajo in kako ga preživljajo* (Leisure of Slovenian primary school pupils) in *Prosti čas mladih* (edited by L. Kalčina Srhoj). Ljubljana: Informacije ZPMS 1, pp. 54-70.

Svetlik, I., Černič, M., Černigoj Sadar, N., Mandič, S., Novak, M., Trbanc, M. and Verlič, B. (1991) *Kvaliteta življenja 1984–1991* (Quality of Life 1984 -1992). Ljubljana: FDV, IDV, Bilten centra za dru'beno blaginjo.

Svetlik, I. (1992) 'Slovenia — A portrait of a new European country', in I. Svetlik (ed) *Social policy in Slovenia.* Avebury: Ashgate Publishing Company.

Not Merely Recreation: Sport as a Vehicle of Political Change in South Africa. An Historical Overview

J.E.H. Grobler
University of Pretoria, South Africa

Modern sport is generally regarded as one of the main components of popular culture. Indeed: sport is, globally speaking, sufficiently meaningful to so many individuals within society that it possesses the potential to be manipulated as a medium for political socialisation. This is especially the case if individuals strongly identify with sport. South African society is often characterised as being sports mad. South Africans, generally speaking, strongly identify with sport, either directly or as spectators. Their involvement transcends class and other boundaries (Hendricks, 1989: pp. 7-8). This reality makes sport as an institution particularly vulnerable to political exploitation.

Commentators on developments in South Africa during the last half century unanimously agree on a number of general statements regarding this country. Nobody would deny that deep cleavages divide South African society. Numerous issues contribute to this state of affairs. Prominent amongst those is the legacy of previously enforced statutory racial segregation — popularly known as *apartheid* — and of race-based class divisions. All agree that the process presently transpiring of dismantling apartheid, is retarded by various elements, including a deeply ingrained aversion to inter-racial social contact exhibited by some groups, especially white South Africans. A further problem is that no single South African nation exists by any stretch of the imagination. On the contrary, there are white South Africans (themselves divided between English and Afrikaans speakers), Indian South Africans, South Africans of African descent (black South Africans, divided between three major language groups) and a rather uncomfortable grouping of South Africans of mixed descent, officially lumped together as Coloureds.

The major political actors in South Africa, and more often than not their followers as well, have differed on the desirability of replacing old racial identities by new ones. Some were or are openly in favour of preserving the racial and cultural identities of their groups. Others regard the cultivation of a single, unstratified South African national identity as of the utmost importance.

South Africans of virtually all political persuasions consider sport to be an important institution in society, like education or religion. It is thus not surprising that, over the last four decades, sports has played a major part in the debate about and clash between exclusive identities on the one hand and a single South African national identity on the other. The point of departure in this paper is that in this process sports has been robbed of its ideal function of being first and foremost a recreational activity. It not only became a political football in contests between conflicting ideologies in South Africa, but has ultimately been utilised as a vehicle of political change.

The main objective of the most prominent black politicians and black political movements before 1940 revolved around "civil rights" and the acceptance of "civilised" black persons as full members of a Eurocentric white society in South Africa. However, since the Second World War the objective gradually evolved into a determination to establish a totally new society in which the values of the black majority would be predominant. Generally speaking the ideal of prominent black organisations like the African National Congress (ANC) and its leaders, as articulated in the famous Freedom Charter of 1955, became the establishment of an egalitarian society. In this society the predominant but foreign Eurocentric culture of the white minority would make room for a broadly based and indigenous people's culture.

The Freedom Charter, in which the word sport is never mentioned, was drafted in the heyday of apartheid. The National Party issued a policy statement in 1956 in which it was clearly stated that:

> Whites and non-Whites should organise their sporting activities separately, there should be no inter-racial competition within South Africa, the mixing of races in teams should be avoided, and sportsmen from other countries should respect South Africa's customs as she respected theirs.

This statement, which the South African prime minister, Dr H. F. Verwoerd, repeated and elaborated in a speech in 1965, in no way represents a programme to utilise sport as a vehicle of political change. It was rather a statement of determination to utilise sport as a force of continuity in a changing world, as well as a statement of warning to all and sundry that the South African government would never tolerate the use of sport as a vehicle of political change. In this sense Verwoerd certainly used sport as a political weapon.

The supreme body of organised sport in South Africa at that time was the South African Olympic and British Empire Games Association. Only white sporting organisations could affiliate to this Association, which was in turn affiliated to the International Olympic Committee as well as to the British Empire Games Association (South Africa left the Commonwealth as well as the Empire Games Association in 1961) . Thus South Africa deprived itself of the possibility of including talented non-whites in its national teams participating in international sporting events. It is therefor no wonder that Sam Ramsamy, the present chairman of the National Olympic Committee of South African (NOCSA), singled apartheid out as the 'real hurdle' in the way of black sportsmen and women in this country (Ramsamy, 1982). White sports administrators did not necessarily agree, but tended in the 1950s and 1960s to regard the colour bar in sport as non-political, as simply one of the customs of the country. They even characterised attempts to remove the colour bar as the intrusion of politics into sport. On the other hand, the more militant black sportsmen regarded apartheid in sport as obviously political — as part of systematic political discrimination (Kuper, 1965: p. 357) .

Resistance against apartheid in sport in South Africa emerged on two levels. Externally campaigns have been launched to isolate South Africa in the sporting world (including specific moves to have South Africa evicted from the Olympic movement and the moratorium on sports contact with South Africa) . Internally various organisations were formed to organise people to boycott apartheid sporting leagues and facilities and to establish alternative non-racial associations (Erwin, 1989a: p. 23) .

During the 1950s, as the non-white sports bodies became stronger, several of their associations formed themselves into inter-racial national bodies. This development towards non-racial sports resulted in the formation of the South African Sports Association (SASA) in 1958. SASA vainly appealed to white South African sports bodies to reject race discrimination and to choose all representative teams on merit. As this approach produced no positive results, the non-white sports bodies formed the South African Non-Racial Olympic Committee (SAN-ROC) in 1962. Its aim was to seek from the International Olympic Committee the right to represent South Africa (Thompson, 1964: pp. 17-19). SAN-ROC was destined to lead the campaign to have South Africa isolated from international sports.

Sport in South Africa remained segregated during the 1960s. That situation led to a number of strange incidents of racial discrimination in the sphere of sports. To mention a few of the most notorious examples: an outstanding South African golfer of Indian origin, Papwa Sewgolum, was granted special permission to participate in the Natal Championships, and won. In terms of the Liquor Act, however, he was prohibited from receiving his trophy within the club house, and it was handed to him in pouring rain outside. An even more ridiculous situation occurred soon afterwards. A local ordinance applicable only in the Orange Free State prohibited Indians from being present in that province for more than 24 hours at a time. Sewgolum was granted special permission to take part in a golf tournament in the Free State capital, but had to stay in a tent on the course when he was not playing or exercising. It was that type of racial incident which led to South Africa's expulsion from the Olympic Games in 1964.

From 1971 the South African government launched the concept of multi-national sport. It implied that black athletes were allowed to participate with whites in international events. A trickle of multi-national competitions immediately followed: a golf tournament in which 15 blacks took part, an athletics meeting in which both South African and overseas black competitors participated, and the tour of a French rugby team, which included a black player, to South Africa, amongst other events. But for all practical purposes sport in South Africa remained segregated and black sports organisations began feeling impatient about the lack of progress towards non-racial sports. Their perception was that virtually all white sport administrators were quite content to "keep sport out of the political arena" in South Africa, because those white administrators felt no compulsion to participate in the crusade to establish egalitarian sport. Most of the black sports administrators were proponents of an egalitarian society and increasingly considered it their duty to fight for egalitarian sport. This resulted in the formation by some of them of yet another umbrella organisation, namely the South African Council on Sport (SACOS) . It was founded in 1973 (Ramsamy, 1982: pp. 13-14) — ironically at a stage when the white sporting bodies were at long last starting to open their doors to non-white sportsmen.

Some of the sports activists who established the alternative sport organisations realised that, as sportspersons alone, they would never manage to change South African society significantly. They had to co-operate with the broad resistance movement in the establishment of a new deal in South Africa. Thus a former SACOS president, Hassan Howa, coined the famous phrase: "normal sport can not be practised in an abnormal society". Many sports activists felt that co-operation with the labour movement was essential. Thus at its conference on "Sport and liberation" in 1983, SACOS accepted that the working class was the force for change and would lead the liberatory movement. (SACOS, 1989a: pp. 32-36) SACOS, which claimed to be the "sports wing of the liberation struggle", was however not prepared to align itself to any particular political organisation or tendency, but insisted that it was composed of people who identified with different anti-apartheid political organisations. Moreover, SACOS was severely crippled by the fact that it lacked a substantial following amongst Africans. By the end of the 1980s Africans in some townships made it clear that they would not join SACOS unless it aligned itself with the ANC-supporting Congress Movement in South Africa. SACOS was under tremendous pressure from its own members to take up a political position, but refused (Carrim, 1989: pp. 37-41) .

SACOS was far from united in this stance. Many of its members experienced a challenge to develop "a people's culture of sport, one that will be mass based and characterised by democratic forms of organisation, accountability and rank and file participation" (Roberts (ed), 1989: p. 1). In other words, the objective has been the establishment of a mass based sports movement with emphasis of workers sports structures and the eradication of gender divisions. It was called "people's sport" (Vawda, 1989: p. ii).

The new generation of sports activists which emerged in the 1980s were not only dissatisfied that SACOS had not developed into a mass-based sports movement. Some regarded SACOS as a rebel organisation consisting mainly of Indians and Coloureds with connections with the Pan-Africanist Congress — a radical, anti-white South African political movement. In their impatience and prompted by the ANC, they established the National Sports Congress (NSC) to assist with the development of non-racial sport, particularly amongst Africans. Although their objective was not primarily to oppose SACOS, strained relations between the two organisation immediately developed. The NSC in 1989 refused to recognise SACOS as the authentic wing of the national liberation struggle. The NSC openly aligned itself to the Mass Democratic Movement (MDM), an internal South African political grouping which included the UDF, which later merged with the ANC, and the trade union COSATU, which became an ally of the ANC. SACOS chose to remain non-aligned. As a result it was superseded in importance by the NSC, which supported the sports moratorium and was against all forms of rebel tours by overseas teams to South Africa (Roberts (ed), 1989: pp. 2-4) .

Especially since 1979, the South African government has attempted to depoliticise sport, partly in an attempt to counter the country's increasing international isolation in sport. From the mid 1980s, South African sport has been regulated by the 1983 constitution. In terms of the constitution government business has been classified as either "general affairs" or "own affairs". General affairs are those "matters" which are not the affairs of a specific population group. By implication, own affairs are matters pertaining to a specific population group. The State President decides what is a "general affair" and what an "own affair". As it turned out, sport became both a "general affair" and an "own affair". Sport practised at school level is an "own affair", but open sport or sport outside the jurisdiction of schools, is practised as a "general affair". As a result of this duality, sport is the victim of fragmentation of administration and has suffered because of that (Zulu and Booth, 1988: pp. 1-2). The major shortcoming was the absence of an all-encompassing, centrally controlled provisioning and financing structure for sport in South Africa. On the contrary, a myriad of structures existed in different degrees of isolation. In the early 1980s, for example, there were 47 first and second level government institutions, including 15 government departments, plus more than a hundred local authorities involved in the control, provision, financing and upkeep of sport facilities. There activities were circumscribed in a total of 48 acts and 26 ordinances. As can be imagined, the result was a complex, fragmented and unco-ordinated setup characterised by duplication and functional ineffectiveness (RGN 1982: p. 91) .

Black participation in sport has always been constrained by the South African system of segregated education. In terms of this system, which is currently being replaced by a more egalitarian structure, almost ten times the amount of money per pupil was allocated to the education of white than to that of black pupils. One of the results of that monetary practice is that most white schools have decent playing fields, including tennis courts and in some cases even swimming pools, while few black schools can afford such facilities. In addition to developed playing space, most white schools have their own equipment, staff qualified to coach a variety of competitive sports and a tradition of healthy inter-school competitions. In black schools, on the other hand, low levels of sport participation has generally been the order of the day. The black South African political martyr, Steve Biko, described the differences between black and white school sport, as he experienced it, shortly before his death in police detention in 1977 in the following words:

> You find for instance even the organisation of sport — these are things you notice as a kid — at white schools to be absolutely so thorough and indicative of good training, good upbringing, you could get in a school 15 rugby teams, we could get from our school three rugby teams. Each of those 15 white teams has got uniforms for each particular kid who plays; we have got to share the uniforms amongst our three teams. (Biko, 1979: p. 19)

To suggest that an easy solution to this problem would be the sharing by white schools of their facilities with black schools, will not really be helpful. The fact is that, notwithstanding their superior sporting resources, most white schools do not have excess facilities (Zulu and Booth, 1988: pp. 3-4). It is for that reason that prominent South African political movements advance the belief that only the total restructuring of the education system will open the use of existing schools facilities to all pupils on an equal basis.

As mentioned, open sport or sport outside the jurisdiction of schools, is in terms of the South African constitution "general affair". This does not mean that the inherent structural inequalities which are clearly visible in school sport are not also present in open sport. The central government has always allocated grants-in-aid to sports organisations. Since the establishment of a Department of Sport and Recreation in 1966, this has gradually changed. From the 1970s the government's attempts to depoliticise sport in fact resulted in the handing over of the sole jurisdiction over sport affairs to the sports controlling bodies. Thus the government abrogated its own responsibility for the provision of sports facilities. The result was that the government made no attempt to alleviate the shortfall of sport facilities for black South Africans. Indeed, in 1979/80 the central government's contribution to total expenditure on sport amounted to approximately five percent of the expenditure, that of local and regional authorities to 8,1 percent and that of participants in sport to 31,1 percent (Zulu and Booth, 1988: pp. 4-6). White local and regional authorities as well as white participants being more affluent than blacks, it is not surprising that white monetary requirements in sport has been more readily answered to.

A survey conducted in one of South Africa's four provinces, Natal (including the black homeland or Bantustan KwaZulu) in 1988, revealed information underlining the backlog in black sport participation. At that time 144 sports were practised in Natal, with 215,708 persons registered with government recognised sports associations. Of those 96,768 or 45 percent were black. The most popular sport in the province was football, with 93,767 players of whom approximately 80,000 were black. The only other sports with significant black participation levels were boxing and road running, while in 40 sports there was no black representation whatsoever (Zulu and Booth, 1988: pp. 8-9).

During the 1980s the government policy of handing sole jurisdiction over sports affairs over to the sports controlling bodies, significantly accelerated the movement towards non-racial sports. Sports clubs were given permission to apply for "international status". which meant that people of all races could become members. Since 1980 a steadily growing number of clubs made such applications and were granted international status, including Johannesburg's Wanderers Club, which was the biggest in South Africa and had 14,000 members who were all whites. However, although the granting of membership by sports clubs to people of all races was considered to be an important symbolic step, it made little difference in practice, as most clubs maintained exclusivity by charging extortionate membership fees and, in addition, demanded countersigns testimonials vouchsafing "civilised" conduct by would-be members (Nyaka, 1989). In addition, SACOS was against blacks joining white clubs, and in one case a black man was physically threatened by SACOS when it became known that he had applied for membership of a white club (*Survey of Race Relations in South Africa*, 1982: pp. 353-354) .

Neo-Marxists in South Africa, taking their cue from like-minded persons abroad, argue that the state's attempt to depoliticise sport indeed resulted in its own extrication from ideological control over sports structures. However, this did not mean that sportspeople then took control over their own affairs. What happened was that corporate capital gained ideological control over both the establishment *and* the anti-apartheid sports structures in South Africa. In that way corporate capital managed to further subordinate the working classes to the capitalist power network in South Africa. Sport thus became an instrument of bourgeois hegemony. Corporate capital commercially developed sport "to give the masses what they want", thus entrenching its domination over one aspect of working class culture, namely sport. Corporate capital sponsored infrastructural developments on a massive scale to ensure that the work force had recreational activities over weekends. Sport was, to borrow a phrase from the eminent French sociologist Joffre Dumazedier, made the real opiate of the working class.

South Africa has indeed, over the last fifteen years, witnessed a virtual mushrooming in the provision of sports facilities for blacks. First-class athletic tracks and football fields, with coaching facilities, have become plentiful — due to a large extent to the exertions of local government institutions and mining companies. It is the official policy of all the large mining groups to promote sports among their workers as part of their welfare programmes. According to a report of the British Sports Council the athletics facilities at mines like Welkom are "markedly superior to any athletic track in the United Kingdom and equal to the best athletic tracks in Europe" (Sports Council, 1980: p. 80).

The provision of this type of facilities by corporate capital is heavily criticised by the proponents of egalitarian sport in South Africa. They argue that the mining companies utilise those facilities and employ qualified coaches to develop the potentials of the worker-cum-sportsperson and then channel them into competitions organised by the establishment controlled structures. The high success rate achieved by corporate capital in controlling sport has enabled the ruling class to counter alternative uses of free time and to prevent the development of a people's culture of sport in South Africa. Until the mid 1980s the anti-apartheid organisations in South Africa had no strategy on sports to counter the actions of corporate capital (Roberts, 1989: p. 14-21). From then onwards, however, anti-apartheid activists realised the importance of sport, transformed it into a major arena of political conflict in South Africa and established numerous organisations to spread the battle for non-racial sport across the whole of South Africa.

One of the many organisations in this category is the South African Tertiary Institutions Sports Council (SATISCO) . It was established in 1986 by students belonging to the South African National Students' Congress (SANSCO) . They readily admitted that they acted first and foremost on a political agenda, and had by 1990 not become involved in the actual practice of sport or in the establishment of sports facilities. Although they claimed to believe in non-racialism, their objective was to provide the black and Coloured students at tertiary institutions with a joint sports body. SATISCO affiliated with the NSC and supported the broad anti-apartheid movement led by the ANC. It supported the moratorium on international sport contact by South Africans instituted in 1990 and was determined to enforce it until all South Africans declare their support for non-racial sport (*KUH Nuusbrief*, Aug 1990: p. 9) .

The international campaign to isolate apartheid sport had a very noticeable negative effect, and that was that the isolation did not differentiate between 'establishment sport' and non-racial sport. The later was also isolated and suffered in the process (Gerwel, 1989: p. 63). However, it is impossible to tell with any degree of certainty to what extent sports was negatively effected by isolation. Participants in sports have experienced the situation in different ways. The experience of the sportsman who participated for purely recreational purposes differed substantially from that of the provincial or potential national competitor. Indeed, the dearth of international competition resulting from South Africa's isolation because of apartheid affected only a small percentage of sportsmen.

The possible negative effects of international sports isolation did not deter the non-racial sports movement. When the South African Cricket Union, which officially became a non-racial organisation in the 1970s, began on the initiative of its managing director, Dr Ali Bacher, to organise so-called rebel tours of international cricket teams to South Africa, it immediately encountered resistance. This culminated in the chaotic tour by Mike Gatting's English rebel team at the end of the 1980s. The NSC not only protested against the tour, but threatened to disrupt it. The South African government, wanting to stay clear of the dispute, announced that it would allow peaceful protest against the tour. Several white groups made clear their intentions to "get at" who ever disrupts the tour. Eventually Bacher had to back down and cancel the last stage of the tour. He also drastically changed his stance on both rebel tours and sports policy by announcing that the Cricket Union would support the sports moratorium until significant political change had occurred in South Africa. Change soon followed. Sport had again been successfully utilised as a political vehicle.

Rugby is arguably the national sport of white South Africans. A number of proposed rugby tours to South Africa was cancelled for political reasons, including a New Zealand tour in 1985. A defiant South African Rugby Board organised a rebel tour by virtually the full national New Zealand team in 1986, but it became increasingly clear to rugby administrators that normal rugby had become an impossibility. As a result two senior members of the Board negotiated with the ANC on the future of South African rugby even before the unbanning of the ANC by the South African government in January 1990. Political pressure was certainly making its mark on established white sport in South Africa.

The major breakthrough for non-racial sport in South Africa followed in 1990 when the ANC was unbanned and the government itself began negotiating with it on a future egalitarian society. White sports administrators who previously were against change now had no foundations left for a policy of segregation. The result was negotiations between white and black sports administrators virtually across the board, coupled with the amalgamation of previously separate sporting bodies like the South African Rugby Board and the South African Rugby Union. New non-racial sports movements were founded, like the Confederation of South African Sports (COSAS), to which 120 national sports bodies affiliated. But an egalitarian and generally accepted system could not and did not emerge overnight. Many a problem still has to be solved.

One problem is symbols. White national teams used to participate as Springboks, and used the official South African national anthem and flag as symbols. Many black administrators reject the future use of those symbols, arguing that they were icons of the former apartheid South Africa. Thus, the South African team participating in the Olympic Games in 1992 used the flag of the newly established NOCSA instead of the official South African flag, and no anthem at all. And when the national New Zealand rugby team played a test match against the South African team in the same year, the latter was allowed by NOCSA to call themselves the Springboks, but not to use the national flag or anthem. A furore erupted when the anthem was played and the mainly white crowd, defiantly waving national flags, joined in singing it just before the match. Ironically, when the South African national football team played Nigeria in Lagos soon afterwards, no significant sports organisation complained when it became known that the anthem of the ANC would be played before the match. A misunderstanding occurred, however, and the Nigerians played the South African national anthem by mistake. Meanwhile, in South

Africa, a backlash against the refusal of sports administrators to allow the use of national symbols in traditionally white sports occurred and resulted in a sudden blossoming of popularity of those symbols amongst whites. The controversy about sports symbols is still going on.

A second major problem is that of development programmes. One of the primary conditions on which South Africa's re-entry into international sport was allowed by NOCSA and other activist organisations was that development programmes should be implemented to alleviate the backlog in coaching and in the provision of facilities for previously deprived groups in the South African society. There can be no doubt that the statutory racial divisions, which were until recently applicable to sports in South Africa, restricted some sportsmen infinitely more than others. Generally speaking most of the white sportsmen, with the possible exception of some potential international competitors amongst them, previously benefited from government intervention in sports, if only because their privileged position in society gave them access to better coaching and facilities than that available to the less privileged, while black competitors on all levels were, relatively speaking, negatively affected. The egalitarian movement in sports demand the rectification of this imbalance.

Rugby, cricket and athletics organisations — to mention only the "big three" — are implementing development programmes. Huge sums of money are pumped into the popularisation of sports — not as prize money for international superstars, but to provide facilities, training and competitions for the benefit of the ordinary people. The success rate achieved has not yet been spectacular, but it is a long-term programme. More people tan ever before get into contact with sport — especially children. Thus the whole concept of "township cricket" has taken off, with many thousands of black youngsters in the townships playing cricket for the first time in their lives. For them at least political involvement in sport has meant a widening of opportunities.

The third problem, or rather controversy, has to do with the administrators themselves. The last three years witnessed the admission of dozens of black sports administrators into managing and decision making positions in South African sports, replacing white administrators who more often than not were vastly more experienced than their successors. This development can be accounted for by a number of explanations. Two major reasons seem to have been the fairly general beliefs that black sports administrators were not only entitled to fill the leading positions in a country where the vast majority of the population is black, but were also better placed than whites were to get South Africa back into international competition. Whatever the explanations, the even more important question in this regard is: did sports in general gain significant advantage from the politically motivated managerial appointments, or were the effects of the latter rather negative? To answer a question like that objectively is impossible. A fact of the matter is that more people than ever before participate in sport in South Africa.

In a comparative sense a number of similarities in the history of sports in South Africa and in numerous other countries can be identified — especially countries where class and ethnic divisions in the population feature prominently. Some types of sports are, in spite of politically motivated attempts at breaking down social barriers, still elitist by nature, while others experience mass support and participation. Fencing and golf are examples of elitist sports, while soccer (football) and road running are mass sports — in South Africa as in many other countries.

Sports has in South Africa played a major (if not the major) role in breaking down barriers prohibiting inter-racial social contact. Twenty-five years ago multiracial sports was illegal in South Africa. Nowadays all sports are officially practised non-racially and it is illegal to bar individuals from participation on the grounds of skin colour. On the sports field the master-slave relationship of old is fast being replaced by a healthy respect of individuals of different races for the ability and sportsmanship of others as competitors and humans. Indeed in South Africa sports is not merely recreation — there is no other society on the globe in which sports has a bigger political role.

Bibliography

Biko, S.B. (1979) *The testimony of Steve Biko.* London.

Carrim, Y. (1989) 'SACOS: Towards player control?', in C. Roberts (ed) *Sport and transformation. Contemporary debates on South African sport.* Cape Town: Township Publishing Co-operative, pp. 37–42.

Erwin, A. (1989a) 'Does sport have a role to play in the liberation struggle?' in C. Roberts (ed) *Sport and transformation. Contemporary debates on South African sport.* Cape Town: Township Publishing Co-operative, pp. 23–31.

Gerwel, J. (1989) 'Towards a disciplined healthy sports movement in preparation for post-apartheid South Africa', in C. Roberts (ed) *Sport and transformation. Contemporary debates on South African sport.* Cape Town: Township Publishing Co-operative, pp. 58–65.

Hendricks, D. (1989) 'The nature of sport in a capitalist society', in C. Roberts (ed) *Sport and transformation. Contemporary debates on South African sport.* Cape Town: Township Publishing Co-operative, pp. 5–13.

Kuper, L. (1965) *An African bourgeoisie. Race, class and politics in South Africa.* New Haven and London: Yale University Press.

NACOS (1989a) 'The sports situation', in C. Roberts (ed) *Sport and transformation. Contemporary debates on South African sport.* Cape Town: Township Publishing Co-operative, pp. 32–36.

Nyaka, S. (1989) 'Challenges and transformation in sport', in C. Roberts (ed) *Sport and transformation. Contemporary debates on South African sport.* Cape Town: Township Publishing Co-operative, pp. 66–69.

Ramsamy, S. (1982) *Apartheid the real hurdle. Sport in South Africa: the International Boycott.* London.

RGN (1982) Sport in die RSA. (Verslag van die Hoofkomitee van die RGN-sportondersoek), Raad vir Geesteswetenskaplike Navorsing, Pretoria.

Roberts, C. (1989) 'Ideological control of South African sport', in C. Roberts (ed) *Sport and transformation. Contemporary debates on South African sport.* Cape Town: Township Publishing Co-operative, pp. 14–22.

Roberts, C. (ed) (1989) *Sport and transformation. Contemporary debates on South African sport.* Cape Town: Township Publishing Co-operative.

Sports Council (1980) *Sport in South Africa.* The Council: London.

——— (1982) *Survey of Race Relations in South Africa 1982.*

Thompson, R. (1964) *Race and sport.* London.

Vawda, E. (1989) 'Foreword', in C. Roberts (ed) *Sport and transformation. Contemporary debates on South African sport.* Cape Town: Township Publishing Co-operative, pp. i–ii.

Zulu, P. and Booth, D. (1988) *Black participation in South African sport: The case of Natal-KwaZulu.* Maurice Webb Race Relations Unit Working Paper. Durban: University of Natal.

Sports and Physical Activities in Leisure Time of Brazilian Adolescent Girls: A Social and Cultural Analysis

Emmi Myotin
Universidade Federal de Viçosa, Brasil

Introduction

The value of sport and leisure for youth as important social and cultural experiences in developing countries is frequently invoked when it comes to establishing priorities for development programmes. It might appear at first sight that Brazil's severe social and economic problems and concomitant alarming rate of poverty would tend to relegate sport and leisure to a position of secondary importance. According to the IBGE (Brazilian Institute of Geography and Statistics), of a total population of approximately 140 million — 80 million under the age of 18 — Brazil has 32 million children between the ages of 0 and 17 living in extreme poverty, i. e., they come from families whose daily wages allow them to buy in São Paulo only three rolls with butter, two glasses of milk with coffee and a single bus ticket (*Veja Magazine*, 1992). São Paulo is the most prosperous city in the country, situated in the state of the same name which has the highest per capita income and relatively well-developed industry and trade. Given this background, one could question whether sport and physical activities should be given priority in the social and economic development of Brazil. Nevertheless, there is a relatively affluent segment of the youth population which should theoretically have access to all the facilities and benefits associated with an industrialised society.

As societies undergo industrialisation, people become less active due to increasingly mechanised technology; they have greater access to mass media communication and as a consequence their attitudes, values, and ways of living and acting usually change, revealing a new physical, cultural and social-psychological complex adapted to the new demands of living. Many studies have shown the importance of sports and physical activities as leisure pursuits in industrial and post-industrial societies as an instrument to reverse the influences of industrialisation. Initially, these studies focused on males only, because it was assumed that their work in factories and other modern organizations caused them to be more affected by industrialisation.

Only in recent decades, with the advent of the women's movement, has attention been diverted to the constraints women face in gaining access to the world of leisure — still considered to be basically a men's prerogative. In general, research investigating women's sports and physical activities as leisure pursuits focuses on adult women; the findings point to marriage, presence of children and domestic responsibilities as major reasons for non-participation in those activities (Woodward *et al.*, 1989). Although young women in their adolescence have not been ignored, the importance they have received is not commensurate with the significance of this stage of life in women's socialisation process into sports and physical activities. This is unfortunate, for not only is adolescence the key stage when much of the women's socialisation process into sports and physical activities takes place, but it is also when concepts of womanhood and femininity are established; these have a great impact on shaping their future behaviour and interest in relation to sports and physical activities as leisure pursuits.

In the course of fourteen years of personal experience as a university lecturer in Brazil working with the community from pre-school to adult level, the author has been in a position to observe that girls usually demonstrate great enthusiasm and interest in sports and physical activities until puberty. At this stage of adolescence the level of girls' participation in those activities was similar to that of boys. However, from this phase onwards girls' participation levels started declining, to the extent that at the end of adolescence it was almost non-existent in some disciplines.

This pattern of behaviour is confirmed by studies of women's involvement in sports and physical activities. They reveal that female participation in sports activities declines with age (Crompton *et al.*, 1979), particularly during adolescence (Kirshnit *et al.*, 1989). In this stage of the life cycle a large number of female adolescents drop out of sports and physical education (Williams, 1988) and continue to avoid these activities for the rest of their lives. Such findings are strongly supported by the continuity theory of ageing (Atchley, 1977), which posits that behaviour and attitudes acquired at one stage in the life-cycle predispose an individual to carry them over at later stages. This means either that participation in sports and physical activities during adolescence tends to prefigure adult sport involvement (Greendorfer,

1979; Snyder and Spreitzer, 1976) or that inactivity in youth tends to inactivity in adulthood (Sofranco and Nolan, 1972; Yoesting and Burkhead, 1973).

This is why many researchers have claimed that motives for dropping out of sports and physical activities, and the consequent low level of participation among girls during adolescence merit particular investigation and understanding (Skard and Vaglum, 1989). Participation in sports and physical activities is thought to promote not only positive feelings about one's body, and higher level of self-esteem (Anthrop and Allison, 1983; Snyder and Spreitzer, 1976) but also "healthy" competition, character building, encouragement of teamwork and providing young people with an area of instrumental achievement unavailable to the non-athletically inclined (Kirshnit *et al.*, 1989). As long as those involved in the health and well-being of adolescent girls do not pay attention to the drop out problem , millions of girls will be deprived not only of all the potential benefits of physical activity and sports during adolescence itself but also of the possibility of carrying over the values of an active life-style from this period into adulthood.

The reasons for the decreasing level of female participation in sports and physical activities during adolescence have been widely investigated in studies on girls' socialisation in sports and physical activities although there has been some controversy regarding the reasons as well as the most probable age at which the decline starts (Bardwick, 1971; Tyler, 1973; Kirshnit *et al.*, 1989). One line of research investigating girls' motives for dropping out of sports adopts a feminist perspective. In these studies the most frequently debated issues have been the psychological constraints related to images of femininity and what is considered to be gender appropriate behaviour (Kane, 1987; Hoferek, 1978; Reis and Jelsma, 1978; Scraton, 1986).

It has been suggested that although attitudes towards women in sport may have changed in the last decades, society still perceives sport as male-oriented and male-dominated (Scraton, 1986). This is why many female participants may feel that their female and athlete roles are in conflict; they then face the problem of reconciling prevailing conceptions of femininity—fragility, dependence, passivity etc.—with their sports behaviour which tends to stress aggression, competitiveness, independence, etc. (Carrington and Leaman, 1986). Another approach in examining why girls drop out of sports during adolescence has been to study motivation and attrition. These studies report that interest in and conflicts with other activities are the major reasons for adolescents discontinuing involvement in sports (Gould *et al.* 1982). This is explained by the fact that, with increasing age, adolescents have less leisure time in contrast with greater opportunities and interests to pursue non-athletic forms of leisure; from this perspective drop out of sports maybe due to interest in non-athletic activities (including boyfriends) and lack of time.

These studies, although focusing on adolescent girls, are contradictory in relation to the age group in which such conflicts and constraints take place. According to Bardwick (1971), while pre-adolescent girls are permitted, even encouraged, to succeed in competitive sport at age 12 to 14, changes in the gender role socialisation and pressures to adhere to gender appropriate behaviour may cause a drop in girls' sport participation (Hill and Lynch, 1983). On the other hand, Tyler (1973) reported that most girls give up athletic pursuits about the age of 15. While these studies disagreed in relation to the most probable age in which girls can be expected to give up sports participation, they fail to discuss how some girls overcome such constraints related to gender stereotypes and do participate in sports and physical activities. Furthermore, these studies are frequently carried out on a small sample of females either in their early, middle or late stage of adolescence; so the restricted age range does not allow a general picture of the changes throughout adolescence. Also, the subjects of the samples tend to be female athletes; this in turn makes it difficult to extrapolate trends applicable to the general population.

This paper seeks to overcome the aforementioned shortcomings of existing literature on female participation in sports and physical activities and will investigate adolescent girls from the general population living in São Paulo and Viçosa whose ages vary from 11 to 20. It is hoped that this age range will allow a more detailed analysis of the variations in sports and physical activity patterns and the impact of self-perceptions of femininity and the stereotyped views of women in sports on these activity patterns at different age groups throughout adolescence.

In addition, the diversity of the sample in athletic ability and place of living are expected to generate data more applicable to the general population. The present study addresses the following questions:

1) What are the patterns of physical activities, outside school, among adolescent girls (11-20 years) attending public schools in Brazil?

2) Are there age differences in participation patterns in sports and physical activities in adolescents from 11 to 20 years of age?

3) Are there differences in participation patterns in sports and physical activities between girls living in a late industrial society and in a rural community?

4) What are the reasons for participation, giving up participation and non-participation in sports and physical activities?

5) Are there any associations between perceptions of femininity and stereotyped views of women in sports with respect to participation and non-participation in sports and physical activities ?

This study worked on several assumptions:

1) It was expected that about 35% of the girls would be participating in some kind of sporting activities, particularly swimming and keep-fit activities (General Household Survey, 1983; Woodward at al., 1989).

2) It was assumed that the indices of participation would decrease with age during adolescence, due to the girls' socialisation process which discourages their participation in sports and physical activities as they grow older.

3) It was expected that the index of girls' participation in sports and physical activities would be higher in São Paulo — as a heavily industrialised city — than in Viçosa — a rural community. It was assumed that the effects of industrialisation not only increase opportunities for and access to leisure facilities, but encourage new attitudes and behaviour mainly through the mass media, including those related to sports and physical activities (Selby and Lewko, 1976). Furthermore, it was found that rural girls tend to be more traditional and conservative in their gender roles attitudes (Hertsgaard and Light, 1984). If this prevails in their attitudes towards sports for women it is expected that rural girls will participate less in sports and physical activities.

4) It was felt that the reasons for participation would be related to needs of affiliation, desire for physical appearance enhancement and health rather than the need for achievement (Graydon, 1987); in addition, reasons for giving up participation would be mainly due to a conflict with interests other than sports (Gould *et al.*, 1982); reasons for non-participation would mainly be related to lack of time, lack of interest in sports and physical activities and other things to do as a result of the socialisation process discouraging involvement in sporting activities.

5) It was assumed that there would be a relationship between participation/non-participation in sports and physical activities and perceptions of femininity and stereotyped views of women in sports: girls who participate in sports and physical activities will tend to perceive themselves to be less feminine than non-participants since the practice of sports tends to develop qualities considered masculine such as muscularity, aggressiveness, competitiveness, etc. ; there are more girls with internalised stereotyped views of women in sports among non-participants than participants (Graydon, 1987).

The results of this study will be discussed against the background of the current ideologies and practices of women in sport in the Brazilian context.

Methodology

Procedures

The data used in this paper are part of a broader study of participation and interest in sports and physical activities among female and male students from two Brazilian communities. The study took place in November/December 1991 and approximately 2,000 students were given a self-completion questionnaire. People over twenty and male respondents were excluded for this particular paper, and the results are therefore based on a sample of 1,497 girls.

The communities involved in the study were São Paulo City (the capital of the state of São Paulo, situated in the south of Brazil, with a population of around 12 million inhabitants) and a small rural town — Viçosa — situated in the state of Minas Gerais with a population of approximately 70,000 inhabitants. These areas were deliberately selected to represent the opposite extremes of the rural-urban-industrial continuum. The girls involved in this study were aged from 11 to 20 years and were attending 15 different public schools in São Paulo and Viçosa. They all participated on a voluntary basis; they were given the right to withdraw from the study at any time if they so wished. The head teacher of each school agreed to take part in the study and PE teachers were requested to select a representative cross-section of students of each school year. Therefore, the sample size of each school partially reflected its size in terms of number of pupils, classes and school years. In the city of São Paulo 1,341 subjects answered the questionnaires of whom 504 were enrolled in first level schools (from age 7 to 14) and 837 in second level schools (from age 15 to 17/18). In the rural community of Viçosa a total of 156 questionnaires were applied in one second level school to all female students attending school at the time the data were collected and who had agreed to participate in the study. This school was chosen for personal interest and convenience, since the researcher has been, over the last 15 years, a member of the staff of the university to which this school is linked and because its sports provision and facilities were similar to those schools from São Paulo.

The administration of the questionnaires was conducted in groups of 15 to 40 pupils in quiet classroom conditions or in the sports hall under the supervision of the author. The pupils took approximately 30 to 70 minutes to complete the questionnaires, with younger pupils, generally, taking longer to finish the task. The questions used were, in general, formulated and defined by the requirements of the present study. Some were borrowed in their original form from studies found in the literature on sport socialisation and motivation adopting a similar theoretical framework and methodology (Gould *et al.*, 1982). Where necessary, after translation into Portuguese, they were adapted to fit the Brazilian context.

Respondents were considered to be a participant in sports and physical activities if they were involved in at least one of the following 21 suggested sporting activities: basketball, volleyball, aerobics, cycling, gymnastics, karate, roller skating, ice skating, sailing, tennis, table tennis, weight lifting, football, handball, athletics, dance/ballet/jazz, jogging, judo, swimming, boxing and baseball. These activities were considered as most likely to be available to the respondents in the community where they lived. Although six categories of frequency in sport participation (never, once, twice, three, four, and more than four times a week) were registered in the questionnaires, only two were used for analysis in the present study: participation (once to more than four times a week) and non-participation (never).

To assess the perception of their femininity girls were asked to answer the following question: "Compared to other girls I know, I would rate my femininity on a scale of 1 to 7 as... 1 (much below average), 2 (below average), 3 (slightly below average), 4 (average), 5 (slightly above average), 6 (above average) or 7 (much above average)".

To investigate stereotyped views of women in sports, girls were presented with the following list of statements:

1) "If a girl is taking sports seriously, it can affect her feminine image";

2) "If a girl is taking sports seriously, it can reduce her dating opportunities";

3) "I think there is a great prejudice against women in sport — they are considered lesbians";

4) Girls should play only feminine sports, i. e. which don't demand strength, violence or speed";

5) "Girls should not play sports because they become muscular";

6) "Girls should not play sports which demand body contact as in basketball and football".

The subjects were asked to say to each of the statements if they strongly disagreed (1), disagreed (2), neither disagreed nor agreed (3), agreed (4), or strongly agreed (5).

In order to assess reasons for participation, a list of statements was presented. Subjects were asked to rate each of them on a 5-point Likert scale as follows: 1 = not at all important; 2 = not very important; 3 = fairly important; 4 = important; 5= very important. The section investigating reasons for giving up participation and reasons for non-participation required the students to indicate how applicable each of the suggested reasons was to their case. In both sections a 5-point Likert scale (1 = not at all applicable, 2 = not very applicable, 3 = fairly applicable, 4 = applicable, 5 = very applicable) was used.

Data analysis

A chi-square analysis was used to determine whether a difference existed between the samples from Viçosa and So Paulo and between age groups. To investigate whether a relationship existed between participation/non-participation and each stereotyped view of sport for women and self-perception of femininity Kendall's tau rank correlation was performed using listwise deletion. For both analyses a significance level of. 05 was adopted. Means were calculated to rank the importance of each reason for participation, giving up participation and non-participation.

Results and discussion

Patterns of participation

The present study examined the participation patterns of 1,497 schoolgirls aged 11 to 20 in 21 sporting activities. It was expected that about 35% of the girls would be participating in keep-fit activities and swimming. The results indicated that 42. 8% of the sample (641 pupils) claimed to have participated in at least one sport outside school during 1991, while 57. 2% (856 pupils) did not participate in any sporting activity. This percentage is slightly higher than expected possibly due to age differences. This figure (35%) was based on studies including basically adult women. Considering that the index of participation decreases with age (Crompton *et al.*, 1989), it could be expected that in the present study the percentage of participation should be slightly higher since its sample is composed of girls from 11 to 20 years old.

Table 1 shows the percentage of participants in each of the 21 sporting activities by age group. Volleyball was the most popular sport, played by 48% of sports participants; this sport was also the most popular for all age groups. The next most popular sports which had more than 10% participants were: gymnastics (24%), swimming (23%), dance (20%), aerobics (18%), cycling (16%), basketball (14%) and handball (11%). Contrary to expectations, volleyball was more popular than either swimming or keep-fit. Although volleyball can be considered by some to be a masculine sport, and for this reason discouraging girls from engaging in this activity, it is possible that the widespread television coverage of women's volleyball competition at national and international level in recent decades in Brazil has encouraged girls to play volleyball. If the presence of female sports role models in television can influence sports participation in girls, it is not surprising that in Brazil, volleyball has recently become the most popular sport among young female adolescents.

Table 1: Percentage of participants in each sport by age- group

Sports	**Age-groups**					**Total**
	11-12 N=78	13-14 N=131	15-16 N=179	17-18 N=201	19-20 N=52	N=641
	%	%	%	%	%	%
Volleyball	12.9	25.5	26.5	28.1	7.1	310
Gymnastics	5.2	11.8	27.5	42.5	13.1	153
Swimming	15.3	22.7	26.0	25.3	10.7	150
Dance	15.0	15.7	33.1	26.8	9.4	127
Aerobics	2.6	8.5	37.6	39.3	12.0	117
Cycling	8.6	21.0	21.9	41.0	7.6	105
Basketball	11.2	21.3	30.3	28.1	9.0	89
Handball	13.2	30.9	23.5	27.9	4.4	68
Table tennis	7.3	12.2	29.3	41.5	9.8	41
Roller skating	22.2	30.6	22.2	22.2	2.8	36
Weight lifting	3.0	6.1	36.4	33.3	21.2	33
Football	——	35.0	15.0	40.0	10.0	20
Tennis	10.5	21.1	21.1	42.1	5.3	19
Karate	5.9	23.5	35.3	29.4	5.9	17
Ice skating	20.0	6.7	40.0	33.3	——	15
Athletics	13.3	46.7	13.3	13.3	13.3	15
Judo	14.3	14.3	42.9	21.4	7.1	14
Jogging	16.7	25.0	8.3	25.0	25.0	12
Sailing	——	——	16.7	50.0	33.3	6
Beiseball	——	25.0	25.0	50.0	——	4
Boxing	——	——	100.0	——	——	1

Age vs sport participation

The assumption of the present study was that the indices of participation would decrease with age during adolescence due to the girls' socialisation process which discourages their participation in sports and physical activities as the age increases. Support for this hypothesis was only partially found. The chi-square analysis indicated that statistically significant differences existed between age groups (χ^2= 53. 66, df=9, p< .0001) in relation to rates of sports participation. The rate of participation was seen to increase from the age of 11 (48. 1%) to 13 (62. 4%). From this age the rate of participation started declining from 57. 6% at the age of 14 to 30. 4% at the age of 20. **Table 2** shows the number and percentage of participants from age 11 to 20 years old.

The explanation could be that in early adolescence girls are still encouraged to participate in sports and physical activities (Bardwick, 1971; Hill and Lynch, 1983), while as they grow older and through sports training develop their sporting skills, this makes them more equipped to engage in a wider range of sporting activities. For example, popular games and sports such as volleyball and basketball are introduced in physical education classes for the fifth year girls, at the age 11. Considering that it takes at least a year for someone to master the techniques of these sports, increases in participation in these sports may be expected from this age.

Table 2: Number and percentage of sports participants amongst Brazilian schoolgirls at different ages.

Age	Participation		Non-participation		Total
	N	%	N	%	N
11	26	48.1	28	51.9	54
12	52	59.8	35	40.2	87
13	63	62.4	38	37.6	101
14	68	57.6	50	42.4	118
15	65	41.7	91	58.3	156
16	114	41.5	161	58.5	275
17	109	36.6	189	63.4	298
18	92	38.2	149	61.8	241
19	38	31.4	83	68.6	121
20	14	30.4	32	69.6	46
Total	641	42.8	856	57.2	1497

However, for the present sample, there is a slight decrease at age 14 and a more marked decrease from age 15 until age 20, reflecting perhaps dramatic changes occurring in the girls' gender socialisation process discouraging sports involvement (Carrington and Leaman, 1986; Scraton, 1986; Hill and Lynch, 1983). Probably at ages 11 to 14 the girls' sports participation is not yet influenced by the prejudices of "appropriateness" of sporting activity for women as was shown by the present study. At later stages, as soon as they become aware that sports participation might affect their feminine image and their relationship with the opposite sex, it could act to prevent them from continuing sports involvement. For the present sample, the ages 14-15 could well be the key ages in which most girls drop out of sports as a result of the their inability to reconcile the prevailing concepts of femininity and sports behaviour (Carrington and Leaman, 1986). This is also confirmed by Tyler (1973) who points out that girls drop out of sports at age 15.

Another reason which could have contributed to the marked decline in sport participation at age 15 may be that, in Brazil, girls at this age generally change their school milieu as they move from first level to second level school. This change in school environment demands adjustments in their new peer-groups, teachers and activities which may affect sports participation (Crompton *et al.*, 1981).

Urban vs rural communities

Since literature on sports participation has reported variations in involvement in different age groups (also confirmed by this study), and the sample from Viçosa consisted only of second level students aged 15 to 20, the chi-square analysis of rural vs urban communities was carried out including only girls over fifteen from São Paulo attending second level schools. The assumption of the present study was that the level of participation of adolescent girls in sports and physical activities living in São Paulo as an industrialised society would be higher than that of girls living in Viçosa. Contrary to expectations, the chi-square analysis did not reveal statistically significant difference (χ^2 = .31, df=1, NS) between the two communities.

One explanation could be related to the characteristics of Viçosa. Although located in a rural area, its population is heavily influenced by the academic community of the Federal University of Viçosa. Many of its members, both staff and students, come from much larger cities all over Brazil, bringing with them different attitudes, behaviour, perceptions and values more pertinent to urban and industrial societies, including those related to sports and physical activities. Perhaps the fact that girls from Viçosa are exposed to these new social psychological complexes via peer-group interaction means that they have acquired similar patterns in their approach to sports and physical activities to those of girls from an urban and industrialised society. Another explanation could be that the relatively good sports provision and facilities offered by the Federal University of Viçosa, near to their homes, is influential in encouraging them to take part in sports and physical activities.

Finally, mass media communication is well developed in Brazil and reaches the most remote areas, including Viçosa. In the last decade women's sports have been widely televised in Brazil, even in sports considered by some to be "masculine" such as basketball and volleyball, in which Brazil has had a good international reputation. At the same time, Brazil "imported" the North-American fashion of exercise and aerobics, and it dominated if not the lives, then the minds of many Brazilian women. It was the theme of a soap opera screened during peak television hours for almost a year and considered an institution in Brazil with millions of viewers. It portrayed the lifestyle of beautiful, sensual, healthy, slim and successful women who frequently gathered in a sports club which acted as the centre stage of the drama. If the presence of female sports role models in television can encourage girls' sports participation and both samples were equally exposed, this could have helped to equalise the index of participation in sports and physical activities of the girls from Viçosa and São Paulo.

Reasons for participation in sports and physical activities

The assumption was that reasons for participation would be related to needs of affiliation, desire for enhancing physical appearance and health rather than needs for achievement. The results confirmed this assumption and findings of other studies (Graydon, 1987). The mean importance ratings calculated to determine the relative importance of the 26 suggested reasons showed that the reasons which were rated by participants as most important were:

"I want to be healthy" (M=4. 50, SD= .84),
"I want to be in shape" (M = 4.17, SD= 1.02),
"I like to make new friends" (M= 4.17, SD= 1.04),
"I want to be with friends" (M= 4.06, SD= 1.13), and
"I want to learn new skills" (M= 4.03, SD= 1.04).

The least important reasons were

"My parents want me to participate" (M= 2.18, SD= 1.34),
"I like to get out of the house" (M= 2.33, SD= 1.23),
"I want to be popular" (M= 2.39, SD= 1. 39) and
"I want to be stronger" (M= 2. 43, SD= 1.34).

Reasons for giving up participation

It was assumed that reasons for giving up participation would be mainly due to a conflict of interest with activities other than sports. The mean importance ratings calculated to determine the relative importance of the 16 suggested reasons confirmed this assumption. The most applicable reasons were " I had other things to do" (M = 2.69, SD= 1.62, N= 533) and " The place/time was not convenient" (M= 1.74, SD= 1.51, N= 533). Reasons rated as least applicable by these dropouts were "I was afraid of making a fool of myself" M = 1.28, SD= 1.08) and "The activity made me too tense" (M = 1.30, SD= 1.07).

Reasons for non-participation

The assumption was that reasons for non-participation would mainly be related to lack of time, lack of interest and other things to do, as a result of the socialisation process discouraging involvement in sporting activities. The mean ratings calculated to determine the relative importance of each of the 14 suggested reasons confirmed this assumption. The reasons which were most applicable were:

"I did not have time" (M = 3. 22, SD= 1. 73, N= 311);
"I had other things to do" (M = 3. 01, SD= 1. 66, N= 311); and
"I was not interested" (M= 2. 48, SD= 1. 72; N= 311).

Reasons indicated as least applicable were:

"No transport to take me there" (M= 1.41, SD= 1.18, N= 311) and
"My friends did not play with me" (M= 1.58, SD= 1.30, N= 311).

Sport participation in relation to self-perceptions of femininity

It was assumed that there would be a relationship between sport participation and perception of femininity: girls who participate in sports and physical activities would tend to perceive themselves to be less feminine than non-participants. This study, however, did not confirm this assumption. Kendall's rank correlation revealed that there is a very low, but significant correlation between sport involvement and self-perception of femininity (t= .08, p< .001, N= 1,429); participants tended to rate themselves as more feminine than non-participants.

To verify whether the relationship between sport participation and self-rating of femininity remained constant in different age groups, Kendall's rank correlation was calculated for the age groups 11 to 14 (group 1), 15 to 17 (group 2) and 18 to 20 (group 3). The results revealed no statistically significant correlation for group 1; for group 2 the correlation remained similar

($t = .07$, $p < .02$, $N = 702$); and for group 3 there was an increase in the correlation ($t = .16$, $p < .001$, $N = 387$). Possibly, at 11 to 14, the girls are not yet as preoccupied with the image of femininity as they are at later stages of adolescence. From this period onwards, due to considerable biological changes coupled with an intensification of the gender socialisation process, girls become more aware of prevailing conceptions of femininity (Hill and Lynch, 1983). If they have enjoyed sporting activities and want to continue with the activities they may feel conflict because, traditionally, sports are still considered a male oriented and male dominated activity (Scraton, 1986).

It has been suggested that the traditional image of women as fragile and delicate is not consistent with the aggression and prowess involved in contact games such as basketball (Ho and Walker, 1982). One clear strategy which the girls use to overcome the stigma of being a sportswoman is either to drop out of sports altogether or choose activities considered to be feminine or asexual/neutral by the general population. For example, the present study found that the five most popular sports were volleyball, gymnastics, swimming, dance and aerobics, usually accepted by the general population as "appropriate" for women. When analysing sport popularity by age group, it became visible that more older girls (fifteen years and over) engaged most in activities considered basically feminine: aerobics, gymnastics and dance; girls between 11 and 14 engaged mainly in volleyball and swimming. As a result of this pattern of choice adopted by the girls over 14, and the fact that the reasons for participation in these "feminine" activities are to develop fitness, grace and to be in shape — in short, to be feminine, it is not surprising that participants reported being more feminine than non-participants.

Sport participation in relation to stereotyped views of women in sport

This study confirmed the assumption that there would be a relationship between sport participation and stereotyped views of sport for women found elsewhere (Graydon, 1978). Kendall's rank correlation revealed a very low negative, but significant correlation between sport involvement and the following five suggested stereotyped views of sports for women: "If a girl takes sports seriously, it can reduce her feminine image" ($t = -.06$, $p < .01$, $N = 1429$); "If a girl takes sports seriously, it can reduce the possibility of finding a date" ($t = -.08$, $p < .001$, $N = 1429$); "Girls should play only feminine sports i.e. which do not demand strength, violence or speed" ($t = -.07$, $p < .002$, $N = 1429$); "Girls should not play sports because they become muscular" ($t = -.08$, $p < .001$, $N = 1429$); "Girls should not play sports which demand body contact such as basketball and football" ($t = -.05$, $p < .03$, $N = 1429$). In all cases participants tended to disagree more than non-participants with the stereotyped views of sports for women presented to them. It can be interpreted that non-participants have in general internalised more stereotypes which could have prevented them from engaging in sports and physical activities and that participants have already overcome prevailing sport stereotypes in order to engage in sports and physical activities.

To investigate whether the associations between sports participation and stereotyped views of women in sports were maintained at different age groups, further Kendall's rank correlations were calculated. The results revealed no statistically significant correlation in any stereotyped view in the age group 11 to 14. Perhaps at this age the girls are not yet so aware of and influenced by gender role socialisation and pressures to adhere to gender appropriate behaviour (Bardwick, 1971). The statement "I think there is a great prejudice against women in sport; they are considered lesbians" , was not significant for the whole sample, or for any age groups. (It may be that the meaning of lesbianism was not yet fully understood by the adolescents of the sample).

Therefore, five aspects remained significant for age groups 2 and 3:

> "Girls should play only feminine sports, i.e. which do not demand strength, violence or speed": $t = -.12$ ($p < .001$, $N = 702$) for group 2 and $t = -.14$ ($p < .001$, $N = 387$) for group 3;
>
> "If a girl takes sports seriously, it can reduce her feminine image": $t = -.11$ ($p < .002$, $N = 702$) for group 2 and $t = -.14$ ($p < .001$, $N = 387$) for group 3;
>
> "If a girl takes sports seriously, it can reduce the possibility of finding a date": $t = -.13$ ($p < .001$, $N = 702$) for group 2 and $t = -.17$ ($p < .001$, $N = 387$) for group 3;
>
> "Girls should not play sports because they become muscular": $t = -.12$ ($p < .001$, $N = 702$) for group 2 and $t = -.11$ ($p < .02$, $N = 387$) for group 3;
>
> "Girls should not play sports which demand body contact such as basketball and football": $t = -.12$ ($p < .001$, $N = 702$) for group 2 and $t = -.09$ ($p < .03$, $N = 387$) for group 3.

In this analysis by age group the correlations revealed that sport participants tended to disagree more than non-participants with some of the stereotyped views of women in sport presented to them. Sport participants might have already felt themselves to some extent to be the subject of the prejudices and stereotypes against women in sports through their involvement; if they felt that in playing sports they were breaking the norms of female appropriate behaviour, as a form of defence or justification of their own involvement in sports they may have disagreed more emphatically with the stereotypes presented to them.

Conclusions

This study was an attempt to analyse Brazilian adolescent girls' physical activity patterns and its interrelationship with self-perception of femininity and prevailing stereotyped views of women in sport. Overall, the findings of this study did not differ substantially from those reported in the literature on female sports participation in Britain or North America. Where consistency with other studies was not found, this was due basically to differences in sports provision and characteristics of the sample regarding age group and category of sport participation, i.e., non-athletes or athletes. Some caution, however, should be taken in interpreting the findings regarding age differences in the correlations. Since the data of this study are not longitudinal, differences between age categories should not be interpreted only as a result of developmental changes. Also, this study did not establish causal relationships; therefore, any possible explanation provided in this study regarding variable relationships was merely conjecture (Hertsgaard and Light, 1984).

As a final consideration, it is recognized that an analysis of girls' physical activities patterns based only on motivation and correlational studies, as was done here, is too narrow to understand and explain female sport involvement. The author is currently working on a broader study on girls' physical activity patterns in which several other variables are analysed simultaneously in an attempt to better understand the nature of Brazilian females' experience in sport and physical activities.

Note: This paper is part of the dissertation to be submitted by the author as a partial requirement for a Ph. D. degree at Loughborough University of Technology, UK, under the supervision of Dr. Duncan Cramer, and of Dr. Sheila Scraton, Leeds Metropolitan University.

References

Anthrop, J. and Allison, M. T. (1983) 'Role conflict and the high school female athlete', *Research Quarterly*, Vol. 54: pp. 104–111.

Atchley, R. (1977) *The social forces in later life*. Belmont, CA: Wadsworth.

Bardwick, J. (1971) *Psychology of women: A study of bio- cultural conflicts*. New York: Harper and Row.

Carrington, B. and Leaman, O. (1986) 'Equal opportunities and physical education', in J. Evans (ed) *Physical Education and Schooling*. Lewes: Falmer Press, pp. 215-216.

Crompton, J. L., Lamb Jr., C. W. and Vedlitz, A. (1979) 'Age and sex differences among adolescent participants in nine outdoor recreation activities', *Research Quarterly*, Vol. 50, No. 4: pp. 589–598.

Crompton, J. L., Vedlitz, A. and Lamb Jr., C. W. (1981) 'Recreational activity clustering among adolescents', *Research Quarterly*, Vol. 52, No. 4: pp. 449–467.

General Household Survey 1983 (1985) Office of Population Censuses and Surveys, Social Survey Division, London: HMSO.

Gould, D., Feltz, D. L., Horn, T. and Weiss, M. (1982) 'Reasons for discontinuing involvement in competitive youth swimming', *Journal of Sport Behavior*, Vol. 5: pp. 155-165.

Graydon, J. K. (1987) 'Psychological research and the sportswoman', in *Med. Sport Sci.*, Vol. 24, Karger, Basel, pp. 54–82.

Greendorfer, S. L. (1979) 'Childhood sport socialization influences of male and female track athletes', *Arena Review*, Vol. 3: pp. 39–53.

Hertsgaard, D. and Light, H. (1984) 'Junior high girls' attitudes towards the rights and roles of women', *Adolescence*, Vol. 19 No. 76: pp. 847–853.

Hill, J. P. and Lynch, M. E. (1983) 'The intensification of gender-related role expectations during early adolescence', in J. Brooks-Gunn and A. C. Petersen (eds) *Girls at puberty: Biological and psychological perspectives*. London: Plenum, pp. 201-228.

Ho, L. and Walker, J. E. (1982) 'Female athletes and nonathletes: similarities and differences in self- perception', *Journal of Sport Behavior*, Vol. 5, No. 1: pp. 12–27.

Hoferek, M. J. (1978) 'Towards wider vistas: societal sex- role models and their relationship to the sports world', in W. B. Straub (ed) *Sport psychology: An analysis of athlete behavior*. Ithaca: Mouvements Publications, pp. 293–299.

Kane, J. (1987) 'The "new" female athlete: socially sanctioned image or modern role for women?', in *Medicine and Sport Science*, Vol. 24, Karger, Basel, pp. 101–111.

Kirshnit, C. E., Ham, M. and Richards, M. H. (1989) 'The sporting life: Athletic activities during early adolescence', *Journal of Youth and adolescence*, Vol. 18, No. 6: pp. 601-615.

Reis, H. T. and Jelsma, B. (1978) 'A social psychology of sex differences in sport', in W. F. Straub (ed) *Sport psychology: An analysis of athlete behavior*, Ithaca: Mouvement Publication, pp. 276–286.

Scraton, S. J. (1986) 'Images of femininity and the teaching of girls' physical education', in J. Evans (ed) *Physical Education and schooling*. Lewes: Falmer Press, pp. 71–94.

Selby, R. and Lewko, J. (1976) 'Children's attitudes toward females in sports: their relationship with sex, grade, and sports participation', *Research Quarterly*, Vol. 47, No. 3: pp. 453–463.

Skard, O. and Vaglum, P. (1989) 'The influence of psychosocial and sport factors on dropout from boy's soccer: a prospective study', *Scandinavian Journal of Sports Science*, Vol. 11, No. 2: pp. 65–72.

Snyder, E. E. and Spreitzer, E. (1976) 'Correlates of sports participation among adolescent girls', *Research Quarterly*, Vol. 47, No. 4: pp. 804–809.

Sofranco, A. J. and Nolan, M. F. (1972) 'Early life experiences and adult sports participation', *Journal of Leisure Research*, Vol. 4: pp. 6–18.

Tyler, S. (1973) 'Adolescent crisis: sport participation for the female', in *DGWS research reports: Women in sports.*(edited by D. V. Harris), Vol. 2. Washington, D. C.: American Association of Health and PE Research.

Veja Magazine (1992) 'Vida brasileira: Infancia maltrapilha [Brazilian life: ragged childhood]. September 16, p. 78–81.

Yoesting, D. R. and Burkhead, D. L. (1973) 'Significance of childhood recreation experience on adult leisure behaviour: An exploratory analysis', *Journal of Leisure Research*, Vol. 5: pp. 25–36.

Williams, A. (1988) 'Physical activity patterns among adolescents — some curriculum implications', *Physical Education Review*, Vol. 11, No. 1: pp. 28–39.

Woodward, D., Green, E. and Hebron, S. (1989) 'The sociology of women's leisure and physical recreation: constraints and opportunities', *International Review for Sociology of Sport*, Vol. 24, No. 2: pp. 121–135.

A History of Sports Policy and Law in Japan since 1945

Kazuo Uchiumi
Hitotsubashi University, Tokyo, Japan

Summary

School curricula enabled ordinary Japanese children to play sport after the end of World War II, but for adults still it was something only the elite and the rich could afford to engage in. Since its formal independence, Japan has been under the umbrella of the USA politically, economically, militarily and culturally. With the 'cold war' Japan was re-militarized and imperialism came to be stressed again.

As hoped and expected, the Tokyo Olympic Games (1964) benefited Japan politically, economically and militarily, and the sports movement emerged. In the 1970s mass participation and the involvement of government grew and a 'right to sport' was born. However, since the 1980s a stingy government policy has been in force, and social welfare has been cut, while in the sporting world commercialization has been gaining power. The characteristics of sports policies are being queried now in Japan as much as in European countries.

Introduction

Since the 1960s in industrialized countries 'Sport for All' has developed, especially in European countries, supported by the idea of the welfare state, and sport has been thought of as a form of recreational welfare. Although Japan has not really enjoyed the benefits of the welfare state, the 1970s were called the decade of welfare. However, since around 1980 the mainstreams of sport ideologies and leisure policies in Japan have been commercialization in economics and imperialism in politics. Generally speaking, sport is conservative and sometimes reactionary. Therefore the democratization of sports policy and the development of the public face of sport are urgent problems in

Japan. A historical review of sports policy since World War II will be needed first, related to several social phenomena (Uchiumi, 1993); it is divided into six periods.

1. Pre- and wartime period

Sports were imported to Japan more than 100 years ago in the Meiji period. Until then there were none other than martial arts, Kendo, Judo, Karate, Naginata and so on. After that sports was enjoyed mainly by university students who formed an elite in society with a Western liberal ideology. There were thus two mainstreams of 'sport' in Japan, western sports and Japanese indigenous sports (martial sports).

During World War II, sports imported from 'enemies' were banned, and every kind of sport and physical education was militarized under the influence of emperor worship. Sport organizations took the initiative in obeying militarism and imperialism. The Great Japan Association of Amateur Sports obtained more than 90% of its financing from the government, and in 1942 under emergency war measures the Prime Minister became its president with the Ministers of Education and of Health and Welfare as vice presidents. The Ministry of Health and Welfare was founded in 1938 to include administering of health and fitness of the people (mainly in order to produce good soldiers). After that the administrative responsibility for sports was shared with the Ministry of Education which was founded in 1872. In 1939 the Peoples' Fitness Act was enforced, by which foreign sports were prohibited and people had to check their fitness once or twice a year, and to devote it to the emperor. The 12th Olympic Games (Tokyo) in 1940 were cancelled, and Japan invaded Asian countries.

2. The first period (1945 –1949)

World War II involved four elements of confrontation, the first being the imperialistic and invasive war by the three allied (developing) nations of Japan, Germany and Italy to re-divide colonies belonging to the developed nations. The second was between fascism and democracy; the third was between capitalism and socialism, and the fourth was between dependent countries (colonies) and occupying powers. After the war the main contested areas were the third and the fourth. The first period of the post-war sport policies was from August 1945 to June 1949, which was the beginning of sports policy, and involved a search for sport's own Act.

The General Head Quarters (GHQ)s of the (British/Commonwealth/ American) allied forces introduced American-style democracy and anti-fascism, which were realized as two occupation policies. Immediately after the end of the war 'passive' democratization was adopted and the GHQ banned many militaristic, imperialistic and reactionary matters, including the martial sports. Some pro-military organizations were dissolved and war criminals were punished. Subsequently 'positive' democratization was established, a great deal of freedom was secured, the new Japanese Constitution was adopted, and people had fundamental civil rights for the first time. Japan abandoned the use of invasive military force under Article 9 of the Constitution. However, the emperor, who was the chief war criminal, was not punished and was given a position as symbol of the nation.

Of course, democratization reflected the historic levels of democracy and the confrontation of democrats and imperialists, the latter being still alive under the surface, as a result of an incomplete experience of a democratic revolution and some abreaction to American democratic styles. The USA maintained the emperor system as an anti-communist force. Around 1948, the USA's Asian policy changed to an overt anti-communism, and then militarism and imperialism were revitalized. A general strike by civil servants seeking to improve their lives was banned by the GHQ by reason of being pro-communist. After that, Japan was regarded as 'an unsinkable aircraft carrier' of the USA in Asia.

Sports were introduced into the school curriculum after 1945, supported by the USA as a good opportunity for democratic experience, and as a result every child including those from the lower classes could experience sports. Even in this period excellence in sport was pursued, but mass participation was ignored. Ordinary people still had not enough leisure time, so sport for them was not something to participate in, but only to watch.

After being dissolved immediately by the GHQ because of its pro-imperialist stance during the war, the Japan Association of Amateur Sports (JAAS, Nippon Taiiku Kyokai) was reorganized. It reopened sport events especially the National Sports Meeting (Kokumin taiiku taikai) which had been held as a form of devotion to the Emperor. The meeting became very a important event for talented athletes, and 80 to 90% of the total financing of the Association derived from government grants after the war, as before it. The Association thus depended on the government and became something like a quasi-governmental organization.

Top athletes wanted to take part in the 14th London Olympic Games (1948), and energetically lobbied the IOC through the GHQ, but the Japanese Olympic Committee (JOC) was not invited. JAAS had two sport policies, the pursuit of excellence mentioned above and mass participation or popularization. However, there were no facilities for sport and no sporting goods, and no leisure time for ordinary people. Some sports leaders who were punished as war criminals returned to the scene and the sporting world was steadily imperialized again in obedience to the government.

Though a Sport Act, desired earnestly by sportsmen for the prestige of sport, was drawn up privately by some officials, the Centre of Information and Education (CIE) in the GHQ did not permit it because of the priority in June, 1949 of the Social (Adult) Education Act. Consequently, the sport and recreation were merely mentioned in the articles of the Social (Adult) Education Act of 1949, but this was anyway the first time sport had been introduced in Japanese law.

3. The second period (1949–1961)

The second period led to the preparation of the Sport Promotion Act in June, 1961. In this period Japan established the fundamental features of its post-war regime. It became formally independent of the allied forces in 1952, but was obedient to the USA politically, economically and militarily, and remained under the umbrella of the Pax-Americana. In 1955 conservative parties were integrated, and since then the so-called conservative monopoly system, which was called the foundation of the post-war regime of Japan, has continued. Supported by the USA, the Japanese economy grew very rapidly from around 1955 till the mid-1970s. Because of its importance as a wall against Asian socialist countries, the USA supported Japan as it did West Germany in Europe. The economy reached its pre-war level in 1955, and after that growth rates were more than 10 % a year on average. The industrial structure had changed from light to heavy industry dependent on oil from the Middle East, while coal mining had been scrapped. The workers' unions were under severe pressures from the employers and the government. In education several notorious reactionary policies were re-introduced.

In 1950 the army was reorganized to protect US military bases in Japan, because the US was fighting in the Korean Peninsula and could not guard its bases itself. In 1954 a Japanese fishing boat was contaminated by radioactivity near Bikini Atoll because of the USA's atomic bomb experiment. From this accident the anti- nuclear weapons movement developed and spread all over the world, as did other peace movements.

In 1960, the Japan-USA Security Treaty was renewed, but strong opposition emerged, as many people hoped that Japan could do without a military treaty. Public opinion was divided, and the conservatives felt a crisis around their regime. Sport was still the amusement of the ruling classes and ordinary people were just spectators. At the end of the 1950s TV became popular. In 1952 Japan came back to the Olympic Games in Helsinki. In 1958 the third Asian Olympic Games were held in Tokyo, and this was the first international sport event in new Japan since the war. After the Asian Olympic Games, the IOC decided to hold the 18th Olympic Games (1964) in Tokyo.

Administrative organizations for the Olympic Games were set up by the government, Tokyo and other local authorities.

After the passing of the Social (Adult) Education Act of 1949, the department of physical education (Taiiku-kyoiku which included physical education in schools, school health services, school meals and sport in society) in the Ministry of Education was absorbed into a Department of Social (Adult) Education. Under this law, organizations like the JAAS could not obtain grants from government under Article 13 of the Act and the Article 89 of the Constitution which prohibited public support of 'private' educational organizations. Such organizations therefore wanted an independent sport Act which would permit grants from government. The disappearance of the Bureau of Physical Education affected the local authorities, which decreased their own sport sections, because they were suffering a lack of finance.

There were three major demands by people involved in sports, especially officials of government, local authorities and governing bodies: reviving the Bureau for Physical Education; inviting the Olympic Games to Tokyo; and making an Act dealing specifically with sport.

The first demand was realised (1 May, 1958) in the course of preparing for the third Asian Games in Tokyo. In 1958 also the school curriculum was drastically revised, accepting the demands of industry, and physical education was given more importance in schools, so a Bureau for Physical Education and Sport was required once more. The second demand was fulfilled by the IOC's decision concerning the Tokyo Olympic Games (26 May, 1959). Some temporary Acts were enacted for the Olympic, and then a movement for enacting the Sport Promotion Act was supported by many people and organizations (June 1961).

This Act was proposed by members of parliament, not by the Cabinet, so that it had no right to offer any financial proposals. The Act was the first and so far the only separate sport Act in Japan and contains four sections. Its twenty-three articles include several aspects for promoting excellence and mass participation. It was characterised by some researchers mainly for its focus on excellence but, on the other hand, this Act supported mass participation after the end of the Tokyo Olympic Games.

4. The third period (1961 –1972)

The third period was from 1961 to 1972, which was the period of formation of the Japanese Sport Regime.

The crisis aroused by people opposed to renewing the Japan-USA Security Treaty made the government respond to anti-government movements. Culturally and ideologically Americanization was introduced and accelerated.

The Tokyo Olympic Games were looked forward to by many organizations for their own purposes. The government regarded them as a means of dispelling people's political frustrations. Industries regarded them as an opportunity to expand domestic demand. The military regarded them as an occasion to obtain the support of the people.

In the latter half of the 1960s, more than a hundred American bases in Japan were used to support the invasion of Vietnam, and the Japan-Korea Treaty was made to support the USA. Okinawa especially, in the southern part of Japan, became a front-line base and Japan was getting involved in the war.

In the same period there were many contradictions in the high economic growth, which stressed not collective consumer goods but only collective producer goods. So far Japan had no experience of the welfare state but had experienced high economic growth with the migration of population into big cities. Consequently those cities faced a severe shortage of collective consumer goods including parks and sports facilities. The high economic growth of Japan was made possible partly by low working standards and loose production regulations, which resulted in many industrial injuries and even deaths from overwork, and a great deal of pollution. Japan was called the 'department store of public nuisances'.

After the late 1960s the political atmosphere became more progressive, especially among local authorities. The frustrations of the people promoted the progressivism and led to the formation of 'welfare local authorities' which influenced the central government from the beginning of the 1970s.

In this atmosphere, it was decided to hold the 18th Olympic Games in Tokyo. In the early 1960s many industries began to include sport as part of their labour management within the high growth of the Japanese economy. The main purpose was to enhance workers' physical fitness and health and to integrate of young workers' thought, which had been influenced by socialism. Through the Tokyo Olympic Games, these industries expected economic benefits through constructing sports facilities, roads and the Shinkansen (bullet-train between Tokyo and Osaka), as well as through tourism. Central government and local authorities reorganized and prepared their administrative order for sport. The Japanese Defence Forces (military) helped energetically in managing the Games, and founded their own school of sports excellence. They gained a better reputation than they had expected; their intention to ingratiate themselves with the people was accomplished, because those forces themselves had been thought of as anti-Constitutional. The Conservative government enjoyed the success of the Olympic Games and employed it also to spread their ideologies among the people, with the result that sport movements (supported by the socialist or communist party) emerged to cope with the government policies and to democratize the sporting world. This they did especially through supporting mass participation, which had been ignored by government although it was the people's demand. The Japanese Sport Regime was formed through the agency of these four elements.

After the Olympic Games (1964) people were much concerned to play sports. Many local authorities began to organise special sections for sport and leisure and began to be involved steadily. In European countries sport and leisure policies had already been incorporated as responsibilities of central and local governments. A committee in the Ministry of Education was asked about programmes to provide sport facilities in the late 1960s. The Sport Promotion Act of 1961 was an influence mainly on local authorities.

5. The fourth period (1970s)

The 1970s was the era of a 'sports right' for people and of recreation as a form of welfare. Since the mid-1960s we have seen that a great deal of pollution occurred, as well as ill health and death from overwork among workers , and collective consumer goods were lacking as a necessary result of the economic miracle which supported mainly collective producer goods. From 1973, the oil crisis and dollar shock battered the world economy. However, Japan exceptionally recovered by expanding domestic demand and by reducing working conditions, with low salaries and long working hours, while reorganizing industry by trimming management and increasing exports. Through the 1960s and early 1970s Japan was ruled by the so-called 'company-oriented society', which would be even more influential in the 1980s.

Politically, progressive mayors were elected in more than half the local authorities from the late 1960s; they promoted welfare policies for the socially weak, leaving the central government behind. Civil rights accompanied by social rights expanded, and it was said that the 'welfare society' began in Japan in 1973. In 1972 a committee submitted a report to the Minister of Education, titled 'Fundamental policies for the promotion of people's physical education and sport'. The report, ruled by the provisions of the Sport Promotion Act of 1961, proposed scales of sport facilities provision which were learnt from *Planning for Sport* (1968) by the CCPR in Britain. Even during the depression investment in sport facilities by the public sector had increased; with the expansion of domestic demand, in many local authorities sport and leisure sections were newly created or enlarged.

Ideologically, 'Sport right' (the civil right of enjoying sport implied by the 1961 Act) was established and spread to many local authorities. A report to the Minister (1972) implied the social right of sport which meant that the people had a right to demand that the public sector provide facilities, coaches and so on. This idea originated by the sport movement (the Shintairen) in 1965, which developed steadily in the 1970s in Japan, encouraged internationally by the 'Sport for All Charter' of the Council of Europe in 1975 and the 'International Charter for Physical Education and Sport' of the UNESCO in 1978. Academically, researchers in law and sport gathered to discuss the 'sport right' in the 1970s.

In this stage, sport showed and revitalized its own 'public' characteristics. 'Sport right' became popular domestically and internationally. Government involvement grew steadily, and the private (commercial) sector became subsidiary.

6. The fifth period (since 1980)

The fifth period runs from the early 1980s to the present, during which the commercialization of sports policy and an injection of imperialist ideology into sport have occurred. So, this period was characterized by confrontation between the 'sport right' and commercialism and imperialism.

In developed countries, mainly the USA, UK and Japan, the new conservatism, new liberalism or monetarism has been adopted and social welfare has been confronted by a severe crisis. In Japan welfare budgets have been cut, and citizens must share expenses themselves. Therefore the main beneficiary has been the classes above the middle. Some roles of local authorities have been under competitive tendering as in the UK.

Japan, like other developed countries, adopted monetarism and a stingy government policy. National companies such as the railways, telecommunications and tobacco were privatized, and the government trimmed itself. The pre-war invasions. With this policy, an ideology concerning Japan's responsibility in the world has been stressed and imperialism has been combined with it.

Economically, Japan's GNP surpassed that of the USA, and Japan became the top creditor country in 1985. This was made possible by Japanese 'company-oriented society', which means that the ethos of serving one's company dominates and governs every phase of life, with long working hours, low salaries, unpaid overtime, poor working conditions, no trades unions and so on. In this situation only competitiveness and performance are evaluated, necessarily resulting in much publicized cases of 'Karoshi (death by overwork)' in the 1980s. **Table 1** shows the still occurring long working and commuting hours in 1991 compared to other developed countries — 18% longer than the USA, 34% more than France, and 42% than Germany.

In schools, children have been evaluated only by their academic test scores, and nearly half of them go to private preparatory schools after ordinary school several days a week. There have been warnings that they have many developmental problems intellectually, morally and physically as a result of overstudying, and lacking the socialization obtained through children's play. The long working hours of fathers and mothers have also separated parents from their families. The nature of affluence in both its material and its spiritual and cultural aspects has been questioned in all phases of life in Japan, reflecting the continuing inadequacy of human rights.

Government expenditure on sport has been decreased from its peak in 1982, and in 1990 it was less than half that in 1982 (**Figure 1).** Instead, the commercial sector has obtained many benefits in local authorities. Governing bodies of sport began to depend on support from companies (direct donations and sponsorship of events, etc.).

Table 1 International Comparisons of Working Hours

Element (hours)	Japan	USA	UK	Germany	France
Ordinary work and overtime	2158	1957	1989	1638	1646
Unpaid overtime	117	—	—	—	—
Commuting	281	214	—	159	187
Total	2557	2171	2150	1787	1833

Source: White Paper on working time (1991)

Figure 1 Central Government Finance for Sports Facilities (excluding school facilities)

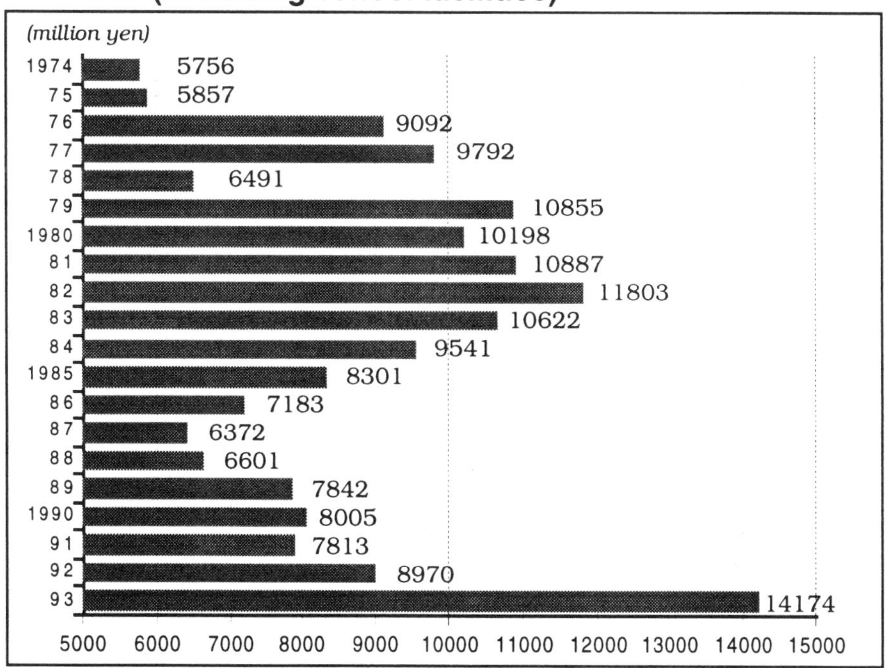

The political and ideological reaction has been strengthened since the mid-1970s. Japanese imperialism was forced on pupils in schools and through the mass media. It has also been stressed in the sporting area by enforced imperial worship.

In 1989 a study group on the sports industry in the Ministry of Trade and Industry submitted a report titled *Sports Vision 21* which intended to accelerate commercialization in the various markets for sports. In the report, sport facilities provision, and suppliers were shown (**Figure 2**). Most sport facilities in Japan have belonged to schools, which have been very slow to accept joint usage of their facilities with the community (compared with the UK, where one third of sports centres are so provided). The expectation about the numbers of facilities by 1987 in the report of 1972 had been realized by only 40–50 % by the early 1980s. Since then the situation has not changed. But the government and the committee thought that sports facilities provided by the public sector are adequate and from now on the provider role will be performed by the commercial sector. As Figure 2 shows, during the 15 years from 1985 to 2000 they emphasized the commercial sector enormously compared with the public sector for which there are no real plans.

In the government there are some 14 departments concerned with sport policies; they came together in the early 1980s under the leadership of the Prime Minister, but no co-operative work has yet been produced. Moreover

Figure 2 Sports Facilities in Japan

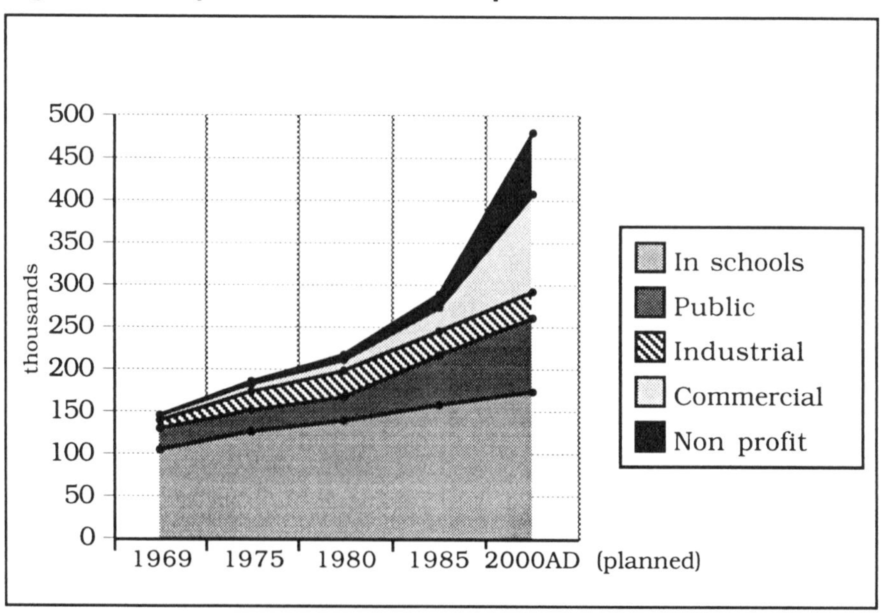

there are conflicts between the Ministry of Education and the Ministry of Health and Welfare, yet adequate co-operation between them is an urgent necessity. So far sport policies have been governed mainly by the Ministry of Education under the Sport Promotion Act 1961. Recently sport policies have been made by local authorities outside the education section, by departments belonging to sections directly governed by the mayor, which makes responsibility for sport policies very complicated.

The confrontation between 'sport right' and commercialism and imperialism, which is in effect a confrontation between the public and individual faces of sport, is a main feature since the 1980s. Society seems to be taking a step backwards and the differences in participation between rich and poor are becoming increasingly serious.

Sport ownership — the public face of sport

Figure 3 shows the history of sport ownership from the view point of the public nature of sport and 'sport right'. In Primitive Common Society sport was played and owned equally by all members of the community. In Ancient Slavery Society all aspects of culture were monopolized by the aristocracies,

Figure 3 History of 'sport right' and public nature of sport

	Sport right	Public nature of sport
Primitive Common Society	**Ownership — common ownership by members of society** Existence of undivided and primitive 'sport right' and public nature of sport	
Ancient Slavery Society	**Ownership — monopolized by aristocracies**	
	'Sport right' of aristocracies Eligibility for sport meetings	Sport meetings as public events
Feudal Society	**Ownership — monopolized mainly by feudal aristocracies**	
	Special right of aristocracies; Prohibition of football for other classes	Public nature in aristocracies
Capitalist Society	**Ownership — monopolized by the bourgeois**	
	Bourgeois' sport right; Amateurism	Public nature in the bourgeois
Scientific Socialist Society	**(Ownership — equal ownership by all members of society**	
	'Sport right' for all	Revival of public nature of sport
	Unity of 'sport right and public nature of sport	

particularly the citizens of Greece and Rome. Sports meetings were held for the first time in history. Eligibility to participate in sport meetings, including the ancient Olympic Games required a certificate of citizenship from the cities involved. Sport meetings were held not as private performances, but as national and public events. This means that the aristocracies monopolized sport, and insisted on their 'sport right' as involving eligibility (a special right), which excluded slaves from sport meetings.

In Feudal Society sport meetings were not as popular as previously. Sport was mainly monopolized by the feudal aristocracies and enjoyed within their own class in public meetings, but without the participation of other classes. Sometimes they prohibited football among the lower classes. Nevertheless, other classes began to own their sports little by little in proportion to the increase of their ownership of land and capital.

In British Capitalism the bourgeois made sure amateurs monopolized sport in order to exclude the proletariat even from public events. Modern society has individualism for its ethos and amateurism combined with it. Therefore the concept of sport as an individual matter has been spread through amateurism.

But recently amateurism has declined and the public aspect of sport has been revitalized both in terms of excellence and of mass participation. In excellence and mass participation the involvement of government has been a necessary historical trend. 'Sport for All' policies in developed countries have demonstrated this. Commercialism was gaining power in the 1980s, but commercial-ism is a typical private sector characteristic; it cannot substitute for the public sector because the essential nature of sport is not private but public (Uchiumi, 1989).

If we see modern Japanese capitalism from the viewpoint of the public finance, it has three phases, 'welfare state', 'company state' and 'military state' (Miyamoto, 1981) (see **Figure 4** opposite). Of course every capitalist system contains all three phases, but one of them tends to dominate at any one time. One of the features common to the three phases is that in modern capitalism the economy of private sectors can not develop by themselves, but needs strong support from government. The expansion of government has been a necessary trend of history, as the public economy has to manage the production and consumption of the nation.

In the case of Japan, the main feature was a company state in the 1960s, a welfare state in the 1970s, and a military state in the 1980s. (For example, in this interpretation, Britain was mainly a welfare state in the 1960s, changing from a pro-military state in the 1950s to a company state in the late 1970s through the welfare state phase of the 1960s.)

Figure 4 Three phases of the Welfare State

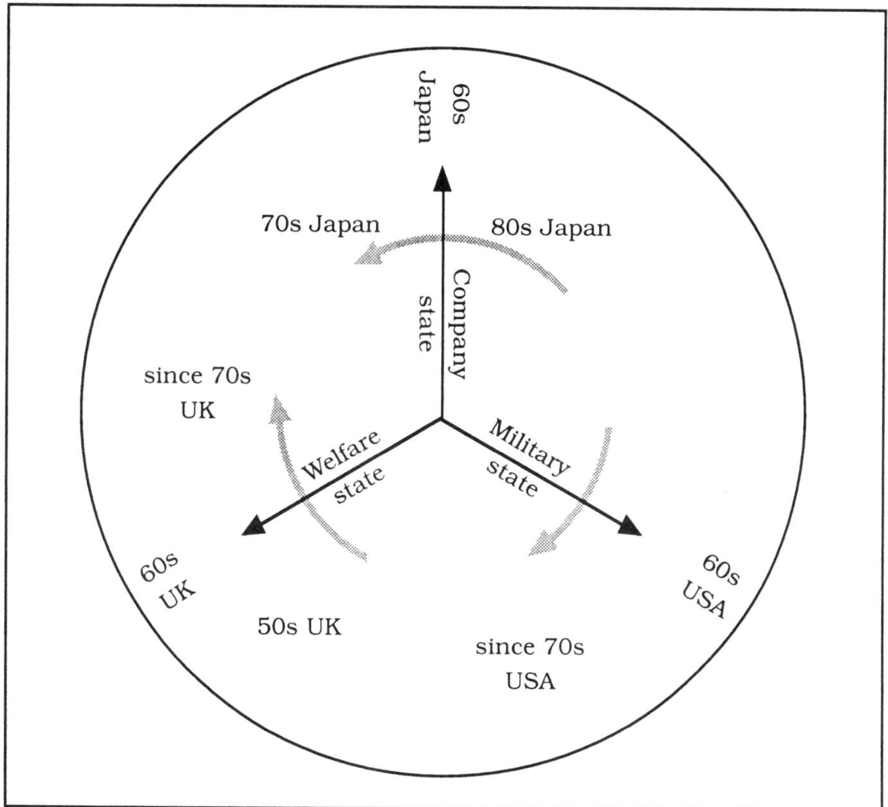

However, Japan did not develop a proper welfare state in the 1970s, so that it has a shortage of collective consumer goods and is weak in fundamental human rights compared to European countries, which have experienced a certain level of the welfare state. Economics has to deal with two kinds of poverty, the old poverty and the new poverty. The former means a high rate of unemployment and low level of wages for many of the working class, while the latter involves all classes. The welfare state cannot solve, and in fact sometimes creates, the following new poverty problems:

1. Difficulties caused by the accumulation of capital in big cities and a shortage of collective consumer goods, thus disasters and public nuisances, land and water problems, housing problems, traffic problems, delays in street cleaning, and shortage of schools, hospitals and nursery schools etc.

2. Social deficits, because the causative agent is unwilling to pay for prevention and compensation.

3. Expansion of the new poverty, which first attacks poorly paid people and then spreads to many of the people in smaller towns and villages as well.

4. Internationalization of poverty, because the welfare state has been made possible by the sacrifices of the developing countries. In general major companies exploit those countries for the benefit of the people of developed nations.

5. The new poverty can not be dealt with either by the welfare state or by monetarism, so another way has to be found.

References

Uchiumi, K. (1989) *Sport no koukyousei to shutaikeisei* [The Public Nature of Sport]. Tokyo: Fumaido Shuppan.

Uchiumi, K. (1993) *Sengo sport taisei no kakuritu* [Formation of Japanese Sport System]. Tokyo: Fumaido Shuppan.

Miyamoto, K. (1981) *Gendai Shihonshugi to Kokka* [Modern Capitalism and the State]. Tokyo: Iwanami Shoten.

The History of the Sports Industry in Japan since 1945

Masataka Ozaki

Hitotsubashi University, Tokyo

Preface

The sports industry in Japan has continued to expand. According to statistics compiled by The Centre for Leisure Development, established in 1970 as a satellite organ of the Ministry of International Trade and Industry, the total sales in sport related industry amounted to Y5,259 billion (US$51.9bn) in 1992. The amount is the total of the gross sales of sporting goods; the volume of enrolment fees and annual membership fees of commercial sport facilities and the charges for sport lessons they promote; and the spectator fees (e.g. for professional baseball games, tennis tournaments.)

The sport industry has a 7% share of the total leisure market, which amounts to Y75,411bn (US$744.4bn). According to the definition of the Centre for Leisure Development, the industry comprises sport; hobbies and culture; amusements; and tourism. **Figure 1 and Table 1** (on the following pages) elaborate the components of each sector.

The sports industry grew by 3.9% in 1991-92; as this was faster than the 2.4% growth rate of the entire leisure industry, it is highly appreciated "as a steadily expanding market sector". Such steady expansion is expected to continue into the 21st century. In this article, I will describe how the Japanese sports industry developed since 1945, explaining the factors that defined its mode of growth; I focus mainly on the active sports service sector. It is useful to read this alongside the paper by Uchiumi on law and policy over the same period (see pp. 97–110).

Figure 1 A Taxonomy of Leisure Activities provided (wholly or in part) by the Commercial Sector in Japan

SPORT	SPORTING GOODS Equipment Provider)		Golf; Ski; Tennis; Baseball; Football; Fishing; Climbing; Diving wear (shoes etc.)
	SPORT SERVICES (Active) Facilities and lessons	Indoor	Tennis; Bowling; Swimming; Fitness; Ice Skating; etc.
		Outdoor	Golf Course; Golf driving range; Boating; Skiing, etc.
	SPECTATOR EVENTS		Baseball; Football; Tennis; Boxing; Wrestling etc.
HOBBIES AND CULTURE	EQUIPMENT FOR HOBBIES		Photography; Music; Gardening; Ceramics; Painting, etc.
	EQUIPMENT FOR APPRECIATION		Radio; TV; Video; Hi-fi; VTR, Records; Cassettes; CDs, etc.
	NEWSPAPERS, BOOKS, MAGAZINES		
	LESSONS IN LEISURE AND LEARNING		Dressmaking; Cooking; Tea-ceremony; Flower arranging; Music; Social dance; Education, etc.
	AUDIENCE APPRECIATION		Music; Theatre; Cinema; Museums; Art galleries, etc.
AMUSE-MENTS	GAMES		TV games; Game centres (arcades), etc.
	GAMBLING		Horseracing; Bicycle racing; Powerboating; Lotteries, etc.
	EATING AND DRINKING		Restaurants; Snack bars; Cabarets; Cafes, etc.
TOURISM	CAR		Car sales; Fuel, etc.
	TOURISM IN JAPAN		Airlines; Chartered buses: Railways; Amusement parks; Travel agencies; Hotels, etc.
	TOURISM ABROAD		International airlines; Cruise ships

Source: Centre for Leisure Development

Table 1 The Changing Japanese Leisure Market 1982–1992 (¥ billion) (%)

Sector	1982	1985	1988	1991	1992	1991-92 Change %
Sport	2,637	2,961	3,747	5,063	5,259	+3.9
Hobbies and culture	7,516	7,889	10,446	10,601	10,501	-0.9
Amusement	22,840	29,365	34,903	45,706	47,884	+4.8
Tourism	65,20	7,531	9,689	12,288	11,767	-4.2
TOTAL	39,513	47,746	58,785	73,658	75,411	+2.4

Source: Centre for Leisure Development (1987–1993)

The sports industry, in the sense of selling and trading equipment for related products, already existed by the 1890s: for example, a document records a sport equipment store opening as early as in 1882. However, it was not until after World War II that Japan became socially conditioned to allow the industry to grow and to achieve such a structure as is established today. Therefore, that is where our historical analysis starts.

The context here is, firstly, the transition to a liberal economic policy which was the basis of the 'economic miracle' of the 1960s and of a higher standard of living which provided the nation with disposable money to engage in sport activity. Secondly, there was a series of democratisation measures enforced by the allied forces GHQ, such as the abolition of the militaristic curriculum of education. A legal condition for sport was also established with the idea that sport should be equally accessible to the whole population.

I have divided the post-war era into three stages of development: (1) From 1945 to the mid 1960s — the preparatory stage; (2) From the mid 1960s to the 1970s — the foundation stage; (3) Since 1980 — the stage of expansion and development.

1. 1945 to mid 1960s: the preparatory stage

The sport industry had to wait until the 1960s to be considered as a subject of debate in Japan. This period began with a nation devastated by war. The living standard was desperately low. Especially during the confusion of the immediate post-war period, the people hardly found the minimum amount of food to keep themselves alive, and even after they survived near-famine, they concentrated for a considerable time on procuring basic goods such as clothing.

However, at the same time, they desired amusement. In those days, the movies was the most popular form of culture, so the cinemas were always full. Additionally, people took pleasure in seeing a play, hearing music, listening to the radio, watching sports games (e.g. professional baseball games and wrestling matches), and gambling (e.g. bicycle and horse racing). By 1955, production had revived to the pre-war peak. As the nation overcame the precarious hand-to-mouth life, they turned their eyes to something more attractive and, at this stage, people desired something new. More active leisure than before attracted their interest (e.g. doing sport, travelling). This interest was further promoted as the government and the business world resolved to expand leisure into an industry, and from around 1960 the term "leisure" began to appear frequently in the mass media.

The central concept in the strategy of the government and the business world was what they called and what became popularly known as the "Consumption Revolution". Although definitions of the term varied, it was defined by the Japanese Productivity Centre (JPC) (Nippon-Seisansei-Honbu, 1961), as "a form of strategy to dismantle what had not yet been integrated into the market economy and to extensively expand the market". Explaining further, it meant "to replace household labour with production through social labour, that is, to dissolve the domestic economy, a form of self-sufficient economy". The context of "production of social labour" here means; processed foodstuffs, ready-made clothing, home electric appliances, furniture, swimming pools, parks, halls, amusement facilities, hotels, and so on. "Consumption Revolution" first appeared in the spread of ownership of durable consumer goods, mainly domestic electric appliances.

The critical points we have to note about this "Consumption Revolution" strategy in relation to sport are as follows; that it is based on the assumption that, if successful, "durable consumer goods and the fun market will be the two largest sectors of high level consumption", and consequently "in accordance with durable consumer goods demand, the fun market such as travelling, sport and social activity, would expand enormously" (JPC, 1961). The JPC assumed that "the diffusion of durable consumer goods consisting mainly of home electric appliances reduces the time taken for household labour, so people have more free time and come to enjoy leisure".

Secondly, the JPC assumed that "the provider (of the durable goods and fun market) will become the future leisure industry". In other words, the "Consumption Revolution" strategy aimed at commercialising "production" of social labour; this idea was modelled on the fun market in the USA.

However, while the "Consumption Revolution" was publicly debated and home electric appliances spread, popular leisure was quite simple. Staying at home, reading newspapers, watching television, or just lying down doing nothing in particular, was how the majority of people spent their free time. Only a limited number enjoyed sports or creative hobbies. The term leisure only gave the impression that free time would most probably increase in future. So there was a substantial gap between the ideal concept of, or the nation's desire for, leisure and its actual experience (Ishikawa, 1979). The sports industry, then, was no more than a few golf courses and tennis courts, which were seemingly for privileged people in the higher ranks of society. So the "Consumption Revolution" strategy did not reach its goal, because of the following factors:

1) People still did not have sufficient free time and spare money to afford sport and leisure activities. By 1955, the Japanese economy was appreciably rebuilt, as measured by GNP and other production indexes, but this was hardly reflected in the standard of people's lives.

2) There was no popular concept of playing sport as free time amusement. The young and middle-aged had been brought up mainly through a militaristic education curriculum, where they had no chance to learn to regard sport as a leisure time activity. There was also a kind of moralistic view of sport as a rather disgraceful activity which said, "work is virtue, but play is vice". Further, sport at that time consisted mostly of physical education in schools or at athletic competitions.

3) Consequently, a consumer sector did not exist to develop and expand sport into an industry. Naturally, in these circumstances, private enterprises could not be motivated to expand sport business beyond the few facilities that served the socially highly ranked.

2. Mid 1960s to the 1970s: the foundation stage

This is the period when changes in Japanese society began to accelerate. Hitherto an agricultural society, Japan urbanised and changed form, with the working population engaged in primary production diminishing rapidly and that in the secondary and tertiary industry increasing. Mass production accelerated. As a result, a self-sufficient economy changed to a commodity exchange economy. So, lifestyle underwent a great transformation. Women formerly housewives started working as paid labourers, firstly because household labour was reduced with the diffusion of consumer goods, and secondly because they had to supplement their household budget as household consumption expenditure increased. As people experienced this transformation of society and life-style, they began to ask for a higher quality of life in several aspects, such as demand for greater leisure time. In fact, free time did increase during this period.

After the mid 1960s, the nation began to seek more participation in sport as an element of this higher quality of life. Those who had never played sport began to take interest. Voluntary sport groups based on sport facilities constructed by local authorities came into operation. The sport movements came into existence in 1965, and organised their own association (New Japan Sport Association, *Shin-Nippon-Taiiku-Renmei*) in 1965.

The government, presumably trying to meet these popular demands, conducted the first poll on the nation's physical power and sport activity (Prime Minister's Office, 1965). According to this poll, approximately 55% of the respondents had enjoyed playing some kind of sport within the year. The rate of participation in sport continued to grow in the 1970s and reached about 65%, but these figures include people who had participated in sport only once a year. Those who participated more than once a week was approximately 20%.

As more people demanded a chance to play sport, a stage was reached when private firms could expect sufficient profit on their capital and they sought not only to meet demand, but also worked to spur new demands. For example, they promoted new forms of sport with which the public sector had never been concerned, such as bowling. There were then a series of booms in tennis (1961), bowling (1963 and 1966–72), golf driving ranges (late 1960s) and golf course membership (1972), and a second tennis boom (1972) (MITI, 1991a, 1991b, 1991c, 1992).

With each of those sport booms, commercial sport facilities were constructed in succession, and they were different from those of earlier days in that they were constructed to serve people of a socially wider range and of all ages. Let us give an instance from bowling. The number of bowling centres increased yearly from 20 in 1962 to 3,882 in 1972, with 124,288 lanes in 1972 when many adults and children played. Consequently, bowling centres became terribly crowded (waiting 2 hours to play was hardly unusual). The factors were, firstly, that bowling was cheap (generally the charge was only Y300 (US$3) per game). Secondly, people of all ages enjoyed bowling more easily than sports such as golf, because it needed neither many skills nor many years' experience. Thirdly, firms made much use of bowling on prime-time TV when professional bowling games were frequently broadcast.

But, we have to note that at the same time as new centres opened too hastily and excessive competition happened, people (especially, the youth) rapidly lost interest in bowling. As a result, after 1972, many bowling centres failed (see **Table 2**).

In the 1970s, large firms began to engage in sport as a new field of economic management, with differing aims. For example, the steel industry aimed to put their idle labour and land into active use, so they constructed

Table 2 Changes in the Number of Bowling Centres in Japan

	Number of Centres	Number of lanes
1959	1	24
1962	20	470
1963	48	1,419
1964	125	3,663
1965	202	5,413
1966	318	7,622
1967	496	11,148
1968	679	15,285
1969	897	21,284
1970	1,287	32,641
1971	2,226	64,022
1972	3,882	124,288
1973	3,515	113,281
1974	2,458	74,401
1975	1,290	36,445
1976	900	25,000
1977	866	23,694
1980	956	27,050
1985	1,079	30,358
1990	1,045	29,385
1992	1,045	29,587

Source : Tamamura (1980)

sports clubs (with gymnastic equipment, swimming pools or tennis courts). In the distribution industry, trying strategically to respond to demands of people's taste, they set up sport clubs too.

In response to the initiatives of private firms, the government resumed a strong interest in further promoting the sport industry. In 1974 the *Overall Survey on Leisure* was published, compiled by the Industrial Structure Council, a subsidiary of the Ministry of Trade and Industry (MITI) and covering the promotion strategy of the entire leisure industry (MITI, 1974). It analysed the conditions of and made proposals for each sub-sector such as sport, films, travelling, pachinko gambling and transportation. Thus people interested in sport were attracted to and woven into the sport industry. Salaried men frequented golf driving ranges while on holidays, young people strode in town with tennis rackets under their arms. New scenes of everyday life emerged and the basis for full establishment and expansion of the sports industry was established.

Factors influencing this phase were:

1) Once conditions allowed people to enjoy longer leisure time and extra money, then they looked forward to a mentally fulfilled life (Ishikawa, 1981, 1989). As the public's feeling changed, they turned their eyes increasingly on sports activities. This resulted in an unexpected population to play sport.
2) The Tokyo Olympic Games were held in 1964. The Olympic Games not only presented Japan before the eyes of the world and its first-rate athletes, but in preparing for the Games Tokyo was introduced to the advanced sport promotion activity of Europe, and so public awareness grew that "sport is an activity for everybody to enjoy", and is "worth enjoying for a better way of life".
3) Public sector policy on sport was unable to catch up and respond to this rising demand for sport activity. Only in legislative measures was public organisation progressing to some extent; the Sport Promotion Act was passed in 1961 (so far the only act concerning sport) and the Sport, Health and Physical Education Council proposals to the Education Minister to promote sport as a lifelong activity for the nation (Ozaki, 1991). However, with insufficient budgets, concrete measures such as constructing new public sports facilities and allocating skilled staff remained at low levels.
4) Private firms powerfully launched measures to arouse demand to play sport, and the government agreed support the movement. The series of sport booms that occurred at this time were the result of the strategic actions of private firms and people responded. Such social reaction led MITI and other government agencies to follow a policy of promoting the sports industry.

3. After 1980: the stage of expansion and development

As Table 1 showed, sales in the sports industry increased rapidly in the 1980s (Hukuoka, 1988). This market expansion was due mainly to the growth of services which as a share of industry rose continuously from 50.4% in 1982 to 58.1% in 1988, and to 61.6% in 1992.

Within this overall growth, I now look at the exceptional expansion of fitness clubs in Japan. As **Table 3A** (opposite) shows, the number of facilities rose sharply since 1980; regionally, they tended to concentrate in densely populated area like central Tokyo at the beginning of the 1980s, whereas in the latter half of the decade, they began to proliferate in other areas and are currently found throughout the country (**Table 3B**: MITI, 1991a). The forms of management changed and diversified accordingly. Clubs were originally mainly small private companies but later were transformed into chain store systems, or into a part of diversified operations of large firms, or run by management consultants.

Table 3: Fitness Clubs in Japan—Growth and Distribution

A. Growth

Period	No. opened
before 1964	13
1965-1969	28
1970-1974	108
1975-1979	256
1980-1984	552
After 1985	611

B. Distribution

District	No. of Facilities	Population per Facility (000s)
Hokkaido-Chiho	31	182
Tohoku-Chiho	81	121
Kanto-Chiho	514	75
Chubu-Chiho	320	71
Kansai-Chiho	304	66
Chugoku-Chiho	95	81
Shikoku-Chiho	41	103
Kyushu-Chiho	182	80
Total	**1,568**	**79**
Tokyo-Metropolis	204	57
Aichi-Prefecture	116	57
Osaka-Prefecture	143	38

Source: MITI (1991)

When we examine government policy, we see it tried to further promote the sports industry; in 1990 MITI released the report *Sports Vision 21* and the Education Ministry also announced their policy to strengthen the connection between the public sector and the sports industry (Ministry of Education, 1987; 1991). With the industry growing and national policy backing the expansion, more and more people chose to play sport through

Table 4 Changes in Monthly Household Income

	Annual Real Household Income (000s Yen)	Annual Real Household Disposable Income (000s Yen)	Real Household Income Annual Change (%)	Real Disposable Household Income Annual Change (%)
1970	112.9	103.6	7.3	7.1
1971	124.6	114.3	4.0	4.0
1972	138.6	126.7	6.5	6.0
1973	165.9	150.9	7.2	6.6
1974	205.8	187.8	—0.3	—0.1
1975	236.2	215.5	2.7	2.6
1976	258.2	233.5	0.1	—0.9
1977	286.0	256.3	2.5	1.6
1978	304.6	270.3	2.6	1.5
1979	326.0	286.8	3.3	2.4
1980	349.7	305.5	—0.6	—1.4
1981	367.1	317.3	0.1	—1.0
1982	393.0	335.5	4.3	3.0
1983	405.5	344.1	1.3	0.7
1984	424.0	359.4	2.3	2.2
1985	444.8	373.7	2.7	1.9
1986	452.9	379.5	1.4	1.2
1987	460.6	387.3	1.9	2.3
1988	481.3	405.9	4.0	4.3
1989	495.8	421.4	0.7	1.5
1990	521.8	440.5	2.0	1.4
1991	548.8	463.9	1.8	1.9
1992	563.9	473.7	1.1	0.5

Source : The Centre for Leisure Development (1993)

commercial sources — for example, facilities where salaried (male) commuters to central Tokyo go and take exercise. More people tend to go to fitness clubs near their work than to public facilities near home, partly because of long journeys to work of somewhere around 2 hours, or because of long overtime. Even housewives who naturally would spend more of their time near home than do their husbands are increasingly going to commercially organized facilities to play sport. Regarding household expenses, the amount of money spent on purchasing sports equipment and using fitness club fees is increasing.

Factors that enabled the industry to expand recently are:

1) Annual growth of household income and leisure time continued. According to the statistics of government agencies, people earned more and worked shorter hours than in the 1970s, so conditions allowing people to enjoy sport improved. **Table 4** shows that real household income grew for 21 of 23 years, and then disposable income grew in real terms for 19 of the 23 years since 1970.
2) Demand for a healthier life began to rise, and sport came to be regarded as a suitable way of maintaining and promoting health. We see in various surveys that "health" is what people cite as their major anxiety in life. In order to confront this anxiety, sport is what most people resort to. The sports industry well understood this public anxiety. Many fitness clubs therefore arrange personal medical check programmes, attracting more people to join them.
3) The popularity of types of sport shifted. Sport that one can easily enjoy alone or with a small group became popular compared to competitive team sports such as volleyball or baseball. Likewise, according to research conducted by our Hitotsubashi University team, more people preferred to play alone or with a few friends than with a large group. The sports industry fulfilled such demands of people because it aimed at individuals as customers.
4) As a result of the strategic advertising by private firms. People began to see a kind of status in playing sport at commercial facilities. Swimming would much be the same at both publicly and privately managed pools, but commercially organised facilities are much more popular, as more people are ready to spend money to enjoy a luxurious atmosphere, and better service. Although an extreme case, there is "a highly-ranked" fitness club where over 1 million yen (US $ 9,870) is required to cover enrolment and annual membership fees. This expensive club is quite popular despite the fee. The expansion of the sports industry in a sense has turned sport into an expensive consumption activity.

5) The environment of support by the public sector still lags behind people's needs. New construction provided by the public sector lingers and has not met the standards proposed in 1972. Moreover, the budget the public sector can currently allocate to sport promoting measures is further restrained than ever before. Moreover, a system of expert officials stationed at public facilities still does not exist.

Conclusions

The sport industry has progressively expanded, What directly prompted the expansion was the nation's strong desire to play sport, and the consequent growth of sport-playing citizens. There were two phases of society in post-war Japan when more people desired to play sport.

Firstly, once Japan had achieved a materially-fulfilled environment resulting from the rising standard of living, the leisure industry expanded as people turned their eyes on sport as an element in of a mentally and culturally higher standard of living. Secondly, the industry itself spurred and created within the people fresh demands for sport. A power to shape the social psychology, or "mass-society", together with the nation's willingness to be manipulated must presumably have functioned (what are called "conforming behaviour" and "group norm behaviour" in social psychology).

A critical feature of the development of Japanese sports industry is its success in assimilating the expansion of demand for sport. This was partly the result of filling a vacuum, because of the inadequate provision of the public sector, which fell behind people's demands; in particular, budgetary support of local government which has been critical in securing sport activity in Europe, has continued noticeably low since the war. Currently, Japan's sport policy continues to restrain the public sector from improving the condition and focuses on promoting private industry.

I have to note finally that, as mentioned before, the expansion of sport industry in a sense turned sport into an expensive "money-consuming" activity. So, if the pre-conditions and formations by the public sector (construction of sport facilities, stationing of expert officials, etc.) continue poor in the future, it will sustain differences in participation of sport activity within the nation. The people who have sufficient free time and spare money to afford sport can play and enjoy, but others without them (especially the aged, the retired, the handicapped, etc.) have little opportunity. This is a great problem, set against the ideal of "Sport for All".

Additionally, the construction of enormous numbers of commercial sport facilities since 1980 is in a sense disorderly. At present, commercial sport facilities, including fitness clubs and golf courses, are failing as a result of excessive competition and of the worldwide business depression. Members of these facilities, as consumers, then sustain severe loss of money and of their right to use the facilities. Some go to law to seek damages. In this sense, the disorderly expansion has led the sports industry to destroy itself. This shows that extreme commercialization is harmful to the sports activity of the nation; so, it is necessary to have some regulation of the industry by government action.

References

Centre for Leisure Development (Yoka-Kaihatsu-Centre) (1987, 1988, 1989, 1990, 1991, 1992, 1993) *Leisure-Hakusho* [*The White Paper on Leisure*]. Tokyo: the Centre.

Economic Plannning Agency (1991) *Kokumin -Seikatsu-Hakusho* [The White Paper on National Life]. Tokyo: Economic Plannning Agency.

Hukuoka. T. (1988) *Sport-Business* [Sport business]. Tokyo: Nihon-Keizai-Shinbunsha.

Ishikawa. H. (1979) *Yoka-no-Sengo-shi* [The history of leisure in Japan since 1945]. Tokyo: Tokyo-Shoseki.

——— (1981) *Yokubo-no-Kozo* [The structure of desire in Japan]. Tokyo: Seibundo-Shinko-sha.

Ishikawa, H. (1989) *Yokubo-no-Sengo-shi* [The history of desire in Japan since 1945]. Tokyo: Koseido Press.

JPC (Japan Productivity Center) (Nippon Seisan-sei-Honbu) (1961) *Shohi-Kakumei-to-Leisure Sangyo* [Consumption revolution and the leisure industry]. Tokyo: Toyo-Keizai-Shinpo-sha.

Ministry of Education (1987) *Wagakuni-no-Taiiku-Sport-Shisetsu* [Report on investigation of sport facilities in Japan]. Tokyo: Ministry of Education.

——— (1992) *Kyoiku-Haksuho* [The White Paper on Education]. Tokyo: Ministry of Education.

MITI (Ministry of International Trade and Industry) (1974) *Yoka-Soran* [Overall Survey on Leisure]. Tokyo: MITI.

——— (1990) *Sports Vision 21* [Sports Vision 21]. Tokyo: MITI

——— (1991a) *Tokutei-Service-Sangyo-Jittai-Chosa-Hokokusho* [Report on investigation of conditions of service industries — fitness clubs]. Tokyo: MITI.

——— 1991b) *Report on investigation of conditions of service industries — golf driving ranges*. Tokyo: MITI.

——— (1991c) *Report on investigation of conditions of service industries — tennis courts.* Tokyo: MITI.

——— (1992) *Report on investigation of conditions of service industries — golf courses.* Tokyo: MITI.

Ozaki. M. (1991) 'Sport-no- Sangyo-ka-to-Shogai-Sport' [The industrialization of sport and life-long sport]. *Ikkyo-Ronso* [Bulletin of Hitotsubashi University], No. 12: pp. 81-97.

Prime Minister's Office (1965) *Kokumin-no-Tairyoku-Sport-ni-Kansuru-Yoron-Chosa* [Poll on the Nation's physical power and sport activity]. Tokyo: Prime Minister's Office.

Tamamura. K. (1980) *Leisure- Sangyo-Seicho-no-Kozo* [Structure of expansion of the leisure industry]. Tokyo: Bun-shin-do.

Sport and the Commonwealth

Barrie Houlihan

Staffordshire University, UK

The Commonwealth and Sport

The changes in the title of the Commonwealth Games over the years reflect the transformation in the relationship between Britain and its Empire. The first British Empire Games were held in 1930 at a time when Britain's status as a world power was still intact. But by 1954 the title had been altered to the British Empire and Commonwealth Games to reflect, less the decline in status of Britain than the rise in status of Canada and Australia. By 1970 the process of decolonialisation and Britain's relative economic decline had radically altered the relationship between members of the former Empire and this was reflected in the new title of the British Commonwealth Games. Finally, by 1978 pressure from member states to give greater public recognition of their independent status resulted in the word 'British' being dropped from the title of the four yearly Games.

Apart from charting the evolution of Britain's relationship with members of its former Empire, the changes in the title of the Games also reflect the capacity of the Commonwealth itself to adapt to the changes in the pattern of international relations in the twentieth century. The quadrennial Commonwealth Games are one of the most visible symbols of the most enduring international governmental organisation apart from the United Nations.

The Commonwealth

According to Groom and Taylor the Commonwealth "is a voluntary association of those states which have experienced some form of British rule who wish to work together to further their individual and common interests" (1984: p. 7). In the early 1990s, 51 states were members of the Commonwealth with Pakistan (rejoined in 1989) and Namibia (1990) being the most recent additions. The evolution of Empire into Commonwealth was due in large part to Prime Minister Nehru who, rather than take the newly independent India out of the Commonwealth, chose to remain within the organisation as an independent republic. Thus instead of the Commonwealth possibly contracting to become a largely white Anglo-Saxon club, each phase of decolonialisation brought new independent members.

The present form of the Commonwealth dates from the early 1970s, when an independent Secretariat was established. The Secretariat was established at a time of great strain within the organisation resulting partly from the conflict between Britain and the African and Asian members over South Africa, but also from Britain's recent membership of the European Community. More specifically, by the 1960s the idea of Commonwealth defence was long forgotten, while the notion of Commonwealth economic preference was fast losing its significance. Of particular importance was the wish among the newly independent Commonwealth members to cast off any remnants of subordinate status. As Doxey observed, "For the Commonwealth to remain relevant to them it had to satisfy national pride as well as national need; to reinforce sovereignty and be seen to do so" (1984: p. 18).

The effect of the establishment of the Secretariat was to weaken the formal Anglo-centricity of the organisation and to facilitate the emergence of non-British political figures within the Commonwealth. The Secretariat took over all the functions previously fulfilled by British civil servants with the primary function being to service the meetings of Commonwealth Heads of Government (CHOG) which take place every two years, but it also coordinated the work of the wide range of non-governmental organisations working within the Commonwealth (Jones, 1991). Well over one hundred organisations, official and unofficial, are associated with the Commonwealth covering development cooperation, culture, education, information and media, youth, and sport. As this list suggests, the focus of the Commonwealth is not on the major dimensions of international relations such as trade and defence, but rather on culture, education and information. While at the formal CHOG level Anglo-centricity is low, it is much more apparent at the NGO level. This may be illustrated with reference to the Commonwealth Foundation, formed in 1965 to facilitate interchanges between professional bodies within the Commonwealth, where the majority of the constituent organisations have a London base with the rest located largely in countries of the 'white' Commonwealth (Chadwick, 1982).

The contemporary Commonwealth is founded upon a mix of value consensus and pragmatic diplomacy, supported by a common language, a broadly similar set of administrative and, frequently, legal processes, and a sense of common identity. The latter factor is described by Groom as a "distant cousin syndrome" which results in a predisposition for cooperation (Groom, 1988: p. 185). In 1971 at the Singapore CHOG meeting the Declaration of Commonwealth Principles was adopted. The Declaration expressed support for the United Nations, a belief "in the liberty of the individual, in equal rights for all citizens regardless of race, colour, creed or political belief, and in their inalienable right to participate by means of free and democratic political processes in framing the society in which they live", a policy of non-discussion of members' internal affairs without their agreement, and a method of operation based on consultation and cooperation (Commonwealth Secretariat, 1987: pp. 156-7). Decision-making is therefore generally limited to making recommendations and avoiding attempts at coercion.

This mix of basic values and operational guidelines is complemented by many members who recognise the diplomatic opportunities that membership of the Commonwealth provides. The Commonwealth has survived some turbulent periods, most notably in 1971 over the British decision to sell arms to South Africa and in the 1980s over Britain's reluctance to pursue a stronger sanctions policy towards South Africa. Despite the tensions that were clearly evident in the Commonwealth it has survived and even at the most difficult times the transnational activity of the NGOs has remained largely undisturbed. Part of the explanation of the durability of the organisation lies in its value to many of its members.

One feature of the Commonwealth is the number of very small states that are members. Of the 55 'states' in the world with a population of less than one million, 20 have a connection with the Commonwealth: indeed, 30 members of the Commonwealth have a population of less than 3 million (World Bank, 1990; Julien, 1992). It provides access to a world stage for those states that would otherwise have little chance of making their views known in other forums such as the United Nations. It also provides small states with a supportive environment in which to try out ideas and policy proposals. Julien notes that those states that have attempted to operate within other transnational organisations such as the Organisation of American States and the Group of 77 have found the experience uncomfortable (1992: p. 48).

Even the larger states, such as many in Africa, despite comprising almost one third of the UN membership find influence on global decision making difficult to achieve. This is particularly the case following the decline of apartheid as a major issue at the UN. The UN Special Committee on Apartheid gave African states a prominent voice within the General Assembly but one which is weakening rapidly. In addition to the marginalisation of the Third World in the UN resulting from the easing of tension over apartheid, there is also the decline in Third World influence resulting from the ending of the Cold War which has reduced the capacity of Third World states to use their strategic location to play one superpower against another (Aluko, 1991). As a result of this decline in leverage it is likely that the Commonwealth will become a more significant point of access to the major forums of world politics.

Yet the Commonwealth is also of value to medium powers such as Australia and Canada. Although Canada in particular sees the UN, OECD and NATO as the major forums through which to pursue its policy objectives, the Commonwealth provides a useful addition. As Delvoie notes, the "Commonwealth is not at the centre of Canadian foreign policy concerns [nor is it] an instrument of the first importance in pursuit of its major and enduring foreign policy objectives" (1989: p. 140). However, the Commonwealth is of use in defining Canada's international personality and differentiating it from the USA. It is also of value in the pursuit of specific policy objectives such as the isolation of South Africa. Finally, the Commonwealth provides Canada with a basis for implementing its development policy towards the Third World (Delvoie 1989: 140-142). Indeed one of the major strengths of the Commonwealth is its acceptability as a link between North and South (Groom, 1988: p. 186).

Attempting to assess the significance of the Commonwealth as an element in the international system, either as an independent actor or as a conduit for its members, is not easy. Its impact on major global issues such as security, trade and the environment is modest, though on the latter issue the Secretariat is hopeful that the Commonwealth can play a more prominent role (Bourne, 1992). Yet it extends the reach of the international system into corners of the globe that the major international organisations often miss and it can claim to have influenced the outcome on some important problems. According to Groom, the Commonwealth "has been successful in easing some of the problems in NIEO (New International Economic Order), in the ACP-EC relationship and in individual cases such as the negotiations between Papua New Guinea and Rio Tinto Zinc" (Groom, 1988: p. 187).

Akinrinade adds to this list the significant part played by the Commonwealth in promoting democracy among its members, for example through the monitoring of elections and in the devising of constitutions for newly independent states. The Commonwealth has also been active in facilitating decolonialisation, both for members and for non-members. the Commonwealth Secretariat played an important part in the negotiations between Portugal and Frelimo over the independence of Mozambique (Akinrinade 1992). Perhaps the most significant contribution of the Commonwealth was in pushing the British government to adopt and retain a policy of firm opposition to the rebel regime in Rhodesia and in moderating Britain's willingness to support South Africa. There is an interesting argument that the controversy over South Africa and the friction between Britain and the majority of Commonwealth states was important in sharpening the focus of the organisation and providing it with a clearer sense of purpose. Thus rather than being a threat to its future, apartheid was an important catalyst in defining the modern Commonwealth (Austin, 1988; Akinrinade, 1992; Chan, 1988).

In summary, the Commonwealth is not a first order international organisation, it is clearly overshadowed by the UN, NATO and OECD. It is not just that the Commonwealth lacks the same prestigious superpower membership, but that the Singapore Declaration of Commonwealth Principles is a long way from being a policy agenda. Yet the Commonwealth clearly has found a valuable niche in the international system. The niche can be defined both in terms of membership and also in terms of approach to issues. The general stability of membership and its shared history, the high proportion of small states, and the geographical spread provide it with a distinctive character. The mode of debate within the Commonwealth, the non-interventionist assumptions and the organisational emphasis on issues relating to culture, information and human rights also add to its distinctive qualities.

However, for an international organisation such as the Commonwealth to survive, it must convince its members of its value and also demonstrate its vitality to the outside world. The key to meeting both these requirements is the achievement of policy objectives, but the maintenance of high international visibility is also important. As will be shown, the Commonwealth Games has an important contribution to make to both achieving policy objectives and promoting the institution's image.

The Commonwealth Games

The idea for a four yearly sports festival for the countries of the Empire was first suggested in 1891. Initially there was some debate about whether America should participate on the basis of its Anglo-Saxon heritage, but the idea was soon dropped in favour of limiting eligibility to the (implicitly white and 'well-born') subjects of the Queen and Empress (Moore, 1986). A limited

'Inter-Empire Championships' were held in 1911, but it was not until 1930 that the first British Empire Games were held in Hamilton, Canada. Some 400 competitors took part from eleven countries. The purpose of the Games is summed up in the following, often quoted, passage:

> It will be designed on the Olympic model, both in general construction and the stern definition of amateur. But the Games will be very different, free from both the excessive stimulus and babel of the international stadium. They should be merrier and less stern, and will substitute the stimulus of a novel adventure for the pressure of international rivalry. (quoted in Commonwealth Games Federation, 1987)

Although this statement seems anachronistic now in the light of the compromises on professionalism and commercialism, it reflects the mix of idealism, social snobbery, and Anglo-centricity that characterised the early Games.

In 1932 the British Empire Games Federation was formed to oversee the organisation of future events and to promote sport throughout the Empire. Its successor, the Commonwealth Games Federation (CGF) has no assets and, apart from a part-time secretary, no permanent staff. It relies on voluntary effort and goodwill to survive. The role of the Federation is to promote and organise the four-yearly Games, to establish rules and regulations for the conduct of the Games, and to encourage amateur sport throughout the Commonwealth. The Games have generally followed the model of the Olympic Games, particularly in terms of the commitment to amateurism and the explicit stand against all forms of discrimination.

But they differ from the Olympics in a number of important ways, most obviously in their explicit political foundation, but also in the way in which they are organised, for example in excluding team sports. In addition, they are limited to only ten sports, of which two must be athletics and swimming, with the other eight selected by the host country from a list of approved sports established by the CGF. Thus over the years fencing and rowing have both ceased to be regularly included in the programme and have been replaced by sports such as shooting, weightlifting and gymnastics. For a new sport to be added to the list of approved sports it must be played in a wide range of countries, have only one International federation, not be solely a team game, not be unduly costly, and not rely on mechanical means. Tennis, table tennis and judo are the most recent sports to be accepted onto the approved list.

Achieving the status of an approved sport is often the result of considerable lobbying by international sports federations seeking participation in the Games, even if some see Commonwealth acceptance as primarily a stepping stone to Olympic eligibility. Karate, handball, triathlon and netball have all attempted to gain acceptance in recent years. There is also increasing pressure on the CGF to admit popular team games such as cricket, volleyball and basketball, and also to allow competitions, particularly regional competitions, outside the Games themselves but under the aegis of the CGF.

The decision making forum of the CGF is the annual General Assembly at which each member country has one vote (in contrast to the weighted voting system of the IOC). The main responsibility of the General Assembly is to select the venue for the next Games. Most other matters are delegated to an Executive Committee comprising vice-presidents of the Regions (continental groupings) and the officers of the Federation. The main source of income for the CGF is from the country hosting the next Games and currently amounts to four annual payments of £100,000. To run a major international multi-sport competition with such a fragile financial base is a tribute to the considerable voluntary effort provided. Unfortunately, the financial weakness of the CGF, by contrast to the IOC which has built up a reserve fund of over $100m, is causing some serious problems. For example, on the question of drug testing, the CGF can only ensure limited consistency of procedure from one Games to the next because it is dependent on the host country to finance and provide testing facilities.

An assessment of the significance of the Commonwealth Games in the pattern of international relations can be approached in a number of ways: first, in terms of its importance to the Commonwealth; second, in terms of its value as a vehicle for the diplomatic ambitions of individual Commonwealth members; and third, in terms of the relationship between Commonwealth sports bodies and other International NGOs in sport such as the IOC and the major International Federations. Two issues provide an opportunity to explore the political role of the Games: the policy towards South Africa, and the current debate about the future of the Games.

South Africa

The policy of apartheid in South Africa dominated the Commonwealth Games (and the Commonwealth) as it did the Olympic Games for much of the 1970s and 1980s. In fact, apartheid in sport had had an impact on the Commonwealth much earlier when the 1934 Games, scheduled for South Africa, were moved to London because of concern with the former's racial policies. Although apartheid was a clear source of tension within the Commonwealth, it was also the issue which helped to define the principles upon which the organisation was based. Given the nature and style of the bi-annual CHOG meetings where votes were normally avoided, direct criticism of domestic policy of members was rare, and a preference for maintaining consensus existed, the opportunities were limited for resolving an issue where there was such a conflict of views . Although this broad consensus broke down partially during the mid 1980s, when Britain's isolation was made clear, the conflict over South Africa was largely displaced to the Commonwealth Games where more aggressive actions, such as boycotts, could be taken without jeopardising participation in the main forum, the CHOG meetings.

The internal politics of South Africa has been a prominent, and often a dominant, issue in the Commonwealth for thirty years from 1961 when South Africa withdrew from the organisation. During that period the black African states sought to isolate South Africa through applying a comprehensive range of sanctions. Sport was a particularly important focus for the campaign partly because of its high public visibility and low cost to relatively poor states, and partly because of the important cultural significance of sport in the Republic and also because the major sports (cricket and rugby union) and sporting partners of South Africa were few in number and the latter were members of the Commonwealth.

It should be noted that neither cricket nor rugby were Olympic sports, and so the Commonwealth could not rely on support from the IOC for its actions. In addition, both sports were among the more commercially successful and therefore were less dependent on government subsidy. Although the issue of apartheid was present as a background to much Commonwealth activity during this period, there were a number of occasions when the issue surfaced and dominated the organisation's agenda. Three such occasions amply illustrate the interplay between sport and politics in the Commonwealth: namely, the formulation of the 1977 Gleneagles agreement, the threatened boycott of the 1978 Edmonton Games, and the boycott of the 1986 Edinburgh Games.

The 1976 Olympic Games was disrupted by a boycott by thirty states because of the refusal of the IOC to withdraw its invitation to New Zealand. The cause of the boycott was the decision by the New Zealand rugby union authorities to send a side to tour South Africa and the clear expression of support given to the proposal by Prime Minister Muldoon. While the black Commonwealth states were incensed at the decision, Canada was also concerned. Canada, although not particularly active on Third World issues until 1984, was motivated by a general antipathy to racism, and also by a concern to maintain both the role of the Commonwealth in protecting western interests during the Cold War and its own reputation as an international peacebroker (Macintosh and Hawes, 1994). The fact that Canada was scheduled to host the Commonwealth Games in 1978 was an additional important factor.

However, matters were likely to come to a head sooner as the next CHOG meeting was arranged for 1977 in London. As Payne makes clear, defusing this conflict owed much to the diplomatic skills of the Secretary-General of the Commonwealth, Shridath (Sonny) Ramphal and the style of CHOG meetings. Ramphal encouraged the African members to moderate their criticism of Muldoon while also persuading Australia, New Zealand's closest political ally, to make clearer its support for the African position (Payne, 1991: p. 417). In this way he made Muldoon's isolation clear. In addition, Ramphal was supported in his endeavours by Trudeau, who embarked upon a vigorous round of diplomacy among the African states.

The technique for getting Muldoon off the hook and building a stronger Commonwealth anti-apartheid consensus was to produce the Commonwealth Statement on Apartheid in Sport (commonly referred to as The Gleneagles Agreement). The idea for the Agreement came from the British sports minister Denis Howell with the support of Australia and Canada, but was largely written by Ramphal. Trudeau, who was seen as instrumental along with Ramphal in getting the Agreement accepted, was also important in obtaining the support of the Organisation of African Unity which he lobbied through Canada's Francophone links (Macintosh and Hawes, 1994). The Agreement drew a veil over previous conflicts while establishing a set of expectations regarding members' response to apartheid which were probably as precise as could be expected from a meeting of over forty heads of state. The document not only saved the Edmonton Games, but also opened the way for the Commonwealth Games Federation to exclude members who failed to live up to its spirit. As a result of some perceived 'backsliding' by Muldoon, Nigeria did not send a team to Edmonton, but it was the only state to withdraw. Yet the issue rumbled on, prompted in part by the decision of the New Zealand rugby union authority to invite the South African Spingbok to tour in 1981. Many members of the Commonwealth saw this proposal as a test of commitment to stand by the Gleneagles Agreement. The fact that the tour took place may be seen as a setback; however, it also provided an opportunity to clarify and strengthen the Agreement.

In 1982 a Code of Conduct applicable to each national association was drafted setting out what would constitute a breach of the Agreement. The Code gave the Federation new powers to exclude a country which seriously breached the terms of the Agreement (Payne, 1991: p. 425). The Code obtained wide support among African states, partly because it was seen as clarifying and strengthening the Gleneagles Agreement, and partly because it was seen as an important step in redefining the anti-apartheid strategy. Until the early 1980s the African states and athletes had borne the brunt of the policy of isolating South Africa. Consequently there was a growing view that the boycotts were harming the boycotting states, and especially their athletes, as much as South Africa, and that the strategy also limited the opportunity to use sporting contact as a political tool for other purposes. Guttmann (1992: p. 141) gives an interesting illustration of the personal consequences associated with the persistent use of the boycott. Youssef Assad, an Egyptian shot-putter, did not participate in the 1972 Games due to his country's desire to show solidarity with the Palestinian cause; he missed the 1976 Games because of the boycott in protest against New Zealand; and he missed the 1980 Games because his government chose to boycott as a protest against the Soviet invasion of Afghanistan.

During the mid 1980s a series of rebel tours took place, indicating the difficulty South Africa faced in arranging official tours. With the election of David Lange and a Labour Government replacing Muldoon's National Party, New Zealand ceased to be the focus of Commonwealth criticism. However, New Zealand's place was quickly taken by Britain, which was sharply criticised for its unwillingness to impose economic sanctions on South Africa. The net effect of the confrontation between Britain and her Commonwealth partners was that 32 states boycotted the 1986 Edinburgh Games. Despite growing scepticism about the wisdom of boycotts the technique presented the black African states with a "relatively cost-free way of demonstrating their displeasure with Britain" (Payne 1991: p. 427), or in other words the costs were borne by their athletes and not their merchants. Despite the attendance of three African states, the remaining participants gave the Edinburgh Games the look of an 'old' Commonwealth club meeting. From 1986 the issue of apartheid began to decline, initially because of the lack of any government-supported challenge to Gleneagles, and later due to the programme of reform ushered in by de Klerk towards the end of the decade.

The future of the Commonwealth Games

By the end of the 1980s South Africa as a political issue for Commonwealth sport was moving down the international agenda. For the institution this was both a welcome relief and also a cause of concern. It was a relief insofar as it removed the issue that had divided the state smost sharply and at times seemed to threatened the Commonwealth's long term survival. But it was a cause of concern because the thirty-year debate over apartheid was the catalyst that had sharpened its identity and sense of political purpose. The declining significance of apartheid also posed problems for the Commonwealth Games. Not only had the Games been one of the most important arenas for the public display of anti-apartheid policy, but it had also diverted attention from other issues related to the role and organisation of the Games. Among the most important of those were the viability of the

Games in an increasingly commercial sports world, the underlying disquiet concerning their traditional location outside the Third World, the role of the Games in the Commonwealth, and their content.

Many of these issues surfaced in the late 1980s when the Commonwealth undertook a review of the Games at the initiative of the Canadian External Affairs Secretary, Joe Clark. The immediate context of the Canadian proposal for a review lay in the recent decision to award the 1994 Games to the city of Victoria in Canada. Since the first Games were held in Hamilton, Canada in 1930 they had only once moved out of the 'white' core of the Commonwealth in Kingston, Jamaica in 1966. Even New Zealand with its small population hosted the Games on three occasions, most recently in 1990. In 1986, when Auckland was chosen as the host for the 1990 Games, there was a widespread assumption that the next hosts would come from a Third World country. New Delhi, India was seen as the most likely contender.

Yet when the Commonwealth Games Federation's General Assembly met in Seoul, it chose Victoria in preference to New Delhi and Cardiff, Wales. Although Victoria's success was based on the votes on many Third World delegates it was also due to the adoption of a style of campaigning for votes that was more associated with the Olympics than the Commonwealth Games. There were strong allegations that Victoria had, on the one hand, bought the Games with promises of financial assistance for teams from poorer countries and promotional visits by delegates to Canada, and on the other scared delegates away from casting their vote for New Delhi with rumours of poor sanitation and health risks. New Delhi's case was strong. It already had the necessary facilities in place and had recently hosted the far larger and more complex Asian Games. However, New Delhi lost decisively on the first ballot, not because of the votes of the 'old' Commonwealth but because the smaller Caribbean and Pacific members voted for the Canadian city.

The Federation decision to select Victoria represented the immediate political context but it is also important not to lose sight of the wider commercial context. The need for the Games to confront the growing commercialism of sport was recognised in the mid 1980s. The success of the Los Angeles Olympic Games in 1984 in attracting commercial sponsorship and making a profit was an important catalyst, but of greater importance was the trend towards professionalism among athletes. The route taken by tennis and golf in abandoning amateurism for their elite sportsmen and women was now being followed by track and field. While the track and field elite have not gone as far as golf and tennis in exerting 'player power' it was clear by the mid 1980s that the assumption that athletes would meekly follow the instructions of their governing bodies was under threat. Part of the source of change lay in the rapid growth in the sponsored grand prix circuit in athletics and the trend for International Federations to organise their own world championships. The Commonwealth Games was therefore under pressure through the growing concern among athletes for prize money and the increasingly crowded calender of competitions.

It was against this background that Canada launched its proposal to review the Games. The Clark proposals stressed the symbolic importance of the Games for the Commonwealth and also the need to involve as many members as possible in hosting and taking part in them (Secretary of State for External Affairs, 1989). The document addressed a set of inter-related issues; the administrative capacity of the CGF, the sports development needs of poorer members, and the provision of financial support to Third World hosts. As regards the CGF, the document included proposals to provide financial assistance via a Commonwealth Sport Trust and also through the adoption of modern marketing techniques by the Federation along the lines of the Olympic movement. The document also suggested that the CGF might be relocated away from London, possibly to Jamaica. In proposing aid to developing countries Clarke gave a high priority to the provision of travel support for teams, through a Travel Stabilisation Fund. However, this would only be one part of a much wider programme of sports development assistance. As regards hosting future Games, the document stressed the economic and sporting opportunities that hosting the Games presented to a country. Clarke also emphasised the importance of the 1998 Games being awarded to a developing country, but recognised the need to provide financial and administrative support to many prospective hosts.

The Clarke document was discussed at the CHOG meeting in Kuala Lumpur in 1989 when the Heads of Government noted the significance of the Games as "a highly visible and important symbol of Commonwealth unity", and agreed to the formation of a working party, under the chairmanship of Roy McMurtry, to consider its suggestions (Commonwealth Secretariat, 1989: p. 43). The preliminary report provided an analysis of the problems facing the Commonwealth. Acknowledging the role of sport in nation-building, the report stressed its similar role in the Commonwealth. It saw sport and the Games reflecting the "core values [of the Commonwealth] of non-racialism, equality and fair play", and identified sport as ranking with other primary Commonwealth links such as language and law. It also highlighted the fact that sport is particularly attractive to the young and that almost two thirds of the Commonwealth's population of 1.6 billion is under 16 years of age. Finally the report recognised that sport might provide a counter-weight to factors weakening the Commonwealth:

> With some Commonwealth countries experiencing significant levels of immigration from non-Commonwealth countries, the traditional Commonwealth bonds are, to an extent, being weakened. These changes in patterns of immigration are matched by diminishing economic ties and the emergence of regional economic blocs. In our view, sport is a powerful antidote for these erosive influences on the Commonwealth association. (McMurtry, [Preliminary] Report 1990: p. 5)

The proposals aired in the report focused on the need to strengthen the Federation, particularly the need to provide a secure source of finance. The report, while noting the difficulty in making the Games self-funding along the lines of the Olympics, clearly saw this as a priority. Thus the marketing of a Commonwealth logo was suggested along with the minting of commemorative coins and the development of sponsorship deals. The report also highlighted the question of the range of eligible sports.

The final report followed closely the issues identified in the preliminary report and made sixteen recommendations, covering a broad range of topics including suggestions for putting the financing and organisation of the CGF on a firmer footing, the establishment of a sports development programme, and alterations to the content of the Games. The basis of the final report's recommendations was an acknowledgement of the importance of the Games as a reinforcement and visible expression of the core values of the Commonwealth.

> Sport imparts values and principles which help form a foundation for broader Commonwealth understanding — principles such as: the equality and dignity of the individual; non-discrimination on the basis of race, sex, colour, creed, economic status or political belief; fair play.... (Commonwealth Secretariat, 1991a: p. 2)

In terms of the content of the Games the Final Report noted the dominance within the programme of western European sports and argued that it was important that the Games reflected the sports most widely played in the Commonwealth. Yet the most popular sports according to the report are team sports such as soccer, netball, basketball, volleyball, cricket, hockey and rugby, most of which have their origins in western Europe or north America. The Report received a warm reception from the 1991 CHOG meeting in Harare, Zimbabwe. The communique welcomed the report and the sports development initiatives and referred to the Games as the cornerstone of the Commonwealth. The meeting decided to establish an *ad hoc* committee, chaired by McMurtry, to meet bi-annually and continue the Working Party's activities over the coming four years.

The successful implementation of the recommendations included in the Final Report is by no means a foregone conclusion. To date progress has been mixed. There have changes in the funding of the CGF which will put it on a much more secure footing, but there has been little progress in the crucial area of sports development beyond the preparation of a distance learning pack for athletes and administrators. Much depends on the willingness of governments, in a time of deep recession, to allocate finance to support the expanded role of the CGF. Many of the suggestions regarding the streamlining of the organisation of the Games and the sports content depend crucially on the success of the 1998 Games to be hosted by Kuala Lumpur. If the choice of Kuala Lumpur proves, like Kingston in 1996, to be an exception rather than a break with tradition the prospects for implementation of the rest of the McMurtry recommendations will substantially diminish.

Conclusions

Assessing the significance of sport, and particularly the Games, to the politics of the Commonwealth is understandably difficult. In such a complex pattern of international relations as surround issues such as apartheid it is not possible to make definite statements about cause and effect. However, while acknowledging the importance of this caveat, a number of observations can be offered. As regards the importance of the Games to the institution of the Commonwealth it is clear that the Games provided an arena where individual members felt that they were able to employ a broader range of policy positions. The restraining protocols of the CHOG meetings were absent from involvement in the Games and members could adopt more radical stances without undermining their participation in CHOG meetings. Thus the Games provide a useful political resource both as an additional medium for policy communication, but more importantly as a safety valve for political positions that the CHOG meetings might not be able to accommodate.

Yet this level of analysis deals only with the rather superficial pattern of behaviour of members not the fabric of values, attitudes and expectations that underpin diplomatic activity. For Wilson the Commonwealth Games like the Olympic Games "began to serve as a public reinforcement of the myths of Western civilisation's superiority over colonial peoples" (1988: 156). In a similar vein, Stoddart argues that "as the formal, political ties with the imperial power have declined, the informal cultural ones have been strengthened to maintain a strong power relationship and a particular vision of social order" (1986: p. 125). While there is much force and substance in both these evaluations, they need to be explored before the richness of the political significance of sport in the Commonwealth is to be fully appreciated.

Wilson is correct in his analysis of the racial politics of the Games, but the impact of the Commonwealth Games is not to highlight the cultural gap between western and colonial peoples, rather it serves to exemplify and, to an extent, set the terms of admission to the modern, developed world. Those terms are not just the commitment to liberal democracy and market economics, but also the acceptance of rational bureaucratic organisation as a basis of social and sporting order. A similar amplification may be made of Stoddart's analysis. He identifies the dominant relationship within the Commonwealth as being between Britain and her former colonies, with the 'old' Commonwealth states forming a set of close allies. Even in 1986 this underestimated the degree of change in the power relations within the Commonwealth. Not only had British power and centrality seriously declined, but other potential focal states had grown in stature, for example Canada, Australia and India. More importantly the content of the cultural message of the Games had changed from one of replicating imperial power to one concerned with wider economic and political values dominant in Britain and North America during the Thatcher and Reagan years in the 1980s. The Commonwealth is culturally significant, but less as a means of retaining imperial domination and more as a means of economic and political assimilation.

In this sense the Games provide highly visible evidence of the presence of the Commonwealth and, according to the McMurtry report, provide a graphic illustration of the core values of the organisation. Here the Commonwealth faces a dilemma. The liberal democratic values of equality, fair play and non-discrimination quoted above are being augmented by the liberal market values of sponsorship, marketing and commercialisation. Yet this development is consistent with trends in the broader Commonwealth. In the Harare Declaration the promotion of sustainable development and the alleviation of poverty is to be achieved through a combination of economic stability and a recognition of the central role of the market economy (Commonwealth Secretariat, 1991b: p. 6). The attraction of a market economy approach to the Games is also reflected in the discussions over the choice of sports for inclusion. The proposal to include a limited number of team games is justified partly on the basis of their popularity within the Commonwealth but also because sports such as limited over cricket would "attract a huge world-wide television audience" (Commonwealth Secretariat, 1991a: p. 7).

However, commercial opportunities are not the only motive for reconsidering the range of eligible sports. The McMurtry Report makes clear its concern to include popularity throughout the Commonwealth as an important criterion for eligibility. But at the very least there is a tension here between commercial attraction and Commonwealth popularity. It will be interesting to see how the Federation balances the highly televisual and marketable cricket, rugby and basketball against hockey and volleyball, which are arguably popular with a greater number of Commonwealth countries. It has been suggested that New Delhi's inclusion of three racket sports in its bid for the 1994 Games lost it votes in the Caribbean, where sport is more strongly influenced by western culture (Ingham, 1988). Breaking the tradition of Commonwealth Games based predominantly on European sports is difficult enough, but will be especially so if commercial considerations become more important.

The Games also fulfill a function in terms of their value as a vehicles for the political ambitions of individual, or groups of, members. Collectively, the African members were able to pursue a policy objective towards South Africa within a forum where their impact was likely to be greater and where the sports politics agenda was not crowded with other issues. It is interesting to contrast the controversy within the Olympic movement prior to the 1976 Montreal Games with that surrounding the 1978 Edmonton Commonwealth Games. In 1976 the issue of apartheid was marginalised due to the controversy over the 'two Chinas' issue and Canada's refusal to accept the Taiwanese team as representing of the Republic of China. Even though thirty states — many of them Commonwealth members— boycotted the Games, the impact on the international debate on apartheid was weak. The Commonwealth Games, by contrast, has not been an arena for east-west tension, nor a focus for battles over diplomatic recognition, and consequently provided a clearer agenda for organising opposition to apartheid.

It is not just the African, and to a lesser extent, the Caribbean states that have used the Games to further political ambitions. Canada has clearly seen apartheid and the Games as political opportunities. According to Macintosh and Hawes (1994) the Gleneagles Agreement was a crucial foundation for Canada's ambitions to adopt a leadership role in the Commonwealth as well as enhancing its influence in the United Nations on the issue of apartheid. From 1984 Mulroney, building upon Trudeau's efforts, adopted a much more interventionist foreign policy than his predecessor. The motivation of the Mulroney government for involvement in this issue lay in the perception of a broad strategic interest in achieving a peaceful transition in South Africa, and a culture within the new government that gave a high priority to human rights issues (Wood, 1990: pp. 284-6). Saul

(1988, quoted in Macintosh and Hawes, 1994) argues that part of the motivation for Mulroney's opposition to apartheid was the view that apartheid's abolition was necessary if South Africa was to be saved for capitalism. Canada also saw apartheid and the Commonwealth as an issue and forum where it could adopt a leading role and move out from the shadow of both the USA and Britain. Canada's choice of sport and apartheid as issues on which to build their diplomatic influence was shrewd as, unlike Britain, New Zealand and Australia, neither cricket or rugby were major domestic sports. Thus an aggressive sports foreign policy could be pursued without arousing internal opposition and without running the risk of being embarrassed by Canadian sports men and sports women breaking ranks.

The third area where the significance of the Games can be assessed is in terms of the relationship between the Commonwealth Games organisations and those of the Olympics and the major International Federations. In general, the relationship between the CGF and other major sports organisations is weak primarily due to suspicion of organisations that are closely linked to political organisations. This suspicion was given substance by the production of the Gleneagles Agreement which, as Coghlan observed, "presented [sports bodies] with a *fait acompli* [which] has been resented ever since" (1990: p. 142). While the issue of apartheid might be fading, an emerging tension relates to the problems of fitting the Commonwealth Games into an increasingly crowded and commercially based sports calender. This is potentially a serious problem for track and field sports in particular.

Among the few areas where there has been cooperation, doping is the most significant. However, this has been limited on the part of the CGF to the adoption of the IOC list of banned substances and practices. As noted earlier the effectiveness of drug testing at each Games depends primarily on the resources of the host state. The one area where cooperation is most promising is concerning sport development. The Commonwealth is clearly keen to support the development of elite and grass roots sports in poorer states, and while few Commonwealth initiatives exist to date it is clear that Olympic Solidarity and the IAAF would welcome any addition to the resources devoted to sports development activity. The advantage that the CGF possesses over the Olympic movement is its contacts with states, for example the smaller islands in the Caribbean and Oceania, that are members of the CGF but are not members of the IOC.

While the membership of the CGF helps to extend the global reach of organised sport, it also provides a voice for smaller nations to raise issues with major sports International NGOs particularly over issues of sports development and travel costs for major competitions. However, it is not only the small states that see the CGF as a useful point of access to the international sports community. Britain, which has gradually lost its leading role in world sports administration, values the CGF as one of the few remaining international sport bodies which retains a strong British influence. As a result the British International Sports Committee (BISC), which has a broad concern to enhance the influence of Britain in international sport, sees the CGF as an important focus for its activities. The payment of a grant by the Sports Council to the CGF from 1990 and the provision of accommodation from 1992 is seen as a prudent investment.

Fourthly, it is important to form some assessment of the impact of Commonwealth membership on the behaviour of the member states. It is clear that the Commonwealth was able to exert some collective influence over New Zealand's policy of support for sporting contact with South Africa. New Zealand has few diplomatic contacts with Third World states and this self-imposed diplomatic isolation is compounded by its geographical isolation and narrow range of trade relations. The Commonwealth was one of the few forums where Muldoon was exposed to a broader range of world opinion. While bringing New Zealand into line with Commonwealth policy was a considerable achievement, the Commonwealth also affected the strategy adopted by the African states. Given that the organisation has little practical involvement in matters of defence or trade, the disputes over apartheid were able to be funneled into the relatively harmless policy area of sport. Commonwealth debates on apartheid were in effect a diplomatic cul-de-sac rather than a springboard for firmer, more aggressive action. The character of the Gleneagles Agreement is ample proof of this. The Agreement undermined any intention that the African states had of pursuing, more rigourously, their challenge to New Zealand's policy. In Payne's words the Commonwealth was effective in urging them "not to demand too much of New Zealand" (1991: p. 419).

The current significance of the Commonwealth Games is not in doubt either to the future of the Commonwealth as an institution or to the majority of participants. It is perhaps fitting that the CGF was discussing with sports officials of the former Soviet Union the possibility of a sports event in May 1994 which would have involved both the Commonwealth and the states of the former USSR. If the event had taken place it would have brought together the two sets of states which have used sport as an explicit vehicle for promoting their respective political ideologies. However, the Soviet Spartakiade sports festivals and the ideology that went with them have disappeared, while the Commonwealth has adapted to change with a considerable degree of success and the CGF is looking forward to the next century.

References

Akinrinade, O. (1992) 'The 1971 Declaration of Commonwealth Principles after 20 years', *The Round Table*, No. 321: pp. 23-35.

Aluko, O. (1991) 'The foreign policies of African States in the 1990s', *The Round Table*, No. 317, pp. 33-44.

Bourne, R. (1992) 'Commonwealth at UNCED', *The Round Table*, No. 324: pp. 457-463.

Chadwick, J. (1982) *The Unofficial Commonwealth: The story of the Commonwealth Foundation 1965-1980*. London: George Allen and Unwin.

Coghlan, J. (1990) *Sport and British Since 1960*. Basingstoke: Falmer Press .

Commonwealth Secretariat (1987) *The Commonwealth at the Summit: Communiques of the Commonwealth Heads of Government Meetings 1944-1986*. London: Commonwealth Secretariat.

———(1989) *Commonwealth Heads of Government: The Kuala Lumpur Communique, October 1989*. London: Commonwealth Secretariat.

———(1991a) *Working Party on strengthening Commonwealth Sport: Final Report*. London: Commonwealth Secretariat.

———(1991b) *Commonwealth Heads of Government Meeting: The Harare Communique*. London: Commonwealth Secretariat.

Delvoie, L. A. (1989) 'The Commonwealth in Canadian foreign policy', *The Round Table*, No. 310: pp. 137-143.

Doxey, M. (1984) 'The Commonwealth Secretariat', in A.J.R. Groom and P. Taylor (eds), *The Commonwealth in the 1980s: Challenges and opportunities*. London: Macmillan.

Groom, A.J.R. (1988) 'The advent of international organisation', in P. Taylor and A.J.R. Groom (eds) *International institutions at work*. London: Pinter.

Groom, A.J.R. and Taylor, P. (1984) 'The continuing Commonwealth: Its origins and characteristics', in A.J.R. Groom and P. Taylor (eds), *The Commonwealth in the 1980s: Challenges and opportunities*. London: Macmillan.

Ingham, D. (1988) 'Olympic-style bidding threatens the Commonwealth Games'. London: Gemini News Service.

Jones, A. (1991) 'The first Commonwealth Forum for Non-Governmental Organisations: A voice for the NGOs of the Commonwealth', *The Round Table*, No. 320.

Julien, K.S. (1992) 'The problems of small States', *The Round Table*, No. 321: pp. 45-50.

Macintosh, D. and Hawes, D. (eds) (1994) *Sport and Canadian diplomacy*. Toronto: McGill-Queen's University Press.

McMurtry, R. (1990) *Commonwealth Heads of Government Working Party on Strengthening Commonwealth Sport: Preliminary Report*. (Chairman Sir R McMurtry). London: Commonwealth Secretariat.

Moore, K. E. (1986) 'Strange bedfellows and cooperative partners: The influence of the Olympic Games on the establishment of the British Empire Games', in G. Redmond (ed) *Sport and politics*. Toronto: Human Kinetics Publishers Inc.

Payne, A. (1991) 'The international politics of the Gleneagles Agreement', *The Round Table*, No. 320: pp. 417-430.

Saul, J. (1988) 'Militant Mulrooney? The Tories and South Africa', paper presented to annual meeting of the Canadian Association of African Studies, Kingston, Canada.

Secretary of State for External Affairs (1989) *A proposal to strengthen the Commonwealth Games: A firmer foundation — a brighter future*. Ottowa: External Affairs and International Trade Canada.

Stoddart, B. (1986) 'Sport, culture, and postcolonial relations: A preliminary analysis of the Commonwealth Games', in G. Redmond (ed) *Sport and politics*. Toronto: Human Kinetics.

Wood, B. (1990) 'Canada and Southern Africa: A return to middle power activism', *The Round Table*, No. 315: pp. 280-290.

World Bank (1990) *The World Development Report 1990*. Washington: World Bank.

Transnational Corporations in the Leisure Industry

Chris Gratton

Sheffield Hallam University, UK

Introduction

There is a large and developing literature on transnational corporations (TNCs). Interest in this area has been further stimulated with the move to the Single Internal Market within the European Community and the creation of a third trading block (in addition to the USA, and Japan) with around 350 million consumers in its 'home' market. It is expected that this development may lead to an acceleration of corporate resructuring to take advantage of new market opportunities in global competition.

But virtually all the literature in the area of transnational corporations and global markets has ignored the leisure industry. Part of the reason for this is that leisure is predominantly a service industry, and the main focus of the literature has been on manufacturing. Where services have been considered, emphasis has been placed on those services that are directly linked to manufacturing such as finanCe and advertising. Also, leisure is rarely treated as an industry in its own right by economists, and therefore is never singled out for special analysis.

This paper attempts to fill the gap, and considers how to approach to the study of transnational corporations in the leisure industry. The first section deals with conventional approaches to such study. The second identifies specific matters relevant to the operation of firms in leisure industries including theoretical issues. The main question addressed is whether there are special factors present in the leisure market that have a particular influence the growth of transnational corporations. The theory is illustrated with several examples from the global leisure market. The third section of the chapter goes into more detail for three specific case studies.

Transnational corporations in a competitive global environment

The development of transnational corporations and the emergence of what is conceived as a global economic system is relatively recent. The first transnational corporations emerged in the primary industrial sector, most notably in the oil industry, but the major development of transnational corporations in manufacturing began in the 1950s with major investments in production capacity in Europe by US firms. In the 1960s and 1970s, European firms followed a similar transnational strategy with major investments in the USA. Japanese firms set up production facilities in Europe and the USA in the 1970s and 1980s and the most recent development is transnational firms emerging from the newly industrialising countries (NICs), most notably Korea and Singapore.

The motivation for large firms to move out of their own home markets and set up production facilities in foreign countries has varied at different phases of the development of the global economic system. The oil companies became transnational through the search for new sources of supply of their primary resource. Initially, American and European manufacturing firms expanded abroad in search of new markets in pursuance of growth. In the 1970s and 1980s, these same firms were switching production out of established areas and into cheaper production countries, most notably in the Far East. At the same time, Japanese firms and firms from the NICs were setting up production facilities in Europe and the USA, in order to overcome protectionist measures in those areas, which were restricting access to these lucrative markets.

An interesting illustration of both these processes is the EC consumer electronics market during the 1980s. The consumer electronics sector consists of manufacturing of audio-visual equipment which makes up a large proportion of the items that represent in-home leisure: video equipment (TVs, videos, camcorders, etc), audio eqipment (hi-fi systems, CDs, etc), and accessories (blank tapes, microphones, headphones, etc). Within the EC the sector is characterised by high growth in demand. Between 1987 and 1988 demand for consumer electronics products grew by 10% in value. Volume growth is often greater than value growth, since prices in this sector in general fall rather than rise. Thus, between 1987 and 1988, volume growth in TVs was up 13%, VCRs 18%, hi-fis 24%, and camcorders 47%.

Despite such strong growth in demand in the 'home' EC market, EC producers have struggled to compete for this 'home' demand with producers from Japan and South-East Asia. The 1980s saw considerable restucturing of the EC consumer electronics industry with a 50 % reduction in plants.

There was a substantial tranfer of production by EC firms to the Far East. At the same time there was a transfer of the production of Japanese and Korean firms to the EC. By 1990, there were 68 Japanese and Korean consumer electronic plants in the EC employing 21,200 workers, compared to 106 plants of EC firms employing 105,000 workers (Eurostat, 1992). This two-way movement of production illustrates the different motivations fuelling transnationalisation of production. EC firms are moving to the Far East in search of cheaper production. Japanese and Korean firms are moving to the EC to avoid EC trade restrictions and tariffs.

The economic motivations for the development of TNCs and global orientation are well documented. The growth of TNCs involves a process of both corporate concentration and territorial concentration. Corporate concentration refers to the tendency of a small number of very large firms to control a large percentage of output. Wallace (1990) summarises the economic forces leading to corporate concentration:

> This corporate concentration of production reflects a number of underlying pressures within a capitalist economy. One is that although the pursuit of profits and the pursuit of growth are not identical goals, they are in many respects interrelated. *Economies of scale* permit larger producers to undercut smaller producers and thereby increase their market share, and this process in itself gives the larger producer more power and flexibility in dealing with consumers. In sectors requiring very large capital investment per unit of output, such as the basic resource processing industries (metal refining, petrochemicals, and pulp and paper), there are often added *technological* arguments for large scale production. *Economies of scope* can be achieved by large multiproduct or multifunction firms which benefit from integrating a wide range of activities internally and reducing their transaction costs. As a firm's competitiveness becomes increasingly dependent on technological sophistication, requiring sustantial investment in *research and development* (R&D) over a sustained period, there are further advantages which accrue to large producers who can recoup these outlays from high volume sales. In many consumer goods sectors characterised by 'mature' products, such as detergents, the volume of sales which a particular firm can achieve depends on heavy *advertising* expenditures to maintain its 'brand image', which again favours large established producers. One or more of these characteristics can represent a *barrier to entry* which makes it increasingly difficult, if not impossible, for new firms to enter a given industry which has become dominated by a few large firms.

These economic forces leading to the growth of corporate concentration inevitably lead to some of the strongest firms expanding outside the original sector of activity (diversification) and/or outside of the original geographical market area (transnationalisation). Dunning (1988) refers to the advantages of large firms discussed above as 'ownership' advantages of the firm. The characteristics of the firms home market and geographical position are referred to as 'locational advantages'. In a situation where ownership advantages are strong and location advantages are weak, growth of the firm leads to expansion into foreign markets through foreign direct investment.

Much of this conventional discussion over the reasons for the growth of transnational corporations has focused on firms in manufacturing, or alternatively on firms operating in the primary sector (agriculture, minerals, and other natural resources). Although some leisure industries are manufacturing industries, such as consumer electronics discussed earlier, leisure is predominantly a service industry. Service industries have received little attention in the literature on TNCs largely because they have been perceived as fragmented, characterised by low entry barriers and diseconomies of scale. However, Segal-Horn (1989) argues that this is an outdated view of service firms:

> The sources of competitive advantage in service industries have shifted as a result of recent environmental, structural, market, and technological changes. This has provided a major shift in the potential for globalisation as a competitive strategy available to service industries. There exists now some evidence that, as already occurred in sizeable segments of manufacturing industry, those companies with clear strategic intent to leverage existing competitive advantage in support of long-term global brand dominance, can establish indentifiable worldwide market presence.

In the next section I concentrate on the forces operating on leisure firms that are leading to a greater degree of internationalisation in the supply of leisure services.

Growth, concentration, diversification, and internationalisation of leisure firms

As indicated earlier, the development of transnational corporations is fuelled by the growth objective of particular firms. I will argue in this section that pursuing this growth objective by leisure firms can lead to a variety of patterns of development in which internationalisation is increasingly involved. The analysis below is based to a large extent on the work of Penrose (1959).

Penrose developed a theory of the growth of firms. She was concerned neither with the internationalisation of firms nor with the leisure industry, but rather with growth and diversification of firms within their home markets. Gratton and Taylor (1987) applied her approach to leisure firms, and in this paper I attempt to extend it to the internationalisation of leisure firms.

Penrose adopted an unusual approach for an economist. She did not look at the firm as a theoretical concept with the cost and demand curves that appear in standard economics texts. Rather, she viewed the firm as a social and administrative organisation, where people are particularly important for success or failure. The most important part of the organisation is the management team, which not only provides the motivation for growth and development, but is also likely to be the major constraint in the firm's rate of progress.

The basic motivation of management is the desire to increase total long-run profits. Since profits increase when investment yields a positive net return, then firms will expand "as fast as they can take advantage of opportunities for expansion that they consider profitable". The management must plan and organise the growth process. They must decide the speed of expansion, the route to growth, and then harness the firm's resources and administer the growth programme.

The initial phase of expansion will be determined by the firm's "inherited resources", that is the productive services it already possesses. A quote from Penrose illustrates the growth process:

> There is no doubt that the growth of demand for a firm's existing products, as expressed through price changes and other sorts of market information, is a powerful influence on the direction of productive activity and on the expansion of firms. The possibility of expanding such demand by advertising and other sales efforts, and the effect of such efforts on the productive opportunity of the firm are not to be underestimated. Other things being equal, it is usually cheaper and less risky to expand the production of existing products than to enter new fields. When, therefore, the market demand for existing products is growing and entrepreneurs expect continued growth, 'demand' will appear as the most important influence on expansion and current investment plans may be closely tied to entrepreneurial estimates of the prospects for increasing sales in existing product lines ... In an expanding economy, therefore, a large proportion of existing firms maybe closely related to increased demand for their original types of product in much the same market area ... demand for a firm's existing products will,

therefore, have an important influence on the rate of growth of firms.

In such an expanding market, the older established firms will have an advantage over newer firms and they will tend to grow faster. Those with the most alert and efficient management teams will grow fastest and we will therefore start to see concentration in the industry increasing. As the larger firms grow, they obtain further advantages from size, which gives them a further competitive edge over smaller firms, thus feeding the cycle of increasing concentration. Penrose argues that such a process cannot continue indefinitely. Even if demand continues to expand at the same rate, as the larger firms increase market share, their growth will be greater than the growth of demand. In order to continue to maintain such a growth rate, either industry demand will have to expand faster, or the firm will have to expand its market share at the same rate. Since market share has a theoretical maximum of one hundred%, and a realistic (or legally binding) maximum much less than this, then eventually it will become impossible to maintain the firm's growth rate without continual increases in the rate of growth in industry demand.

Thus, Penrose argues that demand acts as a constraint in a firm's growth even in industries where demand is expanding, and this constraint leads the firm to expand outside its original market area. There is evidence to suggest that leisure firms may not, in certain circumstances, be subject to this constraint, or rather leisure is a peculiar industry in that the opportunity for rapid expansions of demand over relatively long periods is certainly more feasible than in other industries. That is, I am arguing that it is possible for at least some leisure firms to satisfy their growth objective *without* moving outside their original market area.

The reason for this is that leisure is peculiar in that the nature of demand for leisure is different from that for other commodities. Scitovsky (1976) used arousal theory from psychology to consider two categories of consumer demand: want satisfaction and stimulation seeking. *Want satisfaction* is straightforward. When we are deprived of the essential elements of human existence (food, clothing, shelter) then we demand these essentials and receive pleasure from the satisfaction of these demands. In psychological terms, hunger raises the arousal level: food relieves hunger, lowers the a rousal level back towards the optimum. Pleasure or utility results from the movement in arousal from too high an arousal level towards the optimum level. Being at the optimum level of arousal gives rise to feelings of comfort and well-being. But pleasure results from the movement to the optimum, from an either too low or too high level. Scitovsky critises economists' treatment of consumer demand for only considering the want satisfaction (lowering too high arousal) aspects of demand and completely ignoring *stimulation-seeking* behaviour (raising too low arousal).

There is a limit to the amount of satisfaction that can be obtained from want satisfaction. As the basic demands for material goods are met, there is less and less opportunity for pleasure through want satisfaction since consumers are not sufficiently deprived of anything for their arousal level to increase. Thus Scitovsky paints a picture of the USA as an affluent yet 'joyless economy'. This inability for want satisfaction to generate continuing increases in pleasure places an overall constraint on increases in demand for certain categories of products.

However, want satisfaction is not the only source of pleasure. *Stimulation seeking* behaviour is not concerned with satifying material wants but with seeking experiences that are exciting, novel, and sometimes dangerous. These sort of experiences are demanded precisely because they are *not* essential to human existence. In fact, at times they are demanded even though they threaten human existence. Mountain climbing, skiing, white water rafting, hang-gliding, and many other sporting experiences provide experiences that provide pleasure precisely because they take the consumer out of his or her everyday existence. Such demand is completely different to want satisfaction. Products which fit into this category of demand have a much greater potential for continual increases in demand. Part of the reason for this is that many affluent economies have already reached the limit of further increases in utility through want satisfaction. For many consumers therefore an increasing share of consumption in the future will be in stimulation seeking behaviour.

The overall point of Scitovsky's analysis is that stimulation-seeking behaviour is the motivator behind most leisure demands. This suggests that leisure will command an increasing share of consumers' expenditure in affluent economies. Statistics show that this has been happening throughout the post-war period. This does not mean however that every leisure product will experience continually rising demand. In fact, the pattern over this century is for leisure products to experience rapid increases in demand often from zero levels but then, in some cases to experience equally rapid decline.

An example from the British leisure market will illustrate the point. The cinema industry experienced phenomenal growth in Britain in the interwar years. It was one of the first major mass leisure activities, and — as is often the case with leisure — was a completely new product emanating from developments in technology. Demand grew from nothing to have reached an annual attendance of 934 million in 1934. By the 1930s cinema-going was clearly the most popular leisure activity in Britain. It is perhaps difficult to appreciate today just how popular it was. Richards (1984) quotes a variety of evidence to indicate its popularity. A social survey in Merseyside in 1934 showed that 40% of the population went to the cinema at least once a week and 25% went at least twice a week. For younger people the percentage going to the cinema on a weekly basis was above 70%. Richards entitled his book *The Age of the Dream Palace* and in it he quotes sociologist Seebohn Rowntree on the motivation behind the demand for cinema:

> At a cost of 6d or so a working woman, bored to death by a never-ending round of humdrum household chores, or a factory worker oppressed by the monotony of his work, can be transplanted, as if on a magic carpet, into a completely new world; a world of romance or high adventure.

This quotation reflects the fact that 1930s cinema audiences were predominantly from the working class and also predominantly female. The motivation certainly fits in with Scitovsky's stimulation seeking category of demand, but it was not generated by affluence and the inability to have increased pleasure from want satisfaction. Rather it was a means to escape the frustrations and stresses of economic life in the 1930s, when for the working class satisfying basic economic needs was a major problem.

Attendances continued to grow, so that by 1946 annual attendance for cinemas in Britain was 1635 million. From the end of the First World War to 1946 growth in demand for cinema outstripped every other commodity. Yet by 1985, annual attendances at cinemas in Britain had fallen to 55 million. The market showing the fastest rate of expansion in the first half of the century showed the fastest rate of decline in the second half. This potential for rapid growth of demand and also rapid decline is a peculiar characteristic of leisure markets.

Part of the reason for this volatility of demand is that all leisure expenditures are discretionary; they are the easiest to cut back in times of recession. But there two other peculiar factors that make leisure goods and services prone to experience wider swings in demand than is normal in other markets.

Firstly with increasing affluence, leisure demands become more fragmented. Each individual has the time and money to find that activity that best meets his/her need for stimulation. Some new leisure products may attract a large demand very quickly simply because they are new and have a high novelty value (and hence provide stimulation) for a wide audience. The second factor though may prevent continuing growth of such a market, that is the possibility of repeated leisure experiences providing less and less stimulation. Where the leisure activity requires a relatively high skill level or provides opportunities for skill learning, the stimulation continues through repeated experiences while the nature of the experience changes as skill levels increase. Thus, although the beginners' slope may not stimulate the experienced skier, there are other runs that are challenging and stimulating. Thus skilled consumption activities provide opportunities for continued stimulation. Leisure products that cater to high skill leisure activities may be able to continue with a sustained increase in demand, and may provide an exception to Penrose's argument that for expansion a firm would need to look to new markets.

However, leisure experiences requiring little or no consumption skills depend on the novelty effect for stimulation. With repeated experiences, the novelty wears off. This explains how demand for a new leisure product may increase at a rapid rate as everybody tries the product for the first time, but is also likely to decrease equally rapidly unless a means of retaining the novelty effect can be found (skate-boarding was an example). Also leisure is an area where there is a very high rate of product innovation. New products and activities are constantly being introduced to provide high levels of competition and novelty. It was a new technological development, television, that destroyed the cinema industry in Britain, appealing particularly to the demand for a cheap form of escapism that characterised British interwar cinema audiences.

This tendency for leisure demands to fragment and show high volatility in any one market is a major feature of leisure, and sets it aside from other consumer markets. It also, not surprisingly, presents problems for the supply-side of the industry. It is not an easy job for the firm supplying a leisure product to cater to a demand that may well be expanding at record rates in the early years of the firm's life, only to find, when the firm has grown to a sufficient size to meet this demand, that the demand suddenly disappears.

In these circumstances, to maintain the growth of the firm, it will normally be necessary for the firm to move into new markets. Which will it choose? One obvious direction of expansion is to integrate vertically. Thus the overseas tour operator involved in selling flights and accommodation overseas buys its own airline and maybe hotels abroad (e.g. Thomsons). The firm involved in brewing beer (eg Bass, Scottish and Newcastle) buys the outlets that distribute the beer (i.e. the pubs, bars cafes, and hotels). The film maker (e.g., Cannon) buys up the cinemas in which the films are shown. Growth by vertical integration can provide further economies and cost reductions through improved co-ordination and reduced risk and uncertainty, thus giving a further market advantage to the larger firm. However, the reason why such vertical integration is attractive for the management team is that they already possess the technical expertise to manage the new business because of their base in the existing product area.

Figure 1 Total trip expenditure by hypothetical short-haul international touists (%)

GENERATING COUNTRY		INTERNATIONAL LINK		DESTINATION COUNTRY	
Travel agency services	8	Air carriage	30	Lodging	22
Other services (e.g. information)	3	Goods (e.g. duty-free)	5	Transfers and sidetrips	13
Taxes	2			Personal and souvenirs	12
				Taxes	5
Nontax total	11	Total	35	Nontax total	47

Source: Bull (1991)

Bull (1991) has argued that growth through vertical integration is particular attractive for firms operating in the international tourism industry. He indicates by use of Figure 1, how total trip expenditure by an international tourist can be broken down into expenditures in the generating country, expenditures involved in the international link, and expenditures in the destination country. It is clear that pressure to develop into multinational operations is greatest in the generating countries since the potential gains in revenue are greatest. Also, the operator in the generating country has the first contact with the consumer and also has the expert knowledge of local consumer tastes and preferences. By expanding into the international link and the destination country, the operator can substantially increase revenue and yet still be dealing with the same consumers.

Certainly there has been evidence of such vertical integration within the tourism industry in Europe. Thomsons, the major British package tour operator, also owns Britannia, the biggest charter airline, as well as Lunn-Poly, the largest chain of travel agencies. There are also many examples of foreign ownership of firms operating within a particular national market (see Gomez and Thea Sinclair, 1991). There is some evidence of increasing Europeanisation in the sense that mergers and takeovers of tourism operators in one European market tend to be by a European operator in another market. Thus, Kaufhof AG, a German company, owns ITS the fourth largest German tour operator, has a 80% stake in Holland International, the largest Dutch operator, and a 48% stake in Sun International, which is not only the largest tourism consortium in Belgium but also has operations in France and Luxembourg. ITS also acquired in 1991 a 36% share in Travelplan, a tour operator based in Madrid. In 1992, another major German operator, LTU Touristik, acquired Thomas Cook, the British travel agency chain.

For other leisure industries, growth through diversification *outside* the original product area is the normal pattern. Firms operating in the British brewing industry, for instance, to maintain growth must expand their operations beyond the production and selling of beer, since total consumption of beer has been static or has even declined since the late 1970s; the market is already dominated by six major brewers so that further advances in market share are very difficult; and growth through further vertical integration into public houses has been prevented by intervention of the Monopolies and Mergers Commission which has led to regulations for brewers to reduce their ownership of pubs for reasons of restraint of trade. In such a case, the question is: which market to enter? The standard answer is that the company will continue to draw on its own expertise and knowledge. For a manufacturing firm this will be knowledge of production technology. The obvious direction in which the firm will diversify is towards products that have a similar technological base, and there are many examples of such diversification in manufacturing industries.

However, leisure is primarily, though by no means totally, a service industry. Service industries do not have the technological base to provide the platform for diversification. Management expertise and know-how in service industries is essentially marketing expertise. That is, it is knowledge of *demand* that provides the platform for diversification.

It is not surprising, then, to see leisure firms diversifying into other leisure markets, because these firms have specialist knowledge of leisure demands. They have a market advantage over non-leisure firms. Not only is this the obvious direction of diversification but the peculiar nature of leisure demands, in particular their exceptional volatility, makes diversification across leisure markets particularly advantageous. Again a quotation from Penrose emphasises the need for diversification when faced with uncertain demand:

> The real difficulties occur when fluctuations in demand are not easily predictable.... They are unable to predict these movements with any precision and they often attempt to diversify into the production of products the demand for which is influenced by circumstances different from those influencing their existing markets.

Diversification to deal with temporary fluctuations in demand that are definitely expected but that cannot be estimated with sufficient accuracy to make profit calculations more than informed guesses, comes very close to diversification as a device for coping with generalised uncertainty:

> .... Many a firm has proclaimed the philosophy that its security is greater if it produces a wide range of products instead of concentrating on those products which, even after all practical allowances for risk have been made, seem to be the most profitable. In other words, diversification becomes a hedge, not against those changes that are definitely expected (although it fulfils that function too), but against changes of any sort which the 'luck of the game' may bring. In practice, however, firms recognise that different kinds of products are subject to different types of risk and, within the limits permitted by their productive resources, choose a range of products designed to give the greatest protection against the various definable types of risk.

In the leisure industry we can go further than this. The proportion of consumers' expenditure going on leisure items is not volatile at all in the medium term, although it may vary in the short term due to variations in the business cycle. This proportion grows slowly and steadily over long periods. It is highly predictable. It is the way that expenditure is distributed *over the various leisure markets* that is highly variable. For any firm supplying one of those markets, risk of temporary or permanent adverse changes in demand can be reduced by diversifying *within the leisure sector.* The broader the range of leisure products and services provided, then the greater the chance that the consumers deserting the major product line will be lining up to buy another leisure product that is provided by the firm in another market.

Thus Bass, which has the largest share of the beer market (at about 22%), is also a major hotel operator with the Holiday Inn chain, as well as owning Coral (betting and bingo). Scottish and Newcastle, another major brewing company, also has a diversified range of leisure interests outside brewing including Center Parcs, a Dutch based international holiday company. Ladbroke is the world's largest betting organisation with operations in the UK, USA, and Europe, but is also one of the largest hotel operators in the world, and owns a DIY chain of stores (Texas Homecare) and holiday villages. This process of diversification also often leads to internationalisation. The Holiday Inn chain has hotels in 49 countries, with 81% of its rooms outside the country of its owner, Bass. Ladbroke has hotels in 46 countries mainly through its ownership of Hilton International. Similarly Center Parcs operates in the Netherlands, Belgium, France, as well as Britain.

Of course, if it turns out that the decline in demand for the major product is not temporary but permanent, then eventually it makes sense for the firm aiming to maximise growth and profits to get out of that market altogether. We have seen examples of this in the British leisure market (e.g.,

Ladbroke selling off its bingo halls and slot machine arcades). We can envisage the leisure firm, then, as a management team collecting together a portfolio of business interests spanning the broad leisure market. As demand and profitability change some businesses will be sold off, others will be purchased. Which businesses will be sold will depend on the management team's perception of future demand and profitability. Of course, these forecasts are subject to considerable risk and uncertainty and we often see one leisure firm moving out of a market area, only to see another leisure firm moving into that area (e.g., Rank purchased Ladbroke's bingo halls). Obviously, different management teams have different perceptions of future profitability.

Such moves as this are often accompanied by the "repackaging" of the product — an attempt to create a new product out of the old. Rank took over Ladbroke's bingo halls and immediately tried to revitalise the bingo market with a new national competition. A better example also involves Rank and its creation of Somerwest World out of the old Butlin's holiday camp at Minehead. Somerwest World is still a holiday camp of sorts, but with leisure pools, waterslides, better quality accommodation and a wide variety of sports and recreations, it is a new concept for the fit and active 1980s. Similar redevelopments are also taking place at Rank's other holiday camps. Rank is the subject of one of the case-studies in the next section where an attempt is made to analyse the transnationalisation process for three different transnational leisure corporations.

Case Studies in Transnational Leisure Corporations

1 RANK ORGANISATION PLC.

Rank in fact provides a very good example of a firm that has expanded rapidly within leisure through this process of diversification. Rank was founded in 1935 and quickly became Britain's leading producer and distributor of films. Rank first produced films at Pinewood studios, then established a distribution network, and finally acquired Odeon cinemas, the third largest cinema group after Gaumont amd ABPC (Associated British Pictures Corporation). In 1941 Rank became the market leader in the cinema industry in Britain by taking over Gaumont. Thus from beginning in film production Rank grew quickly through vertical integration.

Rank's growth was severely curtailed in the immediate postwar period as cinema attendances went into long term decline. Bitish cinema attendances dropped from 1.6 billion in 1946 to 400 million in 1963. Rank had achieved a high level of dominance within one industry, the film industry. It had managed to maintain its growth through demand for the cinema and through vertical integration within the industry. Faced with the rapid decline in demand, Rank was forced to look for interests outside the film industry.

There were two strands to the diversification strategy. The first follows the arguments outlined above. Rank sought to move into the new forms of leisure that were competing with the cinema. Many cinemas were converted into bowling alleys, dance halls, and bingo halls. Although demand for these leisure facilities were expanding in the 1950s, again growth was temporary. In particular, large dance halls and bowling alleys were in decline as leisure attractions by the early 1960s.

The other strand to Rank's diversification proved more fruitful. Through its film producing and processing activities, Rank had technical expertise which led it to move into precision instruments and electronics. In 1956, partly as a result of this route of development Rank set up a new company, Rank Xerox, which was a partnership with an American company, Xerox, where Rank used its manufacturing and distribution network to market copying machines throughout the world outside of America. This venture proved amazingly successful. Sales of Rank-Xerox grew from $7 million in 1962 to $276 million by 1969. By 1982 Rank-Xerox accounted for 93% of Rank's total profits, with all the leisure operations together only accounting for 7% (Mirabile, 1990). At this stage it could be argued that Rank was not a major leisure company. What happened in the 1980s and early 1990s was to make Rank again a major player in the leisure market.

Rank is today probably the most diversified commercial firm operating in the leisure industry. Over the 1980s the company became a true 'leisure conglomerate' with core areas of business in holidays and hotels, recreation, leisure, and film and TV. The film and TV services includes advertising, audio-visual, film distribution, video services, and Odeon cinemas. The holidays and hotels division contains Butlins, the market leader in holiday camps, Haven, the market leader in caravan parks, as well as Shearings, Rank Hotels, and Rank Motorway Services. Both the Recreation division and the Leisure division show the importance to Rank's portfolio of activities of the take-over of Mecca Leisure in 1990. In fact, in order to illustrate the process of diversification of leisure firms across leisure markets it is perhaps better to trace the history of another company, Pleasurama, in an attempt to explain, at least partly, how Rank acquired such a diversified structure.

Pleasurama in the early 1980s had its core business in casinos. In the mid-1980s, however, it began to diversify into other leisure markets taking over Associated Leisure (amusement machines, hotels, and holidays) in 1984, Norscot Hotels in 1986, President Entertainments (restaurants) in

1987, and Hard Rock Cafes (restaurants) in 1988. Later in 1988 Pleasurama itself was taken over by Mecca Leisure. Mecca at that time was already a XX major leisure company with a diversified portfolio of leisure businesses including keep-fit centres, snooker clubs, dance halls/discos, bingo clubs, holiday camps, public houses, and hotels. In 1990, Mecca Leisure ran into financial difficulties and itself was taken over by Rank. At the same time as Rank was reestablishing itself in the leisure market, Rank-Xerox was suffering from competition from Japanese firms. By the end of the 1980s, profits were equally split between Rank and Rank-Xerox.

Rank provides us with an interesting case-study that demonstrates the theory of growth, concentration, diversification, and internationalisation of leisure firms developed in Section 2. At the same time Rank illustrates another aspect of Penrose's theory of diversification (expanding into an area of existing technical expertise) through its development of Rank-Xerox.

2 NIKE

Nike dominates the world sports shoe industry, an industry that has shown phenomenal growth over the last twenty years. Total sales of sports shoes worldwide were estimated at $11.3 billion in 1991 and Nike accounts for 21% of this (see Figure 2). Adidas, the European firm that dominated the market in the 1960s and 1970s, has suffered heavily from competition from fast growing American firms such as Nike and Reebok. The growth and development of Nike into a leisure TNC provides an interesting contrast with Rank. Unlike Rank, Nike has not grown through vertical integration nor diversification into other product market areas. Rather, Nike has grown through internationalisation of its product area and greater and greater specialisation within its area of expertise.

Figure 2 World Sports Shoe Sales, 1991 (total $11.3 bn) (%)

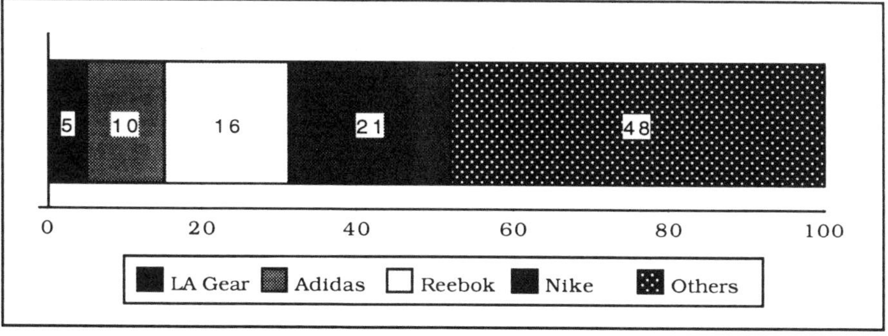

Nike started out as a company called Blue Ribbon Sports, based in Oregon, USA, and distributing running shoes produced by a Japanese company, Onitsuka Sports. By the early 1970s the company had severed ties with Onitsuka and was designing, marketing, and distributing its own running shoes. In 1978 Blue Ribbon Sports changed its name to Nike. This company very quickly established itself at the lead in one of the fastest growing leisure markets in the world. Although Nike produces other sportswear, sports shoes are its main area of activity and 75% of the company's turnover comes from shoes. In 1991, Nike sold 90 million pairs of sports shoes worldwide.

There is some literature relating to the global production, distribution, and marketing approach of Nike (Clifford, 1992; Willigan, 1992). What is perhaps surprising is that Nike is not a manufacturing company at all. All manufacturing is done by contractors, 99% of them in Asia. Clifford (1992) describes how Nike keeps the cost of production down by constantly seeking out lowest cost producers:

> The company is forever on the lookout for cheap production sites. If costs in a particular country or factory move too far out of line, productivity will have to rise to compensate, or Nike will take its business elsewhere. The firm uses about 40 factories; 20 have closed in the past five years or so and another 35 have opened.

This tremendous dynamism and flexibility in the organisation of production is illustrated by Nike's response to soaring labour costs in South Korea over the late 1980s. In 1988, 68% of Nike's shoes were produced in South Korea. By 1992, this percentage had fallen to 42% (Clifford, 1992). Over this period, Nike switched an increasing proportion of production to contractors in the cheaper labour cost countries of China, Indonesia, and Thailand. In 1988, these countries accounted for less than 10% of Nike's production. By 1992, this had increased to 44%.

Not only is Nike able to move production rapidly in search of lower and lower costs. It is also able to alter its global distribution network in response to world events. Clifford (1992) reports that Nike was faced by a potentially dangerous commercial threat in September/October 1992. Having moved much of the production of sports shoes to China, the US government became involved in a dispute with China over demands to open up Chinese markets to American goods. The USA threatened to impose punitive tariffs on Chinese goods unless agreement was reached by October 10th. In response to this threat, Nike planned to switch most of the output from Chinese factories to Europe. It also made an agreement with its Chinese suppliers that any loss resulting from any remaining shoes entering the US market would be split equally between Nike and the Chinese suppliers. In the end the dispute was resolved, and no action was needed.

Clifford's article illustrates that Nike is a fine example of a global corporation with global production, distribution and marketing strategies. Another quote from Clifford illustrates this well:

> Here is how Nike works. At the company's headquarters in Beaverton, Oregon, designers collaborate with the marketing people to come up with the shape and feel of next season's snazzy athletics shoe. There are 1,000 models of shoe in Nike's product range and over 100 new types are introduced each year.

The blueprints are then relayed by satellite to their contractors' CAD/CAM (computer-aided design/computer-aided manufacturing) systems in Taiwan, where the plans are turned into prototype shoes that can be run off a production line. In South Korea, the companies receive the plans by fax. Engineers in both contries work out how to manufacture shoes dreamed up in the US. The shoes can then be produced at the contractor's factories around the region."

Figure 3 the growth of Nike

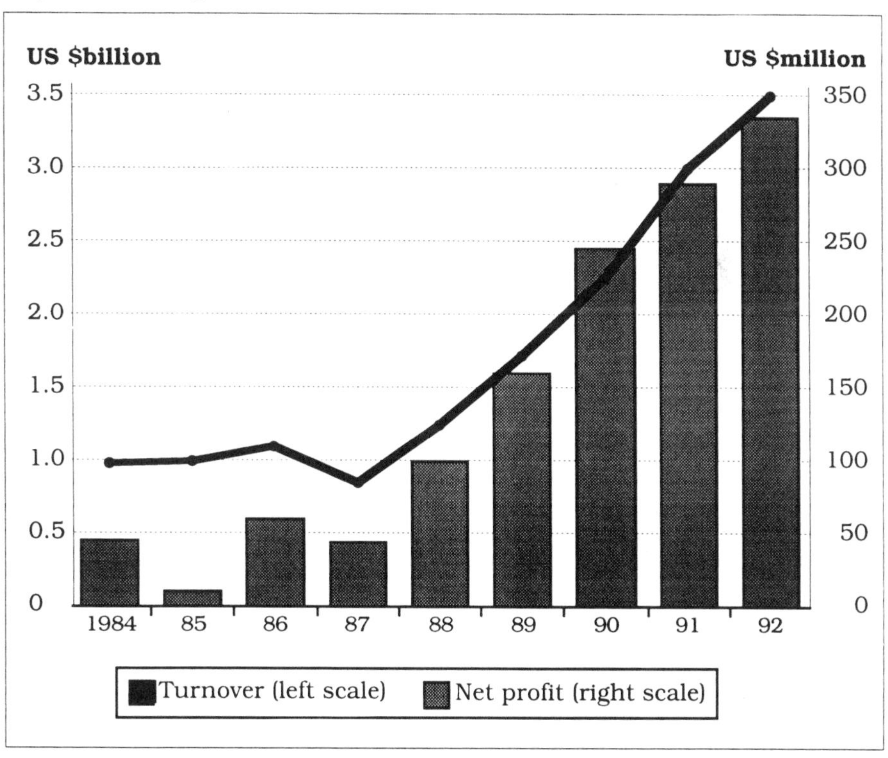

Source: Nike

Willigan (1992) provides further insight into how Nike has been able to continue its phenomenal rate of growth (as illustrated in Figure 3). Willigan interviewed senior executives at Nike and was primarily interested in Nike's approach to marketing which enables the company to promote its products to a global market. Interviewing Phil Knight, founder and Chairman of Nike, she asked him whether Nike was a technology/design company or a marketing company. His response was:

> Nike is a marketing-oriented company, and the product is our most inportant marketing tool. What I mean is that marketing knits the whole organisation together. The design elements and functional characteristics of the product itself are just part of the overall marketing process.

One of Nike's major characteristics in marketing is the association of the product with the athlete: Michael Jordan with Air Jordan the basketball shoe, John McEnroe and Andre Agassi with tennis shoes and clothing. This association is an ideal way of marketing to a global market. The globalisation of sport allows Nike to establish a global marketplace for its products as this quotation from Ian Hamilton, Nike's tennis marketing director, illustrates:

> When I started at Nike tennis, John McEnroe was the most visible player in the world, and he was already part of the Nike Family. He epitomised the type of player Nike wanted in its shoes -talented, dedicated, and loud. He broke racquets, drew fines, and, most of all, won matches. His success and behaviour drew attention on and off the court and put a lot of people in Nikes.

Similarly a further remark from Phil Knight stresses the importance of the association of the product with the athlete:

> The trick is to get athletes who not only can win but can stir up emotion. We want someone the public is going to love or hate, not just the leading scorer....To create a lasting emotional tie with consumers, we use the athletes repeatedly throughout their careers and present them as whole people.

Thus as John McEnroe got older, and Andre Agassi replaced him as the fiery newcomer, Agassi became the promoter of Challenge Court, the exciting and colourful tennis range, while John McEnroe launched a new more subdued range, Supreme Court.

This policy of breaking down each individual sport into smaller and smaller sub-markets is another major characteristic of Nike's marketing approach. Twenty years ago there was only one type of basketball shoe on the market and very few specialist running shoes. A trainer was an all-purpose sports shoe catering to a wide variety of sporting activities. Now there are different shoes and equipment for every sport. The Air Jordan basketball was a concerted effort by Nike to create a completely new market for basketball shoes. It succeeded, and later Nike further segmented the market with two other basketball ranges, Flight and Force.

Willigan's article provides an insight into how a company can sustain massive increases in demand without moving out of the original product area. But Nike and the sports shoe market are still relatively new. It remains to be seen whether such growth within one market can be sustained as the sports shoe market reaches maturity. One factor in Nike's favour is the fact that sport is skilled consumption. Consumers in this market tend to stay in the market rather than try it out and then move on to something different. Nike has built on its detailed knowledge of sports men and women and given the consumer new products that have transformed the nature of the sports shoe market. Because of the nature of the sports market Nike is unlikely to be faced by a collapse in market demand such as faced Rank in the cinema industry.

Nike provides us with a good example of the fragmentation of leisure demands discussed in Section 2. However, in this case the fragmentation has taken place *within* the sports shoe market and the company is actively working on generating such fragmentation and benefiting from it.

3 THE WALT DISNEY COMPANY

The Walt Disney Company, like Rank, started in the film industry. The difference was that Walt Disney himself was a pioneer in the development of the industry and in particular in the development of cartoon films. He created the cartoon character Mickey Mouse and the early success of the company was based on this character. In 1935, the *New York Times* called Mickey Mouse "the best known and most popular international figure of his day" (Kepos, 1992). This remark emphasises the essential international nature of the film industry. Success in Hollywood meant international success.

By the end of the 1930s Disney was making full length feature cartoon films, beginning with *Snow White and the Seven Dwarfs* in 1937. *Fantasia* followed in 1940, with *Bambi* completed in 1942 (Kepos, 1992). Despite the fact that these films were made over 50 years ago, they still attract large audiences today world-wide, and generation after generation of children identify the Disney characters. This particular type of leisure product can look forward to a constant stream of new consumers: the next generation of children.

However, Disney, like Rank, did suffer from the decline in cinema attendances in the post-war period (although the decline in the American market was much less than in Britain). Since the decline was to a large extent due to the growth of a new leisure industry, television, Disney made a major step into this new market by producing *Disneyland* for television, using clips from Disney films. At the same time, Disney expanded out of cartoons and into live-action films. Films such as *20,000 Leagues Under The Sea* had been made in the 1940s, but live-action films became a major area of expansion in the 1950s and 1960s, and in 1964 *Mary Poppins* became one of the top box-office successes of the year (Kepos, 1992).

In the same way that the company had managed to enter the television market based on the popularity of its cartoon characters, Disney pioneered a completely new market when Disneyland opened in California in 1955. Although leisure parks already existed, Disneyland was the world's first 'theme park'. What made Disneyland different was the massive scale of the investment and the theming around Disney characters and films. Within a few years of Disneyland opening, other theme parks started to open across America and a new leisure market started to grow. In 1956, its first full year of operation, Disneyland attracted 4 million visitors. By 1975, the American theme park market had 66 million customers, with Disney accounting for about one third of this after the opening of a second Disney theme park, Magic Kingdom in Orlando, Florida in 1971. By 1980 this had risen to 86 million, with Disney accounting for 30%. Most of the reason for this rapid increase in attendances was massive investment in new theme parks, which saw 16 new parks open in the 1970s including Disney's Magic Kingdom in Florida. The opening of Disney's Epcot Centre in Florida in 1982 further pushed up attendances to 96.8 million by 1985 (Travel and Tourism Analyst, 1987).

By 1985, the theme parks accounted for 70% of the income to Walt Disney Company (Kepos, 1992). In 1989, Disney-MGM Studios Theme Park opened in Florida. The product was also successfully exported to Japan with the opening of Tokyo Disneyland in 1983. The Tokyo is licensed by Disney but not owned by the company, but it attracts annual attendances of over 10 million people.

In 1992, Euro Disney was opened at Marne-La-Vallee, just outside Paris. The Walt Disney Company has a 49% shareholding in Euro Disney and should receive substantial revenue in the future from the park in terms of management fees and royalty payments. However, despite virtually achieving target attendances in the first three years of opening, Euro Disney has failed to be profitable.

Thus Disney has not only managed to create the theme park market but also to lead it. Disney parks account for over a third of US theme park attendances and for about a quarter of attendances at European parks a year after the opening of Euro Disney. In both Europe and the USA Disney theme parks are on a completely different scale with each park attracting more than 10 million visitors annually, whereas attendances at any other theme park do not exceed 3 million, and most have attendances below 2 millions a year.

In the 1980s, Disney further broadened its product base by developing new projects in merchandising Disney products, home video distribution, and hotels. By 1991, it was estimated that these new projects accounted for 28% of revenues (Kepos, 1992).

The Walt Disney Company is still a major film production company, however, and in the 1980s expanded further in this industry by setting up Touchstone Films and Hollywood Pictures, aimed at broadening its film output outside its conventional family audience.

Conclusions

Two models of the development of transnational firms in leisure have been presented above. The first sees internationalisation as a consequence of diversification across leisure industries. The second sees internationalisation as a direct consequence of the development of a worldwide demand for a given product. In both cases the crucial factor is demand.

The second model is appropriate where growth can be sustained through continual expansion of demand. Nike provides a good example of this but also shows that such demand expansion is fuelled by product innovation and the creation of subsegments of the original market area. In many ways demand expansion is sustained by the creation of new markets. This is a peculiar characteristic of leisure industries.

The first model is a response to restricted demand in any one market. Rank is a good example of how a rapidly growing company, riding on the tide of a massive growth in demand for one leisure product, the cinema, can suddenly be faced not by a slowing down in demand but a complete reversal into decline. Again the ability for demand to show such volatility is a peculiarity of leisure industries.Rank's response was to spread the risks across a wide range of leisure markets.

The Walt Disney Company case study has aspects present in both the other two. Disney is an innovative company, similar to Nike in that it tends to create new markets in areas closely related to its original market area. Disney started with Mickey Mouse and Mickey is still there in the theme parks and in merchandising. The company has retained its central focus on cartoon characters but around that focus has moved sustantially out from its original market area of production of cartoon films and into new leisure markets. In doing that, the company has again shown the potential of leisure markets to grow from virtually nothing to massive markets in a very short time period. These markets have also become internationalised. Not only have Disney parks opened in France and Japan, but also Disney parks in the USA and Europe have the largest share of international visitors. Most theme parks cater to domestic audiences, but over 70% of visitors to Euro Disney in the first year of opening came from outside France.

The leisure industries provide an interesting context for studying the transnationalisation process but they have one peculiarity compared to non-leisure industries: the potential of demand to both grow, and decline, at a remarkable rate. This peculiarity leads to different strategies by leisure firms and a different process of internationalisation as a result.

References

Bull, A. (1991) *The economics of travel and tourism*. London: Pitman.

Clifford, M. (1992) 'Nike roars', *Far Eastern Economic Review*, November.

Collins, M. (1991) 'The economics of sport and sports in the economy', in C. P. Cooper (ed) *Progress in tourism, recreation, and hospitality management*, Vol. 13. London: Belhaven Press, pp. 184-214.

Dunning, J. H. (1988) *Explaining international production. London*: Unwin Hyman.

Eurostat (1992) *Panorama of EC industries*. Brussels: Commission for the European Community.

Gomez, V. and Sinclair, M. Thea (1991) 'Integration in the tourism industry: A case study approach' in M. Thea Sinclair and M. Stabler (eds) (1991) *The tourism industry: An international analysis*. Oxford: CAB International.

Gratton, C. and Taylor, P. (1987) *Leisure industries — An overview*. London: Comedia.

Kepos, P. (ed) (1992) *International directory of company histories: Volume 6.* London: St. James Press.

Littlejohn, D. and Beattie, R. (1992) 'The European hotel industry: Corporate structures and expansion strategies', *Tourism Management*, March.

Mirabile, L. (ed) (1990) *International directory of company histories: Volume 2.* London: St. James Press.

Penrose, E. T. (1959) *The theory of the growth of the firm*. London: Basil Blackwell.

Richards, J. (1984) *The age of the dream palace: Cinema and society in Britain 1930–1939*. London: Routledge & Kegan Paul.

Scitovsky, T. (1976) *The joyless economy*. Oxford: The University Press.

Segal-Horn, S. (1989) 'The globalisation of service firms', in P. Jones (ed) *Management in Service Firms*.

Stopford, J., Strange, S. and Henley, J. (1991) *Rival states, rival firms*. Cambridge: University Press.

Travel and Tourism Analyst (1987) *Theme parks in the USA*. London: The Economist Publications Limited.

Wallace, I. (1990) *The global economic system*. London: Unwin Hyman.

Willigan, G. (1992) 'High performance marketing: Nike', *Harvard Business Review*, July-August.

II.

Leisure in Post Industrial Societies

Organisational Structures and Contexts in British National Governing Bodies of Sport

Eleni I. Theodoraki and Ian P. Henry

Loughborough University, UK

Introduction

In the last two decades the advanced economies of the industrial world have witnessed dramatic change. Global change has impacted not simply on local and national economies, but also on the social structure of such societies, their cultures and politics. This affects significant features of the strategic context for individuals, groups, communities, the organisations, or even the nation-states as agencies for change. The types of change to which we allude include the de-industrialisation of many areas of activity in advanced industrial economies; the rise of neo-liberal thinking in political circles in both 'Conservative' and 'Socialist' controlled states; the emergence of global cultural forces, most obviously in the form of new technology-based, transnational broadcasting; and the emergence of new class fragments and the realignment of traditional class, gender, and race structures in the new service economies of the West.

In reviewing the changing social context, one has to exercise caution. Some of these changes alluded to may be more significant than others (see for example neo-Marxist and feminist claims that the social structure is essentially reproducing old forms of exploitation in new guises). Nor should global forces simply be seen as imposing a new context on local actors, since local resistance to, or modification / reproduction of global forces, are important phenomena to understand. Yet clearly structural change has taken place at various levels, and the context of the activity of sporting organisations is therefore different from that obtained in the 1970s. The study on which this paper draws therefore seeks to evaluate how national governing bodies of sport (NGBs) in England have responded to changes in the economic, social, political and cultural environment.

In Britain, it is argued that the collapse of traditional primary sector and manufacturing industries has led to a decline in the size and significance of the working class and a growth in new class fractions, particularly in the service sector (Sarre, 1989). This fragmentation of the class structure is seen as being accompanied by the erosion of traditional collective cultural forms and the growth of new individualistic modes of cultural activity, including individualistic sports (Featherstone, 1987). Changes in the economic structure have not only implied changes in the social structure, and therefore in cultural behaviour, but also in organisational forms as traditional structures give way to flexible 'post-Fordist' forms, with decentralised power, implying greater flexibility of response by organisations to their increasingly volatile environments (Piore and Sabel, 1984). Finally, in political terms the role of the state has changed significantly over the last decade, particularly in Britain with its dominantly New Right governments for whom reduction of state involvement in a wide range of welfare areas, including sport, was a priority (Henry, 1993).

It is thus hypothesised that the NGBs in England, on which this study is based, have faced a number of important changes to their operating context. Firstly, there has been a decline in the significance of communal sports, and an increase in the significance of individual activities. This leads us to ask the question 'is there any evidence of organisational responses to changing demand for sports among either traditional, collectivist sports, or the newer, more individualist sports?' Secondly, there has been a move away from traditional large-scale bureaucratic structures in the commercial sector (which has predominantly led organisational and management fashions in the public, quasi-public and voluntary sectors). Thus there is a need to establish whether such a shift away from traditional organisational forms is evidenced in the NGB sector. Thirdly, there has been a stimulus to move way from relying on public sector support, and to seek a stronger commercial footing, either through sponsorship or through trading activities. This raises the question of how organisations are responding to the changing economic environment and whether for example more flexible, entrepreneurial approaches are evident in the sample. It is with this background that we seek to evaluate the nature of organisational structures and environments for NGBs in England.

The context of the study

The study reported here reflects the findings of the first of a three stage analysis of strategic management in the NGBs of sport in Britain. The analysis developed draws on the results of a questionnaire survey conducted to establish the significant features of NGBs and of their environments. The second stage draws on in-depth interviews with key informants, focusing on organisational processes and procedures and perceptions of the exercise of influence and power. The final stage will be based on participant observation and detailed case studies, and will focus on the reproduction of organisational cultures.

The strategy employed in a sense follows the chronologically developed themes of organisational theory, with its (1960s) emphasis on organisational survival and adaptation to new environments; the (1970s) concern with the political and ideological dimensions of the exercise of power in organisations; and the (1980s) concern with discourse analysis and the reproduction of organisational realities (Reed and Hughes, 1992: pp. 10–12). Such a strategy implies denying the claim that different perspectives deal in incommensurable phenomena. While the post-modern critique makes it clear that "truth'"claims are contingent on theoretical premises and their associated value systems, this is not to assert that objectivity cannot be sustained in arguments drawn from different paradigms, nor is it to assert that what counts as evidence under one paradigm is necessarily inadmissible under another. To reject the scientism of narrow positivist approaches is not to embrace the relativism of naive interpretations.

Thus the "meta-theoretical" assumptions underlying this study are drawn from structuration theory. The project seeks to establish explanations not simply of structural features of organisations and their contexts, but also to clarify how agency reproduces, or modifies existing structural features, and how these act as context / resources for further action. The approach adopted in the first phase of this study and reported in this paper should therefore be viewed in the wider context of the structurational strategy, even though the first stage itself deals in true positivist fashion with structural features of organisations and their environments.

Sports organisations and the organisational theory literature

The organisational theory literature in the field of sports organisations is relatively undeveloped. Except for a burgeoning group of studies in Canada there is an absence of systematic analysis of the sports field in the English language. This may in part reflect historical circumstances, the growth of interest in sport as a legitimate area of serious social analysis coinciding with the intellectual crisis of organisational theory represented in post-modernism. It may also simply reflect the academic interest of those involved in studying sport and sports organisations.

One approach to reviewing the literature relating to organisational analysis and sports organisations is to develop the tripartite, chronological framework suggested above, dividing work relatively crudely between the three traditions in organisational analysis as follows:

a) Work derived from the rationalist, positivist approach developed from Weber's analysis of bureaucracy, which seeks to capture organisational reality by identifying structural features of organisations and their environments and to evaluate the relationship between them, often by reference to statistical association. (We will use the term Weberian to refer to this tradition in this paper, though Weber's own work was in part aimed at clarifying the limitations of such a rationalist/positivist approach.) Seminal work in this tradition would include the contingency approaches of the Aston School (Pugh and Hickson 1976), and of Burns and Stalker (1961).

b) Analysis of power and organisational politics, which partly reflects a radical critique of the one dimensional nature of Weberian analysis; this represents a perspective (or set of perspectives) in which the organisation is conceived, not as a set of structural properties, but as an arena in which agencies compete for valued resources in shifting contexts. Organisational reality is determined by the outcomes of continuing struggles which characterise any organisation. Typical proponents are Clegg and Dunkerley (1980) and, in more applied form, Mintzberg (1983).

c) Analysis of organisations as constituted by symbolic processes, generating social realities by the construction of varying types of discourse. This tradition is influenced by modernist notions of organisational theory. Modernist organisation analysis implies a search for rational scientific theories of a distinctive object which allows us to facilitate the development of stability and control in organisations. The post-modern critique focuses on, not a single, distinctive theoretical object, the organisation, but on the fragmented cultural realities within in it, where theories of management or of organisation are used as legitimating tools for promoting one notion of reality over another. The result of this critique may be to displace the notion of a universal truth as the goal of organisational theory, but it need not mean displacing objectivity and reason. Theories of organisation, like all social theory may be culturally contingent, but that is not to say that they are arbitrary. Gergen (1992) provides an example of this approach to understanding organisation. In prescriptive management theory this approach is linked to the contemporary concern with the construction of organisational cultures, the hegemony of one set of cultural values, one organisational reality over others.

In the field of analysing sports organisation, the main focus has been on the first of these three types of approach. Little has been attempted in terms of analysing of power in sports organisations, except for some material inspired by feminist analysis, such as White and Brackenridge (1985), Slack and Kikulis (1989), and Hult (1989) and occasional case studies such as Ashton's (1992) account of the construction of a new governing body for squash in Britain out of its predecessor women's and men's organisations. Work of the third type outlined above, even in its more applied form of analysis of emerging organisational cultures, has not been seen in the work on sports organisations.

In the British context also there has been little work in the 'Weberian tradition' relating specifically to sports organisations or NGBs. This tradition has however, been very evident in the Canadian work, and research relating to bureaucratisation and related phenomena, has reflected the major research efforts. Four types of 'Weberian' work in this field may be identified:

i) that seeking to clarify the significance of conceptual frameworks relating to organisational structural and environmental variables (e.g. Frisby, 1982; Slack and Hinings, 1987);

ii) that seeking to operationalise theoretical constructs suggesting ways which in principle would allow the structural and environmental dimensions of NGBs to be measured (e.g. Frisby, 1985);

iii) that seeking to establish empirically (by using operational measures) how far the NGBs exhibit bureaucratisation, and related phenomena, such as standardisation, specialisation, and professionalisation (Slack and Hinings 1987; Slack 1985; Thibault, Slack and Hinings, 1991, Kikulis, Slack, Hinings and Zimmerman 1989; Chelladurai and Haggerty 1991); and finally

(iv) that seeking to clarify the relationship between structural features and efficiency of NGBs (Frisby, 1986; Chelladurai, Szyszlo and Haggerty, 1987).

Our own work in this paper relates most clearly to the third of these forms of traditional analysis. It adopts a methodology similar to that of Kikulis, Slack, Hinings and Zimmerman (1989), in that it seeks to derive a typology of British NGBs by reference to structural features of those organisations. It differs, however, in a number of respects. In particular the operational measures employed differ, reflecting in part the different context of the British and Canadian sports systems and their histories, and the availability of data. Some phenomena omitted by the Canadian study are operationalised (e.g. the location in the management structure of ethnic groups and women), while others in the Canadian study are omitted as either inappropriate or impossible to operationalise (e.g. the measurement of specialisation excludes

Table 1. The correlation coefficients and significance levels of all variables employed

	Var1	Var2	Var3	Var4	Var5	Var6	Var7	Var8	Var9	Var10	Var11	Var12	Var13	Var14
Var1	1													
Var2	0.1236	1												
Var3	0.2528	-0.217	1											
Var4	-0.198	-0.158	-.3248*	1										
Var5	0.1452	-.3415*	0.1008	-0.063	1									
Var6	0.1368	-0.115	0.1871	-0.102	-0.145	1								
Var7	0.0518	-0.185	0.0058	-0.091	0.1052	-0.069	1							
Var8	0.0168	0.0979	-0.066	0.1118	-0.056	0.1179	-.7484**	1						
Var9	.4237**	0.1017	0.2594	-0.071	-0.06	0.125	-.3098*	.5002**	1					
Var10	0.0327	0.1216	-0.157	-0.025	-0.105	-0.106	-0.194	0.0768	0.148	1				
Var11	0.1077	0.02	0.0727	0.1	-0.046	-0.118	0.0852	-0.035	-0.005	-.3147*	1			
Var12	0.103	0.0118	0.0463	0.133	-0.086	-0.14	-.3826**	0.2927	.3108*	0.1057	-0.171	1		
Var13	0.0607	-0.082	0.1596	-0.086	-0.138	-0.22	0.1819	-0.112	0.2286	0.0114	0.0039	-0.003	1	
Var14	-0.102	0.0604	-0.034	0.1663	-0.207	0.0617	-0.117	0.0594	-0.176	-.3480*	0.2672	-0.142	-0.092	1
Var15	-0.02	-0.046	0.1672	-0.128	0.1025	-0.131	0.0284	0.0935	-0.049	0.0571	.6332**	-0.233	0.0255	0.229

* Significant at the 0.05 level ** Significant at the 0.01 level

Var1	Size	Var6	% Women employees	Var11	No of events
Var2	Volunteers	Var7	% Ethnic minorities in management	Var12	Sports development
Var3	Age	Var8	% Ethnic minorities employers	Var13	Standardisation
Var4	Professionalisation	Var9	Specialisation	Var14	Formality of objectives
Var5	% Women in management	Var10	Environmental complexity	Var15	Centralisation

in our case specialisation of volunteers, but includes specialisation within the committee structure).

The sample selection and methodology

The nature of this study was influenced by Mintzberg's (1979) classic analysis of organisational structures, and sought to establish whether the analysis of National Governing Bodies would provide support for the existence of Mintzberg's five ideal types as well as for other structural configurations of organisations. The NGBs which were subjects in this study were selected in the following manner. All governing bodies for England recognised by the Sports Council were approached to obtain permission to view any of their files held centrally by the Sports Council. For those which replied positively, annual reports and accounts were reviewed, and each was subsequently sent a questionnaire, and where necessary contacted in person or by telephone, to elicit further information. A response rate of 48.5% was achieved and 45 National Governing Bodies of Sport filled in and returned the questionnaire. Although the sample incorporated a wide spectrum of different sports, some types of sport organisation were excluded. In particular, it should be noted that large and affluent NGBs with a high media profile, such as the Football Association and the Rugby League, were excluded from our analysis at that stage.

The statistical analysis of the data generated by the survey involved two principal stages. The first was a review of the strength and direction of the relationship between the variables employed in the study (a table of correlations is presented in **Table 1**). The second involved conducting cluster analysis to establish whether homogeneous group of cases could be identified. Both analyses were conducted using the Statistical Package for Social Science (SPSS-X). The method employed for the cluster analysis was Ward's method of hierarchical agglomerative clustering with squared Euclidean measures. The variables employed in the analysis were converted to Z-scores, since different scales had been used to generate of raw scores. The number of clusters employed was decided by inspection of a dendogram and a measure of squared error produced by the SPSS-X package, allowing the point to be identified at which including a further cluster would significantly increase squared error. The number of clusters identified was six.

Where composite measures were employed in operationalising concepts such as centralisation, standardisation, formalisation of objectives, and task complexity, Chronbac's alpha was employed as a measure of the internal consistency of such composite measures (with the discriminatory level set at 0.6). Thus measures which generated an alpha score lower than 0.6 were either desegregated or rejected.

Operationalising concepts

The structural analysis of organisations has been dominated by the contingency theory approach, particularly that of the Aston School. The framework adopted by this group employed as key structural variables those of specialisation, standardisation and centralisation, while the key contextual variables employed were environment, task and technology, organisational scale, resources, and organisational age. The application of this framework to an analysis of sports organisations has been articulated by Slack and Hinings (1987) and it allows us to identify separately those variables used that relate to such traditional contingency approaches, those we have excluded, and those we have added (in particular in relation to race and gender).

Contextual variables

(a) *Environment.* The complexity of the organisation's environment was operationalised by referring to the number of bodies (governmental, sporting, commercial etc.) with which the NGB interacted, and the intensity of that interaction.

(b) *Task and Technology.* In this study the tasks of NGBs were conceived as falling in the areas primarily of sports development and of promoting sporting excellence. Operational measures employed therefore fell under the headings of sports development schemes and target groups (alpha = 0.93), and the number of national and international competitions organised. These measures operationalise the notion of organisational task, but not of available technology. The technology associated with, for example motor sport (where the organisation may need to retain a detailed knowledge of automotive engineering), or with athletics (where the specifications for track surfaces and javelin characteristics require the organisation to have access to technical expertise), differs significantly from the requirements of volleyball, for example. However, such measures have not been operationalised in this study.

(c) *Organisational Scale.* This can be conceived as having three different components; the size of the core professional organisation (i.e. staff employed); the volunteer sector of the organisation (the number of volunteers in the organisation); and the size of the membership (whether expressed as individuals, clubs or other member bodies).

In this study we have treated the size of the professional staff (expressed as full time equivalents) as the key measure of size as a structural variable. The other two dimensions of size are problematic, and can be conceived as aspects of the environment with which the core organisation has to deal. In the case of number of volunteers this cannot be combined in a composite measure with core size (a low alpha score reflects the internal inconsistency of a combined measure). The size of the volunteer population is therefore used as a separate measure of size. In the case of membership size, this is incommensurable across organisations because of the different nature of memberships involved. (Some organisations had individuals as members, others clubs and still others were umbrella organisations with a membership effectively of smaller organisations).

(d) *Age.* The length of time for which the organisation has been formally constituted.

(e) *Organisational Resources.* The focus in this study has been on human resources, not simply in terms of professionalisation, but also as indicated by the presence and location of women and Britons from ethnic minorities.

Professionalisation was measured by reference to the formal qualifications of the staff employed. Professionalisation in a range of activities, administrative and technical, were assessed. A distinction had to be drawn between those organisations which required formal professional qualifications of staff, and those who employed qualified staff, the latter population being significantly greater. The measure of professionalisation employed here was that of the proportion of university degree holders in the core organisation in both technical and administrative roles.

For both race and gender the proportion of women, and the proportion of individuals of Asian and Afro-Caribbean extraction, were assessed as was the proportion of women and Britons from ethnic minorities in middle and senior management.

Structural variables

(a) *Specialisation.* This was assessed by the number of committees, and their terms of reference and responsibilities, such that the more complex and detailed the committee structure, the more specialised the nature of the NGB's activities. (Information on the vertical and horizontal specialisation of employed personnel was not available in a consistent and reliable form). The Chronbac's alpha score for this measure was 0.6.

(b) *Standardisation.* Two dimensions to standardisation were identified. The first was how far formal procedures and processes were established for work within the organisation. The nature of the NGBs reviewed was diverse and the range of activities undertaken similarly variable. The standardisation of common administrative tasks therefore was employed for comparison purposes. The second was the development of systems of formal objectives for particular areas of the organisation's work. This measure was employed to identifyhow far formalised goals were set in areas of the organisation's activities such as finance, membership, sports development, elite sport. (This nine item score gave an alpha score of 0.72).

(c) *Centralisation.* The assessment of centralisation involved developing a measure to assess the level within the organisation participating in strategic decision making. Generalised questions assessing which groups are involved in strategic decision-making are unlikely to generate valid and reliable measures (Slack and Hinings 1987), and Kikulis, Slack, Hinings and Zimmerman (1989) therefore focus on specific decisions relating to selection of athletes, coaches etc., and administrative decisions, and assessed them in terms of establishing who was involved and who consulted, and at what level the final decisions were made. In our own study we have focused solely on administrative decisions and sought to establish the levels of the organisation consulted when strategic decisions were made. Measures of centralisation are, however, notoriously unstable and exploration of the concept of centralisation is more amenable to qualitative analysis, as for example Child's work on strategic coalitions illustrates (Child, 1973).

Analysis of findings

It is, of course, a mistake to assume that identifying processes of bureaucratisation and professionalisation in a wide range of organisational contexts should imply some kind of unidirectional organisational development model. This would imply a form of organisational determinism. Indeed, we anticipated that the analysis of NGBs would provide evidence of a variety of structures. This conviction was founded on two factors. First, agents within organisations may react differently to similar organisational contexts, and second, organisational contexts and resources vary from one organisation to another such that similar responses may be inappropriate, or simply not feasible.

As indicated earlier, the statistical analysis of our data included 2 stages. The first was a review of the strength and direction of the relations between the variables cited. Table 1 illustrates the level of association between them. This displays some conformation to, and some deviation from, the classic relationships anticipated by contingency theorists such as Burns and Stalker, or Mintzberg. For example, it was anticipated would that the size of organisations be positively associated with standardisation of tasks and the formalisation of objectives, specialisation, age of organisation and professionalisation of staff; while complexity of the organisational environment, it might be assumed, would be associated negatively with centralisation and standardisation, but positively associated with specialisation. Older organisations would also be expected to exhibit greater professionalisation of staff, and greater standardisation of tasks. The reasoning underlying these anticipated relationships is as follows.

The larger organisations become, the more likely they are to require subdivision of duties and responsibilities to remain effective. Thus, because of problems of control, larger organisations would be expected to be more standardised in the way they operate, to have more formalised objectives, and greater specialisation. They are also more likely to seek to ensure that standards are maintained by appointing professionally qualified staff, as the resources of the organisation increase with size. Age and size might also be assumed to be related as new organisations will tend to be small, until they are able to establish themselves. This rationale is specified more fully in Mintzberg's (1979) derivation of a series of hypotheses relating to expected relationships.

Within the sample of NGBs, size was significantly positively related to specialisation (r=.42), though no other statistically significant correlations were evident in respect of size. The complexity of organisational environment was also negatively associated with the formalisation of objectives as anticipated (r=-.35), and specialisation was positively associated with one measure of complexity of task (that of sports development) (r=.31), though not with the other measure (organisation of national and international events) (r=-.31). These relationships at least might be said to be consistent with the hypotheses promoted by Mintzberg, though in general correlations were weak.

However, some relationships were less consonant with anticipated findings. For example, younger organisations tended to be more, rather than less, professionalised than their older counterparts (r=-.32), suggesting perhaps that newer NGBs were less likely to appoint unqualified staff to management positions. Organisations with a high level of involvement in the organisation of national and international events also tended to be more centralised (r=.63) and to operate in less complex organisational environments (r=-.31).

The proportion of women in management positions was significantly related only to the size of the volunteer population working in the organisation (r=-.34), suggesting that women are less likely to be employed in

Table 2. **The mean and standard deviations of structural and contextual variables in all clusters (expressed as z-scores for total population).**

CLUSTERS	Machine bureau-cracy		Profess-ional bureau-cracy		Decentral-ised simple structure		Typical simple structure		Bureau-cratised simple structure		Specialised simple structure	
VARIABLES	N=16	S.D.	N=7	S.D.	N=7	S.D.	N=8	S.D.	N=5	S.D.	N=2	S.D.
Size	.21	1.36	.63	.97	-.40	.51	-.53	.23	-.06	.60	-.20	.22
Volunteers	.39	1.53	.01	.70	-.27	.19	-.32	.24	-.24	.44	-.30	.23
Age	-.03	1.01	.18	.96	-.63	.52	.27	1.10	.20	1.50	.24	.19
Professionalisation	-.01	1.06	.28	.32	.38	.88	-.02	1.43	-.73	.46	-.32	.56
% Women in management	-.29	1.38	-.08	1.01	.19	.55	.13	.70	.64	.00	-.17	.46
% Women employees	-.10	1.02	.14	.31	.00	.71	.29	1.39	-.87	.80	1.32	.77
% Ethnic minorities in management	.17	.07	-.95	2.29	.17	.07	.17	.07	.19	.00	.19	.00
% Ethnic minorities employees	-.21	.15	1.28	2.03	-.24	.11	-.24	.10	-.28	.00	-.28	.00
Specialisation	-.07	.47	1.85	.33	-.64	.50	-.71	.68	-.62	.28	.73	.93
Environmental complexity	-.69	.93	.60	1.52	-.34	.81	-.18	.75	.10	.98	.01	.86
No of events	.07	.77	.00	.80	-.81	1.39	.75	.38	.40	.50	-1.71	1.00
Sports development	-.04	.76	.72	1.61	.14	1.23	-.46	.31	-.40	.60	.13	1.12
Standardisation	.67	.78	-.02	.64	-.96	.00	-1.12	.47	.89	.72	.36	.00
Formality of objectives	.16	1.23	-.09	.45	-.37	.43	.53	1.21	-.24	.65	-1.23	.00
Centralisation	-.19	.34	.20	.62	-1.42	.00	1.11	.00	1.11	.00	-1.42	.00

managerial positions when larger volunteer populations are incorporated participation in voluntary organisations being generally disproportionately male (Central Statistical Office 1991). Organisations employing managers of Afro-Caribbean or Asian extraction tended to employ fewer people from these ethnic groups (r=-.75), to exhibit less specialisation (r=-.31), and to be less involved in sports development (r=-.38). By contrast, employees from these ethnic groups were more likely to be found in organisations with a greater degree of specialisation (r=.50).

The presentation of the table of correlation coefficients, however, may mask underlying relationships between particular sub-groups of organisations. For this reason cluster analysis was undertaken, identifying organisational groups with homogeneous characteristics. A breakdown of the key characteristics of the clusters with the mean and the standard deviation is provided in **Table 2**.

Figure 1 (following page) illustrates the clusters' scores in the variables used. All variables were standardised for the population of organisations as a whole, such that the mean for each variable is zero, and the standard deviation 1. Thus the means and standard deviations for each of the clusters may be easily compared with those of the population as a whole.

Cluster 1 contained the following 16 NGBs: The National Cricket Association, Tennis and Racquets Association, Petanque Association, RAC Motor Sports Association, British Sub Aqua Club, National Federation of Anglers, Eton Fives Association, Cyclists' Touring Club, National Caving Association, English Women's Bowling Association, the Croquet Association, British Association of Paragliding Clubs, Amateur Fencing Association, Martial Arts Commission, British Cycling Federation and the English Bobsleigh Association. This cluster exhibits the structural configuration which conforms most closely to Mintzberg's *machine bureaucracy*. The complexity of the organisational environment in this cluster was fairly low, and there was a relatively high degree of standardisation. Organisations tended to be large, with some exceptions (Petanque, Eton Fives, Bobsleigh, and Martial Arts), and specialisation and centralisation were limited. The proportion of women in management positions in these organisations was also relatively low compared to figures for other clusters and the size of the volunteer force was significant (though for both variables there was a greater variability than for the population as a whole, with standard deviations of 1.38 and 1.53 respectively). Thus this cluster seems to exhibit some of the classic features of traditionalist NGBs, with standardised work routines, relatively simple organisational environments, predominantly large volunteer work forces, and with traditional gender roles in management.

Figure 1 Comparisons of organisational clusters

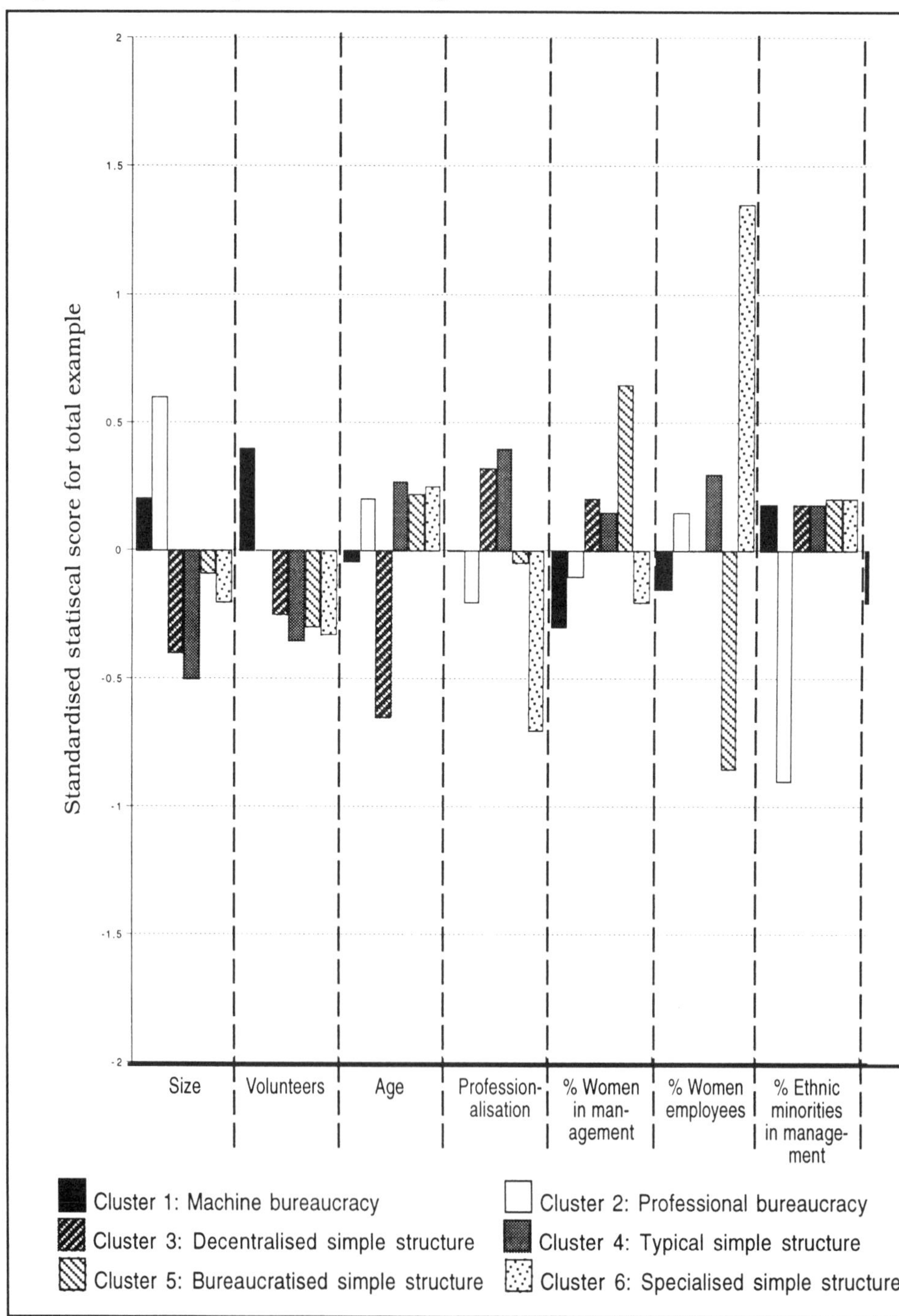

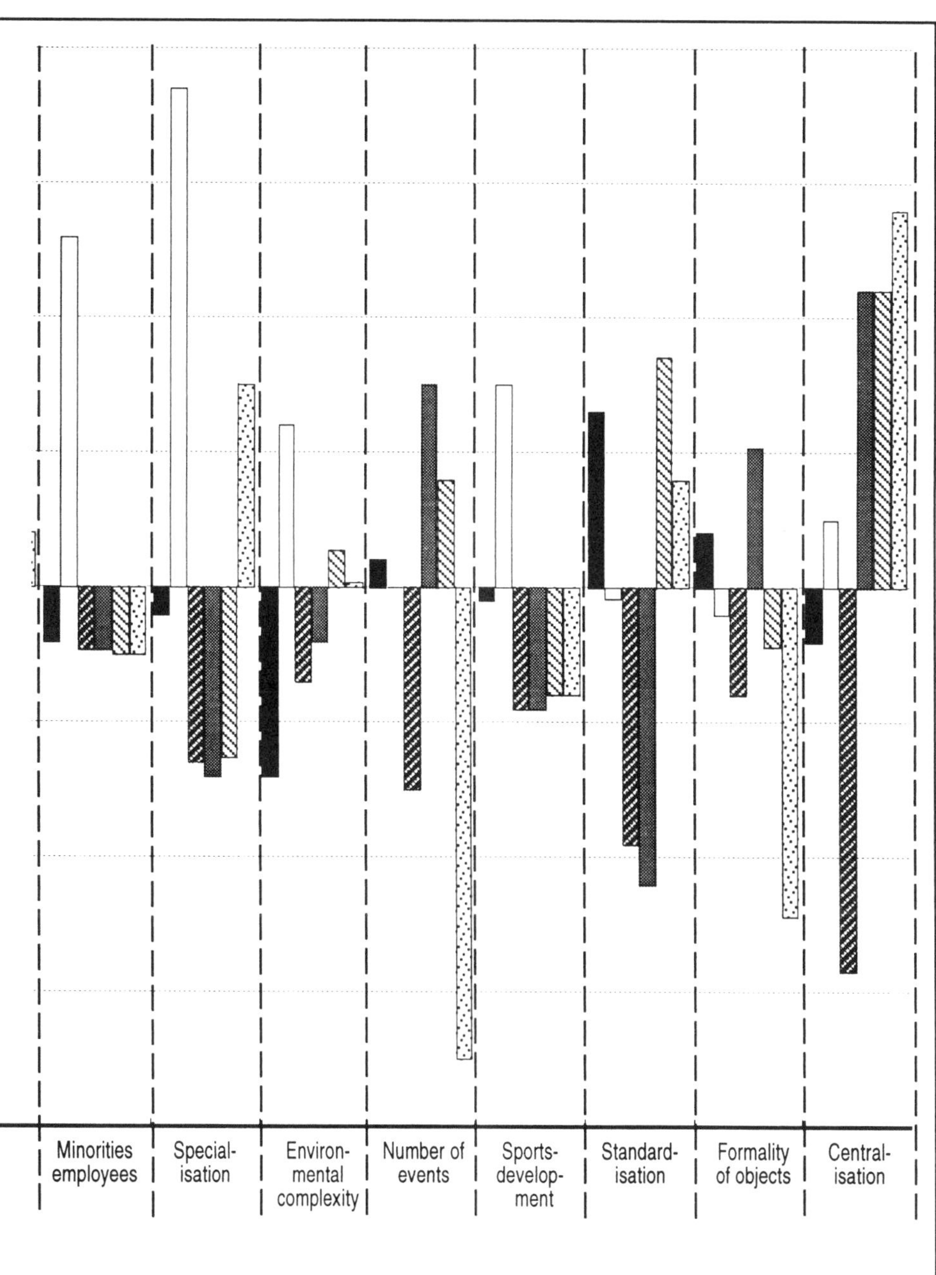
Minorities employees
Special-isation
Environ-mental complexity
Number of events
Sports-develop-ment
Standard-isation
Formality of objects
Central-isation

Cluster 2 contained seven NGBs: The Hockey Association, Amateur Rowing Association, British Water Ski Federation, British Korfball Association, British Mountaineering Council, Squash Rackets Association, British Ski Federation. This was the cluster which most closely resembled Mintzberg's *professional bureaucracy*. The cluster is dominated by established Olympic sports and outdoor pursuits (with korfball as a notable exception). This cluster contains predominantly larger organisations with higher levels of professionalisation together with higher levels of specialisation, and lower levels of standardisation and centralisation, which are consistent with greater professional autonomy. Although these organisations focused more on sports development than the population of NGBs as a whole, and operated in relatively complex environments, there was a high degree of variability in respect of these variables.

Cluster 3 contained 7 NGBs: The English Ski Council, English Basketball Association, the Aircraft Owners' and Pilots' Association, BMX Association, the British Federation of Sand and Land Yacht Clubs, National Rounders Association. These tended to be small, young, professionalised organisations operating with a low level of voluntary involvement, and a comparatively low emphasis on organisation of major events. Although they operated in simple environments they were relatively unbureaucratised, exhibiting little standardisation, specialisation and with formalised objectives. However, unlike Mintzberg's ideal type simple structure, centralisation was low. Thus, this cluster reflected what was in effect a *professionalised and decentralised simple structure*.

Cluster 4 contained eight organisations: The English Ladies' Golf Association, British Surfing Association, British Crown Green Bowling Association, English Folk Dance and Song Society, the Cricket Council, Bicycle Polo Association, and the Road Time Trials Association. These organisations were very small in terms of professional staff, though two, Ladies Golf, and Crown Green Bowls had very large memberships. The organisations were similar to those of cluster 3, being small, with few volunteers, low specialisation and low standardisation. However, by contrast they tended to be younger, and events oriented (rather than sports development oriented) in their activities, and to be less professionalised. More significantly they exhibited a higher degree of centralisation, conforming to the configuration which Mintzberg terms the simple structure but which we will refer to as the *'typical' simple structure* in order to differentiate it from the other simple structure clusters.

Cluster 5 contained five organisations: The English Indoor Bowling Association, British Gliding Association, British Microlight Aircraft Association, the Amateur Boxing Association, and the Hurlingham Polo Association.

These organisations exhibited low levels of professionalisation or specialisation, with high levels of centralisation of decision-making and standardisation of role. The focus of these organisations in terms of task was on organising events rather than on sports development. In addition, though women were evident in management positions, these organisations employed fewer women and workers from ethnic minorities, and operated with a low level of volunteers. Unlike Mintzberg's ideal type simple structure, there is a high degree of standardisation in such organisations, and they are perhaps, therefore, best described as *bureaucratised simple structures.*

Cluster 6 contained two organisations: The League of Health and Beauty, and the English Table Tennis Association. These organisations, though relatively small in terms of professional staff, and using few volunteers, exhibited some bureaucratic features such as standardisation, specialisation, and centralisation. They employed a higher proportion of women than any other cluster, but a smaller proportion of these occupied managerial positions. Perhaps the defining feature of this cluster, which is clearly also an example of simple structure, is the level of specialisation, which sets it apart from the bureaucratised simple structure. Thus we have termed this cluster the *specialised simple structure.*

Discussion

Perhaps the most striking feature to emerge from the clustering procedure is the preponderance of variations on the simple structure. This however is not surprising, in the sense that sports administration in a predominantly amateur set of sports, has traditionally implied amateur management. Such management in relatively small organisations may implicitly rely on the flexibility which simple structures permit.

Related literature suggests that among the conditions associated with variants of the simple structure is organisational age, or the stage of development. New organisations tend to reflect the simple structure because they have not had the time to elaborate an administrative structure. Most organisations, Mintzberg claims, pass through the simple structure in their formative years. Many small organisations, however, remain with the simple structure beyond this period. For them, informal communication is convenient and effective. Moreover, their small size may mean less repetition of work in the operating core, which means less standardisation. In the simple structure, decisions concerning strategy and operations are together centralised in the office of the chief executive. Centralisation has the important advantage of ensuring that strategic response reflects full knowledge of the operating core. It also favours flexibility and adaptability in strategic response.

Nevertheless, the simple structure is also the riskiest of structures, hingeing on the health and whims of one individual (Mintzberg, 1979). As the only, (part time) member of staff of the British Crown Green Bowling Association put it at interview: "if I take two weeks off today I know that there will be two weeks work waiting for me on my desk at home when I come back." However, although the simple structure may be associated with a lack of standardisation, or of professionalisation, and higher levels of centralisation, the types of simple structure identified in the study (with exception of the cluster which we term the 'typical' simple structure) depart from this ideal typical set of characteristics in one form or another. They reflect features such as standardisation, reduced centralisation, as of specialisation. Thus these variants on the simple structure reflect some of the benefits of their compact size, while exhibiting characteristics which, superficially at least, appear dysfunctional.

The professionalised and decentralised simple structure of cluster 3 exhibits a structure which enables professionals to use their expertise with autonomy in an unbureaucratic setting. Cluster 4 on the other hand differs from cluster 3 in that in a typical simple structure the authority is centralised around the chief executive. In addition its small size allows a low standardisation. Cluster 5 exhibits a bureaucratic structure, scores highly in standardisation and is directed towards events production. This is consistent with the lack of professionals in this cluster. Cluster 6 differs from the typical simple structure in that a specialised structure is found. The Health and Beauty Exercise Association is one of the two NGBs in this small cluster and in it the sport development side of the NGB is run by specialist committees of volunteers. The structure of this organisation is reflected in the existence of many specialist committees which have responsibility for specific aspects of the sport.

Although these clusters represented forms of simple structures it was not possible to identify any of the clusters as necessarily moving towards more developed organisational forms. Some had plans to formalise their operations, usually in response to interaction with the Sports Council as a major grant aiding body, and in that sense might be described as "nascent professional bureaucracies", while others gave little indication of impending change. Indeed the average ages of the "typical" bureaucratised and specialised simple structures were greater than those of the other clusters.

The six organisational clusters found in our data operate in a variety of environments. Environmental complexity was operationalised in this study by referring to the number of organisations with which interaction took place and the regularity of such interaction. The organisational cluster operating in the most complex environment was that of the professional bureaucracy.

Machine bureaucracies operated with the lowest level of environmental complexity, while the different types of simple structure fluctuated about the mean. Mintzberg (1979) argued that the more complex the environment in which an organisation operates, the more likely it is that the structure will be an organic one. It is argued that in a stable environment, an organisation is better able to predict future conditions and so, all other things being equal, can more readily insulate its operating core and standardise its activities, establish rules, formalise work, plan actions or perhaps standardise its skills instead. But this relationship also extends beyond the operating core. In a highly stable environment, the whole organisation may take on the form of a protected, or undisturbed system, which can standardise its procedures from top to bottom.

One of the claims rehearsed earlier in this paper is that sporting organisations in advanced industrial societies like Britain, are operating in an increasingly volatile social, economic and political environment. However, it is clear that complexity of environment does vary considerably between organisations and the dynamic nature of the environment in which some operate is by no means universal. If we look into the data from interviews very different scenarios were suggested for NGBs. In relation to the physical environments in which the surveyed NGBs operate, major differences in facilities, resources and opportunities were found. The National Federation of Anglers, for example, had to allocate considerable amounts of money to research in water pollution and the RAC Motor Sports Association Ltd and the British Gliding Association have had to lobby politicians in an attempt to create favourable opinions regarding recreational use of land for motor sport and aviation air space respectively. On the other hand, the English Ladies' Golf Association has recently been benefited from the building of an enormous number of golf courses in England. Land owners are having golf courses built on their land at favourable terms by specialist building companies, often funded in part by subsidy for agricultural diversification or allied to housing or hotel schemes, thus increasing the number of golf courses available.

There are pressures placed on organisations to conform to specific organisational types by the nature of the Sports Council grant-in-aid process. For example, although simple structures will tend to exhibit less concern with formalised goals, objectives and processes, the Sports Council's Grant Assessment Panel evaluates the needs of NGBs on the basis of just such formalised planning, as do those studied in Canada. The preparation of such plans requires therefore some formalisation on the part of the organisation, and to a certain extent requires professionally qualified staff (e.g. financial managers may be required to develop cash flow projections and evaluate market development).

Thus the requirement that the Sports Council be highly formalistic in its grant aid decision making process (to ensure accountability for public money) may be in conflict with the flexibility of response implied in simple structures and 'required' by volatile environments. Mintzberg argues that greater external control of an organisation leads to a more centralised and formalised structure. His data indicated that the two most effective means to control an organisation from the outside are (1) to hold its most powerful decision maker- namely its chief executive officer- responsible for its actions, and (2) to impose clearly defined standards on it. The first centralises the structure; the second formalises it. Moreover, external control forces the organisation to be especially careful about its actions. Because it must justify its behaviours to outsiders, it tends to formalise them. The lack of autonomy means more power concentrated at the strategic apex, tighter personnel procedures, more regulated reporting, more planning and less adapting. In other words, centralisation of power at the societal level leads to centralisation of power at the organisational level, and to bureaucratisation in the use of that power. This process is, however, relatively new to the field and the impact of the formalisation of grant assessment procedures on NGB structures and processes may become more apparent in the near future.

Interestingly, women managers emerge most clearly in simple structures. It is in these types of organisation that traditional barriers evident in highly bureaucratised or professionalised career routes, are likely to be less evident. Those organisational clusters with a lower proportion of women in managerial roles, tended to have a higher proportion of women working at lower levels in the organisation. The position of managers from ethnic minorities is far less clear. Firstly the absolute number of such managers is considerably smaller than those for women, and as a consequence small variations generate larger swings in normalised data; it is worth noting however, that managers from ethnic minorities are least evident in highly professionalised clusters.

The classification of clusters described here does not incorporate examples of either 'ad hocracy' or of 'divisionalised structures'. *Ad hoc* structures are most closely associated with organisations that work on a project by project basis. Typically in such organisations non-hierarchical groups will address particular, mostly one-off problems, and propose solutions. Given that most NGBs face predominantly regular tasks — fund raising, organising events, courses, sports development systems and so on — the project based approach of ad hocracies is less likely to be evident than in, for example, the work of sports management consultancies. Divisionalised structures are also not apparent in the sample of NGBs. Perhaps the single exception to this lack of divisionalised structures is the RAC, where administration of motor sport is simply one of the organisation's many functions rather than its primary task. However, the data obtained from this organisation related simply to the sports wing of the RAC, whose other interests include motor services and insurance. Hence only part of the RAC (one of its divisions) can be construed as a NGB.

Conclusion

In the introduction to this paper we raised three interrelated questions which the research programme should address. These were to consider whether any distinction could be made between the organisational structures and processes adopted by NGBs for what might be described as traditional, collectivist sports, and for new individualistic sports; whether there was any evidence of a move away from traditional bureaucratic organisational forms; and whether there was any evidence of the emergence of new, more flexible, entrepreneurial organisational forms as the economic base of NGBs experienced instability with threatened, and in many instances actual, reductions of public funding. The first stage of the research programme reported here, and which considers organisational structures, rather than organisational processes, provides the basis for some initial observations on these questions.

A clear point to emerge from examining the clusters identified, is that NGBs for both 'traditional' sport forms and new, individualistic sport forms, extend across virtually all clusters. There is no clear differentiation in the data between organisational, structural configurations for 'traditional', and 'new' or 'individualised' sports. These terms are only crudely defined, but it is evident that whether NGBs are for sports which are low cost, new sports (e.g. Petanque Association), 'high tech' high cost sports (e.g. Aircraft Owners and Pilots Association), or for 'exotic', high cost pursuits (e.g. English Bobsleigh Association, Hurlingham Polo Association), no distinctive organisational configurations are evident.

The second issue to highlight in relation to these questions is that new organisations are developing different characteristics (unhampered by the weight of tradition). The data reported here reflect a snap shot of aspects of organisational life at a particular time, and cannot therefore hope to capture organisational processes. The following stages of analysis in this research project will involve data collection exploring the nature of change over time. However, what is already apparent in the responses of NGBs is that pressures of low or declining membership, and therefore of low or declining economic base, together with Sports Council reporting requirements, are prompting a reaction from NGBs. It is perhaps, therefore, not the 'new' sports which are likely to be subject to pressures to restructure, so much as the old sports with a declining base. Thus, for example, the Amateur Boxing Association at the time of writing was considering forming itself into a limited company, while officials of the NGB for Crown Green Bowling and for the

English Folk Dance and Song Society argued strongly for the need to streamline the committee structure to make their organisations more flexible and responsive to the environment. How such organisations respond to environmental change, and/or reshape their own environment, can only be adequately explained if the nature of historical, contemporary contextual, and contemporary internal figurations for each organisation are subject to detailed investigation. This underlines the need for complementary approaches to analysis.

References

Ashton, J. (1992) *Women's Representation in Governing Bodies of Sport: A case study in squash.* (Loughborough University of Technology Unpublished Thesis).

Burns, T. and Stalker, G. (1961) *The management of innovation.* London: Tavistock.

Central Statistical Office (1991) *Social trends.* London: HMSO.

Chelladurai, P., Szyszlo, M. and Haggerty, P. (1987) 'Systems-based dimensions of effectiveness: The case of National Sport Organisations', *Canadian Journal of Sport Science*, Vol. 12.

Chelladurai, P. and Haggerty, T. (1991) 'Measures of organisational effectiveness of Canadian National Sport Organisations', *Canadian Journal of Sport Science.* Vol. 16 , No. 2.

Child, J. (1973) 'Organisational structure, environment and performance: the role of strategic choice', *Sociology* , Vol. 6.

Clegg, S. and Dunkerley, D. (1980) *Organization, class and control.* London: Routledge and Kegan Paul.

Featherstone, M. (1987) 'Leisure, symbolic power and the life course', in J. Horne, D. Jary and A. Tomlinson (eds) *Leisure and social relations.* London: Routledge and Kegan Paul.

Frisby, W. (1982) 'Weber's theory of bureaucracy and the study of voluntary sport organisations', paper presented to North American Society For the Sociology of Sport Conference.

——— (1985) 'A conceptual framework for measuring the organisational structure and context of voluntary Leisure Service Organisations', *Society and Leisure*, Vol. 8.

——— (1986) 'Measuring the organisational effectiveness of National Sport Governing Bodies', *Canadian Journal of Applied Sport Sciences* Vol. 11.

Gergen, K. (1992) 'Organisation theory in the post modern era', in Reed and Hughes (eds) *Rethinking organisation: New directions in organisation theory and analysis*. London: Sage.

Henry, I. (1993) *The politics of leisure policy*. Basingstoke: Macmillan.

Hult, J. (1989) 'Women's struggle for governance in U.S. Amateur Athletics', *International Review for the Sociology of Sport*, Vol. 24.

Kikulis, L. Slack, T. Hinings, B. and Zimmermann, A. (1989) 'A structural taxonomy of Amateur Sport Organisations', *Journal of Sport Management*, Vol. 3: pp. 129-150.

Mintzberg, H. (1979) *The structuring of organisations*. Englewood Cliffs, NJ: Prentice-Hall.

——— (1983) *Power in and around organizations*, Englewood Cliffs, NJ: Prentice-Hall.

Piore, M. and Sabel, C. (1984) *The second industrial divide*. New York: Basic Books .

Pugh, D., and Hickson, J. (1976) *Organizational structure in its context* (the Aston Programme 1). Saxon House.

Reed, M. and Hughes, M. (1992) *Rethinking organisation: New directions in organisation theory and analysis*. London: Sage.

Sarre, P. (1989) 'Recomposition of the class structure', in C. Hamnett, L. McDowell, and P. Sarre (eds) *The changing social structure*. London: Sage.

Slack, T. (1985) 'The Bureaucratisation of a Voluntary Sport Organisation', *International Review for the Sociology of Sport*, Vol. 23.

Slack, T. and Hinings, B. (1987) 'Planning and organisational change: A conceptual framework for the analysis of Amateur Sport Organisations', *Canadian Journal of Sport Science*, Vol. 12: p. 4.

Slack, T. and Kikulis, L. (1989) 'The sociological study of sport organisations: Some observations on the situation in Canada', *International Review for the Sociology of Sport*, Vol. 24, No. 3.

Sports Council (1990) *Programme funding planning guidelines*. London: Sports Council.

Thibault, L., Slack, T. and Hinings, B. (1991) 'Professionalism, structures and systems: The impact of professional staff on Voluntary Sport Organisations', *International Review for the Sociology of Sport*, Vol. 26, pp. 83-99 .

White, A., and Brackenridge, C. (1985) 'Who rules sport? Gender divisions in the power structure of British Sports Organisations from 1960', *International Review for the Sociology of Sport*, Vol. 20, No. 1/2.

Information and the Leisure Professional: The Example of Sport

Peter Taylor

Sheffield University, UK

Introduction: information as a resource

When economists explain the production process, they usually refer to three major resources or factors of production — land, labour and physical capital — and sometimes add a fourth, enterprise. This paper examines the demand for a fifth important resource, information, using as its example people with a professional working interest in sport.

The paper will attempt to judge how far sports information as a resource is assessed and acquired in a manner consistent with efficient decision-making by the professionals who demand it. It examines the rationality of the demand for sports information and from the evidence draws implications for the providers of sports information. Finally it speculates on the transferability of the problems, issues, conclusions and implications concerning sports information to other markets of interest to leisure professions.

A rational demand for a factor of production such as information displays conventional characteristics. Information costs money to acquire; these costs will probably include considerable search costs. Like any input, information is subject to diminishing marginal returns, whereby each additional piece of information is of less value to the user than its predecessor. Information is worth purchasing as long as the marginal returns exceed the marginal costs; any distortion in the market prices of information will move demand and supply away from the market solution. As a durable input, information is subject to the characteristics of an investment good. Its costs include depreciation which requires replacement investment. The acquisition of information can be appraised using standard investment appraisal techniques, and people demanding information can be expected to assess future returns against present costs before making the decision to acquire information.

The research

To address the objectives of the paper, reference will be made to the results of a research project conducted for the UK Sports Information Consortium (hereafter referred to as 'the Consortium') whose members comprised the Sports Council, regional offices of the Sports Council, the Sports Council for Northern Ireland, the Scottish Sports Council, the Sports Council for Wales, the National Coaching Foundation, the National Sports Medicine In-

Table 1: Functional Groups of Sports Information Users

Group:

1. Local authority leisure officers.
2. Local authority sports facility managers.
3. Managers/owners, commercial sports clubs.
4. Governing bodies' administrators.
5. Sports development officers.
6. Sports academics (not sports science or PE).
7. Local authority planners.
8. Sports media professionals.
9. Public representatives with interests in sport.
10. Consultants (not medical).
11. Relevant agencies.
12. Sponsors and sponsorship agencies.
13. Student unions' sports officers.
14. Coaches.
15. Fitness professionals.
16. PE professionals.
17. Performers (elite).
18. Sports medics.
19. Sports paramedics, ie physiotherapists.
20. Sports scientists.
21. Sports officials, eg referees.
22. Groundspersons.
23. Commercial sports products manufacturers and retailers.
24. Building specialists with an interest in sports facilities, e.g. architects, surveyors.
25. Libraries.
26. Sports students.

stitute and the Sports Documentation Centre. The research was conducted in 1991/2 and completed in January 1993 (Taylor and Nichols, 1993). Its main methods were:

- a questionnaire survey, completed by 2,240 respondents with professional interests in sports information (see **Table 1** for a list of the professional interests represented);
- in-depth interviews with 21 people working for organisations in the Consortium (from other functions as well as information officers); and
- in-depth interviews with 57 people from outwith the Consortium who had active professional interests in sports information, principally as users.

The nature of demand for sports information

The so-called 'users' of sports information with a professional working interest in sport are, in fact, producers of services relevant to the sports and recreation industry. Among these users three *roles* emerge as significant according to the qualitative research for the project. These roles are customers, producers and brokers. A major complication for sports information providers is that any one person or interest group may play more than one of these roles in their use of sports information. An academic, for example, may be a simple customer or end user of some information, may use other information to help produce an academic output which is another form of information with added value, and may also use information simply to pass on to students.

Some users are straightforward in demanding information as customers. Customers are often either generalist or interest specific. The generalists (e.g. public sector facility managers) have a wide variety of information needs but often find access to specific sports information sources difficult or inappropriate. Their general and often sporadic demands can involve high search costs and uncertain returns, which limit their demand for information. Those with interest-specific needs (e.g. medics, PE professionals) require very specific information sources and are more easily accommodated by the appropriate specific information services, thus incurring lower search costs and more predictable returns.

Users who are also producers either need information as an input to their own production of information, e.g. academic researchers, or libraries, or they simultaneously use one type of information and supply another, e.g. local authority and governing body administrators. Each role involves a reciprocal relationship with the sports information providers that needs precise communication about the two-way needs. For example, sports academics need to stimulate information providers to make the right research data available, whilst information providers need to encourage academics to produce their information in a form which is accessible for a wider audience than simply other academics.

If the users who are producers reciprocate in the exchange of information with providers such as Consortium organisations, then informal exchange (e.g. bartering) may replace formal market transactions. Sports Councils, for example, regularly sponsor research involving surveys of local authority leisure services expecting and getting a good response rate. In return local authorities receive free or heavily subsidised information on demand. In such cases an important question to address is whether informal information exchange is as efficient or effective as formal market transactions. Informal exchange relies on trust and a collective appreciation of the value of information, but it can be hit and miss in producing exactly the required information to meet demand — the lack of a specific payment for a service relaxes the obligation to fully meet the demand.

The third role, that of brokers, means that some users require sports information primarily to pass on to others. For information providers such as the Consortium organisations these users are arguably the most important because they assist in the flow of information to end users, the customers. They are, in fact, agents of the producers in the distribution of information. However, brokers are typically selective about the information providers they use, the information they pass on and the customers to whom they distribute the information — they do not conform to the multi-access/multi-distribution, 'all things to all people' image that, for comparison, libraries often have.

Flows of information to and between brokers is a crucial determinant of the effectiveness of sports information services. Some of the most important brokers lie outside the Consortium, e.g. governing bodies of sport, professional institutes. Effective communication of information availability to such brokers is important, in order to reach an array of customers who are more used to accessing information via brokers than direct from mainstream information services.

Search behaviour

The survey indicates that search behaviour is characterised by multiple sourcing, informed rather than random patterns of search, and satisficing. On average respondents had searched for information outside their own organisations from more than four sources in the previous year; typically two Consortium organisations and two other organisations.

This multiple sourcing is not normally conducted in ignorance of what source has which information, but rather in knowledge that different organisations have different information and/or services. A multiplicity of information-providing organisations was not universally condemned as unnecessary by respondents. Thirty-two percent of them preferred such multiple sources, because of the greater choice afforded by the competition between the providing organisations and the specificity of particular organisations for particular information needs (and therefore particular client types).

Sixteen percent of respondents did not like the multiplicity of providing organisations, because to them it represented a confusing, uncoordinated approach to information provision with, ironically, many of the providers subsidised from the public purse. This latter view was reinforced by several interviewees, who criticised the lack of coordination between organisations providing very similar information.

Satisficing search behaviour is characterised by search which ceases when a satisfactory outcome is achieved, rather than a longer search for an optimal outcome. According to the research, this search behaviour is conditioned by resource constraints, not simply time and money but also limitations on the number of personal contacts that are available to help the search process.

Precedent is a powerful determinant of search processes. Over half of those respondents who had used a Consortium organisation for sports information in the previous year acknowledged the response 'I have got useful information from them before' as a reason for using the organisation. This finding suggests that search uses reliable, proven sources rather than searching on a broad, uncertain front. Other reasons for using Consortium organisations, cited by about a quarter of the respondents who had used the Consortium organisations in the previous year, were publicity concerning the availability of information, and the low cost of information from these sources.

Any complacency that the finding above might engender in Consortium organisations is quickly dispelled by a reciprocal finding: the most common reason given for not using the information services of Consortium organisations is ignorance of what they provide. So a simplistic but meaningful split in the user market is between realised demand which is based on precedent and therefore knowledge of what information the Consortium organisations provide, and demand which remains unrealised because of ignorance about what they provide.

User constraints

The most important constraint to the use of sports information which emerges from the research is consumer ignorance. The extent of this constraint is demonstrated by the responses to questions which asked current users of Consortium organisations' information services why they did not use these services more and asked non-users why they did not use these information services at all. The most common reason by far in both sets of responses was 'I do not know what they provide'. This constraint also emerged strongly from the qualitative interviews.

Table 2 provides evidence of the ignorance constraint with respect to primary and secondary periodicals produced by Consortium organisations. To be fair, the degree of ignorance expressed by the whole survey sample in this Table is a lot higher than among existing users of the organisations. However, the general impression is that such key publications have not achieved a desirable market penetration. In the qualitative research, even many of those users who could confidently claim to be 'information literate' had an uneasy feeling that they were not fully aware of the sports information on offer, or where to enquire for what.

Table 2: The Awareness Problem: examples of periodicals

% of geographically relevant respondents having not heard of	
a) Secondary Periodicals	
SCAN (Sports Council)	62
Quarterly Bulletin (Wales)	36
Fitness Update (NCF)	62
Sports Documentation Bulletin (U. Birmingham)	68
Sports Medicine Bulletin (NSMC)	65
Leisure Recreation & Tourism Abstracts (CAB)	74
b) Primary Periodicals	
Sport & Leisure (Sports Council)	29
Supercoach (NCF)	47
Sports News Wales	40
Arena (Scotland)	33

A second major constraint for the user is lack of appropriate personal contacts in information-providing organisations, cited by 25% of existing users of Consortium organisations and 17% of non-users. This may be interpreted as a lack of accessibility for the organisations, or it may be an indication that users and potential users face a psychological barrier which prevents them from approaching a stranger for information even if that stranger is an information professional.

A third constraint to the use of sports information from external sources is a lack of time. In the survey, 22% of users of Consortium organisations cited lack of time as a reason why they did not use these organisations more for information. It is also a factor which emerged strongly from the interviews.

Time is becoming a more expensive resource, and time is needed not just for information search, but also for the acquisition, understanding and use of information. Higher time costs increase the likelihood of satisficing search behaviour and sub-optimal demand. It also interacts with both the other constraints identified above, ignorance and lack of contacts; uncertainty over the returns from information search, combined with high search costs can very easily reduce information demands to zero, or more accurately to the status of latent demand. Improved awareness reduces wasted search time, whilst a reliable personal contact can be the most time-effective broker of information.

Implications for sports information service development

If the biggest constraint to the use of Consortium organisations' information services at present is ignorance of what is provided, then a rational response from suppliers will involve enhanced *promotion* of available services. Whether this is done collectively through the Consortium or by individual organisations, marketing development requires a realistic budget as an investment in the growth potential of sports information services. The return from this investment is easily measured, not only in conventional financial terms if direct charging is extended, but also in terms of an increasing volume of service provision.

Promoting services can also help to combat the time constraint for users; reducing time wasted on search. If users could subscribe to different packages of information then some search will be replaced by automatic receipt of information. Furthermore, if search has a higher probability of success then more demand for information is likely.

An apparently indiscriminate 'public service' attitude to sports information provision is not only potentially wasteful of resources but is in fact discriminatory. To treat every type of customer the same is to fall into the trap of discriminating implicitly in favour of the persistent and/or numerous customers (in the UK the best example is students). Such users may not be the priority users for an information-providing organisation. A more logical, acceptable and cost effective form of discrimination is to explicitly *target* certain types of customer. This targeting might be conducted on one or more

of a number of criteria identified in the research, including:
i) priority user groups for the providing organisations,
ii) those with comparatively high awareness and use of information services,
iii) brokers of information,
iv) groups of users known to be interested in specific types of information.
The first of these criteria recognises the political reality that information providers are unlikely to have no priorities among different user groups. In fact Sports Councils typically have users who are of priority 'partner' status, including local authorities and governing bodies; the National Coaching Foundation obviously prioritises coaches; the National Sports Medicine Institute's priority users are medics and paramedics; whilst the Sports Documentation Centre's reputation has been built to a considerable degree on its services to sports science users.

The second criterion targets those users who are already 'information literate' in the sense of being relatively aware of the sports information services on offer and already having used them. In the UK study it appears to be cost effective to concentrate resources on improving market penetration in these responsive markets, rather than trying to break into hitherto unresponsive markets. There appears to be considerable potential for increasing the use of information services by such literate users, since even they have moderate or low levels of awareness and use of information.

Selection of brokers is an obvious consequence of the key agency role of such users in helping distribute information. The project identifies a variety of such brokers, including public libraries, coaches, local authority senior officers, governing body administrators, professional institutes and associations, and sports development officers. Finally, the market research conducted for this project identifies the data appropriate to the fifth criterion,, i.e. which groups of users are interested in what type of information.

Each of these targeting criteria, if appropriate, would help to ensure that sports information is promoted and distributed in a cost effective manner, ie to those users most likely to have latent demand for information services. One note of caution qualifies this recommendation of targeting, however. Users in the market research demonstrate a wide variety of sources through which they seek sports information, and they also often discover relevant information by accident. There is always a justification, therefore, for some non-targeted promotion and distribution.

Charging for information

Consortium organisations typically provide highly subsidised sports information services at present. This subsidy is based on laudable principles, e.g.

encouraging widespread dissemination of information for education purposes and for the better provision and take-up of sports opportunities. However, subsidisation will not achieve such 'merit good' objectives if ignorance, uncertainty of returns and high search costs continue to deter demand. Furthermore, in the current economic and financial environment in the UK it is questionable if blanket subsidies are cost effective; this is the same question as that which has been asked of public sector sports facilities in recent years.

An alternative to blanket subsidies is to increase the scope and level of direct charges for sports information and make subsidies more selectively targeted. Charging has three functions of primary relevance to this investigation: rationing of demand to those of who place sufficient value on the service, raising revenue to offset costs, and discriminating in favour of selected types of user. The research therefore asked users for their attitudes to charging for information services.

Table 3 summarises the willingness to pay for information services of the respondents in the survey. It is important to emphasise that this question was asked of an audience who were used to largely free information services from Consortium organisations. Clearly, resistance to direct charging follows a logical pattern of being high for simple information services, but falling significantly for more complex services.

Table 3: Willingness to Pay for Sports Information Services

% Service	OK to charge		Object to charging	Not interested in service
	Me	My Organ.		
Simple enquiries	2	4	75	10
Standard reading lists	6	15	53	14
Access to Info. centre	7	22	50	11
Current awareness bulletins	11	30	40	10
In depth enquiry	21	45	13	12
Base: Whole UK response (2240)				

Note: Rows do not add up to 100% because some respondents gave no answer.

Respondents were very aware of problems associated with an extension of charging, which also emerged strongly from the interviews. One frequently mentioned problem was that of the user with a clear need for information services but an inability to pay even quite modest prices. Another was the reciprocation involved in information service production and distribution — many professionals in sport give primary information to national agencies so that the agencies' information services can collate and distribute the same information.

In both these situations, and possibly others, there are clear grounds for price discrimination in the form of lower or even zero prices for 'deserving cases'. However, exceptions do not negate the broader principle that at times of considerable resource constraints pricing may be a more cost effective and fairer means of rationing resources and services. The alternative, of non-price rationing, has such characteristics as queues, longer waiting time, access problems, delays in service responses, and poor quality services. These add to the costs and uncertainty of the returns from a search.

One major problem with an extension of direct charging for information is not countered by price discrimination. This is that charging is inconsistent with the principle of encouraging the development of sport, a fundamental *raison d'etre* for many publicly funded sports organisations. The most appropriate response to this problem is that all public policy is constrained by a budget, and charging can help to ensure not only an increased budget but also the cost effective distribution of a publicly funded service.

Any extension of direct charging for sports information is probably best done in conjunction with either a noticeable improvement in a service or the introduction of a new service. Indeed some respondents in the survey indicated that an extension of charging would necessitate an improvement in service quality, to justify the charges. The research identifies several market gaps or opportunities for service development.

Rationalising

The research reveals both production and distribution activities which are duplicated among the Consortium organisations. Such duplication can be seen as wasteful, especially as most of the organisations are financed from the public purse. The organisations are aware of these uneconomic features and are already taking steps to gain economies of scale and cooperation by forming the Consortium and by rationalisation of certain production activities such as abstracting and compiling of bibliographic databases.

Rationalising is, of course, synonymous with cutting costs, which is a necessary strategy in a time of reduced public funding. However, it has other advantages, particularly in making the promotion of services easier and reducing the search time for the consumer.

Networking

The lead organisations in the provision of sports information (in the UK case these are largely the Consortium organisations) head a large array of information providers and brokers. To improve cost effectiveness in the delivery of information to end users it is important that the hierarchy of information providers works. Consortium organisations and others share the responsibility to inform each other and the user of the most appropriate search patterns. This will help to ensure that the user's satisficing behaviour yields the best possible outcome and that the information-providing organisations' resources are not wasted by misdirected or duplicate enquiries.

Information networking lies at the heart of such an improvement. Such networking applies not only to the major information providing organisations, but also to all users with an important broker function. Information flows between brokers is vital to the effectiveness of information services collectively.

Conclusions

The conclusions of this paper necessarily lean towards problems within the sports information market. This is not to be taken to imply that there are no positive aspects to report on. Rather, it enables the conclusions to concentrate on possible ways to improve sports information services.

There are clearly imperfections in the sports information market and this paper exposes the nature of imperfections on its demand side. Users of information with a professional interest, likely to be producers of sports services in their own right, suffer from a lack of awareness and consequently an uncertainty not only about the returns from searching for information but also about the most appropriate search patterns. As a result they satisfice in their demand for sports information, often to the extent of not searching at all. The costs of search for these users are unnecessarily high because of their lack of awareness, lack of appropriate contacts and the increasing cost of time. Somehow appropriate market mechanisms do not seem to be in place to minimise these problems and ensure a rational approach to demanding sports information. The result is an apparent under-valuation and under-use of sports information.

Ironically, organisations in the UK Sports Information Consortium have done their best to reduce costs to users, typically by heavy subsidies for sports information services. Nevertheless the research on which this paper is based points out that in several ways this subsidisation has not been cost effective — e.g. unnecessary duplication of information production and distribution, indiscriminate distribution of services, rationing excess demand by means other than charging, and not exploiting the potential of brokers in the distribution of information. Thankfully, the Consortium is already formulating a development strategy which will attack the problems and hopefully elavate information to its rightful place in the resource management decisions of professionals working in sport.

Finally, how transferable are the issues raised in this paper to other areas of leisure? This is, of course, an empirical question, and to the author's knowledge empirical answers do not exist. Nevertheless it is a testable hypothesis to suggest that the status of information as a resource and the rationality of decision-making with respect to its acquisition are likely to be just as imperfect in tourism and hospitality, arts and entertainments, museums and heritage, and countryside recreation management as they are in sport. The ad hoc experience of the author in acquiring information in these areas suggests that this hypothesis is well worth testing.....

Note

For further information on the work of the UK Sports Information Consortium, please contact

Carolynn Rankin
c/o National Coaching Foundation
114 Cardigan Road
Leeds, LS6 3BJ (UK)
(tel. 0532 744802)

Reference

Taylor, P. & Nichols G. (1993) *UK Sports Information Services: an investigation of demand by people with a professional interest in sport.* London: The Sports Council.

The Devolution Debate: Changing Roles for Leisure Organisations in Britain

Jonathan Long
Leeds Metropolitan University, UK

Introduction

Pluralists appear to consider decentralisation desirable in any form, the general idea being that it allows greater participation by citizens because there are more points of access and greater control over politicians. Over and above that, it is commonly argued that they are better able to make informed decisions because they are closer to the point at which local needs (whether of consumers or producers) have to be satisfied. To Marxist instrumentalists the whole issue of decentralisation is a dangerous diversion that fragments the scope for radical change (Dunleavy and O'Leary, 1987).

It now seems fashionable for some elements of both political left and right to argue for greater decentralisation of state responsibilities. The right profess a natural aversion to centralised state control, and the left advocate empowerment of "ordinary working people". Dearlove and Saunders (1991) observe that:

> It is no coincidence that the regional level should begin to grow in the 1930s at the same time as local councils began to lose some of their powers, for many of the responsibilities that were taken away from local authorities were transferred to the newly created regional offices. (p. 490)

In recent years the British government has advocated returning some of the power of the public sector to the private. But at the same time it has sought to remove power from the local state and to ensure a more centralised state — more centralised than previously, and arguably more centralised than the imagined archetype of the French system. This has lead Crouch and Marquand (1989) to observe that policies in the 1980s have produced an "extraordinary centralism" and the destruction of local government powers. Of course there are exceptions, like the government passing to the local authorities responsibility for community care. But allowing someone else to handle an underfunded hot potato hardly contradicts the general contention of increasing centralisation.

The devolution discussed in this paper refers not to the central-local debate surrounding the relationship between national and local government, but of central-local relationships associated with the leisure agencies. The government's agencies in the leisure sphere have been exhorted to devolve a range of functions to their regional counterparts. If there really is this move towards increasing centralisation within the state, why should there be such attempts to shift the locus of control in the leisure-related agencies? Where decentralisation occurs in these cases it may allow more points of access, but does not increase control over politicians because there is no electoral process associated with these appointed regional bodies. It does, however, afford leisure professionals the opportunity for closer contact with clients, customers and partners. If different tastes, views and values are unevenly distributed spatially then regionalisation allows the opportunity for more people to be satisfied.

This all seemed to suggest that a consideration of the dual state thesis might offer a useful starting point. The dual state supposedly comprises the central state, responsible for accumulation and production through using social investment to reduce production costs, and a local state concerned with the manufacture of legitimation, increasing social cohesion and improving workers' living standards by boosting social consumption (see, for example, O'Connor, 1973; Dunleavy, 1980). However, the previously identified shortcomings of the dual state thesis (see, for example, Dunleavy, 1984; Sharpe, 1984) notwithstanding, there are two particular problems in the current context.

First, it is not clear whether we are examining the role of the state in production/accumulation or in consumption/legitimation. The temptation is to say that the agencies at both levels have a role in both arenas; the distinctions may be between agencies rather than between levels. The tourist boards have long been identified as dealing with an important "industry", and have less commonly seen themselves as being involved with social welfare. On the other hand, the Sports Councils have been much more oriented towards consumption and welfare. Although the Arts Councils have more commonly been associated with consumption and legitimation in the past, there has been much emphasis in recent years on their economic contribution and talk of "the cultural industries" has gained currency. It could reasonably be argued though, that regional arts bodies have tended to place greater emphasis on the social role of the arts while the Arts Council of

Great Britain (ACGB) has emphasised support for the producers to ensure the highest possible quality product. Even so this latter approach has clearly had a strong legitimation component to it.

Second, the agencies and their regional equivalents are not directly politically accountable to the electorate. They represent a kind of corporate state removed from the democratic process — even more removed since central government's recent moves to reduce local authority representation on them.

Changes in the leisure agencies

Devolution has been much talked about, for a range of reasons, in most of the leisure-related agencies. In this paper I intend to focus on those relating to tourism, the arts and sport, but there are many changes afoot elsewhere. For example, recently English Heritage has been engaging in its own version of devolution, trying to pass on responsibility for a large number of historic monuments. Despite the arguments relating to rationalisation, this seems to have been motivated almost entirely by crude economics; there simply was not enough money to go round all the commitments it had taken to itself. Through such desires of a national agency to be rid of liabilities, local authorities may acquire small additional responsibilities.

The Tourist Boards

Among the tourist boards the regional boards are not the regional offices of the English Tourist Board (ETB), but separate legal entities that receive only a minority of their funding from ETB. In the period between 1983 and 1985 the English Tourist Board was supposed to merge with the British Tourist Authority (BTA), and to begin the process of devolving its responsibilities to the Regional Tourist Boards (then 12, now 11). There seems to have been a marked reluctance to implement either of these government directives. Probably in the first instance it was interpreted as a takeover bid by BTA. As an organisation under threat, there was a natural reluctance to give up the marketing that represented the prime moving force in the tourism of the 1980s and 1990s even though the Board's Charter relates to development rather than marketing (and it is in marketing that new appointments have tended to be made).

A report in *The Guardian* (14 Nov., 1992) observed that:

> ...while the Government appears happy for [BTA] -which promotes Britain abroad — to continue to use taxpayers' money, it believes the case for central funding is much less strong for the promotion of tourism in England through the tourist board.

This is almost exactly the same as articles that were appearing almost ten years ago. Perhaps frustrated by the lack of change at ETB, the government is now retaliating by reducing its funding. Under current proposals, by the time ETB has passed funds on to the regional boards, it will have only c. £2 million in 1995/6.

At the same time the regional tourist boards, recognising that some activities can best be dealt with at a supra-regional level, are setting up their own tourism company. Originally established by East Anglia, South East England, Southern and Heart of England, it is now being joined by others, and is hopeful of using the bidding process to take over responsibility for some of the national schemes such as the Crown scheme for grading hotels. From the opposite direction, the regional boards are also looking to acquire other functions from local authorities as they are reorganised and obliged to put further functions out to tender. Rather than setting up tourism departments, some of the new authorities may be encouraged to use the regional tourist boards to fulfil such functions. And the prospect of local authorities having to put marketing functions out to tender is eagerly anticipated by some of the boards.

Interestingly, under the original terms of the Development of Tourism Act (1969) there was to be no separate English Tourist Board. It was only in response to protests at not being treated as the other home countries that ETB was created. Although the Scottish and Welsh Tourist Boards have now been strengthened, the impression that is given is that it is the English regions rather than the English nation that is more nearly equivalent to Scotland and Wales for administrative purposes.

The Arts Councils

As of April 1994 the Arts Council of Great Britain will cease to exist and the Scottish and Welsh bodies will be separately constituted in their own right and funded directly through the Scottish and Welsh Offices. Having wound-up its regional offices in England in the 1950s, the Arts Council of Great Britain was left funding regional organisations that were not an integral part of ACGB. However, the Regional Arts Associations (RAAs) came to receive approximately 80 per cent of their funding from the Arts Council. And recent changes that established 10 Regional Arts Boards in 1992 seemed to tie the regional bodies even closer to the national, though perhaps with more responsibility given to them.

The Glory of the Garden (Arts Council of Great Britain, 1984) may be much quoted, but the delegation of Arts Council clients advocated there went largely unacted upon. The suggestion then was that the Council's 156 revenue clients in 1984/5 be reduced to 94 the following year, with responsibility for the others being given to the Regional Arts Associations. Instead, the number of clients increased, so when the saga associated with the Wilding report renewed arguments around the role of the Arts Council, almost exactly the same debates were rehearsed. Similar proposals for the delegation of responsibilities for revenue clients were made, and the same subsequent resistance encountered. Richard Luce received Wilding's report in September 1989, and over three years later Peter Brooke, the National Heritage Secretary, announced that responsibility for funding 42 arts organisations would pass to the Regional Arts Boards as of April next year (1994). This follows 23 that were "devolved" in April 1992, but still leaves the national body with approximately 140 clients.

Having responsibilities also brings problems. Instead of receiving the 3.5% increase the Department of National Heritage had indicated, Yorkshire and Humberside Arts (YHA), for example, received an increase of only 2% for 1993/4, having already indicated higher levels of grant to clients. YHA has attempted "to soften the blow to arts organisations in the region by passing on an overall 3% grant increase to franchise organisations in line with current rates of inflation" (*Update*, January 1993). The fallout from the government's reduction in Arts Council funding has been a proposal to change the basis for Arts Council spending. For clients this will mean block grants will be replaced by "negotiated funding", a system that appears not unlike the Sports Council's Grant Assessment Process. For the regions the even-handed expansion or contraction of the budget will be replaced by a system of bidding based on an assessment of need (Anthony Everitt in *The Guardian* 22nd May 1993). The implication is that this will be based not on some complex notion of the needs of the population of the region, which is what might normally be assumed to underlie public policy, but the demands made by the artists in the region.

A Creative Future published in January 1993 (ACGB, 1993) as the outcome of the lengthy process intended to produce a national arts and media strategy, appeared to have moved the regional and national arts bodies closer together, recognising the social role of the arts and valuing artforms previously largely ignored by ACGB. However, the arts establishment objected to this liberal interpretation of the arts, fearing that it came dangerously close to embracing cultural relativism. The Arts Council moved quickly to try to recover the situation. Following a two day retreat in May, a press release was issued to reassure the world that it had been agreed that "support for quality was paramount". While few would wish to gainsay the importance of 'quality' in the arts, it has traditionally been the protectionist rallying cry of the elitists intent on defending "high art". The other priorities for the Arts Council and the regional boards suggest that the cries of elitism may be harder to sustain: new work, education (a return to the days of Roy Shaw?), cultural diversity and outreach.

Clearly, tying the regional boards into a national strategy might be a means of ensuring central control. So far, though, the centre seems to be being opened up to at least some influences from the periphery.

The Sports Councils

Unlike the Arts Council and the Tourist Board, in sport the regional bodies are regional offices of the Sports Council, responsible for the implementation of Sports Council policy. Their role, therefore is less ambiguous, though in a recent study we undertook on behalf of the Sports Council, many National Sports Organisations complained of inconsistencies in policy between the national and regional organisations (Sports Council, forthcoming). There is, of course some variation between the Regions because of what already exists there and the advice received from the respective Regional Councils for Sport and Recreation.

An example of this mix of central requirement and regional choice is provided by the initiative on "Focus Sports". All regions are expected to give priority to the four focus sports selected nationally (table tennis, netball, hockey and soccer), but then make further choices for their own region — for example, these may include rugby league in Yorkshire and Humberside, but not in many other regions.

The Minister's Review of Sport has lead to the national administration moving in the opposite direction to that of the tourist boards. There will now be an English Sports Council (alongside those of Scotland, Wales and Northern Ireland) and a UK Sports Commission. In this new set up the chairs of the regional councils will represent 10 of the 18 places on the English Sports Council, so providing a powerful voice.

Who can best do what?

The obvious questions associated with devolution are: Which is the best level for securing government policy objectives? Which is best for satisfying peoples' needs? Which offers the most cost effective solution? These though are not always the issues that drive the debate.

Matters of status

The geographical bases of the structures for the agencies imply much about perceptions of relative status. Although the Scottish and Wales Tourist Boards were given greater powers in the mid-1980s, the recent emphasis given to the Regional Tourist Boards rather than the English Tourist Board suggests that the English regions are seen to be assuming similar importance to Scotland and Wales (in line with comparable populations and volumes of tourism). For sport though the specialness of nationhood has been re-emphasised in line with representation in international competition. The dissolution of the Arts Council of Great Britain suggests a similar position in the arts, founded here on the basis of distinctive national cultures.

The devolution of Arts Council clients is also interpreted by some as a comment on status. Many of the Arts Council's larger clients have resisted the idea of becoming clients of the Regional Arts Boards because it is interpreted as a denial that they are of national significance. In Bourdieu's (1984) terms their cultural capital might be seen to have been devalued by being moved out of the national arena, no longer treading the same corridors of power. It isn't clear though that such distinctions between clients are made on the basis of the production / accumulation vs consumption / legitimation divide.

Devolution to clients

Whereas the previous observation related to the devolution *of* clients, there are also matters that relate to the devolution *to* clients. One of these was highlighted by our recent work on behalf of the Sports Council to examine the services provided to the National Sports Organisations — NSOs are taken to be the National Governing Bodies of Sport and other organisations with a national responsibility for their "sport" (Long, Talbot and Welch, 1993). Many believed that the Sports Council, like the Arts Council should largely be a channel for getting grant aid to its clients. The bald statistics suggest that only a relatively small percentage of the Sports Council grant is passed on to these NSOs. This is because many services are provided centrally (e.g. dope testing, international affairs, advice on facilities, research, planning and development, etc.). This relates to the debate about whether there are indeed economies of scale in providing services centrally from a bank of experience or whether devolution and pluralism should be encouraged by giving each NSO the money to provide or buy these services for itself.

At the same time though the Arts Council has been reprimanded for passing on only 90 per cent of its funding to clients. On announcing the Price Waterhouse proposals for "streamlining" the Arts Council, Peter Brooke (the Heritage Secretary) said, "my desire is to reduce the amount of money that is spent between leaving here and money going into artists' hands" (*The Guardian* 5th June 1993). Observing that frequent changes in structure and funding had imposed considerable burdens, Price Waterhouse included as one of the options for consideration an executive agency with its staff reduced by two thirds and buying in the lost expertise from outside, though that kind of expertise can come expensive.

The argument of some of the National Sports Organisations was that they, and not the Sports Council, knew what was best for their members. This may normally be so, but:

- the Sports Council can reasonably resort to the argument that it is accountable for public money and so must expect to exercise some control over its use;

- there may be divisions within the NSO between what is wanted by different groups;
- the NSO may represent its members, but they may be only a small proportion of those participating in the sport;
- the Sports Council may see the purpose of its grant in aid to be to secure the Council's own aims and objectives for sport.

This distinction between agency goals and client goals can also be convenient. For example, in the past the Arts Council has used this division to its advantage, asserting that it had no need of equal opportunities policies or a consideration of who were the audiences for the arts because that was the responsibility of their various clients to determine and not for the Arts Council to dictate — a bit like their own arms-length principle, allowing difficult questions to be avoided.

Since the ending of Section 4 grants in England the tourist boards cannot really be said to have clients in the same way.

Acting together

While the English Tourist Board seems to be being squeezed out of existence, the regional boards recognise the advantage of having a supra-regional body. Their aim is still to help co-ordinate the tourist industry, facilitate the collation and exchange of information in standard formats, and to ensure that national programmes continue (e.g. the Crowns scheme, the Welcome Host scheme, and professional indemnity and liability assurance). But now the organisation they are setting-up is their own creation, intended to work for them rather than vice versa, a very different power relationship. It is also intended to use the consumer muscle of the collective; together the 20,000 or more members of the Regional Tourist Boards can exercise considerable buying power. In the arts world, although CoRAA no longer exists English Regional Arts Boards (ERAB) has been established to provide collective services for the RABs, particularly where representation has to be made to others.

Other partnerships are also forming. In Yorkshire and Humberside, the regional bodies for the arts, sport and tourism have come together with the Yorkshire and Humberside Museums Council (but not the Countryside Commission) under the banner, "Working Together for the Region". This was prompted in part by the formation of the Department of National Heritage (DNH), which, unlike many other departments has no regional presence. The regional agencies have sought to act collectively on matters like the establishment of the National Lottery and local government reorganisation.

Reasons for regionalism

The foregoing has identified various aspects of devolution, many of them that are strengthening the regional leisure agencies. Why should this be happening?

Does it represent economic efficiency? Maybe, but it is not immediately obvious that this should be intrinsically so, and conventional economic arguments normally seem to argue the reverse. Are the regional agencies more in touch with people's needs? Quite possibly, but this argument has not encouraged the decentralisation of powers to local authorities. Does it further other government policy objectives?

Conclusion

The national agencies have tended to resist the devolution of powers to the regions, seeing in that an attack on their own power and virility, and maybe even a threat to their very existence. If there is a strong government department and strong regions, the need for the central agency is likely to be lessened (a very real concern for those at ETB). However, Dunleavy and O'Leary maintain that decentralisation and deconcentration can displace responsibilities and relieve the load on executive elites. Certainly devolution can be a good ploy in the face of constrained funding; if cuts have to be made let others make the unpopular decisions. In this position, YHA have avoided making uncomfortable decisions about which revenue clients to drop by absorbing the costs elsewhere, but that can only be a short term manoeuvre. They hope to buy enough time to persuade the government of the error of its ways and win greater resources for the arts. This is a high risk approach, as many local authorities banking on a Labour victory in the general election found out.

The abandonment of regional planning and the privatisation of the publicly owned utilities, which had a strong regional dimension, make talk of a regional state seem somewhat exaggerated. What we do have is an increased number of quasi government agencies (despite the supposed Thatcherite antipathy to them), many of which have a strong regional dimension. They tend to have different structures and genesis, and around the country have regional boundaries that may not be coterminous.

Dearlove and Saunders (1991) assert that the regional agency solution allows the centre to control them while keeping them out of the reach of opponents (unlike the local authorities). They conclude that:

> The result has been a regional tier, characterised by central control, managerial autonomy and corporatist closure...part of Britain's 'secret state. (p.497)

This implies that the regional agencies are controlled by what Hutchinson (1982) has referred to in the context of the Arts Council as '"usties" who can be relied on to do "the right thing". This could be true of both appointed board members and of career professionals who have learnt the appropriate language.

Ideological Dominance in Recreation Provision: the Response of Local Authorities in Britain to Compulsory Competitive Tendering

Neil Ravenscroft
University of Reading , UK

Julie Tolley
Sheffield Hallam University, UK

Introduction

Following the British Conservative Party's fourth consecutive general election victory in April 1992, the progressive shift from welfarism to entrepreneurialism witnessed since Mrs Thatcher first took office in 1979 has entered a new, mature phase. In the years since 1979, Britain has undergone what can only be described as a cultural and economic revolution. In the place of the social democracy of the post-war years is a new bourgeois liberalism based on the primacy of the market. Concurrent with this retreat from welfarism has been a shift in government intervention in the economy, from direct production and provision to a strongly centrist, authoritarian concentration on policy direction. The central platform of this policy has, ostensibly, been support for competitive markets as a basis for consumer 'rights' and, consequently, resource allocation decisions. At the production level this has involved the sale to the private sector of many of the former nationalised industries, whilst many areas of provision, traditionally the preserve of local government, have now been subjected to competitive tendering and 'privatised' management.

Although not necessarily promoting competition (Taylor, 1992), nor any automatic improvement in management or choice (Bogdanor, 1992), the politics of the New Right has challenged the construction and range of citizen rights in post-war Britain, distinguishing between 'genuine' rights, traditionally confined to civil and political arenas, and the 'dubious' social and economic rights associated with the creation of the Welfare State (Plant, 1991). Thus the central features of social policy in the 1980s were Mrs Thatcher's rejection of the accepted model of the state in social provision and its replacement by an authoritarian policy stance and a liberal concept of market rationality (Wilding, 1992). The new, mature phase of this process, constructed largely since Mrs Thatcher's demise, has been the reproduction of citizenship as part of that market rationality, both in terms of support for a consumerist imperative and in further dismantling the traditional dual state nature of government in Britain.

In place of the welfarist approach to rights has been an increasing emphasis on the culture of consumerism, with its foundation in the separation of politics from economics (Fudge and Glasbeek, 1992). This culture of consumerism has increasingly fragmented organised opposition to the erosion of welfare rights, particularly from traditional class and gender associations, replacing them with a highly individualistic, decentralised form of work organisation and social process. However, as Herman argues, over-stressing the centrality of rights in this transformation is to miss the more fundamental redistribution of power:

> The 'rights debates', I would argue, are not so much about 'rights' or 'charters', but about underlying political analyses and visions and about who has power to define the terms of equality. (Herman,1993: p. 40)

This sentiment is echoed by de Grazia (1992), who suggests that the growing sense of consumer entitlement engendered by this transformation may actually be antithetical to politics, certainly in terms of its pre-1970s class and party affiliations. At the very least it must signal a departure from the traditional Fordist associations of work and politics towards the conflation of social and political citizenship (Corijn, 1992). This has been highlighted recently in an analysis of the links between class, leisure activities and the political choices of young people, where the outcomes of post-Fordist restructuring are:

> ...low levels of political interest and participation, widespread alienation from political processes and parties, and a lack of ideological coherence and stability in opinions at the individual level. (Roberts, 1992: p. 17)

Having initiated this disaffiliation from traditional politics and welfarism, central government has been able to lay the blame for past inequalities and bureaucracy on local government and its lack of entrepreneurial incentive, whilst simultaneously strengthening its own power and influence (Thornley, 1991). Whilst this process has been applied in all areas of local authority activity, the case of leisure services is particularly interesting given that, in the main, provision has been derived from an era of political consensus about the role of the state in service delivery, such that leisure provision has been predicated more on the basis of 'local socialism' or 'local consumption' than on any statutory mandate from central government (Henry, 1984). Equally, leisure itself has been constructed as a dominant force in the current social and economic transformation (Mommaas, 1992b), a fact not lost on the current central administration when it recently created the Department of National Heritage (see Ravenscroft, 1993a).

Given this origin, with central government determined to regenerate leisure as the epitome of consumer citizenship, and local administrations, seemingly, with a strong mandate to retain the core of local socialist provision, it is not surprising that the attempt to impose new forms of working should have precipitated condemnation and a defence of the local state:

> Leisure services in local government are valued by citizens, customers and communities for their contributions to their health and quality of life. Underlying their success is a well motivated and sincere workforce who understand that the ability to have a rich leisure life is vital for everyone, and that the public service is in a unique position at the centre to guide, support and enable the provision of opportunities for local people. (White, 1992: p. 3)

However, the denial of the rationality of the market has proved to be rather less than unanimous, even amongst those remaining committed to local services:

> ... there quite clearly exists a level of incompetence, a failing to deliver value for money services. (Hodson, 1990: p. 24)

Whilst, at one level, this response indicates a recognition that local authorities have been partially responsible for their own downfall, it also implies a distancing of the management of leisure facilities from local politics and the bureaucracy of resource allocation; a corollary to the separation of politics from economics redolent in the rhetoric of the New Right.

Although rooted in the pluralist basis of politics, the analysis of this apparently paradoxical separation, as well as its implications for the future of local service delivery is hampered by a general lack of understanding of the role of the state in leisure provision (Henry and Bramham, 1986; Stabler and

Ravenscroft, 1993), as well as a tendency to conflate national and local levels of analysis (Henry and Bramham 1986; van der Poel, 1992). In his work on the justification of local government, Young (1986) suggests that its role must be founded on the political basis of pluralism. This implies the operation of a centre/local partnership, with a degree of autonomy at the local level, but with an overriding recognition of the 'superordinate nature of the centre' (Young, 1986: 11).

This construction of centre/local relations is essentially pragmatic, born of a traditional belief in the necessity of local needs being locally defined. However, it is apparent that the growing functional interdependence of government is undermining this traditional separation, such that the boundaries between central and local are now much harder to delineate (Loughlin, 1986). In addition, the relationship between them has become increasingly politicised, due largely to the increase in local power generated by the Labour central administrations of the 1970s followed by the centrist authoritarianism of recent Conservative governments (Goldsmith, 1986). The result of these conditions has been a significant decline in the power and authority of the local state, as an institution rather than simply a tier of government, undermined by what Goldsmith (1986) sees as an 'unholy alliance' between national politicians wishing to reduce the influence and expenditure of local authorities, and civil servants wishing to extend their power through controlling the actions of those authorities:

> Consequently, recent developments have resulted in a significant devaluation in the constitutional status of local government. The object of such reforms seems to be the establishment of rule-bound local authorities with responsibility for limited and specific functions and which are subject to strict central control. (Loughlin, 1986: p. 26)

This reduction in the scope of local authority responsibility can be seen throughout its former functions. The most obvious area of reduction, arguably, is in the responsibility for, and delivery of, the services built around the post-war construction of the Welfare State. Central to this process of reduction has been the introduction, in the Local Government Act 1988, of the Compulsory Competitive Tendering (CCT) of certain local authority services, including leisure provision. Although not the wholesale 'privatisation' that it has been accused of (see Adams, 1990), CCT has involved the regeneration of local authorities away from the traditional role of service provider towards that of facilitator. Associated with this has been an attempt to 'depoliticise' resource allocation and facility management, such that local councillors are to be seen less as politicians and more as business people interested in the efficient and competitive delivery of their services.

Very obviously, this new construction of local responsibilities has met with varying degrees of acceptance from different authorities. In their work on the local state, conducted prior to the existence of CCT, Henry and Bramham (1986) delineated four models of the local political system. These ranged from Marxist and dual state models of local responsibilities, with an emphasis on local authorities having the autonomy to determine their response to locally-defined needs, to democratic pluralism and bureaucratic managerialist models, emphasising the role of local government in resource allocation and demonstrating their 'professionalised' inertia to change and external influence. While accepting the limitations implicit in attempts to reduce local diversity to a limited range of forms, it would be reasonable to expect some variation between these forms in their response to the imposition of CCT. Rather than the quartet of responses suggested above, however, it is proposed to simplify matters still further by assuming a tripartite response to be more appropriate (see **Figure 1**, following page). Considering first the bureaucratic managerialist model of local government, representing the 'reality' of policy implementation in many local authorities (Henry and Bramham, 1986), the response is likely to be an overriding compliance with the dominant ideology of liberalism and authoritarian centrism. Under this 'new urban management' model, termed post-Fordist acceptance in Figure 1, the direct labour force would be either reconstituted in a new commercial organisation or replaced by an outside contractor. In either event new objectives would be derived, along with more 'commercial' working practices and rewards structures.

At the opposite extreme would be a Marxist construction of local statism, combining a rejection of both the market and central government interference in local service delivery. Although popular, particularly among large metropolitan authorities, as a form of opposition to early Thatcherite policies, the extent to which local authorities can continue to adopt this stance has been severely constrained by recent legislation, and is not a realistic option under CCT.

Finally, the third, intermediate, response is that pertaining to the pluralist construction of central/local relations. Characterised in Figure 1 as a post-Fordist rejection of central government intervention in local service delivery, this response (corresponding to Henry and Bramham's (1986) dual state and pluralist models) features a combination of the central elements of the other two responses delineated in Figure 1. While displaying many of the same features as the post-Fordist compliant model, this response refuses to acquiesce in the destruction of local socialism, but without the direct confrontation associated with local statism.

Figure 1 Theoretical response of Local Authorities to the Imposition of Compulsory Competitive Tendering

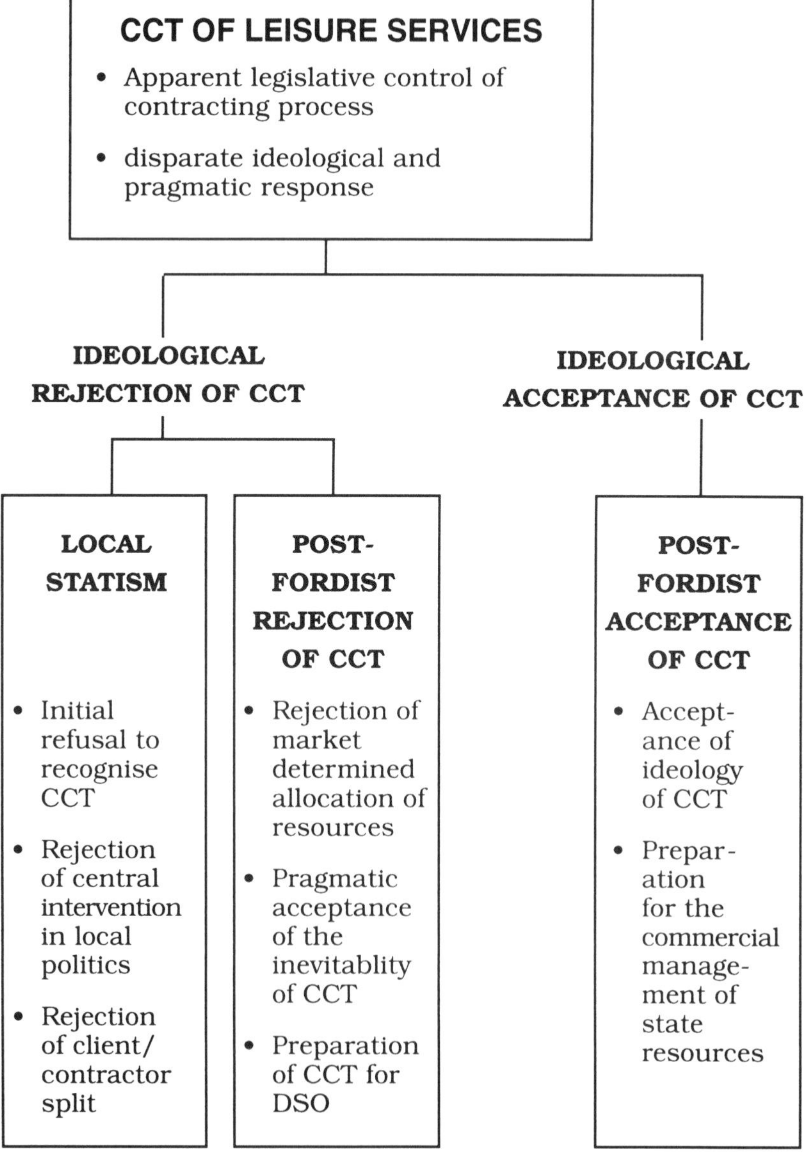

In short, therefore, the intermediate model represents an apparently pragmatic, opportunist response to service delivery, where the emphasis is clearly on the service rather than the politics of provision. This is in stark contrast to the other two models, where political stance has a far higher priority than service delivery, even if exponents of those models would argue that the quality and relevance of the service is a function of the political. Indeed, pragmatism apart, there is a strong argument that technical, 'non-political', responses such as that characterised as post-Fordist rejection, are as harmful to the continuation of an independent local government as the politically compliant models. This is because the very act of recognising the commodification of leisure services, through the creation of pseudo-capitalist structures such as the client/contractor split, compromises the essence and, eventually, the reality of local socialism:

> ... any valid theory of local government must be a *political* theory, drawing from arguments about pluralism and participation, and from arguments about the ability of local government to generate innovation and to maximise public choice. The currently fashionable concern to regard local government as simply nothing more than a convenient mechanism for the delivery of public services is, in the long run, the most dangerous to its continued survival and vitality. (Young, 1986: p. 18)

In seeking to examine the process by which local authorities have responded to political and economic restructuring, therefore, it is important to recognise their broad philosophical origins. Thus, rather than simple models of compliance or rejection, associated with constructions of leisure as commodified or as a 'right' of citizenship, the reality is much more complex. However, what is certain is that the former authority of class, with its leisure activity and political associations, has been replaced by the authority of the market, with its inherent individuality and self-determination.

The Implementation of CCT

The limits of commercial enterprise

In practice it is apparent that the legislation governing CCT impacts on a local authority's ability to embrace or reject the positions found at opposite ends of the model proposed in Figure 1. Even the most entrepreneurial Direct Service Organisation (DSO) managers would argue that the post-Fordist compliance position is unattainable in a pure form, due to the limitations placed on DSOs with regard to establishing fully commercial businesses. The legislation, coupled with the nature of local authority structures and operation, removes many of the benefits available to a private sector organisation. The factors preventing the attainment of a commercial operation include:

- The requirement that DSOs do not make a loss in any one year, thereby preventing them from submitting tenders which may run at a loss in Year 1 and/or 2, with the losses being recouped later. Private contractors are not limited by this rule.
- The need for a DSO's profit to be returned automatically into the authority's General Fund unless the DSO negotiates otherwise. Private contractors can accrue reserves.
- The general rule that DSOs are not capitalised, meaning that any need for capital monies is subject to local authority restrictions on capital expenditure; a basis for investment that private companies could not live with.
- The inextricable link between DSOs and individual local authorities effectively means a future tied to the fortunes of the local authority, implying, as with any other Department, that the DSO could be subject to cutbacks and changes in policy and direction. The operation of the DSO can therefore be subject to non-commercial considerations. Whilst compromising the DSO's commercial freedom, this is one of the primary benefits to local authorities of retaining a DSO, since it will be in a better position to ensure good employment practice and the implementation of equal opportunities policies, for example.
- Finally, DSOs remain publicly accountable to elected Members and citizens — a formidably broad church!

The restrictions on the potential for DSOs to act commercially and achieve a post-Fordist compliant position do not, however, preclude DSOs from acting in a more commercial and financially effective way than in the past. To this end the legislation has been seen as enabling by many managers who wish to work in the public sector but who have been frustrated by some of the restricted practices in the past. An authority such as Hounslow has no qualms about calling its DSO a "Commercial Division" and its officers have pride in the efficient and effective running of the Division. This is not seen as an abandonment of traditions of local socialism. Rather, a more efficient approach to the running of the Division is seen as a way of harnessing facets of commercial enterprise in the service of social policy objectives. The two are therefore not seen as operationally incompatible.

Just under five per cent of leisure management contracts have been won by local authority management buy-outs (Local Government Management Board, 1992). A management buy-out (MBO) involves the setting up of a separate commercial company which operates in the same way as any other commercial company. The principal difference is that the staff running this company are former employees of the Authority and would, in the more usual course of events, be the DSO. It is, perhaps, the nearest an Authority can come to embracing a commercial approach whilst retaining some influence through the Board of the new company. One of the most successful MBOs in leisure management is St Albans Leisure Limited. This MBO was officer-led under a, then, Conservative administration. Interestingly, the motives for encouraging the MBO do not appear to be linked to the retention of any form of control or association between the local authority and the new company, other than via the contract. However, the bond between the authority and its new management remains, witnessed by the MBO, for all its commercial approach, being pro-active in saving the post of a Women's Sport Development Officer due to be cut from the local authority pay-roll. Equally, St Albans Leisure Ltd now have a commercial freedom hitherto unknown in local government. As a result it has formed a holding company called Relaxion Ltd which has tendered for and won several other leisure management contracts.

Minimum compliance

At the other end of the continuum the legislation continues to impede local authorities. Local statism remains no more than a theoretical stand-point because both the legislation and current financial stringencies prevent local authorities from adopting this ideological stance in practice. However, local authorities which did not wish to embrace the philosophy of CCT took a tenacious approach to the CCT process. The only avenue open to them in rejecting central government intervention was to undertake a detailed consideration of the legislation and adopt a number of tactical approaches, within the wording of the law, to advance the prospects of their DSO. This was seen as no more than a means of creating 'a level playing field' in the light of legislation which was overwhelmingly anti-DSO.

It is not in doubt that many authorities did, and still do, resent the advent of CCT. It is too simplistic to view CCT as an isolated phenomenon and imply that a reluctance to specify the service came from a traditional local authority attitude towards the provision of poorly-managed, poorly-monitored and delivered services. Conversely, it is clear that elements of this attitude may have informed the process.

Compulsory Competitive Tendering was and is seen by many local councillors to be part of a wider concerted attack on local government. It is viewed as a tool in the dismantling of local government, but dressed cosmetically in the clothes of a new "enabling" culture. The tenor and format of the legislation was heavily weighed against DSO bids. This political 'red rag' led many local authorities, predominantly labour controlled, to take a very tactical approach to the legislation:

> It is the attempt to take services out of the political arena to which many elected councillors strongly object. It removes critically the accountability of local councillors for local services and fundamentally erodes the democratic process of local government. Compulsion itself weakens local decision-making and prevents councils from being open about DSO performance, for commercial reasons. (Moore, 199: p. 16)

Tactics which local authorities have adopted include:

- Packaging leisure management contracts in large tranches of work or in unattractive combinations. Twenty six per cent of authorities tendered in a single tranche, while 53 per cent tendered between 36 and 99 per cent of the work in the first tranche (Local Government Management Board 1992, 55). The size of these contracts varied, but of those using a management fee contract the average annual contract value was £573,776, with the largest contract valued at £7,950,000 (Local Government Management Board, 1992: p. 57). This average annual figure for leisure management contracts is amongst the highest for any CCT contracts so far tendered, only being bettered by the average annual values of the contracts for catering (education and welfare), at £1,995,245, and refuse collection, at £1,251,087.
- Including staff redundancy payments in the assessment of the cost of private sector tenders.
- Using quality as a ground for the potential rejection of tenders. For example, whilst authorities were not permitted to specify the terms and conditions of staff pay and employment, it was possible to request that tender submissions state the wages to be paid to staff. Comparisons could then be made to the local rate for the job and assumptions made about the tenderer's ability to employ the right staff to deliver the specified service. How many authorities took this to its extreme is not known. However, away from CCT, the quality rather than the cost issue was an argument allowed by the Government in awarding franchises for independent television.

- Applying a fee basis for the contract which was unattractive to private enterprise by giving little leeway for profits to be made without the local authority having a share. The most common form was a management fee contract with an income share on top.
- Requiring that contractors should have a track record of achievement and a credible financial status. For many companies new to leisure management, this requirement precluded them from shortlists until central government insisted that, under certain conditions, they should be included.
- Setting the performance bond fee at a high level. This loophole was closed quickly and replaced by a requirement that the fee was to be 10 per cent of the annual contract value unless the need for higher costs could be justified. Nevertheless, some 34.6 per cent of leisure management contracts have bonds of over 11 per cent of the annual contract value, while nearly eight per cent of them are over 25 per cent of the annual contract value.

The round of central government circulars closing loopholes unforeseen in drafting the legislation gave credence to the binary division between the anti-DSO stance of central government and the anti-private sector/government stance of local authorities. The distinction between private enterprise and the government was not made; the two being treated as virtually synonymous. The legislation, therefore, constrained what could be done. Any attempts to go beyond it raised the spectre of accusations of "anti-competitive" behaviour and the possibility of notices being served under Sections 13 and 14 of the Local Government Act 1988. A further separate but linked factor was the fear, on the part of local authorities, of losing the contract and therefore the workforce.

Whilst local authorities opposed the imposition of CCT in whatever ways were open to them, there was a positive side to the process. This was an express wish to retain DSOs. Moore (1993) lists eight reasons why this should be the case, noting that they relate solely to 'good' DSOs:

1. The ability to determine and influence, through direct management, the quality and standards of service provided.
2. The ability to integrate the delivery of service with the policy objectives of the council and to respond closely to customer needs.
3. The ability to ensure best employment practices and maintain high standards of terms and conditions for employees in the interests of service delivery.

4. The ability to meet the training needs of the council and the community.
5. The ability to ensure compliance with equal opportunities objectives in relation to women, ethnic minorities and other oppressed groups.
6. To re-invest any surpluses in other services.
7. The existence of a DSO alternative influences private sector prices and quality, to the authority's advantage.
8. The security of supply and price without the risk of failure in competitive markets or price-rigging.

Edwards (1993) adds two more:

9. Flexibility — staff can be required to work on other priorities and issues at short notice within the authority.
10. Control and accountability — staff of a private contractor work towards attaining the objectives of the authority only as a means of achieving the goals of their employer.

Within the parameters of the legislation and the consequent options available to local authorities, a different continuum from Figure 1 therefore emerges. This is characterised by being pro-DSO at one end and anti-DSO at the other. This stance has emerged as the polarising one in practice. What has become evident in the CCT process has been a consideration of whether a local authority wishes to retain or reject its DSO. Within this continuum several intermediate positions also appear:

- DSO succeeds at all costs;
- DSO is the preferred supplier and is supported by the council;
- DSO has to stand alone to justify its existence on the basis of price and quality;
- An MBO is allowed or encouraged;
- Any contractor will do, as long as they are the cheapest and are able to meet the specification;
- All contracts must be awarded externally to a private contractor.

Even on this continuum examples of the polar positions remain elusive. Although there are no reported examples within leisure management, the desire to award contracts to the private sector seems to be exemplified in the recently reported case of Brent (Anon, 1993) whose education, arts and libraries and social services sub-committee voted to accept a tender from a private contractor in preference to its own DSO, even when the private contractor's bid was over £2m more expensive.

The "DSO at all costs" scenario is as hard to find. The pressures on local authority resources have had a profound effect on thinking with regard to CCT. Edwards (1993) illustrates a shift in thinking within local authorities, which accepts as read that labour-held authorities will want to retain their DSOs, but that those DSOs must adopt some of the principles of the commercial market place in their operation. The approach implies that the pursuance of social policy objectives should be enhanced by a business-like approach, not achieved at the expense of it:

> It is important for Members to formulate a clear policy framework for White Collar CCT. This should include. Members' criteria for supporting internal provision: support is contingent upon demonstrable efficiency, competitiveness and quality of service. They should make explicit that if the managerial regime proves inflexible, bureaucratic and costly, then Member support for internal provision will be in jeopardy. (Edwards, 1993)

Few of the authorities which have a strong belief in their DSOs now do so as a blind point of principle. The DSOs have to deliver and "justify the faith that members show in them" (Moore, 1993). Delivery means providing an excellent service which is efficient, quality-assured, innovative, close to customer needs, meets with the authority's financial objectives, is co-operative with the client and bears comparison with alternative suppliers.

The consideration of what has happened in practice now allows the theoretical model originally proposed in Figure 1 to be developed into an inter-related model combining both ideological and practical positions. What is immediately clear from the revised model (**Figure 2**) is that while the theorised stance of the Left has been tempered by the legislation, it is the response of the post-Fordist compliant Right that shows more variety and, arguably, a broader ideological base. Whereas local statism and post-Fordist rejectionism have found their expression through a pro-DSO stance, the New Right has had to incorporate the mildly pro-direct labour force, if not DSO, management buy-out alongside the avowedly anti-direct labour stance of the pro-private sector responses.

However, as Figure 2 illustrates, there is, ultimately, an ideological schism between Left and Right that is polarised around the pro/anti local authority stance of the new contractor organisations.

Figure 2: Actual Response of Local Authorities to Compulsory Competitive Tendering

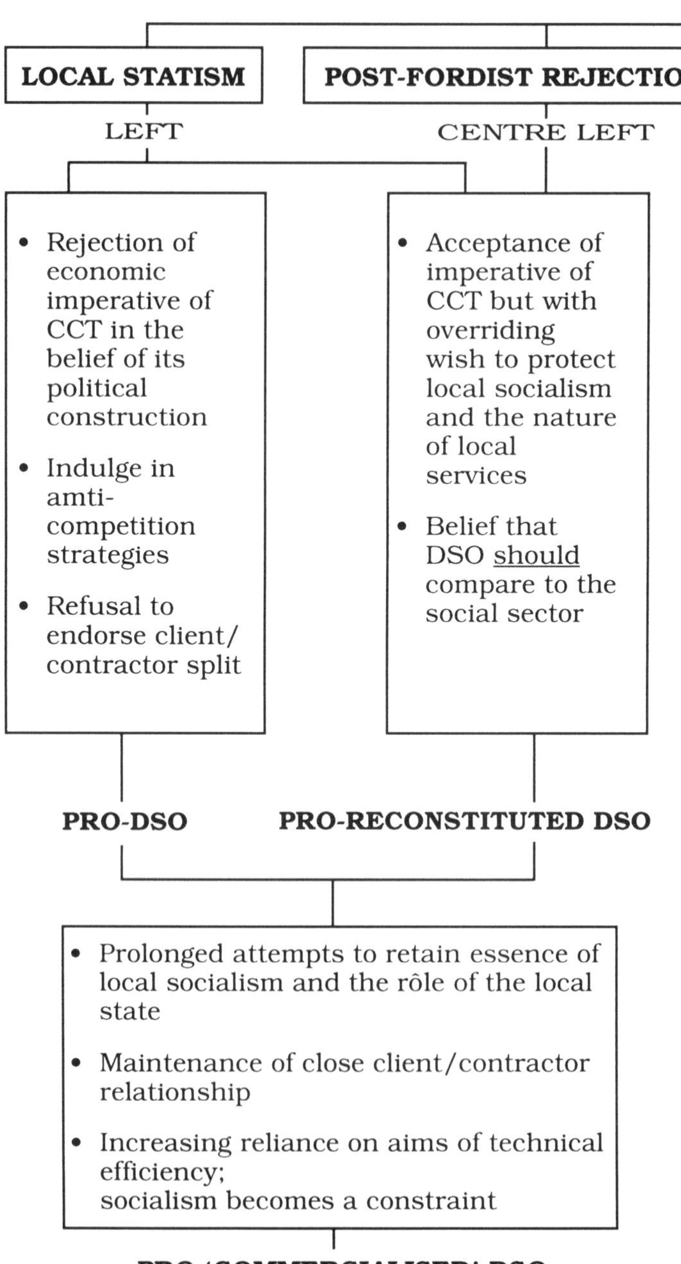

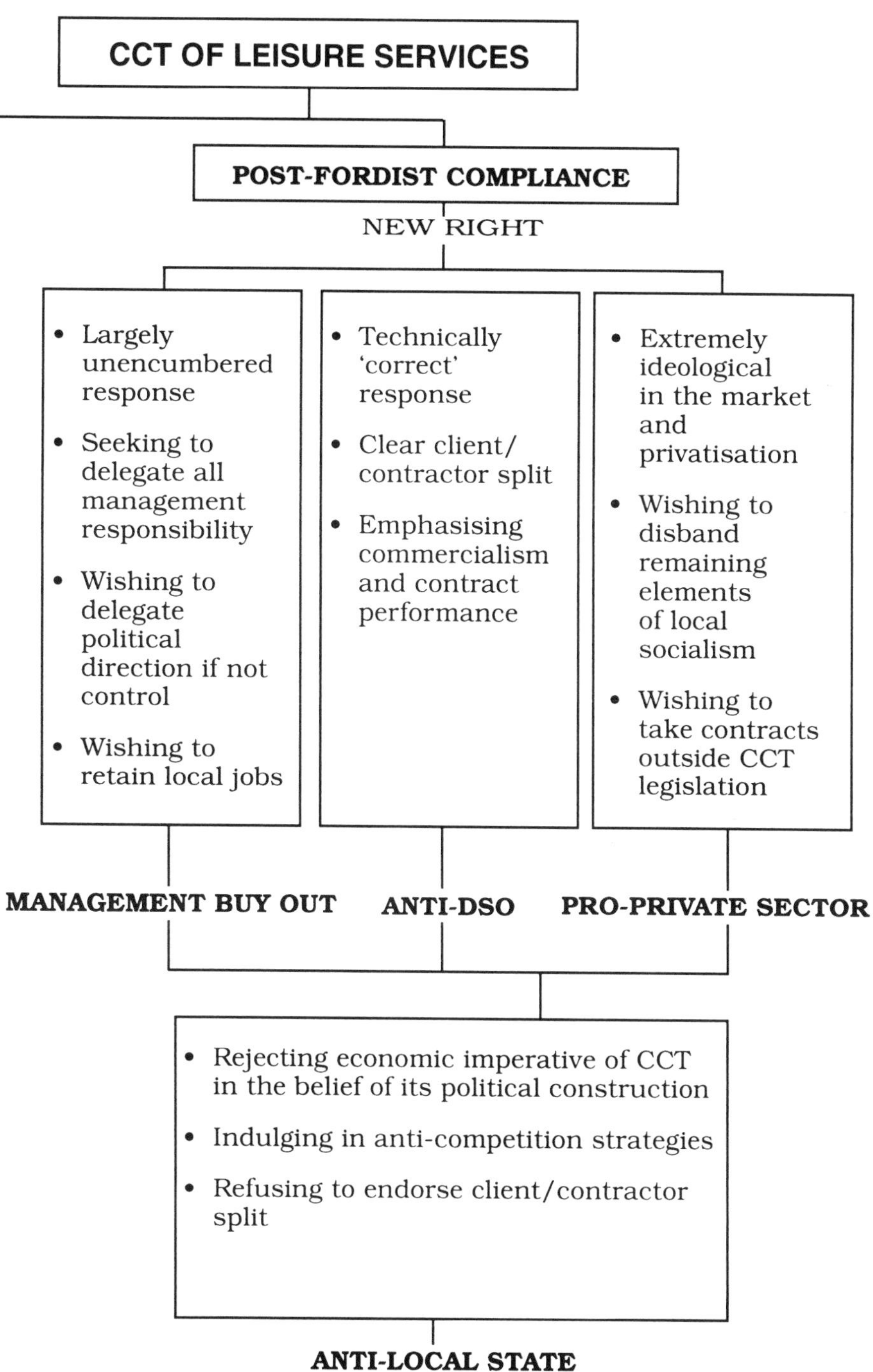
CCT OF LEISURE SERVICES
POST-FORDIST COMPLIANCE
NEW RIGHT
• Largely unencumbered response
• Seeking to delegate all management responsibility
• Wishing to delegate political direction if not control
• Wishing to retain local jobs
• Technically 'correct' response
• Clear client/ contractor split
• Emphasising commercialism and contract performance
• Extremely ideological in the market and privatisation
• Wishing to disband remaining elements of local socialism
• Wishing to take contracts outside CCT legislation
MANAGEMENT BUY OUT
ANTI-DSO
PRO-PRIVATE SECTOR
• Rejecting economic imperative of CCT in the belief of its political construction
• Indulging in anti-competition strategies
• Refusing to endorse client/contractor split
ANTI-LOCAL STATE

Towards a political economy of CCT

With its notions of managerial efficiency, choice and consumer sovereignty, the introduction of CCT has met with a mixed response. Whilst there has been much concern about the changes that would flow from the necessary reorganisation (Clarke, 1992), others have conceded that the outcome has been far from wholly negative:

> In the beginning, CCT was perceived by many to involve cost cutting, reduced standards, higher prices and limited access for 'target' groups. For the vast majority of local authorities, CCT has not created this kind of climate, and in several cases there have been tangible — if not Value For Money — benefits from the process. (Congreve, 1992: p. 9)

However, the fact that the vast majority of contracts have been awarded to DSOs, often uncontested, means that the central element of the process — the competition — has not been increased. Equally, once awarded, the contracts will still represent effective monopolies given the subsidy element implicit in local leisure service provision. The primary outcome of the imposition of pseudo markets on the delivery of local authority services has, therefore, undoubtedly been a recognition of the failure of government to analyse the relationship between supply and social outcomes (Taylor, 1992). Thus although competition may not have increased, there is now, at least, a greater awareness of work practices, objective-setting and accountability:

> There is an advantage in competitive tendering, it will sharpen us up, it will give us a standard to measure ourselves against. (Hodson, 1990: p. 24)

Competitive tendering has, furthermore, questioned the enduring beliefs of both central and local government that social problems can be cured, or at least ameliorated, by the allocation of increasing resources (Hodson, 1990; Wilding, 1992). In the wake of this loss of belief there has been a growing recognition of the importance of structure and agency in service delivery, with a consequent shift in the process, if not the outcome, of resource allocation. The requirement to offer local authority services for competitive tender could be seen in this light, therefore, to be nothing more significant than a technical device for rectifying past allocational and managerial failings:

> The growth of contracting-out and service level agreements has greatly increased understanding of the extent to which outputs and activities can be specified and measured in local authority

> services. The recent contracts prepared by local authority leisure departments for their sports management activities as a result of the CCT procedures imposed by the Department of the Environment, have demonstrated an ability to set out required activity levels and other outputs to a degree rarely before suspected, never mind practised. (Bovaird, 1992: p. 146)

Yet the actual process of competitive tendering can only be described as an abject failure. Rather than generating strong competition for contracts, commercial organisations have been extremely circumspect in their bidding, mainly restricting their interests to large, modern facilities (Thomas, 1991). Even so, of the 59 contracts awarded to the private sector by January 1991, 22 have so far failed, leaving the vast majority of provision to those who were previously undertaking it, albeit often in a different guise. Of even greater significance is the growing recognition that rather than increasing access and opportunity to participate in leisure activities, the imposition of CCT is already having the opposite effect, particularly for some of the most disadvantaged groups in society (Ravenscroft, 1993b).

Rather than the promise of consumer choice and sovereignty, therefore, the reality of CCT has been quite the opposite. Instead of the supposed economic freedom of the market, people are experiencing a highly restricted choice in the political sphere, since to reject the rationality of the market is to reject the very basis of citizenship 'rights'. Indeed, the concept of 'rights' under CCT is largely oxymoronic, as it is in any liberal democracy. But then it is patently clear that the protection of rights, whether via economic or social mechanisms, was not one of the overriding reasons for the introduction of CCT. As Loveland points out, in his analogous critique of Thatcherite council-housing policies:

> Exit is an effective control mechanism only if products in a given market possess a high degree of demand cross-elasticity, a characteristic depending upon the availability of close substitutes, in terms of, among other things, price, quality, and convenience, for the unsatisfactory good. Exit is not a viable consumer strategy (and thus market self-regulation breaks down) in monopolistic or oligopolistic conditions entailing minimal demand-side substitutability and which impose significant entry barriers to potential competitors. (Loveland, 1992: p. 348)

There has never been the chance of significant demand side substitutability for the majority of local authority leisure services. Nor is there ever likely to be, given the costs of entry and the low potential returns. The conclusion must be drawn, therefore, that CCT is not so much a part of economic policy as it is an element in the reproduction of capitalist structures in local government; an attempt to force a shift away from a traditional consumption orientation towards the more pluralist 'objectivity' of pseudo-markets for local services.

While the reception to this form of policy may have varied between authorities, what has become clear from this paper is that all authorities have, to a greater or lesser extent, complied with the ideological imperative as well as the legal requirements of CCT. To have expected any different, even from some of the avowedly left-wing authorities, would probably have to be construed as naive. Regardless of their current political configurations, the structure of local authorities has always been based upon a highly conservative paternalistic professionalisation of 'responsibility':

> Decision making and non-decision making within local politics occurs within the bureaucratic structures of public sector organisations which are unresponsive to change, filter out unacceptable policy options, define 'acceptable' or 'responsible' interest groups, and are constrained by past practices. (Henry and Bramham, 1986: p. 193)

The passing of the Local Government Act 1988 therefore represented an opportunity not only for central government, but for local government professionals as well. In the sure knowledge that Mrs Thatcher and her supporters were wholly dismissive of their managerial abilities (Wilding, 1992), these professionals set about regenerating the defence of local socialism away from the rights debate and towards economic efficiency and the delivery of quality public services. Thus commentators such as Hodson claimed that:

> Leisure services in local government have been streets ahead, both in terms of marketing, in customer orientation and even sometimes when it comes to the question of value for money. (Hodson, 1990: p. 24)

Similarly White (1992), in her defence of local leisure provision, suggests that many of the strengths and successes of public leisure services have reflected the reality, if not the political dogma, of the New Right. Chief amongst these has been an entrepreneurial spirit, together with a willingness to develop new management cultures capable of delivering social benefits within a 'value for money' service. Once again the separation of politics from either economics or management is evident, with the clear inference that public sector leisure professionals are capable of delivering quality product if given an appropriate environment. Calpin supports this belief in suggesting that the adoption of objective service quality criteria, such as BS5750, is as appropriate to the public sector as it is to the private sector:

> For local authority direct labour and service organisations, as for private sector companies, registration to BS5750 standard provides a means of measuring efficiency and competence and of ensuring that they can compete for contracts on equal terms. (Calpin, 1992: p. 33)

It is this very division between the overtly political and the apparently benignly managerial that is at the heart of the imposition of CCT. For whilst outwardly introducing a new system of working practices that mirrors a market orientation, central government has been able to rely on the ideological dominance of bureaucratic conservatism to ensure that politics and management are conflated, but in a passive hegemonic sense rather than anything more alarming or confrontational. Indeed, leisure professionals, mainly working within local government, are at the centre of this apolitical managerialist discourse, in developing what Mommaas (1992a) describes as 'moral standards' that transcend political debate in favour of a detached legitimation of their interpretation of leisure provision. This Foucauldian construct of professional as pastoral is held to be particularly important in leisure provision, as demonstrated by Haywood, amongst others:

> Is leisure supply another area of public provision like housing or waste disposal, or does its conceptual basis of freedom and choice require a radically different approach to service delivery and its management? (Haywood, 1992: p. 43)

Indeed, this discourse of leisure provision as 'professional' rather than 'political' pervades much of public sector thinking, whether in terms of the actions of leisure managers, or in the operation of some of the national agencies such as the Sports Council and Arts Council (Henry and Bramham, 1986). This has occurred largely since the status of local leisure provision was increased, arguably inadvertently, following the reorganisation of local government in 1974. Since that time the move towards what Haywood (1992) describes as 'semi-professionalisation' has tended to focus on issues such as the management of facilities to the exclusion of the more policy- and politically-orientated issues of users and their needs:

> Public sector recreation is emerging in the United Kingdom as an area with an increasingly unified occupational group, promoting its own claims for professional status. This unification process has taken on a number of dimensions facilitating the development of

> ideological corporatism, a system of shared values relating to policy aims and practice which informs the advocacy of policy across a wide diversity of local authorities. (Henry and Bramham, 1986: p. 199)

Central government has therefore been able to use the Fordist underpinning of this ideological corporatism as a 'Trojan horse' for introducing new working practices that enhance the professional claims of those involved. When allied to the traditional conservatism of local authorities themselves, the outcome has been, quite predictably, a wholesale embrace of CCT, regardless of the managerial stance adopted. Rather than an essentially managerialist construction of CCT therefore, the imposition of the market can be seen for what it is; an overtly political policy instrument designed to extend the ideological dominance of capitalism at the expense of the economic and political freedom of individual citizens.

Despite the continued optimism of some commentators, such as Hodson (1990), the future of public leisure services looks bleak. Whilst the immediate threat of a private sector 'take-over' has been averted, the medium-term renegotiation of contracts allows government a renewed opportunity to sever the remaining bonds between local authorities and the management of their facilities. The proposed extension of CCT to theatres, concert halls and art facilities may pave the way for these changes, at least in as far as the issue of pricing is concerned (Tolley, 1992). Although the current practice is to reserve for client authorities politically sensitive issues such as pricing, this will hardly be possible for the individual events, exhibitions and shows that are the predominant use of theatres, halls and galleries.

As Tolley suggests, the obvious conclusion is for client authorities 'to go with the spirit of the law' (1992: p.12) and include programming and pricing in these contracts. Notwithstanding the remaining clauses of the arrangements, contracts of this type should be of considerably greater interest to potential contractors than the politically-constrained variety currently on offer. Assuming that this does prove to be the case and that greater competition for the contracts results, there must be every possibility of this arrangement being extended to the renegotiation of the current leisure management contracts, regardless of any protestation about the differences between community sports facilities and the operation of a theatre or concert hall.

In common with the overall experience of CCT, therefore, it would appear that through a mixture of naivety and duplicity, technical, managerialist considerations could once again reaffirm the ideological dominance of capitalism and the market. That law and legalised politics have the power to ensure this result must be without serious question. However, there are indications that a form of neo-Keynesian political economy is gaining ground, in North America if not yet in Europe, that could undermine the orthodoxy of the market (Hutton, 1993). Quite apart from exposing some of the primary limitations of market models, such as their assumptions about the availability of information and the belief in economies of scale that consequently dominate the relationship between production and cost, the new economics emphasises the centrality of leisure and its relationship to the utility of work. Thus, while market models are dependent upon the assumption that work is a pure disutility, engaged in solely as a means of generating income to spend on leisure, the new economics suggests that leisure is more fundamental to life than the discretion of the market indicates, while work has a utility in its own right, beyond its ability to generate disposable income. Leisure is therefore reconstructed away from the role of discretionary reward towards social centrality, thereby robbing "the new right of its dominance of the economic and political agenda" (Hutton, 1993: p. 11).

For the immediate future, therefore, it is beholden on leisure professionals to ensure that they remain committed to the needs of the community and to deriving the means of separating the quality of their management from the limited rationality of the market, in the hope that political and economic salvation might be at hand and that the 'experiment' of the past decade might finally be seen for what it actually is.

References

Adams, I. (1990) *Leisure and government*. Sunderland: Business Education Publishers Ltd.

Anon. (1993) *Municipal Journal*, No. 6: p. 5 and p. 7.

Bogdanor, V. (1992) 'Going private is the next step to oblivion', *The Guardian* August 29: p. 19.

Bovaird, A. (1992) 'Evaluation, performance assessment and objective led management in public sector leisure services', pp. 145–165 in J. Sugden and C. Knox (eds) *Leisure in the 1990s: Rolling back the welfare state*. LSA Publication No. 46. Eastbourne (UK): Leisure Studies Association.

Calpin, D. (1992) 'Councils walk on the quality street', *Municipal Journal*, Vol. 22: pp. 33–35.

Clarke, A. (1992) 'Citizens, markets and consumers: a post welfare state view of leisure' pp. 109-120 in J. Sugden and C. Knox (eds) *Leisure in the 1990s: Rolling back the welfare state*. LSA Publication No. 46. Eastbourne (UK): Leisure Studies Association.

Congreve, D. (1992) 'Leisure after CCT; working smarter and harder?', ADLO Sports and Leisure Advisory Group. 1992. Second *thoughts*. Manchester. Association of Direct Labour Organisations, pp. 9-10.

Corijn, E. (1992) Leisure and European citizenship. Paper presented to the VIII congress of the European Leisure and Recreation Association: *Leisure and new citizenship*. Universidad de Duesto, Bilbao, Spain. 9-14 June 1992.

Edwards, C. (1993)*Towards a corporate and strategic framework for white collar CCT*. Draft Briefing Paper. Manchester. Association of Direct Labour Organisations.

Fudge, J. and Glasbeek, H. (1992) 'The politics of rights: A politics with little class', *Social and Legal Studies* Vol. 1, No.1: pp. 45-70.

Goldsmith, M. (1986) The status of local government. pp 31-44 in Goldsmith, M. (editor). 1986. *Essays on the future of local government*. West Yorkshire Metropolitan County Council and Salford University.

de Grazia, V. (1992) 'The politics of leisure, 1930-1990: historical perspectives'. Paper presented at the VIII Congress of the European Leisure and Recreation Association: *Leisure and new citizenship*. Universidad de Duesto, Bilbao, Spain. 9-14 June 1992.

Haywood, L. (1992) 'Community recreation and local government in the 1990s', in J. Sugden and C. Knox (eds) Leisure *in the 1990s: Rolling back the welfare state*. LSA Publication No. 46. Eastbourne (UK): Leisure Studies Association, pp. 41-44.

Henry, I. (1984) 'An analysis of the determinants of the expenditure of English local authorities on leisure services.' Paper presented at the Leisure Studies Association conference *Leisure: politics, planning and people*. University of Sussex, Brighton. 4-8 July 1984 (unpublished).

Henry, I. and Bramham, P. (1986) 'Leisure, the local state and social order', *Leisure Studies*, Vol. 5: pp. 189–209.

Herman, D. (1993) 'Beyond the rights debate', *Social and Legal Studies*, Vol. 2: pp. 25–43.

Hodson, D. (1990) 'Life after CCT. The public sector in the 21st. century', *The Leisure Manager*, Vol. 8, No. 1: pp. 24–25.

Hutton, W. (1993) 'New economics hits at market orthodoxy', *The Guardian*, 19 April: p. 11.

Local Government Management Board (1992) *CCT Information Service*. Survey Report No 6. London: Local Government Management Board.

Loughlin, M. (1986) 'The constitutional role of local government', pp. 21–30 in M. Goldsmith (ed) *Essays on the future of local government*. West Yorkshire Metropolitan County Council and Salford University.

Loveland, I. (1992) 'Square pegs, round holes: the "right" to council housing in the post-war era', *Journal of Law and Society*, Vol. 19 No. 3: pp. 339–364.

Mommaas, H. (1992a) 'Leisure and the intellectuals: the end of the legislator?'. Paper presented at the 10th anniversary conference of *Theory, culture and society*. Champion, Pennsylvania, USA. 16-19 August 1992.

Mommaas, H. (1992b) 'The city and cultural diversity'. Paper presented at the joint conference of the Leisure Studies Association and the Vereniging voor de Vrijetijdssector: *Internationalisation and leisure research*. Tilburg University, the Netherlands. 10-13 December 1992.

Moore, G. (1993) 'Sorting out the many hats a member has to wear', *Municipal Journal*, Vol. 14: pp. 16–17.

Plant, R. (1991) 'Welfare and the enterprise society', pp. 71–88 in Wilson, T. and Wilson, D. (eds) *The state and social welfare: the objectives of policy*. Harlow: Longman Group UK Ltd.

van der Poel, H. (1992) 'Analysing leisure policy. The development of an idealtypical model'. Paper presented at the joint conference of the Leisure Studies Association and the Vereniging voor de Vrijetijdssector: *Internationalisation and leisure research*. Tilburg University, The Netherlands. 10-13 December 1992.

Ravenscroft, N. (1993a) *Paradise postponed? The UK Department of National Heritage and political hegemony*. Working Papers in Land Management and Development No. 5. Department of Land Management and Development, University of Reading.

——— (1993b) 'Public leisure provision and the good citizen', *Leisure Studies*, Vol. 12, No. 1: pp. 33–44.

Roberts, K. (1992) 'Young adults in Europe'. Paper presented at the joint conference of the Leisure Studies Association and the Vereniging voor de Vrijetijdssector: *Internationalisation and leisure research*. Tilburg University, The Netherlands. 10-13 December 1992.

Stabler, M. and Ravenscroft, N. (1993) *The economic evaluation of output in leisure services*. Discussion Papers in Urban and Regional Economics, Series C, Volume V, No. 80. Department of Economics, University of Reading.

Taylor, P. (1992) 'The contracting of leisure management'. Paper presented at the joint conference of the Leisure Studies Association and the Vereniging voor de Vrijetijdssector: *Internationalisation and leisure research*. Tilburg University, The Netherlands. 10-13 December 1992.

Thomas, K. (1991) 'CCT: round one', *Leisure Management* Vol. 11, No. 3: pp. 46–47.

Thornley, A. (1991) *Urban planning under Thatcherism: the challenge of the market.* London: Routledge.

Tolley, J. A. (1992) 'Extension of CCT to theatres, concert halls and arts facilities: the spirit or the letter of the law?', in ADLO Sports and Leisure Advisory Group Second *thoughts.* Manchester: Association of Direct Labour Organisations, pp. 11–13,

White, J. (1992) *Leisure: the cornerstone of local government. A discussion paper.* Telford: University of Birmingham in association with the West Midlands Chief Leisure Officer's Association.

Wilding, P. (1992) 'Social policy in the 1980s: an essay on academic evolution', *Social Policy and Administration,* Vo. 26, No. 2: pp. 107–116.

Young, K. (1986) 'The justification for local government', pp. 8–20 in M. Goldsmith (ed) *Essays on the future of local government.* West Yorkshire Metropolitan County Council and Salford University.

Leisure Services in Britain and the Management of Change

Jeff Abrams

Leeds Metropolitan University, UK

Introduction

The pressure for change over the last ten years has had a significant impact on public sector organisations. This can be seen in the health service with its shift to internal markets in education with the national curriculum, education forum, the incorporation of Further and Higher Education establishments, and in the Local Government Act 1988 which has had a direct impact on local authority leisure provision. There is a similarity in all these cases: all the changes are driven by external influences, primarily government intervention. In each case the quality of the implementation and the value of outcomes are questionable. The purpose of this paper is to explore some of these issues as they relate specifically to local authority leisure provision. This will be a achieved by relating theoretical perspectives on organisation structure, culture and change to local authorities.

It is clear that if employers and employees agree with need and strategies for change that conflict is reduced and implementation is less problematic. The reality of organisational life is rather more complex, often with competing interest groups in conflict. The mainstream literature in the area of leisure management (Torkildsen, 1985, 1993; Borrett, 1991; ILAM, 1993; Gratton and Taylor, 1985 etc.) although excellent in many ways, tend to be either descriptive or perspective and do not really address the less tangible yet no less important area of organisation behaviour, culture and change. In fact much of the literature in the area of leisure management tends to focus on the functional aspects of management (marketing, human resources, finance and law).

The importance of understanding the softer management theories is amplified by the rapid pace of change and the effect that this has on all concerned. A case in point is the implementation of quality assurance (QA) and British Standard BS5750. The processes and ideas underpinning these initiatives are admirable, however a recent dissertation study of Calderdale Leisure Facilities (Beaver, 1993) concluded:

1 QA is complicated due to its implementation on the back of Compulsory Competitive Tendering (CCT);
2 Staff are being asked to do more for lower wages and less recognition;
3 Motivation and morale are low;
4 Staff feel they must resist change and make their voices heard by management;
5 QA is seen as another "big stick" with which management are forcing changes on staff;
6 Accountability is increased due to QA which is seen as coercive; and
7 There is a "them and us" attitude amongst staff.

The problems of implementing organisation change in the public sector leisure context was also highlighted by the recent Institute of Leisure and Amenity Management Study (ILAM, 1993) which attempted to identify if CCT had improved quality from the customers' perspective. On balance, over a range of criteria, the study indicated that there was in fact a slight reduction in quality overall. What was particularly interesting here was the fact that fewer staff were being paid less to do more. Even the best traditions of Taylorism would find the motivational effect of this scenario rather limited! What we are left with in the two examples above is a dependency relationship between manager and managed which can only lead to a coercive power dynamic.

What is clear is that successful introduction of organisational change has to recognise the micro political, and cultural realities of the organisation. To impose change without thoroughly considering these factors ultimately leads to conflict a win/lose situation and poor organisation health. Berg (1979) comments, "change programme never occurs in a vacuum. It is implemented in a social system characterised by emotional and political bonds between the members easily changed by artificial and human relations training". He goes on to argue that "the meaning of a change programme in relation to the network of power relations is of particular importance. Life in organisations is political and competitive and this is a fact which must be taken into account in the design of programmes of planned change". The problem is, however, that change is rarely planned and the need to change is often imposed. This inevitably creates tensions within organisations which will need to be resolved if change is to be successful.

Mastonbroek's (1989) ideas may be of relevance here. He characterises organisational negotiation in terms of the following dilemmas:

1 Relatively strong mutual dependence;
2 Pronounced self-interest on each side; and
3 No clearly superior power on one side or the other.

The tactics of negotiation range from compromise through negotiation to fighting. In the public sector leisure context, however, there is a power imbalance, given the nature of the structure of local authorities and the need to be publicly accountable. The political dimension within local authorities requires not only management but political management.

This is further complicated by the nature of public sector objectives as highlighted by Coalter, Long, and Duffield (1986) who identify multiple objectives — for health, quality of life, personal achievement, equity of access, affirmation action for disadvantaged groups etc. as central to the public sector. In addition there is an increased pressure to improve efficiency, value for money, customer service, quality etc. Chayton (1993 p.31) reinforces this "new reality".

> Leisure management in the public sector is, through necessity, more commercially aggressive than it had been. Long gone are the days when a leisure centre opened its doors, welcomed its customers, bought from its regular suppliers and regraded its budgeting situation as an after thought.
>
> Maximising income, minimising expenditure and 'managing the bottom line' are now key phrases for every manager, and priorities in very organisation.

Henry (1993) also suggested that their has been a shift from the welfare models of the 1970s to a more commercial approach within local authority leisure services.

Herein lies a significant dilemma for local authority leisure services during a period of significant change. Local authorities have a very definite organisational culture. This is categorised by strict rules and procedures which are reinforced by public accountability. Structurally local authorities are hierarchical, with clear lines of responsibility. Due to the political nature of local authorities there is a requirement to be bureaucratic, sticking very closely to set rules and procedures. Front line managers work to tight financial controls and are given little incentive to be entrepreneurial. Handy (1985) would describe this type of organisation as a role culture which is reinforced by job descriptions, authority definitions, set roles and procedures, significant accountability etc.

Burns and Stalker (1971) distinguish two sorts of organisational structure. The mechanistic organisation is more appropriate for stable circumstances. The organismic in which roles, responsibilities and authority are more diffuse and less hierarchical are more appropriate to the change situation. A strong argument could be presented suggesting that local authorities exhibit primarily a role culture, have mechanistic structures and find change extremely difficult. Argyris (1982) suggests individuals who are brought up in bureaucratic organisations become so entrenched in the culture that it is nearly impossible for them to shift attitudes sufficiently for there to be a change in culture.

The need for change can come from a variety of sources: these include changes in technology, political and social frameworks, size and complexity of organisations, poor performance, and the competitive environment. As already suggested, the primary motivation for change with local authority leisure services is external-political legislation and pressure. It could be argued that without this intervention in the form of CCT, the type of change local authorities are experiencing would not have occurred.

In order for the implementation of change to be successful and for there to be commitment to change, a number of factors need to be considered.

1 *A perceived need for change.* If there is a general consensus within the organisation that change is inevitable, or better still beneficial, then implementation becomes less problematic. It is often the case, however, that it is not absolutely clear that change will be beneficial. This leads to the perception that change is imposed and irrational and should be resisted.

2 *Appropriate resources.* If it appears that sufficient resources are not invested during a period of change conflict and tension becomes inevitable. This can be seen in the ILAM (1995) study outlined above where staff are being asked to do more for less pay. The net result is a lack of commitment to change reinforced by poorer performance.

3 *A supportive organisational culture.* If there is a congruence between organisational culture and the need to change, again implementation is less problematic.

It must be stressed that resistance to change is almost inevitable and can be expected in most circumstances. There are a number of reasons for this:

1 If the organisation culture is strong and deep rooted change becomes more difficult. It then becomes a matter of shifting organisation culture.

2 If change has been too rapid in the past uncertainty fear and the lack of stability create a need to slow down.

3 If change is not seen as legitimate. It has almost become the expectation

that organisations should be in a constant state of turbulence and change even if there seems to be no rational explanation for this.

In the case of local authority leisure services change has been imposed from outside. There has been a series of attempts to contain and reduce local government to intervene in the process of local authority expenditure and raising of finance (Henry, 1993). For local authority leisure services this was manifested in the form of Compulsory Competitive Tendering. The operational requirements of such a change has had a significant impact on leisure services. There is widespread uncertainty, fear that jobs will be lost, pressure to maintain and improve both the quality of service and efficiency within service resource constraints. In addition local authorities are driven by public accountability and bureaucratic systems and as a consequence will find change difficult. In fact taking each criteria for successful implementation of change in turn illustrates this point:

1 A perceived need for change: The change (CCT) was imposed and it could be argued would not have happened otherwise. Generally staff have not internalised the change (ILAM Study, 1993), and there is little evidence of improvement in quality. There is evidence (ILAM Study, 1993) that morale has been negatively affected by the changes.

2 Appropriate resources: The commercial sector has not been widely interested in bidding for local authority leisure facility contracts. The management of local authority leisure facilities, is not seen as a profitability activity. Collins (1990) states:

> I have seen five assessments by major commercial consortia over that last decade and all were unanimous that they could not run profitably on the current basis: the objectives had to be reduced, fewer markets selected, fewer activities offered at a simpler price structure. (p.3)

The reality of CCT is that it imposed efficiency measures which resulted in the deterioration of pay and conditions. This is supported by the Public Services Privatisation Unit study (PSPU, 1992) which highlighted that nineteen local authorities had reduced pay and/or conditions even though there was limited competition. Although it can be agreed that this is in fact healthy in terms of improving efficiency it is clear that the impact of a reduction in pay and conditions has very real human consequences. These competing objectives become almost unmanageable. In addition if the reduction is both capital and revenue allocation to local authority leisure providers then the successful implementation of change leading to improved quality becomes near impossible.

3 A supportive organisational culture: There is a fundamental conflict between the bureaucratic orientation of local authorities and the changes imposed by CCT. Authorities will have to generate an organisational structure to accommodate the change. Henry (1993) describes this change: "This will require the establishment at officer level either of separate sections within a department (one to undertake the client role, the other to manage the facility a service) or of separate departments or 'management boards' (of officers and members) which would act in a way analogous to the board of a private company employed to carry out the terms of a management contract" (p.99). The development of contrast specifications, monitoring of contract performance, and the management of contract compliance will also need to be considered (Henry, 1993).

We have already established that local authorities tend to be bureaucratic and generally are slow to adapt to change. In addition the organisation culture of local authorities are somewhat entrenched (Argyris 1982). Rather than creating a vehicle for significant change within local authority leisure services I would suggest that CCT will provide an opportunity for local authorities to behave even more bureaucratically. The client now has a detailed specification to beat the contractor with. If specifications are not thorough accounting for all of the diverse range of objectives and customers served by local authority leisure providers then the quality of the service suffers.

Ultimately if staff at all levels do not internalise the change the old system and culture will just manifest itself in a new way. What we will be left is a coercive/compliance relationship between manager and managed with casualties on both sides and no appreciable improvement in service quality."

Conclusions

Local authority leisure providers have been experiencing significant change which has been externally imposed. They are now having to be even more accountable, identifying explicitly what their objectives are and how well they are met. The imposition of CCT has required organisations to focus on efficiency, the net result being a reduction in conditions and pay for staff with little evidence of service quality improvement.

The cultures of local authorities which tends to be bureaucratic and hierarchical are somewhat incongruent with the requirements of significant and rapid change. The operational implementation of change therefore is strained, with little organisational support for change and significant resistance to change from workers. The strength of culture is reinforced with the old way resurfacing within the new systems and procedures.

It seems the potential of mistrust, uncertainty and hostility is great. When this prevails communications become difficult and agreement near impossible. We are left the in coercive/compliance dynamic with all of its inherent limitations.

References

Argyris, C. (1982) *Reasoning, learning and action: Individual and organisational.* Reading, Mass.: Addison-Wesley.

Beaver, J. (1993) *The Implementation of Quality Assurance and BS5750.* BA (Hons) Leisure Studies Dissertation: Calderdale Borough Council.

Berg, PL-Olof (1979) *Emotional structures in organisations.* Stockholm School of Economics: Student Literature.

Borrett, N. (1991) Leisure *services UK. London: Macmillan.*

Burns T., and Stalker, G. N. (1971) *The management of innovation.* London: Tavistock.

Chayton S (1993) 'The bottom line', *Leisure Manager*, Vol. II, No. 4: p. 31.

Coalter, A., Long, J. and Duffield, B. (1986) *The rationale for public sector investment in leisure.* London: Sports Council/Economic and Social Research Council.

Collins, M. (1986) 'Shifting icebergs: The public, private and voluntary sectors in British sport', in A. Tomlinson (ed) *Sport in society: Policy, politics and culture* (LSA Publication No. 43). Eastbourne: Leisure Studies Association.

Gratton, C. and Taylor, P. (1985) *Sport and recreation: An economic analysis.* London: E & FN Spon.

Handy, C. B. (1985) *Understanding organisations.* Aylesbury: Penguin Books.

Henry, I. P. (1993) *The politics of leisure policy.* London: MacMillan.

ILAM (1993) Guide to good practice. Reading: Institute of Leisure and Amenity Management.

ILAM Leisure Features (1993) *Has CCT led to better quality services?.* Reading: Institute of Leisure and Amenity Management.

Mastonbroek, W. (1989) *Negotiate.* Oxford: Blackwell.

Mounzelis, N. P. (1985) *Organisation and bureaucracy, An analysis of modern theories.* London: Routledge and Kegan Paul.

PSPU (Public Services Privatisation Unit) (1992) 'CCT: The story so far', *Leisure Management*, Vol.12, No. 3: p. 21.

Quinn, J. B. (1980) *Strategies for change, logical incrementation 1981*. New York: Irwin.

Torkildsen, G. (1983) (2nd. ed.) *Leisure and recreation management*. London: E & FN Spon.

The Emerging New World of Leisure Quality: Does it matter and can it be measured?

Mike Stabler
University of Reading, UK

The importance of quality

The long-term trends of rising incomes, more non-working time, and the advent of what might be termed a recreational and sporting culture, have engendered higher expectations by consumers regarding the quality of leisure products, services and experiences. On the supply side, a fiercer competitive environment, domestically and internationally, often arising from over-capacity, particularly in the tourist industry, has led to organisational and market structural changes and technical advances in providing leisure accommodation, facilities, goods and travel. The investment in more, and more various, leisure opportunities has anticipated the desire for higher quality and reinforced consumer expectations. Moreover, these expectations have spilled over into public sector provision as compulsory competitive tendering (CCT) has demonstrated in acknowledging quality as an element in contractual arrangements.

A key feature of the supply trends is that in many instances quality is often of greater importance than price. In effect there is non-price competition based on quality differences which holds implications for the marketing and management of leisure for both commercial and non-commercial providers.

The multi-dimensionality of quality

The consideration of quality has mostly occurred in a practical context for specific purposes, and has generally been fragmented. This has given rise to a proliferation and somewhat confusing array of terms reflecting the attention now being devoted to the concept, for example: quality; assessment; assurance; commitment; control; improvement; management; maximisation;

optimisation; standards; systems; total. Of these some are of fundamental importance and underpin the more fashionable terms currently being coined. The term quality control is the longest standing and best understood, being of particular significance in manufacturing, where targets are set on the proportion of output of goods which should meet specified standards both in manufacture and subsequently when used. Quality assurance is a more recent term, becoming familiar in the UK as a result of Compulsory Competitive Tendering (CCT) in the provision of public services in which a client/agent relationship exists whereby the latter contractually undertakes to supply facilities and/or services to the former of a given standard. Quality management is essentially concerned with the process of delivering quality, i.e. how to set up, maintain and monitor a system for providing goods or services of a predetermined and consistent standard. The terms maximum and optimum quality are largely economic in origin, reflecting the opportunity cost of attaining specified goals. Maximum quality is where the total benefits associated with it are maximised irrespective of costs, whereas optimum quality is attained where marginal benefits equal marginal costs. However, the term of most significance is quality assessment or measurement because, unless appropriate methods can be devised and agreed upon, no other objectives concerning quality can be achieved.

Remarkably, most studies have investigated aspects of quality without attempting to define it. Many duck the issue by stating that it can be recognised once seen or experienced, thus inferring that it is possible to discuss quality improvement, standards and systems without knowing what quality *is*.

Defining quality

It is argued that the quality of products and services is not easily defined as each individual has a different perception of what it is: therefore, the concept is too subjective to be amenable to a precise definition. It is certainly a multidimensional phenomenon from a perceptual as well as a practical viewpoint. Perceptually, for example, quality can be equated with luxury for some customers, for others with the range of facilities and services available, and for yet others with the competence and attentiveness of staff. Considered in its practical sense it may be concerned with the consistency, reliability and specification of a product or service, or it might embrace grading or again the nature and range of facilities and services provided. Clearly many of these dimensions are interrelated and not easily individually identified.

The British Standard, BS5750, which has gained widespread recognition and formed the basis of both European regulations and international guidelines for the delivery of quality (Pearce, 1992) suggests three definitions which can facilitate its objective assessment. In a comparative sense, it states that products/services should be ranked relative to each other or an agreed standard. Quantitatively, as in production processes, quality should fall below a given standard in only a specified number of cases, such as once in a thousand. The products/services should be fit for the purpose of satisfying a given customer need.

The focus of the paper

The main purpose of the writer's research into quality has been to derive objective methods of assessing it. To an extent it parallels the aim of BS5750 to secure the adoption of common quality delivery systems, but applied solely to leisure provision.

In this paper the notion that objective measures of quality cannot be realised is challenged. Initially, however, it is necessary to suggest an acceptable analytical framework which might enable a working definition of quality to be identified and an agreed method for its assessment derived. Currently there is neither an established nor common theoretical foundation for measuring quality, approaches tending to depend on the requirements of each study. With the aim of assessing performance, most progress in deriving measures of quality has been made in the fields of education (Sizer, 1980) and health (Feldstein, 1979), although some work on the hospitality industry has been conducted (for example, Haywood, 1983). Reflecting long-standing theoretical and empirical issues regarding both consumer behaviour and production, economists have recently paid greater attention to the issue of quality. An essentially economic stance is taken here as it holds out the promise of contributing to the resolution of the problems raised. However, this does not imply that the examination of quality will be abstract and theoretical. The objective of this paper is to suggest a way forward by exploring means by which quality may be categorised and measured, with the specific aim of facilitating its assessment by practitioners, and to indicate to the leisure industry the importance of doing so. The measurement of quality is illustrated by examples from leisure facilities, mostly from the field of tourism.

Towards a theoretical framework for assessing quality

To indicate how demand and supply theory can contribute to deriving an analytical framework for assessing quality, a brief review and evaluation of developments relevant to it within economics is undertaken. Then a framework reflecting an economic viewpoint is related to those emanating from elsewhere. Subsequently it is shown that an economic approach to quality measurement is helpful in a practical context.

Traditionally, the analysis of both consumer behaviour and supply in economics has been concerned with quantity rather than quality. However, over the last 20 years, that it has been more closely studied is partly a manifestation of the shift in the theoretical ground within the discipline.

Issues hitherto unresolved in consumer behaviour theory, such as explanations of tastes and preferences and changes in them, the inclusion of new goods into behavioural models, consumer actions in the face of uncertainty and the lack of information and the existence of widely varying prices for ostensibly the same good are now being addressed (Roth, 1987). It is increasingly being recognised that these issues relating to consumers' perceptions of product, very often reflect quality differences. The result has been the introduction of greater flexibility and subtlety in modelling consumer behaviour which, together with debate on the approaches which should be adopted, offer pointers as to how to define quality and assess it.

A key development in economics was the reconsideration of the basic utility theory by Lancaster (1971). The essence of his concept of demand theory is that certain products such as houses, cars and holidays consist of bundles of characteristics. This permits the estimation of price differences which arise from variations in the combination of characteristics, or perhaps more correctly explains why the prices of similar products are different.

Applied to natural and built leisure resources, the approach raises the possibility of quantifying variations in the characteristics which occur, such as facilities, activities, services, the size of the establishment, location etc. By standardising for price, differences in these characteristics can be identified to assess quality variations. The Lancaster approach to demand has been developed into what is now known as the hedonic pricing method (Rosen, 1974) which has been used to evaluate amenity resources (Garrod and Willis, 1991a, 1991b; Michaels and Smith, 1990). The method suggests that price differences are a tangible manifestation of quality differences, which with reservations will be posited below in considering its application to evaluating leisure facilities.

Another consideration which economics can make to assessing quality is its categorisation of goods. A simple system is the distinction between necessities and luxuries which can be determined by reference to the price and/or income elasticity of demand, i.e. the responsiveness of quantity demanded to changes in price or income. Necessities (which can be equated with lower or standard quality) generally have a low price/income elasticity which means that demand is not very responsive to price/income changes. Luxuries (higher quality goods) on the other hand are much more responsive to such changes. In economic terms, they have high elasticities.

However, consumers lack knowledge of many kinds of goods or are uncertain of their suitability and performance. Irrespective of whether they are necessities or luxuries, a more useful categorisation is to distinguish between *inspection* goods, generally those bought regularly with which consumers are familiar, can examine and evaluate prior to purchase, *experience* goods, which can only be assessed after purchase and use and *credence* goods, which it may be possible to examine but which it is not possible to adequately evaluate however long the experience of them. Examples in the leisure field of these three categories are, respectively, most sports clothing and equipment, a holiday at a destination new to the tourist, and the health benefits of a course at a fitness club or spa. The value of these categories is that not only do they exemplify many leisure products, particularly the last two, but the means by which consumers can and do evaluate them offers some insight into how their quality can be assessed.

Where consumers lack knowledge they can adopt strategies either to improve it themselves before purchase or rely on others' assessment of the product. This may be in the form of evidence provided by past purchasers. Promotional material produced by the seller or the brand name may also be an indicator. For example, many sports equipment suppliers such as Dunlop, Head, Reebok and Slazenger are acknowledged as providing products of a consistent and reliable quality. In the travel and tourism field, Quantas (carrier), Cooks (travel agency and services), Saga (tour operator) and Forte (accommodation) are reputable names. The opinions of experts on certain products or services and assessments by 'watchdog organisations', such as the Consumers' Association in the UK, may be other means of gaining information.

Developments in the theory of consumer demand increasingly acknowledge that perceptions of a product or service are as important as what is purchased. In particular, economic psychology suggests, notwithstanding the lack of differentiation of goods and services by any objective means, that if consumers perceive differences including quality, then they actually exist. This highlights the necessity of taking cognisance of perceptions and attitudes as determining preferences and tastes. In short information must be obtained from consumers themselves rather than merely observing the choices they make, thus indicating the need for social surveys. This approach is particularly important where new goods and services are introduced. However, it is of even more significance in evaluating non-priced public goods, for example open access natural amenity resources which are not traded in the market. In order to make decisions on allocating such goods on a like-for-like basis with market priced resources, it is essential to ascertain consumers' willingness to pay for them. In the case of unique resources the community may attach high prices to them, reflecting option and existence values over and above willingness to pay to use them.

The contingent valuation method (CVM) is a recently developed technique, which through direct questioning, attempts to ascertain the value consumers' place on non-traded goods and services. It has been used widely in studies concerning conservation, recreation, and pollution issues. It appears to be suitable as a technique for assessing quality which possesses similar intangible characteristics.

The economic analysis of supply acknowledges that technical change in the production of goods and services is akin to improving the quality of inputs employed. It has proved difficult to incorporate such improvements into production theory because it appears to have a number of effects which are not easily identified. In economic growth theory a technical improvement is usually seen as a means of increasing output with unchanged quantities of inputs of labour, capital or land. The transmission of technical change is designated as 'disembodied', i.e. not specified, in crude models. In more sophisticated approaches the transmission is 'embodied' in the stock of capital which results in the production process being classified as either capital or labour saving or neutral (not changing the capital/labour ratio).

Growth theory has not progressed much beyond this classification stage, so that its contribution to explaining improvements in the quality from the supply side is limited. Nevertheless, it does indicate that improvements in productivity arising from technical change is not costless and cannot take place unless it is embodied in new capital. This suggests that analysis of the capital inputs over time in the leisure industry is necessary to establish changes in its quality. Moreover, it infers that the employment of higher quality inputs, and consequently an improvement in production methods, enhances the quality of the product. For instance, not only can quality control be enhanced but the product can be of a higher specification to satisfy customers' needs. The classification of technical change also provides a framework which to examine the labour and management inputs in the same way as capital. Thus, an improvement in the management input can be related to what is known in economics as 'X efficiency', the term coined by Liebenstein (1966) and applied to the manager-worker relationship. This kind of efficiency is a function of weakened competitive pressures where there is a degree of market power exercised by an organisation.

Analysis of market competitive conditions and possible non commercial intervention, (to which oblique reference has already been made concerning branding and reputation) is another area where economics can contribute to assessing quality. In pursuit of their objectives suppliers attempt to exploit perceived differences in goods and services where they have some control over the market. The economic analysis of monopoly, particularly where it is possible to discriminate between different groups of consumers, and oligopoly throws up a number of instances which reflect quality differences.

For example, product differentiation, market segmentation and share and niche marketing are all features of actions by suppliers to promote sales of their own products. The impact of such actions on price depends on how suppliers see it as influencing demand.

Any consideration of quality observed in the market must begin with its association with price. The old aphorism 'one gets what one pays for' suggests a positive relationship. Empirical evidence (see for example Hjorth-Anderson, 1981) confirms this relationship, but it is somewhat weak. No one would deny that a five-star hotel provides better quality than a guest house, but for a holiday costing twice as much as another similar one it cannot be supposed that the first offers twice the quality. Two observations can be made with respect to the two examples given. In the first concerning accommodation, information on the relative size of rooms, range of facilities and services, i.e. the specification of the product, helps in ranking the quality of hotel and guest house accommodation. In the second example regarding holidays, the price differential may reflect not only quality but also the level of demand or scarcity of supply or the relative prices of complementary and substitute products.

It is often possible for a monopolist with spare capacity to discriminate on price by segmenting the market temporally, for example tour operators selling cheap off-season holidays in winter to retired people but charging what the market will bear when there is likely to be excess demand in the summer months. However, there are numerous leisure examples which illustrate price discrimination which reflects quality differences, for instance carriers, such as airlines, have various classes of fares — first, business, economy or tourist. A factor in the ability of suppliers to do this is the distribution of income, a principal determinant of willingness to pay.

While, with certain reservations, different prices for essentially the same product signify differences in quality, non-price product differentiation is a stronger indicator. The main objective of differentiation is to distinguish one firm's product from another's in order to maintain or increase market share. In some cases, a company may endeavour to serve different segments of a market by further differentiating its own product. Differentiation is reinforced by a brand name, logo, trademark, packaging, labelling etc. to give individual businesses a degree of control over their respective markets. As a differentiated product can be readily identified, it tends by reputation to give consumers greater certainty and confidence to buy. This is of particular importance where they do not have the requisite knowledge or the search costs to gain it are too high.

Examples in the leisure field of differentiation by branding have already been given but in many instances, especially in the hospitality and tour operator sectors, this is not always possible because the product is an experience good. Moreover, where there are health and safety considerations or financial risks in what is a largely fragmented industry, intervention may be necessary to protect consumers or to set quality standards. Legislation concerning the storage, handling and preparation of food, fire regulations, and bonding schemes to safeguard holiday deposits and prepayments are examples of such intervention. Where no legislation exists, an industry may voluntarily institute its own system of standards, perhaps accompanied by grading. The purpose of voluntary schemes is to maintain or enhance an industry's reputation and to increase revenues and profits.

This illustrative examination of how quality might be discerned in the operation of the market suggests a number of possible dimensions along which it might be measured. Why suppliers differentiate their products by price or non price means is the main focus of economic analysis, but how this is done offers much information on the characteristics of products which reflect quality differences. The descriptions and specification of goods to effect differentiation is of value here. This idea is pursued below in considering how the concepts can be made operational.

Making economic concepts operational

From the foregoing review of a number of economic concepts and methods of analysis, it is possible to indicate how the discipline can contribute to identifying and measuring quality in an operational/practical way. Reflecting the discussion in the previous section, to give structure and focus to the task of deriving a quality assessment method, it is instructive to maintain the economic taxonomy of:

- demand factors
- market indicators
- supply measures: input
output

An examination of quality assessment entirely within each of these frameworks cannot be strictly adhered to as there is a degree of overlap between them. For example, hedonic pricing has been viewed as part of demand theory but can also be considered as both a market indicator and supply measure as it is concerned with the characteristics of products. In the leisure field primary (natural) and secondary (human-made) resources, such as buildings, equipment, and staff are outputs as well as inputs, as they represent the products and services which users experience or consume.

The value of the economic approach is that it extends the analytical framework, making it more holistic than the emphasis on supply measures prevalent in most empirically based studies. For instance, in assessing the quality of publicly provided services such as education and health, which has drawn on techniques used in measuring the performance of organisations, most attention is concentrated on the process (inputs) and structure of supply, particularly where it is difficult to measure the outcome (output). This is exemplified by research referred to earlier by Sizer (1980) on education and Feldstein (1979) on health. In the leisure sphere, most effort has been directed at quality assurance, control and management so that understandably studies of these aspects are supply based.

A recent review of quality management in the tourism and hospitality industry by Gilbert and Joshi (1992) epitomises these approaches. In addition to quality they identify the range of services, price, uniqueness and ease of availability as ways in which a leisure supplier can exploit a differentiated competitive position. Gilbert & Joshi's consideration of the conceptual foundations of quality management is very much set in what they term the technical and functional process, meaning respectively what is delivered and how. However, to be fair to these authors in their appraisal of the work of others, they relate the management of service quality to consumer perceptions and satisfactions.

As well as widening the analytical framework to embrace the consumer in addition to the market and supply side, the economic approach implies that no single method of assessment is adequate. This is a reflection not only of the multidimensional nature of quality and of leisure as a product or service, but also of the information problems compounded by the shortcomings of the available methods of analysis. Moreover, the *purpose* of the exercise will tend to determine the choice of method. For example, if the objective of the assessment is to decide on the closure of a number of a company's hotels to cut costs, then the study would tend to concentrate on the inputs, whereas if the purpose is to consider a firm's competitive position in the holiday village market, the emphasis would be on demand and the market.

To illustrate how the relevant elements of economic demand, market and supply theory can be made operational, a hypothetical example of the assessment of a large-scale leisure resort is examined. These kinds of leisure developments normally embody a wide range of facilities and services such as serviced and self-catering accommodation, restaurant, bar, shops, swimming pool, gymnasium, health and fitness rooms, outdoor sports and recreational activities and very often extensive gardens and grounds. Thus it is possible to demonstrate the variety of approaches necessary to assess their quality. To facilitate this **Figure 1** (p.259), which has no pretension to being a model, presents a flow chart of a suggested sequence for assessing quality; it also includes some feasible methods which could be adopted. **Figure 2** (pp. 262-263) complements Figure 1 by setting out in edited form the inputs/outputs of a large leisure resort likely to be amenable to quality measurement. It indicates the components of the most appropriate methods identified in Figure 1 in an empirical context.

The left side of Figure 1, which traces the stages of quality assessment, suggests what might be accomplished in a practical context, virtually as an internal company exercise. The right side shows at what stage in the sequence of the assessment exercise it can be more intellectually based by indicating the methods which might be appropriate. Clearly the framework allows for feed-back to earlier stages and in and out of the theoretical approaches as necessary.

After identifying the purpose and objectives (Stage 1) and delineating the scope and framework of the investigation, in Stage 2, where the information can be collated as far as is possible in categories reflecting consumer, market and supply aspects held internally, the assessment should then consider the secondary data available (Stage 3). This is an important stage on two counts. Accumulated comparable evidence may be sufficient to carry out an assessment in circumstances where there are close parallels to be found in types of facility or constituent parts. For example, though there may be quality variations, holiday centres, holiday villages and timeshare are very similar in their type and range of provision. The self-catering elements of these may well, where quality measurement methods have been set up, be suitable as a framework for assessing chalet or caravan parks. Likewise, methods adopted for leisure centres could be applied to the same facilities incorporated in holiday provision. In a more theoretical approach the secondary data collection would be embodied in a systematic literature search which would include a review of methods. In the light of previous studies, Stage 4 would involve a revision in the scope and analytical framework of the investigation. The literature search will also tend to determine the necessity for and form of the primary data collection (Stage 5). In almost all cases, except the most simple, it will be found that some primary data will be required, if only within an organisation. To avoid errors and bias, whether a practical or more academic study is contemplated, the data collection methods should be carefully defined. The elements of these methods are indicated at Stage 5 in the right hand column of Figure 1. The procedures are widely known in the social sciences and will not be considered in detail here.

Stage 6, as is shown in Figure 1, represents the heart of quality assessment. In practice, in the leisure industry, for the reasons outlined earlier, it is likely to be difficult to distinguish consumer behaviour/demand, market and supply determinants as clearly as economic theory would dictate.

Since the ultimate aim of leisure provision is to meet consumers' requirements, the product or service should be both fit for the purpose and should meet defined standards. What those standards are will vary for different consumers. For example, perceptions of and expectations regarding excellence, perhaps in the sense of comfort and luxury, will depend on socio-

Figure 1: A suggested sequence for the quality assessment of leisure provision

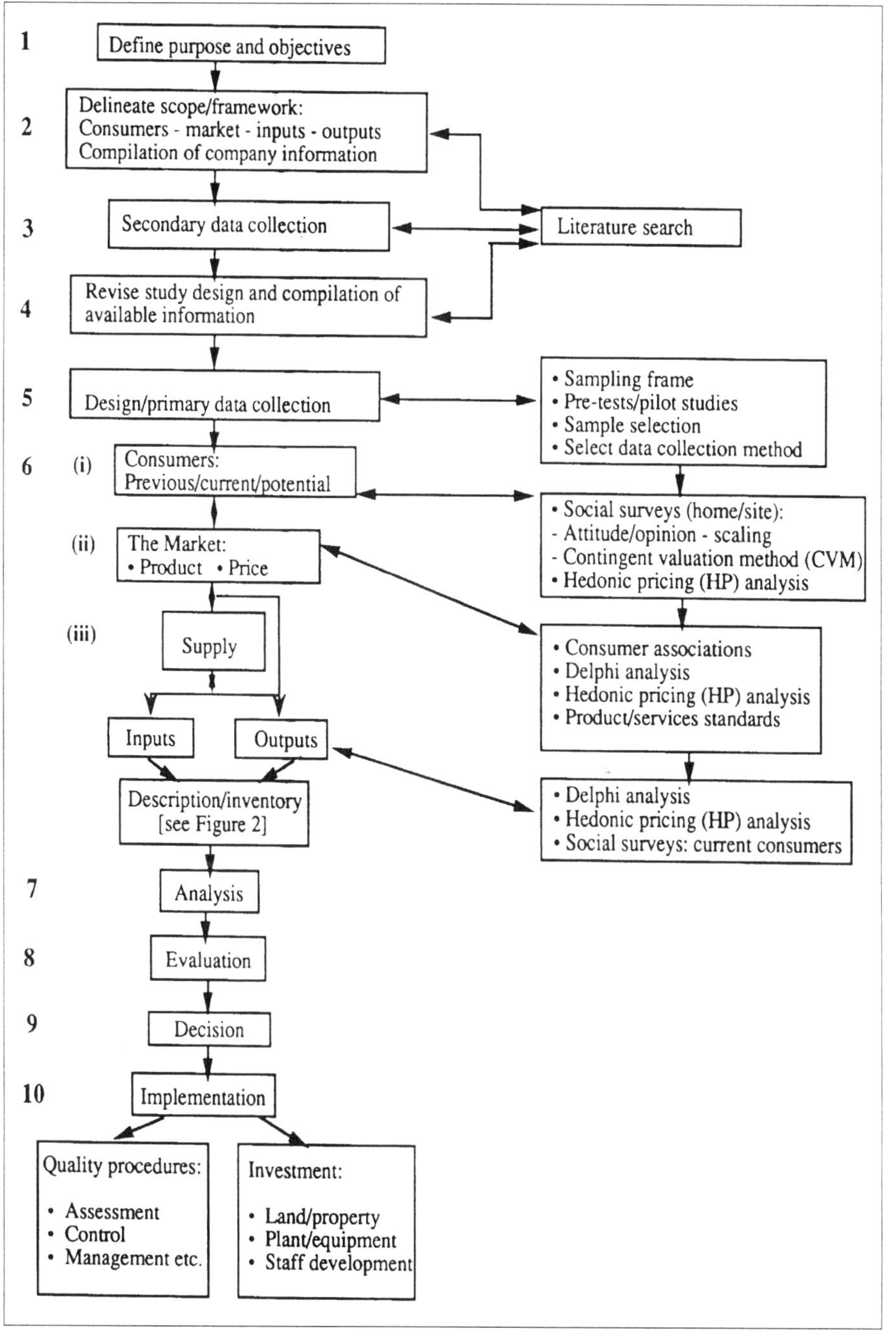

economic characteristics. Therefore, it is imperative that the assessment of quality should focus initially on consumer preferences, tastes, attitudes and behaviour at a disaggregative level on a cross-sectional basis. Hence Stage 6 (i) is headed by the focus on eliciting information on or from consumers.

Many organisations collect information on consumers' behaviour and attitudes, especially users of facilities, as a matter of routine, but attempts to measure quality are virtually unknown, either at a practical or theoretical level. The discussion earlier in the paper has adequately outlined the problems and solutions. At this point, therefore, attention will be directed at filling out the detail of possible methods.

Given the intangible nature of quality, which is not a variable in its own right but is 'attached' to various factors determining behaviour and choice, two lines of approach to measuring it are seen as capable of being developed. Understandably the thrust of development will come theoretically via deriving methods, which may incorporate applications of those employed for other purposes.

The first approach, which has been widely adopted by market researchers, is the social survey to ascertain attitudes and opinions and the strength with which they are held. In a recent review (East, 1990), concentrating on changing consumer demand, the state of the art has been summarised . The basis for assessing quality could be initiated through a ranking of products and services rather than attempting to measure it directly on a scale of, say, 10 as excellent and 1 as very poor, although there is no reason why this direct approach should not be attempted. Traditional scaling techniques, such as the established ones by Lickert and Thurstone, suggest themselves as appropriate.

The second approach, in which two related techniques are considered fruitful, conforms more closely to economic theory where price is given prominence. The techniques differ in their emphasis in that the first, the contingent valuation method (CVM), like attitudinal studies involves surveys to question consumers directly on their willingness to pay, while the other, hedonic pricing (HP), directs attention at the product and does not require consumer surveys to identify the characteristics of products which are included in the analysis. This choice is normally made by the researcher in which, on an iterative basis, variables may be added or removed from the regression equation.

The CVM approach, as indicated earlier, has been used in estimating people's willingness to pay for non-traded goods. It is easy to see the relevance of the method by inspecting Figure 2. Many items listed contribute to the overall quality of the resort but are not owned by the company operating it. For example, the site evaluation concerning physical features includes what are in effect public goods if the community at large, which embraces those staying at the resort, cannot be excluded from gaining access. The CVM technique, through both home and site surveys, asks consumers for their willingness to pay for goods such as a landscape of high scenic value, an equable climate, water courses, lakes, nature reserves etc. It is possible to conceive of different prices (willingness to pay) emerging for these goods which reflect quality variations, if standardised for the socio-economic characteristics of the respondents, especially their income. The technique is currently being developed and is continually evolving ways of ensuring that it is unbiased and valid (Garrod and Willis, 1990).

In some senses the CVM method should be viewed as being embodied in the HP approach. It can be argued that many of the goods listed in Figure 2, including the public goods, carry implicit prices because the overall payment is likely to reflect variations in their quality. This is the essence of HP, for it posits that a good or service consists of a number of attributes which cannot be directly priced but which contribute to the overall price. For instance, two identical resorts in terms of accommodation, facilities, services, etc., may have different charges because one is in an outstandingly beautiful area while the other is near a large urban conurbation. Thus it can be posited that consumers will be willing to pay more for a holiday where the accommodation is larger and more luxurious, there is a wide range of and easy access to required services, the site is well located with good views, tree cover, water frontage, etc., and there is both a high ratio to customer and well trained staff.

Taking HP further, it is a means whereby the implicit prices of individual attributes can be identified. Thus, for example, a holidaymaker may be willing to pay an additional sum for a second bathroom in a specific holiday accommodation. An interesting feature of HP, however, is that it may be possible to predict the overall price of a holiday as accurately with as few as 10 or so variables (individual attributes) instead of including exhaustively all variables, say 50 or more. This has been demonstrated in studying house prices from estate agent's particulars, an area of research where HP has been widely used.

Although the method has been applied to assigning values to amenity resources, as an aid to making allocation decisions, to which reference was made earlier (Garrod and Willis, 1991a, b) it has not been employed in the assessment of quality as suggested here. It does suffer from technical problems, a key one being the assumption of equilibrium in the market (hardly a feature of the leisure field) which will not be investigated. However it does appear to be an appropriate technique for considering quality and so warrants further investigation.

Inspection of Figure 1 reveals that at Stage 6 HP analysis in the right-hand column appears three times — against consumers, the market and

Figure 2 Leisure Resort: Example of a physical description/inventory

Brief description of regional location: e.g. coastal, lowland, upland, urban		
Site evaluation:	**Physical**	**Aesthetic**
	Primary resources Size (hectares); Land form/relief; Land use; Climate; Geology/soil; Vegetation; Ecological/wild life habitat; Water courses/lakes Secondary resources Site infrastructure Heritage artifacts **Built environment*** **Facilities****	Scale Diversity Detractors Views in/out Horizons/skylines
Built environment* (i) exterior		
General description	***Buildings***	
	Service	***Accommodation***
Built area **Setting** **Design/style**	Function: reception recreational storage etc.	Style: chalet/cottage/apart't Design; Materials; Spacing between units; Patio/garden; Parking/garage etc
Built environment* (ii) interior		
Service areas		***Accommodation***
Physical:	• Area • Decoration • Fixtures and fittings • Furniture • Toilets etc. • Layout • Flooring • Lighting • Heating	***Physical*** • Area – total; each room (incl. service areas) • Number and function of rooms • Layout (inc. no of floors) • Services: heating, double glazing, etc. • Decoration; flooring; fixtures and fittings, • Furniture, lighting
Overall evaluation:	***Specification of rooms:***	
*** Cleanliness**	• Bedrooms: twin/double; dressing table; bedside tables; easy chairs; en suite; linen etc.	

Figure 1 (cont.)

*** Atmosphere** *** Ambience** *** Service**	• Bathrooms:	bath; jacuzzi; shower; bidet; heater rails; hairdryer.
	• Living:	open fire; TV (teletext; video; (note manufacturer); books; games; cocktail cabinet/bar etc.;
	• Kitchen:	hob/cooker/grill; microwave; refrigerator; freezer; dishwasher; food mixer; utensils etc.
	• Services:	drying cabinets; sauna/solarium; washing machine; tumble drier; iron and board etc.
	• Other:	patio; garden area; barbeque; garden chairs/tables/parasol; games equipment etc.
	• Overall:	• Ambience; • Noise; • Service.
Facilities:**		
• Shops/services:	food; off licence; pharmacist; gifts; sports equipment; launderette; hairdressing; health and beauty; banking; safe deposit; postbox; fax/telex/photocopying; travel; chapel; medical centre; creche/nursery/play area; baby sitting; security; insurance; car hire; equipment hire etc..	
• Indoor:	*leisure:*	swimming pool; toddlers pool; jacuzzi; sauna; solarium; steam bath; fitness; weight training, gym etc.
	sport:	badminton; squash; table tennis; billiards/snooker/pool; ten pin bowling; roller/ice skating; basket ball; tennis etc.
• Outdoor:	*leisure:*	childrens pool; putting; crazy golf; croquet; petanque; sailing; sub aqua; pedalos; horse riding; pony trekking; fishing; jogging; cycling; walking; nature trail etc..
	sport:	football, golf, sailing, tennis etc.
• Entertainment:	discos; show/cabaret; cinema;	
• Catering:	snack bar; restaurant; pizzeria; barbeque; bar; pool bar; wine bar etc.	
• Adjacent to site:	i.e. off site but concessions etc., e.g. fishing; golf; marina; shooting	
• Staffing:	Appearance; courtesy; service efficiency; training etc..	
• Prices:	Clarity of quoted prices, service charges, taxes, surcharges, additional service charges, management fees; insurance; meals; drinks; hire etc.	
• Service:	Reservations; reception and checkout; requests; complaints etc.	
• Environmental impact auditing/monitoring:	use of materials and energy; extent of recycling	

supply respectively. This reflects both how HP has developed and its role in the consumer-demand-price-product/output-input continuum. The technique has grown from being an innovation in consumer behaviour theory to explaining prices in certain markets, with the attention being on the characteristics of the product without reference to consumers. In the leisure field, as already argued, the product/output and input are essentially the same, so that HP can be viewed as applying to supply also.

The earlier examination of the theoretical underpinnings of assessment in the market showed that price and the characteristics of the product (hence the contribution of HP) gave some indication of quality. What emerged was that there is a weak relationship between price and quality and that non-price competition via product differentiation often reflected variations in quality. A crucial factor in whether consumers could identify such variations was the extent of the knowledge and the information available to them. Economics has no clear theoretical approach to assessing quality from the supply side at Stage 6(ii) in Figure 1; it can only offer partial explanations of the strategies producers adopt in different competitive situations or to attain given objectives. However, in conjunction with other approaches it can contribute to making progress in deriving methods of assessment. The Delphi technique is one such approach.

The Delphi technique is best known for making forecasts of events when certain data is unavailable, originating in the 1950s (Dalkley and Helmer, 1963) in the United States. A panel of experts selected by the researcher estimate the likely future situation with respect to a specific topic such as recreation in a number of rounds of questionnaires, where the results of each previous round are made available to each panellist for reconsideration, until consensus is reached. A panel can consist of up to 50 experts but in a study of likely leisure environments in the future Shafer, Moeller and Getty (1974) used over 900.

The approach seems eminently suitable, from the supply side, to complement consumers' assessments of quality. Rather than considering future scenarios, the experts can make assessments of the product/outputs based on inspection of facilities and their experience of them. However, in doing this the exercise should be conducted individually by each expert in order to avoid conferring and being subject to peer pressure to reach consensus. The process is little different in practice from inspection, acting on behalf of different organisations representing consumer interests, who anonymously evaluate products, facilities and services. Well known examples in the UK are the grading systems compiled by the tourist boards and the motoring organisations for hotels and other forms of holiday accommodation. Additional notable examples are guides to good restaurant food and the Consumers' Association's assessments of a wide variety of products and services. Even industries set and endeavour to enforce standards, usually because it is in their own interests to do so, for instance the Association of British Travel Agents (ABTA) bonding scheme which is aimed at safeguarding tourists' advance payments and ensuring a reserved holiday is secure should a holiday trader fail. Where such voluntary schemes do not, or cannot operate the government may legislate to set and maintain specified minimum standards, referred to earlier in the paper.

The Delphi technique, therefore, is a rather more independant and theoretical approach to quality assessment which could not only contribute to the development of methods by being incorporated into economic consumer and production theory, but could be applied more universally and systematically using an agreed formula, in the leisure field. The uniform approach which should emerge could be adopted by the many organisations which currently give a fragmented coverage of quality assessment and use methods tending to reflect their own, often vested, interests.

Consideration of the Delphi technique completes this review of theoretical approaches and the core stage of assessing quality. Stage 6(iii) in Figure 1 shows in the left-hand side that description/inventory approaches might be employed in a practical context, particularly if firms are constrained by limited resources; social surveys of consumers, and the Delphi technique are both expensive and protracted. Inventory methods of assessing inputs, as illustrated in Figure 2, are in accord with grading systems, such as those compiled by the Automobile Association which ranges from listing basic accommodation (no stars) to a five star rating. These are concerned as much with the number and range of facilities as their standard and constitute one dimension of quality. In Figure 2 the checklist of accommodation suggests that the degree of luxury can be ascertained by reference to the specification of equipment. For example, under living rooms, the make, model and range of electrical appliances supplied would indicate the standard.

The remaining stages of the quality assessment procedure presented in Figure 1 are concerned with analysis, evaluation, decision and implementation respectively and clearly relate primarily to practical aspects. Accordingly, since they are not central to the theoretical discussion of this paper, and will not be considered further.

Conclusions

The central aim of this paper has been to raise the awareness of quality and its assessment as an important issue in the leisure sphere, by considering both its theoretical and practical aspects. An attempt has been made to construct an operational framework for measuring quality which links theoretical concepts and methods to its empirical context.

This link should not be considered a one-way relationship from theory to practice but an interactive process. Although economic demand theory and market and supply analysis offer insights into definitions of and the assessment of quality, practical approaches, such as product specification and grading, and methods used for other purposes, for example the Delphi technique, suggest ways in which the economic theories of consumer behaviour, production and growth could be developed to incorporate quality change.

Moreover, practitioners undertaking quality assessment should be able to do so with different degrees of sophistication depending on whether the exercise is conducted 'in house' or by engaging professional researchers. At its most basic, it is akin to an inventory or audit of the quality of inputs and outputs while carrying out surveys of users in seeking outside, perhaps expert opinions, it can be more wide-ranging and comprehensive.

For the reasons given at the outset, quality is likely to continue to be a significant issue, certainly in the UK. The adoption of the British Standards Institution's (BSI) BS5750 for quality management by leisure providers is perceived as conferring benefits, particularly in the commercial field, and certification will undoubtedly be increasingly sought. To achieve such certification requires an organisation's systems to be approved by BSI quality assurance, which also signifies compliance with European and International standards. The standard involves implementing periodic quality reviews, recording procedures and introducing systems for process control, training, auditing and corrective action. The BS 5750 scheme, for which guidelines for the hospitality industry were published in 1992, also holds implications for the leisure provision in the public sector under Compulsory Competitive Tendering. Providers will need to introduce quality management schemes in order to conform with local authority contracts which specifically refer to quality. Currently, however, this conformation has not been defined in a way which makes it susceptible to measurement, perhaps a reflection of the state of the art.

Irrespective of the marketing advantages of implementing a recognised standard or meeting contractual obligations, attention to quality and its assessment is of value in other directions. In the present fiercely competitive climate, especially in tourism, the long-run viability of entities may depend on their setting and on maintaining high quality standards. The very action of adopting an ethos of delivering quality forces a leisure organisation to review a host of operational factors such as its strategies, objectives, marketing, management, recruitment and training, purchase policies, maintenance programmes and control mechanisms.

Undertaking an assessment, if done on a standardised basis, allows comparisons to be made with other companies which might demonstrate examples of good practice. The exercise tightens the effectiveness and efficiency of organisations, and consequently quality assessment, and its management constitutes a performance indicator. This will very likely be reflected in the prices of products and services which in a competitive market can be a crucial determinant of success. While consumers may view a higher priced product as of higher quality, they are also interested in obtaining value for money. If consumers perceive that the quality offered does not match its promotion or meet their expectations, they will consider it overpriced and buy an alternative. Finally, with the increasing recognition of the environmental impact of leisure provision, systems of environmental auditing can be conceived as part of the quality assessment process.

The assessment of quality in the leisure field is still in its infancy; therefore what can be done to speed its progress to maturity? Key issues are to reach agreement on definitions and terminologies as prerequisites for establishing a framework in which to make assessments in conjunction with common approaches on quality control and management systems. The academic investigation of the phenomenon requires more attention than has been given to it hitherto, particularly in economics, which has avoided the issue of attempting to measure it. Given the need for a customer oriented approach, a multidisciplinary effort which draws on the contributions of psychology, social psychology, sociology and statistics, as well as economics, is called for. However, the impetus for such co-operation will undoubtedly have to come from practitioners who, to meet vitally important needs, should press academic researchers to construct and refine appropriate means for assessing quality.

References

Dalkley, N. and Helmer, O. (1963) 'An experimental application of the Delphi method of the use of experts', *Management Sciences*, Vol. 9, No. 3: pp. 458-67.

East, R. (1990) *Changing consumer behaviour*. London: Cassell.

Feldstein, P. (1979) *Health care economics*. New York: Wiley.

Garrod, G. D. and Willis, K. G. (1990) *Contingent valuation techniques: A review of their unbiasedness, efficiency and consistency*. Countryside Change Initiative Working Paper 14, Department of Agriculture and Economics and Food Marketing, University of Newcastle upon Tyne.

——— (1991a) *The Hedonic Price Method and the valuation of countryside characteristics*. Countryside Change Initiative Working Paper 14, Department of Agriculture and Economics and Food Marketing, University of Newcastle upon Tyne.

——— (1991b) *The Environmental economic impact of woodland: A two stage Hedonic Price Model of the amenity value of forestry in Britain.* Countryside Change Initiative Working Paper 15, Department of Agriculture and Economics and Food Marketing, University of Newcastle upon Tyne.

Gilbert, D. C. and Joshi, I. (1992) 'Quality management and the tourism and hospitality industry', in C. P. Cooper, A. and Lockwood (eds) *Progress in tourism, recreation and hospitality management.* Vol 4., London: Belhaven, pp. 149-168.

Haywood, K. M. (1983) 'Assessing the quality of hospitality services', *International Journal of Hospitality management*, Vol. 2, No. 4: pp. 165-177.

Hjorth-Anderson, C. (1981) 'The price and quality of industrial products: some results of an empirical investigation', *Scandinavian Journal of Economics*, No. 83: pp. 372-89.

Lancaster, K. (1971) *Consumer demand: A new approach.* New York: Columbia University Press.

Liebenstein, H. (1966) 'Allocative Efficiency versus X efficiency', *American Economic Review*, Vol. 56, no. 3: pp. 392-415.

Michaels, R. G. and Smith, V. K. (1990) 'Market segmentation and valuing amenities with hedonic models: The case of hazardous waste sites', *Journal of Urban Economics*, No. 29: pp. 232-242.

Pearce, E. (1992) 'Taking quality on board: BS 5750', in C. P. Cooper, A. and Lockwood (eds) *Progress in tourism, recreation and hospitality management.* Vol. 4, London: Belhaven, pp. 195-198.

Rosen, S. (1974) 'Hedonic prices and implicit markets: Product differentiation in pure competition', *Journal of Political Economy*, No. 82, pp. 34-55.

Roth, T. P. (1987) *The present sate of consumer theory.* Lanham: University Press of America.

Shafer, E. L., Moeller, G. H. and Getty, R. E. (1974) *Future leisure environments*, Forest Research Paper NE 301, USDA Forest Experiment Station, Pennsylvania.

Sizer, J. (1980) 'Indicators in times of financial stringency, contraction and changing needs', in D. Billing (ed) *Indicators of Performance Papers presented at the fifteenth annual conference of the Society for Research into Higher Education.* London: The Society.

Putting Clothes on the Invisible Man: The Audit Commission, the Citizen's Charter and Local Authority Leisure Services*

Bob Lentell

University of North London, UK

Uncovering the Audit Commission

Why might the efforts of a body such as the Audit Commission, which neither makes leisure policy nor delivers leisure services, be of interest to leisure scholars? One may apply here Simon's concept of "bounded rationality" to leisure services management (Simon, 1947). Leisure managers are seen as attempting to function through "rule of thumb", "common-sense" rationalities within the universe given to them. The Audit Commission is one of the key players in the translation of ideology and policy into boundaries. I suggest here that the importance and interest of its work as a subject of inquiry, lies precisely in its occupying the territory between government policy imperatives, local politics, and professional management cultures. It is one of the key lenses through which the light of governmental policy initiatives towards public services is passed. Whether the pattern retains the clear (and often overly-simple) focus desired by Ministers, becomes distorted or unfocused, depends upon the exact approach adopted by the Commission. As McSweeney (1988) has pointed out, the Commission's work usually appears uncontentious, even anodyne, but the principles underlying it may be controversial, or intellectually unsatisfactory.

It is this "Audit Commission culture" which public leisure services managers experience and which engages local political cultures and the emergent "professional-managerial culture" in local authority leisure services. Perhaps leisure studies is in danger of neglecting the importance of cultural change amongst public service leisure managers in the midst of examining the sea-changes wrought by Compulsory Competitive Tendering (CCT) and other high-profile legislation.

It is difficult to fully understand the Citizen's Charter and the Commission's response to it, without also studying the background of the Commission's dealings with local government. The Commission itself (full name: the Audit Commission for Local Authorities and the National Health Service in England and Wales) was established in 1983. In addition to running the District Audit Service, which provides auditors to individual local authorities, the Commission is charged with carrying out various central studies designed to improve the economy, efficiency and effectiveness (the three "E"s) of local government.

The Commission has a third role, to examine the impact of central government policies, practices and legislation on the ability of local authorities to deliver value for money. It was this work which put it in a good position to develop the Performance Indicators (PIs) for local government services in the wake of the Citizen's Charter.

A fundamental critical analysis of the Commission has been articulated by McSweeney (1988). Here the significance of three aspects of McSweeney's case are highlighted. First, it is argued that achieving a balance between the three "E"s is a highly contentious area and cannot be presented as managerial or technical question as the Commission so often does.

> How, and on the basis of what other values, can, or should, the relative importance of each of the three "E"s be decided and evaluated? Are each of equal status? What additional criteria should be, or are, used in evaluating trade-offs between them? (McSweeney, 1988: p. 42)

As much of the literature has done, McSweeney argues that the Commission has emphasised economy and efficiency at the expense of effectiveness:

> Its neglect of effectiveness is caused not merely by the undoubted technical and political difficulties of identifying and determining the impact of some local authority outputs, but also more fundamentally as a greater focus on effectiveness could weaken the Commission's attempts to change local authorities. Influencing acceptance of reduced funding and a reduction in scale of organisations also means cutting back on purpose. Identifying unmet needs and demands would have the opposite impact. (McSweeney, 1988: p. 42)

Second, the much of the Commission's work is grounded in comparative studies. This is necessary because for many of the issues studied by the Commission, there are no generally agreed standards. The attempt to render visible the relationships between inputs and outputs through changes in the management regimen, such as establishing a small number of performance indicators or measures, is complex and difficult. Establishing universal standards for minima or maxima against indicators involves another order of difficulty. However, for several years, the Commission has doggedly pursued the institution of PI regimes, following through by suggesting that authorities performing in the "lower" quartile should move their performance towards the "upper" quartile of responses.

The criticism of this approach is that it understates the limitations of audit itself. Given the large variety of local circumstances, is it really possible to squeeze comparison into a few numeric indicators, without introducing more artefact than substance into the end result? McSweeney suggests that these systems are wide open to error and manipulation through the minutiae of local accounting practices. Whilst he may overstate the case, his polemic is refreshing to those who would wish to see the Commission exercise a little more humility about the figures it uses.

Moreover, if one does accept the validity of the figures, there is still room for contention about what they actually mean as a guide to action:

> Comparing performance will almost always indicate a distribution of results. Some local authorities will be better or worse than the mean. To conclude from such comparisons, for example, that if all local authorities were like the best there would be £x million savings (as the Commission has done) may be statistically correct but not a true indication of possible savings. Of the £492 million potential savings identified by the Commission by using comparative studies, only 16%(£80 million) are said by the Commission itself to have been achieved in four years. (McSweeney, 1988: p. 38)

The third critique of the Commission is perhaps most fundamental. The assumption is that those responsible for the management of local authorities can know the causal relationship between their actions and the consequences of those actions, both ex post and ex ante. In practice, however, local authorities work in situations of rapid change and unpredictability. We have already observed that this is particularly true in the case of leisure services.

> The links between organisational arrangements and organisational outcomes which local authority auditors must now evaluate, are

> far less direct, predictable and understood than the Commission's evaluation criteria presume. (McSweeney,1988: p: p32)

In these situations the Commission's insistence on finding straight-forward, planned relationships looks less like good management and more like a mechanistic organisational model. Management literature overwhelmingly concludes that mechanistic models are unsuitable for rapidly changing organisational environments, or for fostering innovative culture. Since the popularisation of such work by Kanter (1983), Peters and Waterman (1982) and Peters (1987) many organisations seeking to change have become aware of the characteristics of successful organisations. This would imply a far looser relationship between organisational goals, inputs, and results than the Commission contemplates.

The invisible man

The above issues come to the fore when analysing local authority leisure services. The manifestations of such services are particularly prominent in the forms of parks and built leisure provision. However, the rationales for providing through the public sector, the level of provision that constitutes a citizenship right, and the level of contribution citizens should be expected to make for it through taxation, fees or charges, are all rather hard to define or agree. In this sense leisure services have been the "invisible man" of local authorities. The contract between citizen and the local state in respect of leisure has been unclear. The relationships involved in leisure services need to become more visible. It is unsurprising therefore, that hitherto the Commission's work in this area has been generally welcomed by local authority associations and by leisure management professionals.

The Commission took the momentum of the Financial Management Initiative into a series of Value for Money studies on leisure services (Audit Commission, 1989, 1990, 1991a, 1991b). The Commission adopted a simple systems model whereby measures of input (mainly financial) were linked to measures of output, and, at least in principle to outcomes (the actual impact of output upon the locality). Using this approach the Commission was able to suggest a suite of PIs addressed to service economy, efficiency or effectiveness, from which authorities could choose according to their own pattern of leisure service objectives. However, it is doubtful that this work has had the impact the Commission would wish for, as research indicates that many authorities have yet to develop social policy objectives for their leisure services.

In the period of consultation about the Citizen's Charter, the local authority associations, the Sports and Arts Councils expressed the wish that

PIs be sensitive to locally determined priorities and policies. Bovaird (1992) reflected these concerns, producing recommendations for 22 "compulsory" PIs, and a further developmental and voluntary list of PIs which could be collected by local authorities on a purely voluntary basis.

In consultation there was much disagreement about PIs from organisations and individuals. In fact, the eight PIs eventually adopted for leisure services (not including libraries as they have their own set) were more basic than much of what was mooted in the consultation phase. They are listed below (**Table 1**) with the "Citizen's Question" each is designed to answer.

Table 1: Citizen's Charter Performance Indicators for Leisure and Recreation

How many people visit swimming pools and sports halls? How much does this cost the Council?	
1.a.	The net expenditure per head of population on swimming pools and sports centres
b.	The number of swims
c.	The number of other visits
d.	The net cost per swim/ visit.
How many playgrounds does the Council provide?	
2.	The number of playgrounds which meet minimum standards.
How many sports pitches does the Council provide?	
3.	The number of sports pitches available to the public.
How much park land and open space does the Council provide? How much does it cost to maintain this?	
4.a.	The hectares of parks and open spaces provided or managed by the authority
b.	Annual cost of managing and maintaining parks and open spaces.

Source: Audit Commission (1993a: p. 23-24)

Three points need to be made as a result of the above discussion. First, we can see the process described above as an illustration of McSweeney's (1988) assertion that:

> The Commission is not a regulatory body in the sense of ensuring that regulees maintain a direction and meet specified criteria. Rather, it aims to change them. (McSweeney,1988: p. 40)

Second, it is very difficult to predict how information collected against the above set of indicators will impact upon local authority leisure services. Reference to the Health Service, where the Commission's writ also runs, shows how the Commission attempts to influence the agenda. Comparative studies of the performance of the different Health Authorities, for example of their purchasing arrangements, are given maximum publicity. This contributes to a perception that the key issues are waste and inefficiency rather than funding levels and organisational arrangements. Once some aspect of a public body's performance is established in the public eye it acquires a degree of independence and may return, like Frankenstein's monster, to trouble its parent (viz. — health service waiting lists).

Third, what is clear is that the Commission had considerable difficulty in applying the Citizen's Charter approach to local authority leisure services. The reasons for this are discussed below through an analysis of the Charter's principles.

The Citizen's Charter

This is not the place to add to the not inconsiderable literature on what the Citizen's Charter represents in terms of Conservative ideology and policy. However, many would agree with Oldfield (1990) that the basis of the Charter is in liberal individualism not civic republicanism.

The Charter's citizen is consumer, customer and taxpayer. The Charter's citizen has no interest in participating in the political process to create social realities; the citizen merely has an individual contract with the state. It is this individualism which leads to the emphasis on Customer Service Standards expressed in Service Charters. Because Service Charters impose duties on providers (perhaps to reimburse consumers when the Standard has not been attained), providers will choose the contents with care, and there may well be differences between such contents and the actual concerns of citizens as they express them in the polity.

A pre-requisite of a leisure provider establishing Customer Service Standards is the definition of output standards for the service. This implies a performance indicator regime, but it is likely to be one closely tailored to local conditions. The establishment of arrangements on which local Service Charters can be built does not of itself aid the Commission's task, since this aspect of the legislation requires it to establish a basis on which the performance of local authorities can be compared.

The Commission has insisted that its aim is to collate information which will be of interest to the citizen and not just to politicians, professionals and managers. Thus it has predicated its work on questions which the citizen might ask about local services, and then attempted to develop a few indicators for each service which might assist in answering the citizen's question.

Value

It is unsurprising, therefore, that one of the most prominent of the four themes within the Charter as identified by the Audit Commission, is that "services must be able to give value for money within a tax bill the nation can afford" (Prime Minister, 1991: p 4). One of the declared purposes of the Charter is to make visible the relationship between costs and benefits. Whilst the assessment of costs in the form of tax inputs to sustain a leisure service is easy, the outcomes from it are inherently difficult to define and measure.

Coalter*et al.* (1988) have pointed to the various underlying, and to some extent competing, rationales upon which public sector investment is based. These include desire to achieve improvements in the health of the populace, as well as social control, through limiting crime and disorder through diverting energies into "rational recreation". Another significant view has been of the leisure activity as a "merit good" which public provision makes more widely available than would be the case if left to market forces. This "recreational welfare" view contends with a view of "recreation as welfare" in which public leisure provision is seen as compensating for disadvantage manifest in other areas of life.

The last three of these rationales would lead one to conclude that in order to gauge the performance of the service one would need to know much more than the number of visits to leisure facilities, which appear as Charter PIs 1b and 1c. We would need to know how many visitors, who the visitors were, and whether they reflected local diversity or were the intended service recipients in terms of gender, ethnicity, class, age, residential status and so on. According to these rationales, effectiveness could not be judged without measuring equity, that is the fairness in the distribution and take up of the service.

A further flavour of the difficulties in this field can be gained by considering the long pedigree stretching from the Victorian seaside resorts to the Sheffield World Student Games, and Manchester's Commonwealth Games, of muncipalities undertaking what could be regarded as "leisure infrastructure" work. The initial dominant rationale for such investment is local economic development, in which case one would need to consider local area development indicators to see how effectively the investment had "performed". This is itself a difficult and controversial subject. However, as time passes the rationale for continued support from the local purse may change, perhaps recreational welfare becoming dominant. A humorist might remark that in future years the indoor leisure centres of the 1970s may become regarded much as we regard seaside piers today, to be maintained as part of conserving our heritage.

Even where there is agreement on the desired outcomes, relating the efforts of leisure services to changes in any indicators (health, crime, community development, quality of life, economic development) is notoriously risky. There are far too many uncontrolled variables.

Even measuring leisure service outputs is far from straightforward. An indubitably helpful indicator is the number of user visits to a leisure facility; though in itself this does not tell us how developmentally useful these visits are (i.e. how far they contribute to achieving desired outcomes). Some authorities already publish figures on a grossed output, such as numbers of users of indoor facilities, or a relation of input to grossed output (e.g. subsidy per user). The interpretation of these figures is all important, as, for instance, a high subsidy per user may be due to inefficiency, or a policy decision to subsidise low prices to users. Little has been done to produce PIs based upon user-related output in facilities where users do not pay (such as parks) owing to the cost of data collection.

The Chartered Institute of Public Finance and Accountancy (CIPFA) has for many years collated information on net inputs (subsidy) to leisure services. It relates these figures to the numbers of citizens (spend per head of population) and calculates the mean. CIPFA does not publish such information in the "league table" form favoured by the government and Audit Commission. Whether "good performance" is constituted by a high spend per head or a low one depends on your point of view.

However, given the ease of measuring inputs it is unsurprising that a disproportionate emphasis on costs appeared in both the proposal of the Audit Commission and its Scottish counterpart.

Standards

> The citizen must be told what service standards are and be able to act where service is unacceptable. (Prime Minister, 1991: p. 4.)

Unlike some other areas of local government activity, such as benefits administration, it is not possible to put forward meaningful PIs based on caseloads. It is therefore not possible to put forward a credible standard based on a minimum acceptable caseload handling criteria. Two sorts of standards are available leisure, provision standards and operational standards.

An example of a provision standard is the National Playing Fields Association standard for the area of play space per thousand population. Unfortunately, provision standards are seriously flawed as detailed by Veal

(1982). Two points are made here. First, provision standards have little meaning to the citizen as customer. Second, provision is the product of many factors including ones of past history; it is often very difficult for authorities below standard to reach the standard (e.g. as in open space provision), and certainly major capital spending might be needed so to do. So in practice provision standards do not allow the citizen to implement the principle of redress. It is unsurprising that the trend in a public leisure provision is away from the use of such standards.

Individual leisure facilities can have operational standards, perhaps the local swimming pool defining the standard pool temperature or the cleanliness of the changing rooms. But given the diversity of leisure facilities and services there are as yet no standards which could sensibly be offered up on a national basis. Comparisons between leisure facilities are fraught with difficulty since each one is different in usage pattern if not in specification.

Quality

The Charter has been presented as "a sustained programme for improving the quality of public services" ((Prime Minister, 1991: p. 4). Once credible indicators are established upon which a standard can be based, customer and management attention can be focused on those aspects of the service which fall below standard. Quality should be an aspect of indicators, or have its own dedicated indicators. Some aspects of quality are subsumed in indicators which cover all local authority services (such as handling complaints and time taken to answer the telephone). Others may need a special measurement to be made. The problem is that even collecting data on "proxy" measures of leisure services quality, such as the proportion of return visits to leisure facilities (fidelity) can be expensive, and interpretation of results is complex.

Management good practice requires that customer satisfaction surveys should be undertaken at regular intervals. Recent data collected by the Commission (Audit Commission 1993-b) suggest that a large majority of authorities have undertaken such a survey for sports and recreation within the last three years. Whilst the Commission records the proportion "satisfied" according to such work (median values 80-85%) it is not clear what significance can be attached to this comparison. In the absence of a common format for the questionnaire and its administration, the cautious instincts of leisure researchers would come to the fore.

39% of authorities had undertaken non-user surveys in the last three years (Audit Commission 1993b). The perception of leisure services from non-users is a most significant indicator both for management and citizen. But in its approach to the Charter the Commission has hitherto been reluctant to impose new data collection duties (and concomitant expense) upon local government.

Another approach might be to record the percentage of facilities that were covered by quality management systems, and this has been the subject of Commission enquiry (Audit Commission 1993b). There has been considerable discussion in the industry about this topic and a proportion of authorities (ranging from 38% of the Districts to 65% of London Boroughs) have achieved or will seek registration under British Standard 5750/ ISO 9000 (Quality Assurance) for all or some their sport and recreation facilities. However, there will not necessarily be a correlation between level of service supplied to the customer and registration under the Standard. BS 5750/ ISO 9000 is in effect a "consistency management" system, which should ensure that the customer knows what the service is, and that the providing organisation can show that it can deliver it.

Choosing as an indicator the proportion of facilities covered by local Service Charters, is a related approach. At present, the downside of such an approach is that it might encourage a proliferation of rather meaningless (to the customer) Charters, as local authorities strive to score better under the Commission's indicator regime.

Choice

The last major theme within the Charter, as identified by the Commission, is choice. "Choice, wherever possible between competing providers, is the best spur to improvement." ((Prime Minister, 1991: p. 4). Insofar as local authority leisure competes with other, perhaps less "meritorious" leisure forms, it is already competing with other "providers". In general there can be little choice available to the customer as to which local authority leisure facility to use. The opportunity costs of travelling further afield to an alternative provider's facilities become prohibitive in many cases. Choice then, is likely to become the local authority client's prerogative in choosing a contractor to provide services at the best value for money.

Public performances

The difficulties of translating the intentions of the Charter into a meaningful set of leisure service PIs highlights the folly of transplanting a simple view of performance measurement in the commercial sector into the public sector.

The period since the "Thatcher revolution" beginning in 1979 has been one in which the public sector has been contrasted, usually unfavourably, with the private sector. The former has been caricatured as unresponsive, revenue-consuming bureaucracies, whilst the latter are seen as customer-led, entrepreneurial, lean and wealth producing. Many of those in the public sector have resisted such unfavourable comparisons, but have gradually come to use paradigms which have apparently come from commerce. As Stewart and Walsh (1992: p. 511) note:

> The public service, it seems, can only retain legitimacy by changing the way that it is managed, to reflect ideas about what constitutes good management, which will typically be based on private sector ideas.

However, it is salutary to question how accurately the private sector is portrayed:

> The image presented of the private sector is seldom based on empirical observations of how this sector actually works. Rather it is taken from how introductory text books in business administration say it should work.

Olsen (1987: p. 3) is writing about the Scandinavian experience, though many will recognise the UK in the quotation. All too often, what is offered for consumption by the public sector are not sound management principles at all, but an ideological construct, managerialism, of discredited flotsam and jetsam discarded from the ship of management studies.

Performance measurement is an area full of misconceptions. Carter (1991) records that civil servants implementing the government's Financial Management Initiative were virtually unanimous that performance measurement in the private sector was different and easier. The private sector has the famous "bottom-line" — profit, and thus it is assumed that performance measurement will therefore be "a straight-forward, incontestable technical procedure". In the real world this is seldom the case; for example high profits may have been achieved at the expense of investment in research and development, or of market share which will have implications for future profits. Moreover, even a cursory reading of the financial pages of the newspapers will bring home the point that profit figures themselves often raise more questions about performance than they answer. Accountancy is more an art than a science and there is often room for dispute about the accounting practices adopted.

> To assess the meaning of profits (or of alternative key indicators such as market share or return on capital) involves forming a judgement on the performance not just of the firm in question but of its competitors, as well as strategic judgements about the long-term effects of current pricing and investment decisions. In short,

> the 'bottom line' turns out, on closer inspection to be a plasticine concept, both malleable and movable across time. (Carter, 1991: p. 86)

Various theories of the firm have stressed that the audience for performance is not only made up of stockholders (for example, see Freeman, 1984). It can be difficult for managers so to set performance that all such stakeholders are satisfied. This problem is considerably magnified in the public sector, and certainly so in the case of local authorities. The underlying reasons for the existence of local authority services are often complex and even contradictory; they are affected by social and political pressures which are in their very nature hard to predict. Thus the audience for performance is likely to be more diverse than is the case with the private sector, and is less likely to agree about what constitutes good or bad performance.

Again, if the following equations were true —

Private/market sector = easy performance measurement

Public/welfare sector = difficult performance measurement

— then it would follow that local authority leisure services, would be amongst the most easy to subject to a performance indicator regime. As Coalter*et al.*(1988) have pointed out, leisure services are part of the public sector which operate between welfare and the market. Those parts of the sector, such as leisure centres, which produce an income from paying customers, have in recent years sought to behave more like market-oriented organisations. Whilst in most cases, subsidy from the public purse remains substantial, income generation has been maximised through the introduction of 'market-like' pricing and marketing strategies. Yet the problems of finding credible performance measures for this sector are particularly acute.

However, Carter (1991) suggests that the problems of finding and introducing performance indicators may also reflect organisational characteristics which cut across the public-private divide. He has developed an organisational typology for the study of the evolution of indicator systems in the private and public sectors. The dimensions of the typology are shown in **Table 2** (opposite).

The Carter study highlights the significance of the last four dimensions when assessing the difficulty of introducing indicator systems. The National Health Service, for example, stands out as having a high degree of heterogeneity (a multi-product organisation), and extreme complexity (the skills of many different professionals in complex relationship one to another are required). The goals tend to be very general as prioritising is difficult and controversial; and the work of the NHS is only one factor effecting the general

Table 2: Factors influencing the ease of introducing Performance Indicator regimes

Ownership:	Public or Private.
Trading Status:	Trading or non-trading.
Competition:	The degree of competition between organisations providing similar products or services.
Accountability:	How far the organisation is politically accountable.
Heterogeneity:	The variety of products or services offered by the organisation.
Complexity:	How far the organisation has to mobilise different skills in order to deliver the service.
Uncertainty:	The level of difficulty in defining objectives, and relating the means of achieving them to the desired outcome.

Source: Carter (1991: p. 86-87)

health of the populace. So it is also characterised by high uncertainty. The structure of accountability is also diffuse. All these elements make the development of indicator systems difficult.

How do local authority leisure services measure up on the Carter typology? They are clearly a heterogeneous bundle of services, even when only sport and recreation are considered. Some elements, such "play as you pay" sport are traded in a situation of low to medium competition. Others, such as parks provision are provided without charge, and there is little competition from other providers. Again, the services are reasonably complex since the local authorities have a variety of roles in leisure, not only as direct providers of services, but also as creators of services indirectly through work with the voluntary and private sectors. The Carter studies also prompt us to consider the uncertainty inherent in public sector leisure provision. There is a high level of uncertainty which flows from the variety of provision rationales, and the difficulty of translating them into measurable work outputs.

Local authorities are clearly politically accountable to the locally elected Council. But the Citizen's Charter attempts to introduce a new pattern of accountability and this makes the issue of performance assessment more complex.

A view

The PIs developed for the Charter make a very modest contribution to making visible the inputs and outputs involved in leisure services. They have nothing to contribute to the visibility of outcomes. Those PIs which relate to the quantity of open space provision (3 and 4a.) are arguably not indicators of performance at all, since they are largely the product of geography or history, rather than of management factors. Three PIs can be taken as economy related (1a, 1d, 4b), and one of these (1d) might also serve as a very blunt efficiency indicator. However, the indicators for effectiveness (1b, 1c, 2, 3 and 4a) are collectively weak. Although indicator 2 (playgrounds) is a provision indicator, it is an area where there are well-established standards and it is to be hoped that its existence will persuade Councils to invest the relatively small sums need to bring their fixed play provision in line with them.

Whilst the leisure PIs may be of interest to the citizen taxpayer, for reasons of clarifying leisure expenditure, they cannot be used as the basis of a Value For Money evaluation because the output indicators are so weak. The usefulness of the PIs to the citizen consumer of leisure services is surely very limited.

A great problem in the conception of the Citizen's Charter is the stipulation for a common format for the indicators, with the intention for national publication of a "league table" of performance. It is one thing to collect data and use it longitudinally to measure change from year to year. It is quite another to adopt a comparative mode. It charges the Commission with finding a simple framework to compare dissimilar facilities and services, working towards differing objectives. It is very difficult to see how this can be done without doing violence to a balance between the citizen as in the polity, the citizen as customer and citizen as taxpayer. One is forced to conclude that the stipulation for national league table of performance represents the arsenic in the Audit Commission's chalice.

Moreover, in the sense that the Charter pays insufficient attention to the current accountability of local authority services, to an elected Council through the polity, and overlays another accountability, to the customer through the Charter, it risks muddying the accountability of services and making the institution of a performance regime more, rather than less difficult.

Stewart and Walsh (1992) have pointed out the danger of assuming that there is a generic approach to management which can be applied to all circumstances. Not only are there distinctive tasks, in the public domain, which require distinctive organisational approaches, but also there are "distinctive purposes and conditions". Stewart and Ranson (1988) have summarised these differences of conditions as shown in **Table 3** (opposite).

Table 3: The Public Domain Model

Private Sector Model	Public Sector Model
Individual choice in the market	Collective choice in the polity
Demand and Price	Need for resources
Closure for private action	Openness for public action
The equity of the market	The equity of need
The search for market satisfaction	The search for justice
Customer sovereignty	Citizenship
Competition as the instrument	Collective action as the market instrument of the polity
Exit as the stimulus	Voice as the condition

Source: Stewart and Ranson (1988: p. 17)

In essence, the Citizen's Charter applies itself to a private sector model of public services. At a superficial glance, when one considers operations and outputs, the private sector model appears reasonably applicable to local authority leisure. But appearances are deceptive. When one examines the rationales for investment, when one considers outcomes, only the public sector model is sufficient for devising a performance regime for these services.

There is a certain irony, that in the name of introducing "private sector" styles of management, the Commission finds itself arguing, in the wake of the Citizen's Charter, for grafting a customer orientation onto a simplistic, mechanistic prescription for local authorities. The most successful commercial organisations have moved away from such models and are experimenting with organic, self-organisational or holographic metaphors for organisational design (Morgan, 1986). These would appear to have far more potential for achieving local authority services which are learning organisations, aware of their environment and responsive to customers.

From a management studies viewpoint, a major problem with the Citizen's Charter PIs is the way in which they substitute for actual research on citizen's perceptions of the service they receive. The concerns of citizen's have already been pre-defined by the Commission and there is no incentive for local authorities to find out what its citizens actually think. As an alternative one could suggest that local authorities should conduct an annual "mini-General Household Survey" in order to ask citizens for their views according to a pre-set and uniform questionnaire. The form of question to be asked, the sampling pattern used and the interpretation of the results, would all need consummate care, but in principle such an exercise would be a way of tracking citizens' perceptions. It would enable a view of quality and value for money to be expressed. However, there are two obstacles to such a course. The first is the sheer complexity and diversity of local authority services which implies that a service such as leisure would only be able to take up a very small number of questions. Thus the view of leisure services would be painted with a broad brush and would tend to be shallow in consequence. The second obstacle is the sheer cost of such an exercise; hitherto the Commission has been unwilling to impose onerous data collection duties on authorities. It would be difficult to argue for the expenditure on this kind of survey at a time when many essential services are being cut. Nevertheless the Commission is piloting a "Standard Consumer Survey" (Audit Commission, 1994), which includes some questions on aspects of leisure services quality.

One avenue for progress would be for the "Citizen's question" to ask if the local authority had analysed local leisure needs and demands, if it had consulted on objectives designed to meet those demands and had allocated resources towards these ends. Such an approach would take the "organisational environment" as the starting place for the assessment of performance, and thus would be fully in tune with management thinking. By suggesting this as a responsibility of local Councils, the evaluation of the performance of the whole raft of local authority activity in leisure is placed within the local polity.

The Carter study drew attention to the difference between using performance indicator systems as "dials" and as "can-openers". The Citizens Charter leads the Commission to stressing the former, that is as a means of "reading-off" performance from a scale. This is because the assumption is that this what the customer will want to do. However, if one has a view of the citizen as interested in improving social realities, interested in the development of an educated polity, then one is forced to travel another path, which is also far more relevant for managers. This is where the role of indicator systems is as can-openers, initiating a process of iterative questioning. This role requires the recognition of the necessity for, and value of, a pluralist local polity. It is only such a polity that, in the final analysis, can provide a framework in which the performance of leisure services against desired outcomes can be assessed.

Outside that context, and in spite of the work of the Audit Commission, the invisible man of local authority leisure services remains only very partly dressed — rationales and relationships invisible to politicians, public, and in no small measure, to practitioners.

*Author's note: This paper was first drafted in 1993 before the Audit Commission had finalised the Local Authority Citizen's Charter Performance Indicators (PIs) for Leisure and Recreation. It has been altered to address the PIs adopted for use from 1994/95.

References

Audit Commission (1983) *Code of Local Government audit practice for England and Wales*. London: Audit Commission.

——— (1989) *Sport for whom? Clarifying the local authority role in leisure and recreation*. London: Audit Commission.

——— (1990) *Local Authority support for sport*. London: Audit Commission.

——— (1991a) *Local Authorities, entertainment and the arts*. London: Audit Commission.

——— (1991b) *The road to Wigan Pier: Managing local authority museums and art galleries*. London: Audit Commission.

——— (1993a) *Citizens Charter Indicators — staying on course*. London: Audit Commission.

——— (1993b) *The Quality Exchange — leisure services sports and recreation*. London: Audit Commission.

——— (1994) *Quality counts — a standard consumer survey of aspects of local Council services*. London: Audit Commission.

Bovaird, T. (1992) *Citizen's Charter: Local Authority Performance Indicators — recreation and leisure*. Aston University Business School: Public Sector Management Centre.

Carter, N. (1991) 'Learning to measure performance', *Public Administration*, No. 69: pp. 85-101.

Coalter, F., Duffield, B., and Long, J. (1988) *Recreational welfare: The case for public sector investment in leisure*. London: Avebury/Gower.

Freeman, R. (1984) *Strategic management: A stakeholder approach*. Boston: Pitman.

Kanter, R. (1983) *The change masters*. New York: Simon and Schuster.

McSweeney, B. (1988) 'Accounting for the Audit Commission', *Political Quarterly*, No. 59: pp. 28-43.

Morgan, G. (1986) *Images of organisation*. California: Sage Publications, pp. 40-111.

Oldfield, A. (1990) *Citizenship and community: civic republicanism and the modern world*. London: Routledge.

Olsen, J. (1987) *The modernisation of public administration in the Nordic countries*. Bergen: University of Bergen.

Peters, T. and Waterman R. (1982) *In search of excellence*. New York: Harper and Row.

——— (1987) *Thriving on chaos: Handbook for a management revolution*. New York: Alfred A Knopf.

Prime Minister (1991) *The Citizen's Charter: Raising the standard*. London: HMSO.

Simon, H. (1947) *Administrative behaviour*. New York: MacMillan.

Stewart J. and Ranson, S. (1988) 'Management in the public domain', *Public Money and Management*, Vol. 8, Nos. 2/3: pp. 13-19.

Stewart, J. and Walsh, K. (1992) 'Change in the management of public services', *Public Administration*, No. 70: pp. 499-518.

Veal, A. (1982) *Planning for leisure — Alternative approaches. Papers in Leisure Studies No. 5*. London: Polytechnic of North London.

Leisure and Recreation Programmes for Young Delinquents: The Non-Custodial Option

Motoaki Tsuchiya
Loughborough University, UK

Introduction

There has been a long debate on the effectiveness of leisure, recreation, and sport programmes as a means of preventing and rehabilitating young delinquents. Numerous studies have been carried out to investigate the effects of such programmes (for example: Segrave, 1983; Segrave and Hastad, 1984; Sugden and Yiannakis, 1982; DeBusk and Hellison, 1989; Maitland and Keegan, 1987). Yet there is still some uncertainty associated with it, as Segrave and Hastad (1984) describe: "the efficacy of sport...as an antidote to delinquency is by no means settled."

As Purdy and Richard (1983) explain, "previous research has often been plagued by inconsistent measures of delinquency, weak theoretical conceptualization, poor methodology, inadequate samples, and an over-reliance on official records". These problems are also recognised by many other researchers (Segrave, 1983; Purdy and Richard, 1983; Sugden and Yiannakis, 1982; Robins, 1990). Thus, even though the majority of leisure and recreation professionals feel that those activities and programmes contribute to the prevention and rehabilitation of young offenders, proving their effectiveness is still to be accomplished.

While proving the cause-and-effect relationships, like a negative relationship between the provision of leisure, recreation, and sport programmes and occurrence of reconviction, might not yet be confirmed, there are some encouraging findings to support the effectiveness of such programmes. Furthermore, there is evidence of growing recognition for the using of such programmes as a tool of prevention and rehabilitation. The national voluntary organisations, the National Association for the Care and Resettlement of

Offenders (NACRO) Juvenile Crime Committee makes recommendations to help the development of local youth policies and strategies for crime prevention with regard to leisure, recreation and sport (NACRO, 1991):

1 Play and youth provision should be made a statutory requirement for local authorities.

2 In allocating resources to youth and leisure provision, both central and local government should give recognition to the contribution which they make to reducing and preventing youth crime.

Research Method

In this research, the case study approach with interview was used to analyse different schemes separately. Several schemes in UK were contacted by telephone to collect basic information regarding their operation. Within those schemes, four schemes established or supported by the local Probation Services were selected for interview.

Interviews were conducted either by meeting with one of the scheme leaders, or by telephone. A check list was made to use during the interview; items included: date of establishment, targeted groups, aims and objectives, numbers and types of staff, number of clients, nature of the programme, financing of the scheme, and the evaluation techniques used. Also, any current managerial difficulties were identified.

Case 1: Sherborne House Day Centre, Inner South East London

This scheme became a part of the Inner London Probation Service in 1982. Sherborne House was originally established by Sherborne Public School, Dorset, while the school had set up a Sherborne Trust for pupils to work with disadvantaged young people, and bought a facility in London to provide arts and craft classes for them. This volunteer work was very popular until the late 1960s. Yet, because the style of the class was authoritarian (pupils from the school were Cadets who would become officers in military service), the scheme became outdated, and started to lose its popularity. At this time, the Trust decided to work with another organisation which might be able to manage the facility more effectively to meet its purpose. Thus, the Inner London Probation Service was selected by the Trust as its partner.

i) **Target Group**. The Sherborne House's target group was both males and females aged 16 to 20 — 'serious' and also 'persistent' offenders. More than 80% of those who participated in this scheme had more than six previous convictions (Maitland and Keegan, 1987).

Clients were referred by the Courts, as a result of being assessed before trial for custodial sentence or attendance at Sherborne House. Thus, all clients served a non-custodial sentence by participating in this scheme. Any clients who refused to participate during the course of programme were sent back to the Court for further sentence.

ii) **Aims and Objectives.** Five were identified by Maitland and Keegan (1987), to:

1) provide the court with a credible alternative to custody for persistent or 'serious' offenders;
2) help young people to reduce their offending behaviour;
3) help young people to develop their capacity to make choices and to enable them to accept responsibility for their actions;
4) improve their communication skills in dealing with both officialdom and personal relationships; and to
5) link young people with community resources, especially in relation to employment and education.

iii) **Staff Involvement**. Six Probation officers, four craft instructors, two administrative staff, and one cook worked as full-time staff. Several other specialist tutors, such as instructors for outdoor pursuits, were arranged according to need. However, no volunteers were involved, although the scheme was interested in working with them, and was making approaches to several different organisations.

iv) **Number of Clients.** A maximum of 132 clients could be accepted within one year. Clients were divided into eight groups, of which two operated simultaneously. So every three months, two more groups started the programme.

v) **Programmes**. The clients had to complete 4.5 days per week for 10 weeks, a total of 45 days. The programme started at 9:00 am and lasted to about 3:00 pm. Lunch (also breakfast for those who needed it) was provided for every client as well as commuting expenses.

There were four basic types of programme offered at Sherborne House: 1) offending behaviour group work, 2) craft workshops and education, 3) life skills sessions, and 4) sports and outdoor pursuits. Offending behaviour group work focused on the coping skills for possible offending situations and reflection on their own experiences in offences. Craft workshops and education provided a variety of activities such as working in wood, plastic, and metal, carving, upholstery, T-shirt making, machine maintenance, and many others. Life skill sessions covered areas such as drug/alcohol education, contraception/family planning, HIV/safe sex, child care, coping with prejudice, and planning for the future.

Various leisure, recreation, and sport activities were provided in the scheme, including racquet sports, bowling, snooker, weight training, water sports, karting, rock climbing, and horse back riding. These were an essential component, and took about one third of the total programme. The House owned a mini-bus so clients could be taken to various sites for their activities.

Although the structure of the daily programme was fixed, there was great choice of activities. This seemed to be an important factor in encouraging participation since the clients were ordered by the Courts to attend. Staff also tried to create a friendly atmosphere and close relationships with clients by eating, playing, and participating in many other activities with them.

Clients' participation in the programme was monitored by a points system. Each client started the scheme with a fixed amount of points. Anyone who was late, missed a class, or did not show up for the day lost a certain number of points. However, this system did not focus on punishment, but rather tried to provide encouragement by also giving points for regular attendance and performing certain tasks and behaviours. Thus, the system tried to incorporate positive reinforcement to clients.

vi) **Finance**. The scheme was funded by both the Inner London Probation Service and the Sherborne Trust. The Sherborne Trust, which was the owner of the facility, was responsible for financing facility maintenance and diversification.

On the other hand, the Inner London Probation Service allocated an annual revenue budget of £67,000 (excluding full-time staff salaries). This covers the cost of food, materials, transportation, and other items. It was estimated that the non staff cost of the programme was £50.80 per client per week, or £508 per 10 weeks.

The scheme also tried to support the future planning of its clients by applying for grants offered by various other organisations. For example, if a client was interested in a certain sport, then Sherborne would try to find any grants which would provide personal sports equipment. Of course, it was not always successful, yet Sherborne House was able to raise total of £30,000 in 1992 for future opportunity of their clients.

vii) Evaluating the Scheme. In 1987 extensive research was conducted by the Research and Intelligence Unit of the Inner London Probation Service (Maitland and Keegan, 1987) to look into the effectiveness of the scheme by asking 81 participants to complete questionnaires and interviews with clients, home probation officers, and staff.

It found that 66 (81%) of the sample actually started the programme, and 40 participants (61%) completed it. The conviction rate during the programme was 10%, and twelve months later, a follow-up study of those 40 showed a reconviction rate of 36%. Sherborne House was ready in 1993 to conduct similar research again to explore further its understanding of effectiveness.

Case 2: Probation Action: Challenge and Training (PACT), Bristol

The Probation Action: Challenge and Training (PACT) was another scheme which used leisure and recreation as a key element of the programme. It was established in autumn 1989 by the Avon Probation Service to provide a non-custodial option to the Courts. The original assumption of the scheme was that "active sporting participation can engender greater self-confidence, well-being and relief from stress and pressure" (Avon Probation Service, 1992). However, through experience gained during the operation of the scheme, it was diversified by adding educational programmes.

i) Target Group. PACT set the target group for serious offenders aged 17 to 20. Very similarly to Sherborne House, the scheme focused on serious and persistent offenders referred by the Courts, and so the clients were serving out a Court order.

ii) Aims and Objectives. PACT set specific aims and objectives, to:

a) provide the Courts with a programme of activities which substantially restricts the liberty of offenders (aged 17-20) where offences were so serious that a custodial sentence might otherwise be made, and to

b) develop work in partnership with statutory and voluntary organisations to reduce both the rate and seriousness of re-offending amongst the target grou. (Avon Probation Service, 1992).

To achieve this, it set out to:

1) provide the Courts with an individually planned programme of activities based on the offender's educational and training needs, sport skills and interests and specifically designed to deal with offending behaviour;

2) help develop a range of skills, changes in attitudes, increased self-confidence, and personal responsibility. The long-term aim of such a programme was to try to break into the cycle of offending in which many young offenders appear trapped, and from which they were unmotivated to escape; and to
3) target 50 orders per year.

It was interesting to see that the programming's approach was client-centred, where the scheme would actively try to meet the needs and interests of individuals. Yet as general aim (a) indicated, it was not an easy or soft option to a custodial sentence. It was slightly different from the Sherborne House scheme which was more fixed. PACT was a totally individualised programme which required considerable amounts of time and money involved in programming.

iii) **Staff Involvement**. Three probation officers, one seconded police officer, and two administrative staff worked full-time. No part-time staff were needed to serve a scheme of this size. Thus, clients who participated received considerable attention from staff.

iv) **Number of Clients**. There were 45 clients participating. Usually, about 100 referrals were made annually, about half of whom participated. The main cause of non-participation after referral was a conviction before the programme started.

v) **Programmes**. Each client had to complete 40 to 45 days of activities within six months, in order to meet the requirement set by the Courts. Every time clients turned up for the session, either a half-day or full-day was credited toward the completion of the sentence.

As explained before, the main component of the programme was a sports and "Outdoor Challenge residential programme". This Outdoor Challenge was a compulsory programme which consisted of five-days of residential activities run by Fairbridge Drake (now the Fairbridge Trust). A compulsory sports programme was provided at Leyhill Prison with supervision by a physical education instructor and selected inmates. Activities were such as: 1 km run, 5-a-side football, basketball, circuit training, volleyball, weight training exercises, trampolining, minor games, and other activities chosen by the clients. Other sport activities such as running, swimming, weight lifting, judo, and racquet sports were arranged.

The second part of the programme was education. The scheme co-ordinated with the LOOP project (Learning Opportunities for Offenders Project) established by the Local Authority, Avon County

Council. LOOP assessed clients' educational needs, and connected them to adult education classes, further education colleges, and the Open Learning Centre — a so-called, "second chance education". Clients were also placed into some form of community service to encourage them to link up with their local community. Depending on the clients' preference, they were allocated to places such as junior youth clubs, youth hostels, adventure playgrounds, working with the homeless, or in day centres for people with disabilities.

The Probation Service's Employment Team also provided courses to impart some vocational skills and information to prepare unemployed offenders for their future. Even though the economic climate was not favourable, PACT hoped that clients would be ready to take up a job when the situation improved.

vi) **Finance.** The scheme was funded by the Avon Probation Service, which provided an annual budget of £24,000 excluding full-time staff salaries. Even though the total cost of operating this programme was unknown, the cost per client reached £533.

vii) **Evaluating the Scheme.** Because the scheme had started fairly recently, any detailed evaluation was yet to be done. However, the officer reported the completion rate of those who started the programme to be about 40% (i.e. only 18 to 20 clients). Sherborne House had a 61% completion rate with total of 132 clients per year. It seems that PACT's completion rate was low, considering that those clients received a fair amount of attention from staff.

Case 3: Greater Manchester Probation Service's Projects Unit, Manchester

The Greater Manchester Probation Service's (GMPS) Projects Unit had been operating successfully for almost 20 years, although there was a movement to reorganise to further enhance the quality of its services.

i) **Target Group**. The target group for the Project was anyone who had received a probation order by the Courts. Thus, the scheme had a much wider range of clients than Sherborne House or PACT. There were eleven Probation Field Offices within Greater Manchester, and the Project covered them all.

The scheme was operated by voluntary participation, which was a major difference from those two already described. A variety of programmes was promoted at each Probation Office in the City, usually by using simple colour posters. When a client became interested in attending any of the programmes, the appointed Probation Officer filled in a referral form containing a description of the client, and sent it in to the Project before the starting date. Project officers made up a list of participants for the first day to see how many of the referred clients would turn up. For those who did not turn up for the first session, the Unit contacted the Probation Officer to see whether he/she still wished to participate; one officer described this as the "screening process". He believed the voluntary participation was extremely important for the success of the programme, since commitment to sign up for the programme and being on time for the first session indicated the client's level of self-motivation.

ii) **Aims and Objectives**. It was surprising to find that there were no formally agreed aims or objectives in this scheme. The Unit had tried to put together the 'mission statement', yet could not reach agreement on its content. One of the Unit's officers had stated the major objectives as "personal development through building self-esteem and self acceptance, at the same time, to provide the opportunities for self-reflection and self-evaluation", and "empowering clients", or precisely, the client-centred approach.

iii) **Staff Involvement.** There were four probation officers who worked full-time. Most of one-day programmes were run by part-time or contracted instructors. There were also about 12 regular volunteers involved in provision of programmes to clients.

iv) **Number of Clients.** Robins (1990) reported that 3,000 clients were referred to the Unit during 1988-89. However, the figure for 1 April to 31 October, 1991 indicated that the target population eligible to participate was 2,274, of whom 600 were referred, and 287 actually took part. From October, 1991, the Unit, curiously, decided not to keep records of these figures: staff estimated that referrals were about 1,000 cases a year, and participation at 490.

v) **Programmes.** Various programmes were offered by the Unit, such as personal development courses, day and residential outdoor skills courses, organised group work, video, drama and music workshops, advice and consultations, as well as individualised packages. Some residential programmes such as narrowboat trips and family camping were also popular. Programmes were also flexible with demand: if more people sign up for a particular programme than could be carried, then arrangements were made to provide extra sessions for those on a waiting list.

vi) **Finance.** The Project Unit was allocated an annual budget of £30,000 (excluding staff costs). Usually, £10,000 was set aside for innovative programmes which might come up in future, and £20,000 was spent on regular programmes to pay instructors, transportation, food, equipment, and other minor expenses. Thus, the cost per client was calculated to be £61.

The Unit also tried to raise extra funds from private organisations. Extra revenue was needed, for instance, to pay for a crèche. As a result, GMPS did not acknowledge this to be necessary, and women with young children become constantly disadvantaged. The Unit's officer stated "if we want to take women with children to one of the residential programmes, the cost becomes double or triple, depend on how many children the woman has".

vii) **Evaluating the Scheme.** Surprisingly, no formal evaluations of the scheme had been conducted during its 20 years' operation. It was disappointing because the clients were numerous, and there was so much experience. The movement of reorganisation, however would introduce a systematic approach to monitoring the clients of the Scheme as well as other offenders who became involved with the GMPS.

Case 4. Sports Counselling Scheme, Southampton and Portsmouth

In December 1983, a pilot project, Solent Sports Counselling Scheme, was set up by Southampton magistrates funded by the Manpower Services Commission. It was later funded by the Sports Council as one of its National Demonstration Project Programmes. Later, Hampshire County's Probation Service became involved in this project, and after the Sports Council funding had finished in 1990, the project was formally 'mainstreamed' by the Hampshire Probation Service as one of their units. Since it was monitored by several different organisation, management of information and organisation was highly refined, and known to be one of the most well-known sports oriented schemes in UK.

i) **Target Group.** The scheme targeted offenders aged over 17. It was a voluntary participation programme, which did not necessarily relate to a Court order or to probation, even though the scheme was run by the Hampshire Probation Service. SCS accepted referrals from a variety of sources such as Juvenile Justice Units, attendance centres, Social Services officers, courts, hostels, and Probation day centres. This increased its accessibility to youth in general.

ii) **Aims and Objectives.** After three years of the Demonstration Project, an extensive monitoring report given by the Research Unit (North West) of the Sports Council (The Sports Council, 1990) recommended a revised version of aims and objectives which were accepted by the current scheme, to:

1) provide a programme of sport and leisure activities, using resources within the community of the participants;
2) enable offenders to participate in sport and leisure activities at their own level in a friendly and supportive environment;
3) allow participants the opportunity to have a positive experience through the medium of sport and leisure activities during their time in the scheme;
4) introduce participants to various facilities within the local community so that the activities introduced through the scheme may be continued on completion of their programme;
5) enable participants to develop social skills through the medium of sport and leisure;
6) contribute to programmes for offenders in the community where appropriate including Probation Day Centres and other institutions; and to
7) develop the goodwill and co-operation of the appropriate agencies within the local community, and wherever possible use resources on a shared basis.

The key message again seemed to be the client-centred approach where participation was in activities "at their own level" which allowed participants "the opportunity to have a positive experience". Also, close ties with the local community were essential in SCS, as well as working with local community to promote the understanding of the scheme which represents delinquent youth. This latter aspect became extremely important, as will be discussed later. It seems that the aims and objectives of this scheme were very clear, which helped in measuring its performance.

iii) **Staff Involvement.** There were seven full-time staff with six regular volunteers involved in this scheme. Because the scheme had expanded to different areas, it required more manpower, especially volunteers.

iv) **Number of Clients.** The SCS Annual Report for 1991-92 (Hampshire Probation Service, 1992) indicated very encouraging figures. There were a total of 483 people referred to the Scheme from April 1991 to March 1992, of whom 94% were male and 6% female. 64% of those referred were clients aged 17 to 21. As could be predicted, 95% were unemployed. Of 483 referrals, 260 (54%) clients signed up to start on the programmes. However, 67 (14%) clients failed to show up for the initial interview, 104 (22%) clients did not show up for the first session, and 52 (11%) clients were either not interested in taking part or not able to take part for other reasons.

Numbers were also encouraging when compared with figures from 1990-91, when there were 312 clients referred; that was an increase of 155%. Also, even though the proportion of clients who started the programme dropped from 57% to 54%, the absolute number increased from 177 clients to 260. This tremendous increase in referrals was due to opening new sites in North/Central Hampshire, in Andover and Winchester. Opening new sites obviously increased the accessibility for the targeted youth.

v) **Programmes.** The scheme established several 'drop in' centres within the Southern part of the county to encourage youth to keep in touch with staff more frequently. When clients were referred to the scheme, staff met them one-to-one at drop in centres to find out their interests, and explain how the scheme could help them. At this interview, the staff would design the eight weeks programme according to the client's wants and interests, then the programme would be agreed by both parties. Also the staff would select the objectives or the goals to be achieved for the client through the participation. The Scheme had identified ten objectives, as follows (Hampshire Probation Service, 1992):

1) introduction to new sports/activities
2) introduction to new community facilities
3) initial introduction to club/team
4) gain membership of club
5) increased ability in activity
6) arrange to go on course/outward bound programme
7) assistance with job hunting
8) contact with other support agencies
9) help with diet/health/fitness
10) gain grant/equipment from other agency for referral.

Note the strong emphasis on linking clients to the local community by using the facilities available, and through membership of different clubs. It was not only the sport and leisure aspect of counselling, but also the vocational assistance as that was important. Similarly to Sherborne House, the Scheme also tried to obtain extra support from many other agencies to assist the clients in furthering their leisure and recreation pursuits.

Regular daily programmes included snooker, darts, table tennis, pool, weight training, board games, and computer games; regular weekly programmes involved badminton, squash, football, swimming, volleyball, circuit training, and judo. One-off events included dri-skiing, boxing, rifle shooting, sailing, cycling, and fishing. Thus, the scheme provided a variety of options, from daily activities to special events.

vi) **Finance.** The annual budget of the scheme in 1992-93 was £165,000, which included salaries for seven full-time staff. No details were available with regards to staff salary, but if the average salary was estimated to be £15,000, the running cost of the scheme would have been £60,000 per year. The unit cost of participation would then be estimated at £231 per client.

vii) **Evaluating the Scheme.** An evaluation of the scheme was conducted annually, and the 1992 report (Hampshire Probation Service, 1992) showed that the rate of successful completion was 41% (260 clients started the programme, and 107 completed), a 7% increase from 1990-91.

The scheme also conducted a survey to find out the cause of failure to complete, which showed the major reasons as 1) moving from the area, and 2) finding part time or full time employment.

The monitoring report from the Sports Council (The Sports Council, 1990) also indicated that the regular attendants were not re-offending while on an eight-week programme, and also about 50% of the clients had maintained a crime-free record over a two year period following participation in the programme. As Maitland and Keegan (1987) reported the result of Sherborne House was 36% after a one year follow up. It will be interesting to see the result of a two year follow up study, to compare results of the two different schemes.

Major Issues

This research covered four schemes currently operating in the UK. The summarised comparison of different schemes is shown in **Table 1**. Each scheme was unique, yet certain common issues arose from them. These were 1) cost analysis, 2) type of participation, 3) commitment to leisure and recreation programme as a non-custodial option, and 4) public acceptance and awareness.

1) Cost Analysis

Table 1 also compares the cost of different schemes investigated in this

Table 1 Comparison of Different Schemes

	Sherborne	PACT	GMPS	SCS
Target Group	"serious" and "persistent" offenders aged 16 to 20	"serious" offenders aged 17 to 20	anyone who received a probation order, no age limit	offenders older than 18
No. of full time staff	13	6	5	7
No. of part-time staff	sports instructors are contracted individually	none	sports instructors are contracted individually	none, several regular volunteers
Financial sources	Inner London P. S.; Sherborne Trust	Avon Probation Service	Greater Manchester P. S.	Hampshire P. S.
Annual Budget (Salaries excluded)	£67,000	£24,000	£30,000	£60,000 (approx.)
No. of clients starting programme	132 / year	45 / year	492 / year (approx.)	260 / year
Cost per client	£508 / 10 weeks	£533 / 24 weeks	£61 (programme)	£231 / 8 weeks
Cost per week	£50.80	£22.21	£61	£28.88
Reconviction rate	36% (1 year)	Unknown	Unknown	50% (2 years)
Type of participation	Compulsory	Compulsory	Voluntary	Voluntary

research. The average weekly cost for four schemes was £40.72, with a range of £28.88 to £61.00. On the other hand, the weekly cost of youth custody centres was estimated to be £311 (Home Office, 1990). The cost of sentencing the custodial orders to youth was almost 800% more than those non-custodial options.

2) Type of participation

Participation was of two different types: compulsory and voluntary. The SCS and GMPS Project both believed strongly that the key element of success was the voluntary participation. They believed that the programme would lose its effectiveness when the clients were forced or ordered to participate. This might be a reasonable assumption, yet Sherborne House reported a reconviction rate of 36% after one year follow up (Maitland and Keegan, 1987). Thus, it was difficult to conclude that voluntary participation was better than compulsory participation. The national reconviction rate of adolescent offenders who served custodial sentence(s) was reported to be higher, from 54% within one year (Maitland and Keegan, 1987), and up to 85% within a two year follow up (Broadcasting Support Services, 1993).

From the interview with the Senior Probation Officer at Sherborne House, it was very clear that the staff expended tremendous efforts to have close, trusting, and friendly relationships with clients. For the staff of Sherborne House, winning the trust of the clients was the first step to the provision of programme. The officer stated "we [the staff and clients] practically do everything together, eating lunch together, talking while on the move to activity sites in our mini-bus, and playing together. The only thing we don't do is sleep together". Also the GMPS Projects officer shared the experience of doing different activities with clients to earn their respect.

Ideally, the clients were self-motivated to participate in any of these schemes, yet in reality, offenders ordered by the Courts had no choice. They were required to attend the session or go back to custody. Whether the participation style was voluntary or compulsory, creating a comfortable, friendly, and trust-worthy environment was a must for any schemes to be successful.

3) Commitment to Leisure and Recreation Programme as Non-Custodial Option

The managers of all four schemes believed that personal commitment for the scheme was very important. This was just like counsellors who acquire the special knowledge as well as personal involvement and care for their clients. The initiative to trust must come first from the staff, since clients were sceptical about the scheme. It seems almost the same as in any other service industry where staff commit themselves for customer satisfaction, quality service, and value for money. One might argue that the non-custodial programme did not belong to the service industry, yet lessons from service industries might be valuable.

4) Public Acceptance and Awareness

Acceptance in the community of clients as people, as well as of the scheme was very important. The schemes usually focused on their own target group so that clients would be motivated to take active part, achieve set goals through the programme, and reform well in the community. However, the scheme also focused on the local community, and its various agencies including the police, as well as the Courts. To accept the clients back as citizens, people and organisations need to be aware and understand the intent of the scheme. PACT faced a major challenge in this area, since one of their programmes was to put clients into various types of community services. The officer interviewed complained that it was very difficult to find any agency willing to accept their clients. In theory, it was a good thing to co-operate with such a scheme, so that in long run, reduction of local crime might be achieved. However, the reality was that the community still doubted the value of accepting offenders at the end of such programmes that operate without a direct supervisory presence.

Sherborne House had another type of problem relating to the acceptance of the scheme. As mentioned before, Sherborne House targeted 'serious' and 'persistent' offenders just about to receive custodial sentences. The Criminal Justice Act 1991 contradicts the intention of such a scheme. The Senior Probation Officer explained that the Act would seek to punish such serious and persistent offenders, and to provide community-based sentences for less serious offenders. This seems to make sense, yet because of this Act, the number of referrals to Sherborne House were dropping dramatically. He had been trying to invite judges from the Courts to see the programme in action, so that they might be convinced that to offer a non-custodial sentence was not a soft option, but hopefully worked as well as (or may be better than) custodial sentences.

Clearly, public acceptance was a crucial aspect for achieving the success. It is worth noting one of the aims of the SCS; "to develop the goodwill and co-operation of the appropriate agencies within the local community" (The Sports Council, 1990). While such schemes must be promoted to eligible clients, external promotion to raise the awareness of the public is equally an important issue.

Conclusion

The concept of leisure and recreation programmes as non-custodial option requires much more investigation. There were also some fundamental questions, such as how we measure delinquency (Segrave, 1983), which must be answered to uncover its full aspect. Specific aims and objectives, as well as strategies must also be identified to monitor and measure its performance.

However, the case studies in this research suggest that such leisure and recreation programmes seem to have characteristics of 1) requiring less finance than custodial sentences, and 2) as great, or even more effectiveness than custodial sentences in terms of reducing conviction rates.

References

ACRO (1991) *Preventing youth crime. Juvenile Crime Committee Policy Paper 3*. London: The Association.

Avon Probation Service (1992) *PACT information package*. Bristol: The Service.

Broadcasting Support Services (1993) *Crime and prejudice: Straight thinking on sentencing*. London: Derek Jones Publications.

Debusk, M. and Hellison, D. (1989) 'Implementing a Physical Education Self-Responsibility Model for delinquency-prone youth', *Journal of Teaching in Physical Education, Vol.* 8, No. 2: pp. 104–112.

Hampshire Probation Service (1992) *Sports Counselling Scheme Annual Report 1991-92*. Winchester: The Service.

Home Office (1990) *The sentence of the Court: A handbook for courts on the treatment of offenders* (5th ed). London: HMSO.

Maitland, P. and Keegan, A. (1987) *The Sherborne House Day Centre Activity Programme for young offenders*. London: Inner London Probation Service Research and Intelligence Unit.

Paraskeva, J. (1993) 'Purposeful Leisure: Prevention Not Punishment'. Unpublished paper presented at ILAM 1993 conference, Blackpool.

Purdy, D. A. and Richard, S. F. (1983) 'Sport and juvenile delinquency: An examination and assessment of four major theories', *Journal of Sport Behavior*, Vol. 6, No. 4: pp. 179–193.

Robins, D. (1990) *Sport as prevention: The role of sport in crime prevention programmes aimed at young people*. Oxford: The Centre for Criminological Research, The University.

Segrave, J. O. (1983) 'Sport and juvenile delinquency', *Exercise and Sport Sciences Reviews*, Vol. 11: pp. 181–209.

Segrave, J. O. and Hastad, D. N. (1984) 'Future directions in sport and juvenile delinquency research', *Quest*, Vol. 36: pp. 37–47.

Sugden, J. and Yiannakis, A. (1982) 'Sport and juvenile delinquency: A theoretical base', *Journal of Sport and Social Issues*, Vol. 6, No. 1: pp. 22–30.

The Sports Council (1990) *National Demonstration Projects: Solent Sports Counselling Project*, Final Evaluation Report. Manchester: The Council.

Imported Sport on British Television: A Feast of Sport?

Garry Whannel

Roehampton Institute London, UK

Introduction

The starting point for this paper is the awareness that the amount of foreign or unfamiliar sport on British screens grew significantly during the 1980s. There are indeed some interesting parallels between typical British attitudes to food and to foreign sport. In the fifties foreign food was for many an exotic novelty; something to be wary of. By the sixties the more adventurous were getting the restaurant habit in growing numbers. As the awareness of other cuisines grew during the seventies, so in a balancing fashion, the process of globalisation began to produce a standardisation of international cuisine. The hamburger, the pizza, and the curry became established as the centre-pieces of a limited lexicon. The post-modern eighties appeared to offer us a rich cultural feast of diversity, yet on closer examination a superficial *avant-garde* experimentation often merely served as a gloss, masking a return to classicism, to tradition and to nostalgia: in short, a flight back to the familiar. This brief history in caricature serves well to describe the place of the "foreign" in television sport.

There was a time when an annual calendar of major sporting events seemed as fixed and permanent as the stars in the sky. The Grand National, the Boat Race, the FA Cup Final, the Derby, and Wimbledon all still come around in regular rotation in the broadcasting year, although in the last few years they have been augmented by events like the World Snooker Championships and the Superbowl. Such a calendar, though, is in part a constructed product of broadcasting's own particular history (see Peters, 1976; Whannel, 1992). While such traditions may seem permanent, they are always subject to processes of change. Our sense of the world of sport is continually being modified by television's selections and by changes in the world of sport itself. Events like the World Athletics Championships, the Superbowl, or the World Snooker Championships now seem part of the tradition yet none were features of British television a mere 15 years ago.

Major supra-national events like the Olympic Games and the World Cup are no problem for television — their combination of cultural familiarity, spectacle, global appeal and peak performance make them ideal sources of television. However, as competition and de-regulation have intensified the search for new material that can fit television's confining economics, imported sport has become an increasingly important component in British television sport (Barnett, 1990).

One way of understanding the kind of changes that have occurred is by examining the importing of coverage from overseas, both from the perspective of internationalisation and globalisation, but also from the perspective of foreign-ness and other-ness. The ways in which sport from overseas is framed have changed dramatically during the last fifteen years as the universalisation of television conventions has ironed out some forms of cultural difference.

Popular culture thrives on the tension between familiarity and innovation. To become popular at all, material must be accessible; that is, it must appear in a form that audiences can readily comprehend, utilising established conventions. However audiences are neither static nor passive, but are also active generators of meanings, which are also subject to processes of change. Out of the relation between the market imperative for new product and the changing character of audiences comes innovation.

In introducing new events, and more especially new sports, television is dealing with the relation between the familiar and the strange. To build an audience for Sumo, American football or Australian Rules football means searching for a delicate balance between excess strange-ness (and hence audience bafflement) and over-familiarity (and hence audience dis-interest).

The economics of television provide a massive incentive towards globalisation. First-copy costs are substantial but replication costs are minimal — almost all the budget of a programme has to be committed to produce a first copy, which can then be distributed world-wide for a minimal additional outlay (Whannel, 1985).

In principle, sport has a big advantage over some other forms of television — much of the message is in the visual level. Language is not a major barrier and it is a lot easier to produce a new commentary in another language than it is to dub a drama series like *Dallas*. So the producers of sports as diverse as baseball, Australian Rules football, and Kabaddi are keen to exploit the global market. But the audience cannot be taken for granted — cultural work has to be done when importing material. It could hardly have been predicted in 1982, when Channel 4 started, that Sumo would be more successful than basketball. In this paper, I offer a skeletal periodisation of imported sport since 1954, and some comments on Channel Four, Italian Football and Olympic Opening Ceremonies.

A skeletal periodisation

1. 1954-1962: The novelty of the Other (the whiff of garlic)

In this phase of television the very technology itself was still a subject of wonder and marvel. So the very fact that live pictures could be brought from continental Europe, via Eurovision, was in itself exotic and strange. The technology itself was an event, with its own intrinsic fascination. Part of the original impetus of the Eurovision Song contest grew precisely out of technological display. Like Chesterton's dog walking on its hind legs, the point was not so much that it was done well, but that it was done at all. The development of the Eurovision link aided the transmission of live pictures and recorded material, giving a boost to the European Cup. However, whilst the rest of Europe began to embrace some of this potential, British television remained remarkably insular. Where continental sports like ski-ing or cycling were broadcast they were often overlaid with light jangling music, which seemed to signify their "trivial" status. Like a British tourist who is fascinated by the smell of garlic, but wouldn't dream of tasting it, British television stuck to the good old staple fish and chip diet of football, cricket, racing and rugby.

2. 1962-1974: The Other as routine (eating out)

This period saw dramatic and rapid innovation, in the course of which the technological marvel became routinised. The era begins with the launch of telstar and those first flickering and indistinct images from across the Atlantic. In 1966 the first action replay shuddered erratically into life, In 1970 Cliff Michelmore still found it necessary to jokingly pray before ushering in the live pictures from Mexico. But by 1974 television had reached the stage where high quality live colour images from around the world were a standard audience expectation. Sport had entered the era of the global spectacle.

But a global medium still typically established parochial relations with its audiences. The major regular sport programmes of British television, Grandstand, Sportsnight and World of Sport remained focused on major

British sports and events, straying overseas only for big events or British interest. The Asian Games and the Pan American Games could as well have been taking place on Mars. "Foreign" sport got little air time. The one regular exception was within *World of Sport* on International Sport Special. This section of the programme, built on the back of cheap imported material from ABC and other North American sources, was heavily framed by the notion of foreign sport as strange exotic novelty. So American Football appeared, cheek by jowl, in brief snippets along with the World Log Rolling Championships and Acapulco Cliff Diving.

Viewers did, however, get far more exposure to events from overseas, even if the sports were firmly rooted in the familiar. To persist with the culinary metaphor, it was as if the audience were becoming used to the occasional meal out, even if they still preferred roast beef to Bolognese.

3. 1974-1982: McDonaldisation of the visual

During the eighties there were signs that the diverse menus of world sport were being streamlined. The growing technical sophistication and the expanding global trade in television was producing a heightened control over the image and a growing homogenisation of style. The rigidity of distinctions between live and tape, studio and location began to become more blurred. It was in this period that the globalisation of the image became well established. Regional variations in stylistic conventions were smoothed out in the interests of the production of an acceptable international feed. For instance, for the 1978 World Cup coverage, Argentine television dropped their own camera positions in order to adopt positions favoured by European broadcasters (Tomlinson and Whannel, 1986). Just as a McDonald's hamburger tastes the same in Milwaukee, Milan and Manchester, so sport began to look the same whether it was filmed in Buenos Aires, Bologna or Bolton.

4. 1982-1992: Post-modernity (sport as global smorgasbord)

However, globalisation has brought with it many paradoxes — internationalism alongside localism; modernity in constant montage with tradition; foreign-ness as the familiar. To some it has begun to reverse the old certainties so that the centre is now marginal and the peripheral central. Clearly, there are great dangers here for analysis. Those who proclaim the arrival of post-modernity all too easily confuse appearance with substance, sever representations from their modes of production, and analyse the signs of society as it they existed independently of any conditions of existence. It is undoubtedly important to analyse the role of consumption. The argument that consumption involves the working through of mechanisms of pleasures and desires in a form that constantly eludes total control by the market-place is a valid and important antidote to some of the flaws of mechanistic and one-dimensional versions of Marxist analysis. However, much recent analysis has focused on consumption and its surface appearances to the exclusion of any attempt to analyse the processes and relations of production, that beneath the glossy post-modern *bricolage*, continue to structure the cultural marketplace. Enthusiasts for post-modernity all too easily acquire a blind-spot that allows them to evade, rather than resolve, problems of the relationship between phenomenal forms and real relations.

Having said that, there is no question that the global expansion of television, its rapid technological advance, and the growing cultural and technical consolidation that links the various information technologies; along with the production of a sophisticated, media saturated audience, has had a dramatic and transforming effect on the field of representations.

Part of this process is that cultural imports such as Sumo can suddenly assume a cultural accessibility, whilst British sports that are indigenous but virtually non-televised (e.g. netball, speedway) can seem remote, strange by comparison. Global television enables a kind of postmodern cultural smorgasbord in which Australian Rules football, Kabbaddi, and Sumo are potentially all equally "ours".

However, this is only one half of the process. While global media systems seem to promote the growth of an international culture, the continuing strength of, indeed resurgence of nationalisms and localisms, has helped enable diverse readings of this material in different contexts. Slain, Boyle and O'Donnell (1993) have vividly demonstrated how the same events can be covered in dramatically different ways within different linguistic communities. There is, then, a complex interaction of internationalism, nationalisms, and localisms, that underpin the ways in which this media material can be read. The willingness of British youth (mainly male youth but not exclusively so) to proclaim their identification with American Football and Baseball teams or Italian football teams can be measured in the expanding markets for the appropriate hats, sweatshirts and replica kits. However this appears to supplement, rather than supplant identification with British football, cricket and rugby. It is then, highly relevant to examine which sports gain television coverage, and to explore the underlying economic circumstances that help to determine the selection process.

The peculiar economics of television have meant, for Channel 4, that it is far more practical to import sport, second-hand, and then sell it to the audience than it could ever be to develop minority British sports. American

Football, Tour de France cycling, Sumo, and Australian Rules, bought in, offer great spectacle, yet are probably far cheaper than the costs of covering British volleyball, or women's football. The English women's cricket team won the World Cup in 1994, in striking contrast to the abysmal failures of their male counterparts in the Test Series against Australia. But the women's game continues to exist in almost media-free isolation. It is the strange accomplishment of television to have popularised a Japanese sport with no British interest, whilst neglecting international success in a major British sport. Clearly this is partly a consequence of the long-term neglect of women's sport, which has its own complex roots in the historical impact of patriarchy (see Hargreaves, 1994), but the particular impact of television economics have also played their role.

5. 1992 onwards: Dump-vision or global citizenship? (Junk-food for the gourmets)

The future might appear to offer more of the same — much more of the same. The massive start-up costs of satellite television, its need to fill extensive hours, and the long run-up to break even point has limited its programme budgets. Typical costs per hour, sometimes less than £10,000, are much less than terrestrial television. As with Channel 4, this has led the sport channels to draw heavily on the second-hand market, buying up American Truck Racing, wrestling, and college football — a kind of grunge television.

Yet ironically the growth of television sport has arguably produced an audience more sophisticated than ever before. Television's close up eye, focusing with endlessly-replayed sharpness, allows a particular insight, the access to major events is greater than ever, and the consequent familiarity with elite level sport can be assumed to have produced an audience with a keen appreciation of sport at its finest. Much of the sport now offered to this audience is, in objective terms, dross. It is as if a convention of gourmets are regularly served up junk-food, with only the rare *cordon-bleu* item slipped in. In the context of communication gluttony, quantity is always threatening to subsume quality.

Channel Four and after

However, from the British perspective it is undoubtedly the case that, during the 1980s, Channel 4 revolutionised the representation of foreign sport.

In this paper I am focusing on foreign material, by which I mean foreign to the audience. So I include baseball and Sumo, but not coverage of traditional British sports such as cricket from Australia, or athletics from

Europe. So when I refer to imported sport, I mean the introduction to the British audience of unfamiliar sports or competitions. In this category I am including sports such as cycling and basketball that have no established tradition of being British television sports, but are well established elsewhere. I am also including in this category the coverage of new competition events such as Channel 4's coverage of the Italian soccer league.

In 1980 I would estimate that less than 1% of sport on British television was imported in the sense I am using the word. This 1% included cycling, basketball, and Gaelic sports. By 1989/90 this figure had jumped to around 9% and included American football, baseball, Sumo, Australian Rules Football, and volleyball. Much of this increase was directly attributable to Channel 4. Between 1982 and 1987 around 27% of Channel 4 sport fell clearly into my 'imported' category, and of the 850 hours that went to the top five sports (racing, American football, snooker, cycling and basketball) 37% were devoted to imported material.

There are three noteworthy features of Channel 4's policies towards sport. First, for hard economic reasons they chose to foreground foreign sports, using American Football, repackaged by Cheerleader, almost as a brand image. (It was no surprise to discover that it was Adrian Metcalfe, C4's commissioning editor for sport, who gave Cheerleader their name). Second, they rejected the previous dominant frame (exotic novelty) used to present foreign sports to the British audience. Third, they chose instead, to take the sports seriously, give them regular hour-long slots and take the time to try and explain some of their finer points, thus building an audience by slowly educating it.

In this last endeavour they have had some success, at least with American football and Sumo. When Channel 4 opened in 1982 with American Football as one of its first season attractions, a lot of care was taken in introducing the sport. The early programmes contained regular items on aspects of the rules, the tactics and the formations of the game. American Football had at least the benefits of comprehendable spectacle and sufficient familiarity to other sports (Rugby, Soccer) that were central to British sporting cultures, Sumo posed greater problems, having both a more unfamiliar structure as a sport, but also being located within a complex culture that was largely unfamiliar to the British audience. Great care was taken to try and explain aspects of this culture and the presentation of the sport constantly emphasised the ways in which an understanding of this culture was central to an appreciation of the sport itself (see Watson, 1988).

This is of some significance, because the professional common sense of British broadcasters places little faith in the ability of television to educate its audience. I have talked to sports producers who are quite convinced of the futility of audience education. Sadly, there is little evidence that the example of Channel 4 has had any great effect on dislodging this dispiriting corporate philistinism. However in two ways, the Channel has had a significant impact on its rivals. First it has pushed them towards a greater preparedness to experiment with different imported material. Second, some of Channel 4's characteristic conventions — greater use of graphics, and montages, use of music, more youth oriented presentation — have been adopted and adapted by the others.

Case Study: Italian football

The adventure of Italian football on Channel 4 has been a fascinating tale in which the familiar and the other have been held together through the unlikely mediating figure of Gazza.

The deal was a minor inspiration — bringing together the right sport and the right channel at the right moment. Chrysalis noticed that satellite television, gorged on the rich dark roast beef of old England and its Premier League, had lost its appetite for the pasta and sauce of Serie A. Negotiating a quick deal at the last moment, they had teamed up with Channel 4 before anyone had fully realise the significance of the deal.

The delicate balance of football on British television was decisively altered by the Premier League deal. Television football has always been a commodity, but was always also something more — part, if one wished to be pompous, of the national heritage. The Sky deal marks a new phase — a major element of the English football game was to disappear onto what is, in size terms, a minority channel.

Satellite television has spread more slowly than many media analysts predicted. Indeed the relative failure to penetrate the market decisively, and the destructive war between BSB and Sky, led ultimately to the fusing of the two companies in a traumatic episode that became known around BSB's Marco Polo House headquarters in Battersea as "the merge-over". Premier League football presented Sky with an opportunity to boost dish sales. It is well known that only movies and sport are significant pull factors in persuading people to buy dishes.

But impressive though the deal seemed at first, Sky lacked a unique selling proposition. It didn't have the only Premier League action — BBC had the rights to highlights. It didn't have the first weekend slot — BBC's Match of the Day did. It didn't have the only live action — having been frozen out of the major action, ITV naturally did a cheap deal with the Football League, allowing it to offer a live alternative to Sky. Finally, Sky did not even have the only elite live action: Channel Four's Italian Football gave viewers a further interesting choice. Indeed, if anyone had the unique selling proposition it was Channel Four. They were offering the first regular terrestrial broadcasts of live games of a major foreign league. Even better, not just any foreign league, but the one universally thought to be the highest in quality, the one with the majority of the worlds stars playing in it. As a bonus, many of these stars were known to the British audience through the 1990 World Cup and 1992 European Nations Cup. For the *coup de grace*, the biggest British star, Paul Gascoigne, and two others, David Platt and Des Walker, were also available to build in audience appeal.

In informal conversations with around 30 football fans at the start of the season, I discovered no-one who intended to go out and buy a dish, but a majority who looked forward to Sunday afternoons on Channel 4 with great enthusiasm.

Italian football has built a solid audience of between 2 and 3 million viewers. It must be assumed that this has had a significant effect on the ability of BSkyB's football to sell satellite dishes (see Endnote). The disappearance of live football onto BSkyB was a shock to football fans, but it certainly seemed that for many a regular opportunity to watch Italy's Serie A — unquestionably the strongest league in the world, and certainly the greatest assemblage of basic talent available — was sufficient to dissuade them from dish purchase. Channel 4 has been able to offer the audience top quality live football at no cost, at precisely the moment when there is a widely perceived lack of talent and flair in English football.

Even given the favourable circumstances, the problem was to market the unfamiliar. English players who had gone to Italy offered invaluable scope for audience identification, and the centrality of Gascoigne was almost inevitable. His lack of prominence on the field was handled by drumming up a magazine programme, in which glimpses of Gazza could be interspersed with round ups, goals and some attempt to familiarise the audience with Italian teams and players.

As if in fear that Gazza alone would not make it English enough, they further anchored the basic British-ness of the operation by turning to veteran commentator Ken Wolstenholme to read the results round up (in an ambience so acoustically dead that Ken could have been in a flotation tank, or an anechoic chamber). Wolstenholme's voice is rich in connotations — as the voice of the World Cup he of course uttered the immortal "some people are on the pitch, they think it's all over — it is now" and so shares in the glories of English football triumph over foreign-ness. But he also commentated on Matthews' Cup Final in 1953, although on this occasion he could only manage the rather less inspired "it's there...Perry...it's Perry". So his voice is also redolent of football on flickering black and white sets, long shorts, sodden leather balls, and cigarette cards. In short, it is almost the exact antithesis of modern Italian football.

Having anchored down Englishness, they needed also to build on our fascination with the exotic-ness of "foreign". But here the coverage has been deeply disappointing in its general lack of Italian-ness. Despite the rather lame sidewalk cafe material, it has done little to capture the intensities, the commitment, the colour, the peculiar combination of discipline and passion of the ultras, the tension between extravagant skill and regimental discipline that Italian footballers have to handle. The coverage, with commentary seemingly done off-tube in London, has failed to evoke Italian-ness. Quite simply, there is not enough foreignness, not enough "other", not enough garlic.

Seoul and Barcelona: the global and the other

Since regional variations in visual conventions have increasingly been ironed out, international sport now bears few traces of its origins. However there is one notable exception and that is in Opening Ceremonies of major events like the Olympic Games (Tomlinson, 1989; Gruneau, 1989). These hugely expensive and elaborate rituals have little direct connection with sport, yet attract massive audiences on account of the compelling visual spectacle that they offer. Such spectacles constitute the meeting ground of complex and contradictory elements. Two major meaning systems are in collision. Global television, which in this case is dominated by the financial muscle of the American network that has the rights, requires a television spectacle, just exotic enough to fascinate without being so "other" as to confuse and alienate the viewer. The host nation wants to use the opportunity to make a statement. However this statement is inevitably the product of conflicting concepts. Tradition and modernity must be shown as the two sides of a nation, yet how are these to be signified ? In the case of Seoul and Barcelona, there was a strong desire to make a cultural statement — to reflect a depth and richness — in uneasy co-existence with the impetus to make an economic statement — "we are powerful, resourceful and efficient".

In the event both Seoul and Barcelona produced Opening Ceremonies of an extraordinary visual richness. Yet little of the underlying connotations and significances were made accessible by the verbal level supplied by the BBC. No sports commentator does his homework more conscientiously than David Coleman; but he is no expert on myth, ritual or tradition. He has no real insight into the symbolic lexicons of either Korean or Spanish cultures —

indeed there is no reason to expect that he might. So much of the ceremonial dimension was inevitably compelling but incomprehensible. Indeed its very impenetrability ironically contributed something to its polysemic power. Yet neither the hot spice of Kimshi nor the subtle fishy blend of paella successfully made it through the mediations of the media kitchens. The globalisation process renders up a superficial impression of difference, but one that is paper thin. Small variations of content have always to be placed within the formal structure of the familiar in order that the communication process works to the maximum effectiveness. Familiarity may breed contempt, but it also breeds large audiences. Whether their appetites are enriched, or merely temporarily assuaged, is a different question.

Endnote

On the day I completed the revised version of this paper, England beat Poland 3-0 in a key game at Wembley. Although the complex deal between the Football Association, the BBC and BSkyB allowed the BBC to show this match live (on the grounds that it was a match of major national importance), they elected not to do so on the grounds of the expense of exercising this option. Considerable anger was expressed on at least one radio phone-in at the decision. It could prove a highly significant moment for Sky, coming as it did only a week after Murdoch's bullish announcement of the new expanded range of channels, and other future plans. It sent a clear and readable message about the potential future, in which major live sport could typically be only available on satellite. The audience response to this remains to be seen, although the expense of renting access to satellite sport in the middle of a recession could be a deterrent. My guess is that in the short term the real winners will be publicans with dishes.

References

Barnett, S. (1990) *Games and sets: The changinq face of sport on television.* London: BFI.

Blain, N. and O'Donnell, H. (1993) *Sport and national identity in the European media.* Leicester: Leicester University Press.

Gruneau, R. (1989) 'Television, the Olympics and the question of ideology', in R. Jackson and T. McPhail (eds) *The Olympic Movement and the mass media.* Calgary, Canada: University of Calgary Press.

Hargreaves, J. (1994) *Sporting women.* London: Routledge.

Peters, R. (1976) *Television coverage of sport.* Birmingham: CCCS.

Tomlinson, A. (1989) 'Representation, ideology and the Olympic Games: A reading of the opening and closing ceremonies of the 1984 Olympics', in R. Jackson and T. McPhail (eds) *The Olympic Movement and the mass media*. Calgary, Canada: University of Calgary Press.

Tomlinson, A. and Whannel, G. (eds) (1986) *Off the ball: The 1986 Football World Cup*. London: Pluto.

Watson, L. (1988) *Sumo*. London: Sidgwick and Jackson.

Whannell, G. (1992) *Fields in vision: Television sport and cultural transformation*. London: Routledge.

——— (1985) Television spectacle and the internationalisation of sport?, in *Journal of Communication Inquiry*, Vol. 2, No. 2.

Service and Volunteerism: An Emerging Leisure Lifestyle

Lei Lane Burrus-Bammel and Gene Bammel

West Virginia University, Morgantown, West Virginia, USA

Introduction

Although "service" and "volunteerism" appears to have received more attention recently than in previous years, it is not a new concern. A number of famous individuals have made service statements that are notable quotes. Theodore Roosevelt said "this country will not be a good place for any of us unless we make it a good place for all of us to live". Probably the most often repeated John F. Kenedy comment is "ask not what your country can do for you but what can you do for your country". Martin Luther King is often remembered for saying "everybody can be great because everybody can serve". President George Bush will be remembered for his "Thousand Points of Light" programme.

The United States has a long history of volunteerism and community service (Hertzel, 1993). Co-operation in the colonies, as early as the 1600s, was a must in order to provide food, shelter and defence — individuals were not able to overcome the hardships alone. An expression of this commitment to voluntary co-operation was the Social Compact of 1620 which bound the governed "to all care for each other" (Ellis and Noyes, 1990: p. 18). The Pilgrims believed that performing good deeds helped one attain grace, and the survival activities of clearing the land, erecting buildings, farming and harvesting, and quilting and spinning, became community ventures (Ellis and Noyes, 1990: p. 19). Civic problems not under the government's control became by 1775 the responsibility of voluntary organizations.

Community efforts for survival continued after the Revolutionary War as people left the east and moved westward for the new frontiers. Over time, volunteer efforts branched out from the private sector and became part of government and business. There appears to be increasing volunteerism.

Not only are a greater number of people involved, but those people are starting earlier and devoting increasing proportions of their life to volunteer experiences. Special efforts are also being made to increase the diversity of the volunteer pool.

The purpose of this paper is to examine the increasing role of volunteerism in American's lives, and to examine why people engage in the activity, what are emerging trends, and does this represent leisure? The case will be made that service and volunteerism appear not only to be an emerging leisure lifestyle, but are very desirable forms of leisure. The form of research for this paper will be historical, with supporting content analysis from student reports on "field placements" with special populations.

The US literature on volunteering — A historical perspective

Various important events stimulated volunteerism. About 1850 the Fugitive Slave Law was enacted and those opposed organized to help slaves escape by forming the Underground Railroad. Women made significant volunteer efforts during the Civil War to help care for the soldiers — the beginning of the Ladies' Aid Societies (Hertzel, 1993: pp. 106-107).

Wealthy individuals donated funds to support projects for the tenement poor, but the efforts were not very efficient. The need for better organization and a systematic approach led to the development in the late 1800s and early 1900s of charitable volunteer organizations such as Community Chests, the United Way of America, the Salvation Army, Volunteers of American and the Children's Aid Society. Many associations concerned with social and health welfare, such as the National Easter Seal Society, City of Hope, and the Rockefeller Foundations, started as volunteer institutions. The need for volunteer sponsored clubs especially for children was recognized. The Cub Scouts were founded in 1937 and the Little League in 1939 (Ellis and Noyes, 1990:pp. 225).

The government, in 1933, as a response to unemployment during the depression, sponsored the idea of community service on a large scale during the New Deal era with the Civilian Conservation Corps (National Governors' Association, 1989). Before it ended, three million had served in the corps. Twenty eight (28) years later, President John F. Kennedy created the Peace Corps to provide developing countries skilled American volunteers. This program started in 1961, has had over 125,000 young adult participants and, according to Eberly, "is viewed by many of the world's people as American's best program". American volunteers were so effective in other countries that XX President Johnson in 1966 initiated VISTA (Volunteers in Service to America) to help solve problems at home in the United States. During his War on

Poverty, the Job Corps, the Neighborhood Youth Corps, and the College Work Study Program were started.

Government support of community service and volunteerism continued in the 70s. A federal umbrella organization called ACTION was organized to foster a major American volunteer force and house individual programs such as the Peace Corps, VISTA, the Foster Grandparent Program, RSVP (Retired Senior Volunteer Program), the Service Corps of Retired Executives (SCORE) and the Active Corps of Executives (ACE) (Ellis and Noyes, 1990:267). During this same time the results and values associated with volunteerism were being recognized by private business — corporate America was becoming involved with community service. Staff positions were created to co-ordinate employee volunteerism as part of the company's public relations effort.

Over the years volunteerism moved from being supported primarily by private citizens to being funded by the government and encouraged by business. Volunteerism had become entrenched in American life. By 1974 the U.S. Census Bureau reported that annually, one out of every four citizens over the age of thirteen did organized volunteer work. As further evidence of volunteerism being a part of American life, in 1983 volunteerism was the theme of the Rose Bowl Parade, and it was adopted as an Ad Council cause with the slogan "Volunteer — Lend A Hand." There was even a commemorative stamp issued using the Ad Council's slogan (Ellis and Noyes, 1990:291). It is difficult to determine the exact popularity of volunteerism, as estimates of the share of the population that volunteer vary widely. During their research, Fischer and Banister Schaffer found estimates ranging from 18 to 55 percent for all people aged 18 and older and from 11 to 52 percent among adults aged 60 and older (1993:6). This wide range of results might be due to lacking a standard definition of volunteerism. The U.S. Bureau of Labor Statistics considered a volunteer as "a person who performed unpaid work for an organization ... persons who did work on their own such as helping out neighbors or relatives are excluded." "Persons who worked in some way to help others for no monetary pay" are included by the organisation INDEPENDENT SECTOR, Washington D.C. The reporting difference from those two definitions is around 30 percent, the range being from a low of 20 percent to around 50 percent during the 1980s. Three variables however, appear to be associated with higher levels of volunteering: higher levels of education, income and occupational status, and good health (Fisher and Banister Schaffer, 1993).

Following corporate America and the federal government, volunteerism's next arena of conquest was the educational system. A National School Volunteer Program (NSVP) was established. NSVP reported that 79% of all public schools had some form of volunteer program by 1983 (Ellis and Noyes,

1990:294). Other indications of major support for service was President Bush's creation of The Points of Light initiative, and Congress passing the National and Community Service Act of 1990, which authorised a variety of national community and service-learning programs. In 1992 The Commission of National and Community Service provided US $16.3 million in grant money to forty-seven states, the District of Columbia and Puerto Rico in order to implement service-learning innovations in elementary and secondary schools. Higher Education received US $5.2 million to help at least 175 institutions undertake innovative community service efforts. American Conservation and Youth Service Corps Programs were given US $21.5 million and Subtitle D made provisions of US $20.1 million for programs related to education or housing benefits upon completion of service for individuals aged 17 and older.

Service and volunteerism in the school system

The earliest reference found during this research that connected the idea of volunteerism to education was Charles Elliot's 1869 inaugural address in which he asked, "And what will the University do for the community?" His response was, "It will foster the sense of public duty — that great virtue which makes republics possible." The idea was that institutions of higher education ought to support those activities which develop generosity, civic mindedness and the capacity for conscientious action. Campus Compact was founded as a national organization in 1985, to tie institutions of higher education to a clear-cut service mission. Composed of visionary presidents, Compact members help integrate student involvement in public service and into education's central mission and goals. During 1992, there were 305 member institutions, including West Virginia University. Survey results indicated that 11% of the responding 112 institutions had a formal graduation requirement related to public service (McCarty and Schwartz, 1992).

Public schools appear to have faced the issue some time later. William Kilpatric, about the end of World War I, advocated a form of school-based community service which emphasised that "learning should take place in settings outside the school and involve efforts to meet real community needs" (Conrad and Hedin, 1991: p. 744). Evidence of the recognition of the importance of volunteerism and community service is the fact that it is now a graduation requirement for an increasing number of high schools (Lesko, 1992: p. 3) and it is a statewide graduation requirement in Maryland.

Statistics on student volunteers

Yearly, the number of schools and students participating in volunteer activities and programs is increasing. Campus Compact had 202 member institutions listed in their 1988-89 report (Hicks and Walsh), 260 in their 1991-92 report (Zivi), and 305 in 1992-3 (McCarty and Schwartz). In the 1988-89 Campus Compact, survey results from member institutions indicated that Dartmouth College had a 66 percent increase in the number of student volunteers over the previous year and a half. The number of participating students at Norwich University grew 100 percent while both Brookhaven College and University of Utah had at least doubled their student numbers (Hicks and Walsh, 1989).

Why do people volunteer?

Four major reasons are reported as to why people volunteer: 1) a desire to help others, 2) to make a difference, 3) to give back something, and 4) to make a statement or a point. Volunteers also receive benefits from their efforts. Ninety-five percent reported that regular giving gives them an immediate physical feel-good sensation. Other reported benefits included increased self-worth, improved self esteem, better general health, a sense of belonging, developed leadership skills, a better understanding of the real world, and participating in a meaningful activity. One volunteer said that volunteering wasn't work, that is was the highest form of fun! (Ferrell, Ferrell and Wakin, 1985).

Volunteerism and leisure

Leisure has three preconditions: some capacity for free choice, some time left over once life's necessities have been satisfied, and the availability of experience that departs from the ordinary routine (Bammel and Bammel, 1992). The same appears to exist for volunteerism. Both leisure and volunteerism can be considered non-obligatory but Roberts pointed out that "the fact is that leisure is often interwoven with the obligatory, elements in people's lives" in that it is "not rigidly segregated as an isolated compartment of life. " Rather, "leisure pervades, and is pervaded by, numerous other types of activities" (Roberts, 1970: p. 7).

No one definition of leisure has been generally accepted (Roberts, 1970: p. 6), but it is a phenomenon common in some form to every society. Leisure, in ancient Greece, "referred to the opportunity to develop the human body, mind and soul" (Roberts, 1970: p. 6). A more modern version views leisure as a way of living, and in leisure occur most of the important events of one's life. Leisure has the connotation of attitude, time, experiences that enable personal growth or development. Leisure activities are ends in themselves, they are intrinsically rewarding. Leisure can be actualised each day by the person who cultivates what leisure has to offer. Like leisure, volunteerism has no standard definition but "there's general agreement that it is a freely undertaken, unpaid activity intended to help others" (Fischer and Banister Schaffer, 1993: p. 6). Volunteerism then, can be considered a leisure activity/ experience and it might be argued that it is the ultimate leisure experience.

Godbey and Parker indicated that leisure is determined not by a period of time but by the quality either of an activity or of the person engaging in the activity. Josef Pieper thought leisure to be "a mental and spiritual attitude ... a condition of the soul" (Godbey and Parker, 1976: p. 4). Leisure in this classical notion included contemplation. Contemplation, wrote Pieper, "means to open one's eyes receptively" (Dare, Welton and Coe, 1987: p. xviii). Leisure, by some definitions, contains aspects of personal growth or development (Bammel and Bammel, 1992), relaxation, diversion, and social achievement (Godbey and Parker, 1976). Dumazadier described four characteristics of leisure. One of these was hedonistic, in that leisure is the search for a state of satisfaction (Dare *et al.*, 1987). The literature on volunteerism and community service clearly documents that personal growth and development occurs through such activities. A study conducted by a West Virginia University professor investigated growth in terms of the characteristics listed by Maslow, Loevinger, and Kohlberg. Maslow (1968) established a hierarchy of needs, Loevinger (Loevinger and Wessler, 1970) was interested in ego development, and Kohlberg (1972), like Loevinger, described the sequential stages of development. His conclusions on volunteerism and growth were that "the volunteer experience emerges clearly as highly contributive in all areas but more contributive to ego development, self-actualization, and moral development" (Peterson, 1975: p. 46).

Conrad and Hedin (1991) stated that the outcomes of youth service programs include three major areas of growth and development: personal, intellectual, and social (Hertzel, 1993). Personal growth and development included, among other things, self-esteem, sense of personal worth, competence and confidence. Improved communication skills, tacit learning skills, basic academic skills, and more positive attitudes toward education were some of the aspects under intellectual development and academic learning. Social growth and development was expressed in concern for the welfare of others, knowledge and understanding of others as well as better attitudes toward living and working with people with diverse backgrounds.

Another connection between leisure and volunteerism is the effect on the family. Leisure activities have been reported to play an important shock-absorbing role during periods of change and may have a stabilizing influence over an entire marriage (Witt and Goodale, 1985). In fact, a positive relationship exists between marital satisfaction and leisure participation (Crawford and Godbey, 1987). Advantages of family-based leisure include increased communication between family members, greater consideration for others, and lessons in responsibility (Bammel and Bammel, 1992:339). A News Release from the Points of Light Foundation, stated that "American families continue to voluntarily reach out to help others in need" and that "volunteerism was one important way that whole families could enhance their home life and strengthen the family unit" (1993). Families have long been considered a type of institution. President George Bush proposed a three part community service strategy, the first part including changing the nation's attitudes about service, seeking to "call every individual and institution in America to claim society's problems as their own." He further commented that "from now on in America, any definition of a successful life must include service to others" (Anderson, 1992).

Content analysis of student reflections

Majors in West Virginia University's Recreation and Park Management program are required to take Recreation and Parks Course 241, Introduction to Special Populations. A "field placement" of three hours a week for 10 weeks of community service with an approved agency or organization that provides recreation/leisure opportunities for special populations is the lab part of the course. After the 10 weeks, each student writes a three part paper. The first part is devoted to a description of the agency, the second part is library research on the type of population selected, and the final part is an evaluation/reflection section.

The case has already been presented that volunteerism and community service can be considered as a form of leisure and that the number of people participating is increasing, as is support from the government and private sectors. The purpose of the content analysis is to add support to the notion that volunteerism and community service are forms, and perhaps very desirable forms of leisure.

Twenty-seven student papers from the 1991 Fall semester were included in this content analysis. Three parts of the analysis are of interest to this paper. Frequently recurring key words and their derivatives (see **Table 1**) were recorded, expressed themes (see **Table 2**), and selected phrases/sentences. Results appear to support the premise that this community service-service learning activity is viewed by the students as volunteerism; that the activity contains characteristics of leisure; and that the activity is viewed in a very unique, positive and desirable light.

While technically considered a community service, service-learning experience — many students think of themselves as volunteers and participating in volunteerism. Nine students used the word "volunteer", and the word or its derivatives appeared 14 times (Table 1). Of the words tallied, "volunteer" tied for seventh place with "good" for the most frequently used words. The

Table 1: Word Tallies, Content Analysis of Park & Recreation Majors' Field Placement Papers, West Virginia University, Fall, 1991

Word	Total Frequency	Number of Papers
I	409	27
learned	75	26
work	47	19
feeling	24	15
experience	23	14
enjoy	18	13
help	18	11
good	14	11
volunteer	14	9
friend	7	5
sad	6	5
fun	6	5
happy	5	5
love	5	5
patient	5	4
proud/pride	3	3

Table 2: Themes, Content Analysis of Recreation & Park majors' Field Placement Papers, West Virginia University, Fall, 1991

Theme	Number of Papers
Positive experience	25
Active	16
Awkward beginning	13
New, eye opening	9
Future	9
Larger than local concern	8
Continue to volunteer	6
Made a difference	6
Sad/Sadness	5
Reinforced major/career	3
Clients strong/brave	3
Greater appreciation	3

thoughts about volunteerism were probably best expressed by student 6: "before, I never knew what kind of person it took to offer their personal time in this busy world, but after I felt the good feelings of helping others I quickly found out what volunteering means."

Definitions and connotations of leisure contained reference to personal growth and development as well as experiences that departed from the ordinary routine (Table 2). Student number 6 wrote: "at first I was scared of the whole idea of volunteering but now realize that I wasn't as complete a person as I am now. The field placement has opened up my eyes and given me a whole new perspective on life." Student 26 commented that "this field placement was the most beneficial experience that I have ever done." The expression that something extraordinary had been experienced was not limited to a few. Student number 1 expressed it in the following way: "it was [a] mind expanding journey. It raised questions within myself that will require further self-exploration ... It was inspiring." The field placement was just not a continuation of their previous existence, it fulfilled one of the three preconditions of leisure by departing from the ordinary routine (Bammel and Bammel, 1992). Two of the tallied themes address this, the theme of something new/ eye opening/enlightenment and the theme of being concerned or mentioning something beyond the student's normal area (global concerns, the larger world, the 'real world'). Thirty percent or more of the students mentioned each of these themes. A good example would be from student number 1: "the quality of life for individuals, our country, and the global community is dependent on equality of services and resources for all citizens regardless of the ability to pay."

Besides growth and development, satisfaction and enjoyment are included by some in a definition of leisure. Nearly half, 48 percent, of the students selected the word "enjoy", "enjoyed", "joy" etc. a total of 18 times. Over half (55%) of the students included either a derivative of "enjoy" or "fun" a total of 24 times and nearly 60% when either the word "happy" or "love" is added for a total of 29 words. Student number 6 stated "this personal growth and learning that I have experienced through the field placement has given me great satisfaction and a better self-worth ... the field placement has opened up my eyes and given me a whole new perspective on life." Another student (number 7) said, "the greatest thing I feel coming out of this experience is a sense of accomplishment." Number 8 wrote, "this was definitely a positive experience for myself [sic]. I would recommend this to anyone that has some spare time. Being a volunteer is a rewarding experience and it also makes you feel good." "This field placement made me feel real good inside," was written by student number 14, and number 15 indicated that the field placement "was an uplifting and exciting experience." Number 24 summed it up with the words, "I had a great time ... it made me feel good."

Another indication that the experience was very well received by the students, even though it was required, is the fact that all but two (93%) wrote some kind of statement rating the placement in positive light and six (or 22 %) even included comments about either continuing with the placement or contemplating continuing as a volunteer. One negative comment was made and one problem was discussed in the 27 papers. Student 2 concluded the paper with these words, "I felt proud about what I was doing. I liked the field placement very much ... I have volunteered my services again at the hospital for the remainder of the school year." Student 4 ended the paper with the following statement, "I enjoyed my work so much that I am going to keep doing [it] for as long as I'm able." An intent was expressed by Student 6, "I am seriously going to make a sincere effort to continue to volunteer some of my free time to help Kramer because of the new outlet I now have."

Leisure is a very individual, personal experience. The students reacted in a very personal way to this assignment and recognized that it was an "experience". Some form of a personal pronoun (I, me, myself) was used at least 8 times by every student and the average was 15 with a high being 30. The word "experience" appeared a total of 23 times from 14 or slightly over half (51.9%) of the papers.

Summary and conclusions

The United States has had a long history of volunteerism and community service. This has been expressed in many forms from the Social Compact of 1620 to the National and Community Service Act of 1990. Volunteerism was initially supported by private individuals for a local cause. Over time, other larger interest groups became involved, and the effort evolved to a higher more organized level with worldwide concerns. First the government joined the effort and then the business sector. More recently, an educational movement called service-learning has started sweeping the country. Both secondary schools and institutions of higher education have added a community service component to their list of graduation requirements. Maryland is the first to have a state wide High School requirement.

Volunteerism and community service, while of long existence, has for the past 30 years or so been picking up speed in the number of people participating, the degree of participation, the number of businesses starting corporate programs, the amount of federal support, and the role given it in all levels of the educational system.

According to the various definitions, notions, and preconditions of leisure, volunteerism/community service can be considered a leisure activity.

Content analysis further supports the premise that volunteerism/community service not only constitutes a leisure activity but perhaps is a very desirable form of leisure. Volunteerism /community service is an experience that offers a natural high that record numbers seek and seek in increasing amounts. Volunteerism/community service is becoming part of people's thought and behavioural pattern — an emerging leisure lifestyle.

References

Anderson, R. (1992) Letter and Points of Light material from Serve-America to Commission on National and Community Service Grantees. Washington DC, June 17, 1992.

Bammel, G. and Bammel, L. (1992) *Leisure and human behavior* (Second Edition). Dubuque, IA: Wm. C. Brown.

Conrad D. and Hedin, D. (1991) 'School-based community service: What we know from research and theory', *Phi Delta Kappan* June, p. 744.

Crawford, D. W. and Godbey, G. (1987) 'Reconceptualizing barriers to family leisure', *Leisure Sciences*, Vol. 9, No. 2: pp.119-27.

Dare, B., Welton, G. and Coe, W. (1987) *Concepts of leisure in western thought*. Dubuque, Iowa: Kendall/Hunt.

Eberly, D. J. (nd) 'Milestones on the road to national service', in J. C. Kielsmeier and R. Willits (eds) *Growing hope: A sourcebook on Integrating Youth Services*.

Ellis, S. J. and Noyes, d K. H. (1990) *A history of Americans as volunteers*. San Francisco: Jossey-Bass.

Ferrell, F., Ferrell, J. and Wakin, E. (1985) *Trevor's place. The story of the boy who brings hope to the homeless*. San Francisco: Harper & Row.

Fisher, L. R. and Banister Schaffer, K. (1993) 'Seeking answers about volunteers', *Modern Maturity*, Vol. 36, No. 4: p. 6.

Godbey, G. and Parker, S. (1976) *Leisure studies and services: An overview*. Philadelphia: W. B. Sanders Company.

Hertzel, D. (1993) *Brooklyn Community Youth Service Learning Program*. Brooklyn, Ohio: Brooklyn City Schools.

Hicks, L. and Walsh, J. (1989) *Campus Compact: Members' Report 1988-89*. Providence, RI: Brown University.

Kohlberg, L. (1972) *The concepts of developmental psychology as the central guide to education*. Washington, D.C.: Special Education Leadership Training Institute, U.S. Office of Education.

Lesko, W. S. (1992) *No kidding around! America's young activists are changing our world and you can too.* Maryland: Information USA.

Loevinger, J. and Wessler, R. (1970) *Measuring ego development.* Volume One. San Francisco: Jossey-Bass Inc.

Maslow, A. (1968) *Toward a psychology of being.* New York: D. Van Nostrand Company.

McCarty, L. P. and Schwartz, L. H. (1992) *1992-93 National Members' survey and resource guide.* Providence, RI: Campus Compact: A Project of the Education Commission of the States.

National Governors' Association (1989) *Community service: A resource guide for States.* Washington DC: The Association.

Peterson, V. (1975) 'Volunteering and student value development: Is there a correlation?', *Synergist* Vo. 3, No. 3: pp. 44-51.

Points of Light Foundation (1993) News Release: *Year Long Study Shows Volunteerism Benefits Families.* Washington, D.C., April 30.

Roberts, K. (1970) *Leisure.* London: Longman.

Witt, P. A. and Goodale, T. L. (1985) 'Barriers to leisure across family stages', in M. Wade (ed) *Constraints on leisure.* Springfield, Ill: Charles C. Thomas.

Zivi, K. (1991) *Campus Compact: 1991-92 National Members' survey and resource Guide.* Providence, RI: Brown University.

Serious Leisure — A Middle-Class Phenomenon?

Stan Parker

University of Brighton, UK

In this paper I aim to explore the extent to which the concept and practice of serious leisure is correlated with middle-class values and behaviour. I shall first say something about the types and criteria of serious leisure, then discuss middle-class values. I shall place the criteria of serious leisure and middle-class values side by side to see to what extent they are compatible. Finally, I offer evidence from fieldwork that middle-class people do more often have serious leisure pursuits than working-class people.

Stebbins (1992) defines serious leisure, in contrast to the causal variety, as "the systematic pursuit of an amateur, hobbyist or volunteer activity that is sufficiently substantial and interesting for the participant to fond a career there in the acquisition and expression of its special skills and knowledge". I have argued with Stebbins that the concept of career is really variable, rather than a defining characteristic, in the explanation of serious leisure. Indeed, the concept hardly appeared in his earlier work on the subject, and he admits that it "has evolved over the fifteen years of this project".

I want to make two points about Stebbins' insistence that the concept of career is a defining characteristic of serious leisure. One is that 'career' is essentially a *work* term. There is no reason why it should not be imported into fields other than work (we hear, sometimes, talk of a delinquency career, for example), but we should be aware of the dangers of conceptualising leisure in works terms rather than in its own (leisure) terms. Godbey in 1975 rightly drew attention to the phenomenon of 'anti-leisure': treating leisure in such a competitive, goal-seeking and compulsive way is to take all the fun out of it.

My second point is that "career" is essentially a middle-class concept. The term 'middle-class ' is controversial in its meaning, and I do not wish to take part in the still-raging debate about whether class analysis has anything useful to contribute to sociology. My point is simply that people who would generally be regarded as middle class talk a lot about 'career' and their own work histories usually follow Stebbins' five stages of progression. Working-class people, however, don't have careers — they simply have jobs, if they are lucky enough to get them. At best they have what Wilensky (19760) calls "chaotic" — as opposed to "orderly" — careers. Of course, some middle-class people these days are forced to have "chaotic" careers — but that is another story.

I want now to focus attention on middle-class values, or standards of behaviour, because I think they have a lot to do with serious leisure. One of the best, if not *the* best, discussions of middle-class values is to be found in a book on delinquent boys by Cohen (1955). He lists and discusses nine such values, which I propose to expand to ten:

1. Ambition
2. Individual responsibility
3a. Cultivations and possession of skills
3b. Tangible achievements
4. Deferred gratification (he also calls it worldly asceticism)
5. Rationality
6. Manners, courtesy and personality
7. Control of physical aggression
8. Leisure spent constructively
9. Respect for property.

Only one of these refers specifically to leisure. "Leisure spent constructively" means that recreation should be 'wholesome'; time should not be 'wasted'. But if we look at some of the other middle-class values in relation to *serious* leisure we can see that at least some degree of correspondence.

Besides "possibility of career", Stebbins lists five other characteristics of serious leisure that distinguish it from casual leisure. These are:

- the need to *persevere*;
- *effort* based on knowledge, training or skill;

- *durable benefits* (Stebbins has found eight different types of these, ranging from self-actualization to lasting physical products);
- a *unique ethos* or social world that grows up around the activity;
- and finally, a strong individual *identity* based on the chosen pursuit.

The next step in my argument is to compare these two lists of serious leisure characteristics and middle-class values. Of the six serious leisure characteristics, five may be seen to relate to middle-class values:

1. Interest in the possibility of a career is clearly a type of ambition: one is ambitious to climb the career ladder.
2. A need to persevere is involved in the cultivation and possession of skills.
3. Effort put into a leisure pursuit is equivalent to spending the leisure (time) constructively.
4. Durable benefits include tangible achievements.
5. Constructing an individual identity from a leisure pursuit is an expression of individual responsibility.

There appears to be no middle-class value approximating to the serious leisure characteristics of a unique ethos or social world. Indeed, if anything this comes closer to the working class value of solidarity with one's mates. And several of Cohen's middle-class values (deferred gratification, rationality, manners, control of physical aggression, respect for property) seem to have no direct counterparts among the criteria of serious leisure. However, some of these middle-class values are arguably more likely to be expressions of serious than casual leisure. For example, a person spending much time learning to become an amateur musician surely exhibits more deferred gratification than a person who simply presses button for casual music.

I suggest that my reasoning so far points to a correlation between serious leisure and middle-class values but not to a one-to-one relationship. The next step is to see how far empirical research confirms this hypothesis.

Recently I interviewed 30 men and women in Australia about their leisure (Parker *et al.*, 1993). The interviews were semi-structured and allowed informed judgements to be made both about their class (dichotomised crudely into middle [n=21] and working [n=9] on the basis of a mixture of education and job criteria) and their leisure (serious; casual; and partly serious, the latter scoring on three of Stebbins' six criteria).

Figure 1 Types of leisure activity or interest of 30 selected Australians

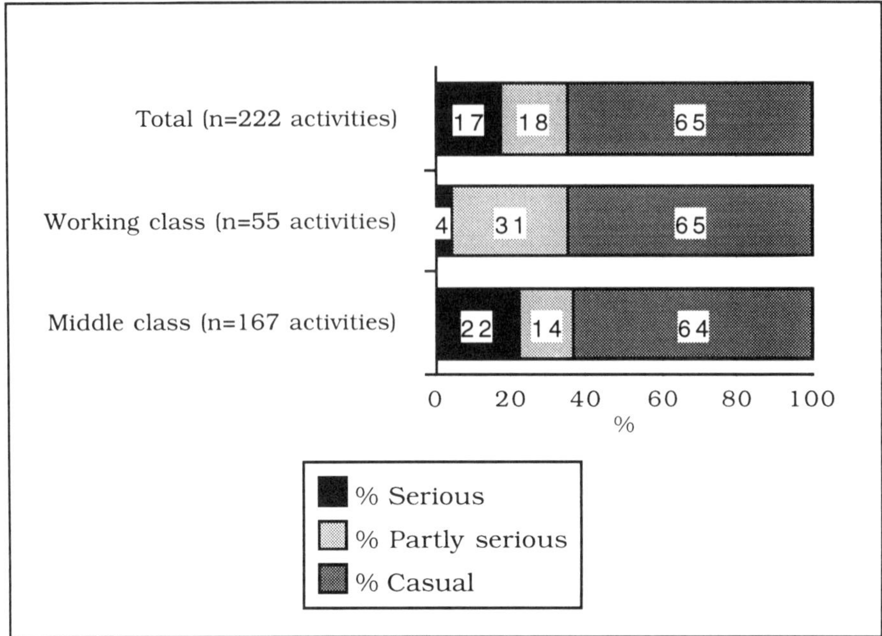

Figure 1 is based on the 222 leisure activities that the 30 interviewees collectively mentioned, and shows that serious leisure was indeed more common among the 21 middle class people than the 9 working class. However, the working-class people made up for this by having more partly serious leisure.

Figure 2 (opposite) shows how this works out in terms of broad groups of leisure activity, which is clearly a middle class concept in all classes of activity except handicrafts. Further:

1. Arts and Cultural activities are mainly middle-class, both as serious leisure.
2. Handicrafts are more often partly serious leisure, especially for working-class women.
3. Volunteering, unpaid teaching and coaching, socialising and being with friends in a 'serious 'way are mainly middle-class activities.

Figure 2 Types of serious and partly serious leisure, by social class

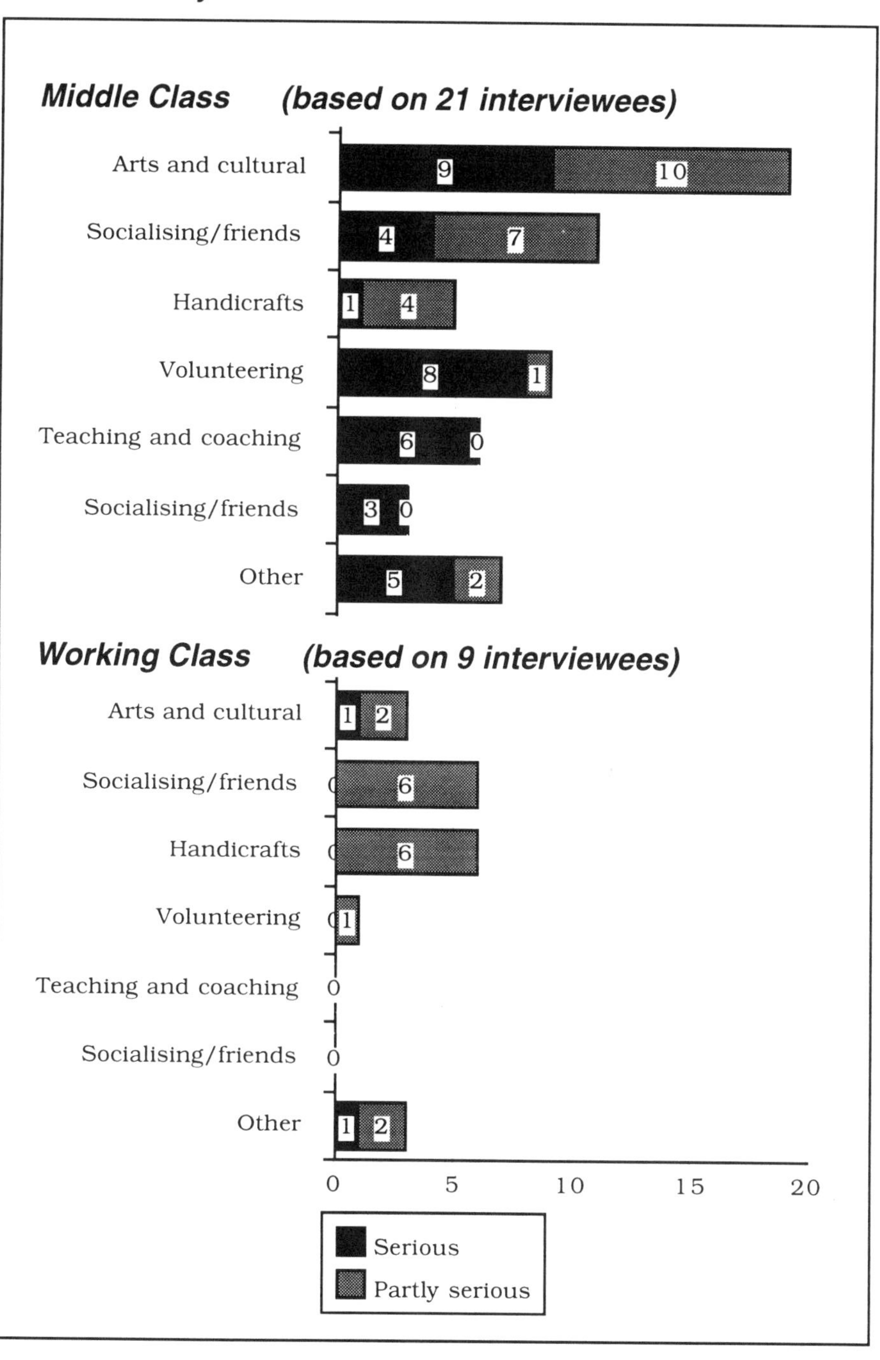

Conclusion

This paper has the modest aim of seeking to show that the concept and practice of serious leisure is mainly a middle-class phenomenon. Theoretically, the characteristics of serious leisure and the content of middle-class values have much in common. In practice, middle-class people do seem more often to have serious leisure activities and interests than do working-class people.

I disagree with Stebbins' claim that career is a defining characteristic of serious leisure because I think it is possible to be a good amateur, hobbyist or volunteer with little or no thought of career. but I agree with him that for a significant minority of the population there is "a serious orientation toward leisure". If casual leisure is mainly the province of the public and commercial providers (as I think it is), then the working class seem to be the most avid consumers of what is provided for them. If serious leisure is to grow in the future then it seems the middle class will be primarily responsible for that growth. Or perhaps I should say "People with middle class values will be responsible".

References

Cohen, A. K. (1955) *Delinquent boys*. Glencoe, Ill.: Free Press.

Parker, S. *et al* (1993) 'Serious and other leisure: thirty Australians', *World Leisure and Recreation*, Vol. 35, No. 1: pp. 14–18.

Stebbins, R. A. (1992) *Amateurs, professionals and serious leisure*. Montreal: McGill-Queen's University Press.

Wilensky, H. L. (1960) 'World, careers and social integration', *International Social Science Journal*, Vol. 4.

Family and Leisure in the Netherlands: A Literature Review

Jan W. te Kloeze

Wageningen Agricultural University, The Netherlands

Introduction

"Sunday is *the* day for joint recreation, reflection and recreation for the members of a family. A joint holiday can have the nature of a 'final rehearsal for marriage', whereby sexuality has to be considered as a taboo" (Smelik *et al.*, 1962). In these terms a group of Dutch Protestant authors formulated in the 1960s their hopes and fears about family and leisure affairs. After more than 30 years this quotation is intriguing at the very moment the new Dutch governmental coalition [1994; political colour 'purple' — this means Conservatives + 'New' Liberals + Social Democrats *without* Christian Democrats] starts a discussion about free opening and closure times shops on Sundays. Further, the quotation nicely indicates the norms and values regarding family life and the role of leisure.

As far as I know, the first empirical study in the Netherlands dealing with aspects of family and leisure was done by Litjens (1953). He described the use of leisure of 'unsocial' families. According to this author most of such families lacked every trace of home comforts. Before the Second World War, Andries Sternheim (1939) – who was murdered by the Nazis in Auschwitz – had already written about the intervention of the totalitarian state in family life and the misuse of sports and recreation by the regime for political goals, in order to retain the cooperation of the mass.

Studies and literature in the sixties on family and leisure in the Netherlands can be characterised by questions about the integrative or disintegrative function of leisure for family life. I briefly quote the results of those studies:

- spending the weekend is strongly family oriented (Vries-Bastiaans, 1966);
- the family design is important with regard to leisure spent by the family (Versteegh, unknown);
- parents are of the opinion dancing is important for making contact with other people, they directly link up between dancing and courtship (Dussen-Van Dongen and Van der Heiden, 1965);
- family structure and culture at the camp site and at home hardly deviate (Dom, 1971).

In many studies on recreation and leisure as a social phenomenon, leisure is regarded as the opposite of work, or as a compensation for it. Leisure is also seen as complementary to an individual's line of work. However, a number of scholars questions whether these views of leisure as the antithesis of work are the most fruitful approaches to gaining insight into recreation and leisure. According to Philipsen (1963), Roberts (1981), Kelly (1983) and Te Kloeze (1985a) a family or household approach is more productive. Only a few studies have made use of these suggestions.

Several authors supplied theoretical and empirical reviews about leisure, recreation and tourism in the Netherlands (Beckers, 1981), Mommaas and Van der Poel (1984, 1985), Beckers and Van der Poel (1990), Beckers and Mommaas (1991), Dietvorst and Spee (1991). New theoretical insights have been provided about the meaning of complexes and networks for the tourist-recreative sector Dietvorst (1989), the structurationist critique of leisure studies (Van der Poel, 1993; Mommaas, 1993), the application of a transformation model for tourist recreation product development (Dietvorst, 1994) and the idea of 'contra-structure' which refers to everything that falls outside the concept of everyday reality such as leisure (Lengkeek, 1994).

Even a review of the theme 'family and leisure in the Netherlands' has been published before (Te Kloeze, 1985a, 1985b), ending with a plea for using the concept of lifestyle in family and leisure studies. In this contribution relationships between family aspects and leisure practices and experiences, focused on the Dutch case, are described and an integration between family styles and leisure styles will be discussed. Attention will be paid to the macro social developments, especially individualisation and technological processes and their influences on family and leisure. The international literature on family and leisure deals with the following issues (Van Betuw & Van Dijk, 1993; Van Betuw, Van Dijk & Te Kloeze, 1993):

1 definitions of leisure by family members and by women in particular, and values, meanings and ideals of leisure;
2 daily paths and biography in terms of actual experiences of family members;

3 the family as a social context; individuality versus togetherness;

4 family functions of leisure, the leisure functions of the family;

5 power and control, decision-making, rules, organisation and task-sharing in families with regard to leisure, and the conflicts that arise;

6 caring position;

7 the home as spatial context.

The first six issues have been found in the literature in the Netherlands too, and are examined here; no studies on the home as spatial context for leisure have been found. Finally, new theoretical approaches to help understand the relationship between family and leisure will be discussed. Before I examine these, I shall look at theoretical approaches and the macro-social trends of family leisure in contemporary Holland.

The literature on family and leisure in general and in the Netherlands in particular can be regarded from several points of view. On the one hand, there is the scarce literature in the sociology of leisure studying aspects of leisure in the family context empirically (Van der Heiden, 1966, 1968, 1972; Van der Heiden and Smeding, 1967; Te Kloeze, 1994a) or, theoretically, the household context (Van der Poel, 1993). Besides, themes such as recreation styles of different households – mainly families – (Andersson and De Jong, 1987), leisure of housewives (Van 't Eind *et al.*, 1981), "househusbands" (Te Kloeze, 1990a) or several categories of women (married) housewives, working mothers (out of two career households or singles) and single women (Karsten, 1992)), camping styles of households in the Netherlands (Hout, 1993), and central aspects of family life such as socialisation into leisure (Kamphorst and Spruijt, 1983) have been studied. Hardly any attention has been paid to the family or household context of tourism in Dutch literature.

On the other hand, studies in sociology on marriage and the family in the Netherlands have also paid little attention to leisure and recreation. The mainstream in this subdiscipline has been for years the institutional approach (Van Leeuwen, 1976). Kooy, one of the founders of the sociology on marriage and the family in the Netherlands, theoretically described the recreative *function* of the so-called modern Western family (Kooy, 1977). In addition, Douma (1975) constructed on an empirical base the modern Western family and described the contours of what he mentioned the 'plastic' family, including recreative aspects shifting to a modernised meaning of leisure. In the tradition of this 'Wageningen school' of the sociology on marriage and the family, Weeda (1982) described ideal images of lifestyles. She showed the relationship between the extent of individualisation of both the lifestyle and the leisure domain. Weeda studied the impact of leisure and conflicts in the leisure domain on divorce and marriage too (Weeda, 1983a, 1983b, 1984).

Komter's study on the power of the obvious showed the obvious task-sharing between husbands and wives in the leisure domain (Komter, 1985). Recently, Te Kloeze *et al.* (1995) showed the relationship between family domains and leisure domains. To the present day, family sociologists in the Netherlands have not studied tourist aspects of family life.

Theoretical approaches

Quite often leisure is just one of the aspects taken in consideration when studying the family or family life. In the Netherlands there are in fact only two comprehensive studies, already mentioned above: Van der Heiden (1966, 1968, 1972; Van der Heiden and Smeding, 1967) and, recently, Te Kloeze *et al.* (1995). Van der Heiden's studies deal with the familial factors influencing leisure behaviour and with family camping and day recreation. These studies originate from the ideology of the sixties: family integration. Family leisure and specifically family camping were seen as a means of achieving this integration. Te Kloeze *et al.* (1995) were able to construct a general family typology and a family leisure typology in terms of modern Western, transitional and post-modern family types.

Another study that is considered to be a comprehensive study in fact solely examines the leisure of housewives, although within the family context (Beckers *et al.*, 1980; Van 't Eind *et al.*, 1981). This study is more feminist-oriented and deals among other things with a housewife's definition of leisure. Karsten's study (1992), mentioned above, is similar to the Van 't Eind *et al.* study, although not restricted to housewives' leisure, but is distinguished by its challenging theoretical approach, on which I will elaborate here.

The main theoretical divisions in sociology today reflect the different approaches established in earlier periods, the most important currently being the system oriented 'family' of approaches (*functionalism, structuralism, institutionalism, some conflict approaches, operationalism and Marxism*) and the actor oriented 'family' of approaches (*symbolic interactionism*, some *role theories, ethnomethodology, phenomenology*, some *exchange theories*, the *situational approach* and the *life-cycle approach*). To escape from the actor-structure dilemma, in the last few decades new theoretical approaches have been developed in sociology: *figurational sociology* (Elias), *lifestyle approaches* (Bourdieu), *theory of structuration* (Giddens), *contextual approach of leisure* (Beckers and Van der Poel), *theory of communicative action* (Habermas). Because of influencing the theory of structuration and of its importance for the study of leisure, *time-space-geography* (Hägerstrand) has to be mentioned as well. The theoretical bases in the sociology on family and leisure in the Netherlands refer to the following approaches.

The institutional approach, more or less future oriented, is the central guideline in the studies of Kooy (1977), Douma (1975), Weeda (1982) and Te Kloeze *et al.* (1995). The family is regarded as an institution in which human behaviour has been established in patterns, but which can change; therefore, the family is interconnected with other institutions. This institution meets two fundamental needs: reproduction and socialisation. Historical comparison is necessary to understand developments in the family as institution. Kooy (1967) said in his study on the evolution of family functions, that the development of a "society of provision" created more room for the development of the "cherishing" function of the family — that is, the increases in leisure time provide room for "being there for each other". This has become more and more important to family members. Kooy (1977) stated that the "modern Western family" is becoming more and more a recreation unit instead of the production unit as in the past, but he described the recreational function of the family as more or less non-problematic.

Orthner (1975) too indicated that the family has not lost its recreation function. He noticed that families are not prepared for the leisure explosion and should therefore be socialised so that they can learn how to deal with the increasing possibilities of leisure. Douma (1975) saw mainly a qualitative change in the importance of the recreation function, namely a shift toward modernisation (e.g. holidays abroad instead of staying with relatives). Douma saw the core function of the "plastic" family as striving for identity. Weeda (1982) described the extent of the need of togetherness for different lifestyles and both traditional and new types of relationships. The extent of the need of togetherness is strongly connected with the lifestyles studied: the more people belong to an individualistic lifestyle, the more they prefer to undertake leisure activities apart from their partner or with other persons. Te Kloeze *et al.* (1995) developed a framework to study the relationship between family domains and leisure domains. The authors concluded the housewives interviewed were more traditional on the leisure domain than on the specific family domain, which conclusion was contrary to the expectations. Typical for all these studies is the diachronic approach. Family typologies have been constructed, and changes from one type to another has been understood in terms of long term social developments such as individualisation processes.

Kamphorst and Spruijt (1983) studied the influence of socialisation on leisure behaviour by means of structured interviews with 420 males *and* their mothers. The males were asked about their present leisure behaviour, the mothers about various aspects of socialisation in the past, 20 to 25 years back, i.e. when their sons were 5 to 10 years old. This study can be criticised because reliability of the data is questionable (much depending on answers about situations 20 years ago) and, more seriously, it lacks a theoretical framework. They showed many relationships between variables but hardly explained the findings within the context of a social theory. Therefore, Mommaas and Van der Poel (1984) classified this study under the heading of operational approaches. Nevertheless, these authors have shown the importance of socialising effects adequately from the empirical point of view. Unfortunately, the institutional approach is not able to give adequate insight on the micro level of the family.

Therefore we need an actor-centred approach, which gives weight to the active, creative individual. This approach have been used by Van der Heiden (1966, 1968, 1972; Van der Heiden and Smeding, 1967), Van 't Eind *et al.* (1981), Weeda (1983a, 1983b, 1984), Komter (1985), Te Kloeze (1990a) and Hout (1993). Van der Heiden held extended interviews with parents, which offered many insights into family life in the 1960s. Some studies were focused on outdoor recreational behaviour and experiences such as camping. One of the conclusions was that families keep their structure and much of their culture during camping (Van der Heiden, 1966). As well as home interviews, participant observations of camping situations and interviews with campers were applied. These studies focused on interaction and communication patterns, integration, socialisation and family images. Being together as a family defines leisure as a joint project. A starting point in the study was: the family has its own style; the subjective experience is essential.

While the Van der Heiden studies breathed the preoccupation with the family ideology of the early 1960s, those of Van 't Eind *et al.* (1981), Weeda (1983a, 1983b, 1984), Komter (1985) and Te Kloeze (1990a) were focused on power relationships between the sexes, and were more or less feminist oriented. Van 't Eind *et al.* (1981) intensively interviewed housewives about the meaning of leisure; the authors stressed the oppressed position of women, and of working class women in particular. Among other things, Weeda (1983a, 1983b, 1984) studied the impact of leisure on marriage and divorce. For example: many a marriage is put to the test by time consuming activities of husbands such as attending football matches (Weeda, 1984). The same author found leisure was one the important problems experienced as causes of divorce (Weeda, 1983b). In many cases divorce was experienced (particularly by women) to be a liberation from oppression by the (male) partner.

Komter (1985) studied the relationship between husband and wife from the balance of power point of view, drawing on Lukes' idea that power is a result of conflicts, and Gramsci's that the consequence of power is consensus, and consensus maintains power. Among other things she studied the power relationship between husband and wife in the field of leisure where task-sharing is self-evident. So to say, the obviousness of power leads to the power of the obvious (Te Kloeze, 1990a). Komter's approach nicely contradicts the opinion that actor-centred approaches cannot be compatible with structural concepts such as power relationships.

Te Kloeze (1990a) studied the gender differences between the leisure practices and leisure experiences of people having one and the same caring position: housewives and "househusbands". The results were discussed within the framework of structural developments such as the deeply rooted male dominance in western society, and individualisation processes, and are described as part of issue 6.

Hout's study into the dynamics of camping styles showed the importance of the transitions in the family life-cycle in explaining the changes in camping behaviour (Hout, 1993). Information derived from extended interviews helped to construct a typology of campers on the basis of two continua: the extent of variation versus familiarity to the destination , and the extent of privacy wanted versus social orientation during the holiday.

While the institutional approach is not able to theorise about the actor's feelings and experiences, the actor centred approach fails in linking these experiences with an institutional context. To transcend this actor-structure dilemma, a theory of action such as the theory of structuration (Giddens, 1981, 1984) and its 'translation' to leisure studies: the contextual approach of leisure (Beckers and Van der Poel, 1990), is necessary. In the field of household and recreation, Andersson and De Jong (1987), Karsten (1992), Van der Poel (1993) and Te Kloeze (1994a) based their studies on this approach, as I will elaborate later.

Macro social developments

The developments in the field of family and leisure proceed from changes in society as a whole. This is why it is important to examine macro social developments that have most influenced the mutual relation between family and leisure. The influences of individualisation, technological processes and emancipation seem to have been considerable. Other main developments such as secularisation and social differentiation (Kooy, 1977), commercialisation, pacification and uniformation (Rojek, 1985; Te Kloeze, 1989), and economic developments will not be discussed here.

In this contribution on family and leisure, individualisation *of* the family can be understood as a process whereby the family becomes increasingly independent of surrounding institutions, like relatives, the neighbourhood and the church. This means that leisure takes place more within the family context than in the more traditional contexts just mentioned. Yet, there is individualisation *within* the family itself. Members of the family are seen as individuals rather than just as a particular member. Individualisation expresses itself in a more individual leisure pattern. Family members no longer undertake the same activities at the same time and place. It is possible that while father reads the newspaper, mother has gone to her fitness class and the children are doing their homework. The cultural undercurrent of these potential developments has been described earlier in similar terms: as an ongoing process of individualisation.

Hofstee (1980) formulated the idea (and fear of) 'hyperindividua(lisa)tion': a strongly ego-centred individualisation, an extreme form of individualisation. "Hyperindividualisation" results in, among other things, a decreasing interest in establishing a family and the family context for leisure becomes less relevant: family leisure ceases to exist or family members focus on themselves only ("cocooning"). However, "hyperindividualisation" is hardly likely to occur.

Te Kloeze (1989) discerned the potential of this, but saw indications of a more socially directed variant of individuation which could be interpreted as 'association'. Association means that the individual's fulfilment and value are dialectically related to his or her orientation to other people and things in the social and natural environment. Neither the development of one's own personality is at the cost of the others, nor do others or the social setting dominate the individual to such an extent as to suppress fulfilment and consciousness-raising. By extrapolation it can be postulated that the consciousness-raising of the value of the self is only 'possible' if one gives room to and is involved with the social setting. "I as human being will be a human being only if I give others the space I myself need" (Te Kloeze, 1990a). The *common* factor of hyperindividuation and association is the feature of individuation: the consciousness-raising of the perception of one's own personality. The *difference* is that hyperindividuation can be considered an extreme form of ego-centric individuation, and association a more socially directed variant or dimension. It is interesting to note that similar thinking has been expressed recently by Bauman in mentioning 'moral responsibility': "being *for* the Other before one can be *with* the Other" (Bauman, 1993: p. 13).

In the 'associative' case both individual and joint leisure are attractive options. The two alternatives of individualisation bear similarities to Yankelovich's three ethics: of self-sacrifice, self-fulfilment and commitment (Yankelovich, 1981). Individualisation has not only made people more independent of certain institutions, it has simultaneously made them more dependent on other (anonymous) institutions. The social security system, for instance, is no longer seen as a favour, but as a right. However, there may be a tendency towards a feeling of greater responsibility with regard to others, society and oneself. According to Weeda (1992), social processes based on developments in gender paradigms are individualisation (the process indicating the individual is more and more responsible for his own choices) and 'solidarisation' (the process indicating people are taking responsibility for others in a new way, entering into new relationships).

The process of individualisation is boosted by technological and economic developments. New technological techniques are used to extend recreational possibilities. As a result of the vast range of leisure activities and leisure possibilities, a great variety of leisure patterns occurs. Families are more mobile because of the increase in car ownership and mobility in general. The aspect of mobility is of great importance to the spending of leisure time. The arrival of the car has influenced the choice of location of the (annual) holiday(s). It has become easier to travel longer distances. Besides, for singles the car is an important means of maintaining their contacts. The mobility of the family has also been made easier because of the decreasing size of the family as a result of birth control.

Parents have now more (free) time for their children and also for each child. Another typical example of the influence of technological inventions on family leisure time, is the introduction of television. Almost every household in the Netherlands has one or more television sets: in 1991 95% of the households owned a colour television set (CBS, 1994). In 1975, 10.2 hours per week were spent on watching television; by 1990 this had advanced to 12 hours per week. Of housewives interviewed in rural areas, 90% reported television watching every evening in their families (72% always or sometimes in the afternoon). Nevertheless, 70% of these families played 'round' games a few times a month or more often (Te Kloeze *et al.*, 1995). The poor watch TV more than the rich (De Hoog and Van Ophem, 1992, 1994a). Furthermore, the invention of the video recorder enables people to choose when and what to watch. In 1985 a quarter of the households had a video recorder and since then this number has only increased, in 1991 to 50% (CBS, 1994); in 1986 31% of the families in rural areas had a video recorder (Te Kloeze, 1988).

Another invention that has brought about changes in leisure time, is the (personal) computer. In 1986 13% of the families in rural areas had a personal computer (Te Kloeze, 1988), in 1991 25% of all households in the Netherlands owned a PC or home-computer (CBS, 1994). Children can enjoy themselves playing video games alone, whereas previously the parents played, for example, board games with their children. The computer also allows freedom of location so that people can work from their homes and can be free of regular working hours. In this way they could have more control over their own (free) time.

Some authors criticise these developments. Ritzer (1993) typifies the changing character of contemporary social life in terms of 'McDonaldization' and Postman (1985) discusses the transition from a reading culture to an image culture. We are amusing ourselves to death. Everything is going to be 'amusementised'. Children in western societies have been educated from childhood with the image culture. In the United States a second generation has been educated and grown up with TV. In his more recent study Postman (1993) describes the United States as being a 'Technopoly', a system in which technology of every kind is a cheerfully granted sovereignty over social institutions and national life, and becomes self-justifying, self-perpetuating, and omni-present. Writing on the impact of the electronic media, he says that children come to school having been deeply conditioned by the biases of television: "There, they encounter the world of the printed word. A sort of psychic battle takes place, and there are many casualties – children who can't learn to read or won't, children who cannot organise their thought into logical structure even in a simple paragraph, children who cannot attend lectures or oral explanations for more than a few minutes at a time" (Postman, 1985: pp. 16-17).

At a recent congress Trouw stated that family life will revive through interactive television: teleshopping, video-on-demand, interactive medical services and advertising, with TV as the life-line to the outside world. These processes of consumption are examples of what Van der Poel (1993) calls modularisation of daily life.

Finally, emancipation of women, which is related to the individualisation process, has influenced the relationship between family and leisure. In modern society people strive for a more equal distribution of tasks between women and men, whether household, educational, labour or leisure and for a balance of authority between both sexes. Emancipation has also brought about an increase in the number of working women. In the Netherlands, the percentage of women working in 1971 was 30% and that of men about 85%. In 1991 this figure was about 55% for women and 81% for men. The Netherlands used to be quite unique with its low percentage of full-time working married women. Although this is no longer the case, one thing that is still unique in the Netherlands is the high percentage of *part-time* working married women. Two thirds of all working women (and mothers) in the Netherlands, are part-timers.

Issue 1: Definition, meaning and value of leisure

The individual approach is applied in most, what we call, isolated studies on family and leisure. The individual member of the family was often taken as the research unit on which statements were based applying to the whole family. Besides, it was often the supposition that leisure activities are free from normative constraints. "Leisure is time free from obligations to self or to others – time in which to do as one chooses" (Parker, 1983: p. 64). In this context Karsten (1992) talks about control; she thinks that in daily life people claim each other's time (spending). Leisure time can only exist when people are able to protect themselves from the claims other people place on their spending time (Karsten, 1992). In this way, leisure can be defined in both objective terms (participation, activity and time) and in subjective terms (experience and satisfaction). The subjective definition includes terms such as: free choice, absence of obstructions, enjoying, relaxing, free from obligations to self or to others. Not only do claims by other people influence the choices made in leisure time, but social factors over which people have little control, such as age, family stage, sex and time structures determined by society (school hours, closing hours of shops, etc.), also effect these choices. Therefore, free time is not available as leisure time for everybody in the same measure. From that point of view it is understandable that housewives define several types of leisure:

- leisure for mothers (role-determined leisure);
- leisure for oneself (intrinsic leisure);
- leisure for housewives (compensatory leisure);
- leisure for a spouse (relational leisure) (Van 't Eind *et al.*, 1981; Te Kloeze, 1985d, 1985e, 1985f).

It is striking that "househusbands" define leisure solely intrinsically, and according to them leisure starts after the household chores (say after 7.00 p.m.) (Te Kloeze, 1990a). With reference to the qualitative methods, used in the study of Van 't Eind *et al.* (1981), Te Kloeze *et al.* (1995) tried to measure these definitions of leisure quantitatively. Housewives define 'being alone and able to do what I want to do, without husband and children' as paramount leisure, while 'drinking a cup of coffee after having done the household chores' is hardly experienced as leisure.

Issue 2: Life-cycle, daily path and biography

The shift of attention from life-cycle to life course or biography is also partly an expression of the trend of individualisation. First some attention will be paid to the concept of life-cycle. In 1975, Rapoport and Rapoport studied the importance of the life-cycle in the design of leisure. During the life-cycle people's preoccupations, interests and activities change (Rapoport and Rapoport, 1975). They used the family life-cycle as the framework within which they analyzed change: individuals change their occupations, interests and activities as they develop through the course of their life stage. They change because of social roles, in relation to the family stage and the family structure (Rapoport and Rapoport, 1975). There are a number of family variables that influence leisure behaviour:

- the family life-cycle;
- the presence of children;
- employment of the spouse/parent ;
- other family variables, family type, family size, family's socio-economic status (see also Holman and Epperson, 1984).

Not much is known about children's leisure in the Netherlands. Te Kloeze (1988) provides a review. The impact of the presence of a TV-set at home is unmistakable. Nevertheless, playing outside is still important in children's play, which can be concluded from a content analysis of essays written by school children (Te Kloeze, 1995). Apart from the family (see further on), the peer group is one of the most important socialising agents into leisure (Kamphorst, 1988). Young people claim their own time and space (Naber, 1985; De Waal, 1989), sometimes hanging around together (Hazekamp, 1985), creating their own specific and sometimes secret lifestyles (Ter Bogt, 1987), having their own secret language, rites and codes. As mentioned before, parental control over several leisure domains is still ahead, but is decreasing in case of 'less dangerous' leisure practices such as the choice of sports, things to do on holiday or the choice of TV programmes (Te Kloeze, 1994b).

Starting a relationship takes place in a recreational context in 60% of cases (De Hoog, 1982), while for young adolescents 'going out' can be described in terms of flirtation and marriage market (Van Duin, 1983). Until far into this century complete '*noaberschappen*' (Saxon dialect for neighbourhood) in the Province of Gelderland were busy days, and days to celebrate punctuated the time span between publication of the banns and the '*broedlachte*' (wedding-party): the '*boksenbier*' (a sort of beer-party), the '*schutten*' (a party outdoors accompanied with drinking a lot of Dutch brandy, while the bride was leaving her parents' home), the '*brulfteneugen*' (invitation party for the wedding) and the '*halemoal*' (a meal, at the end of the ceremony, just before the wedding-party itself) (Wildenbeest, 1982).

Family members have different amounts of time (for leisure) and different interests at different stages in their life-cycles. Two specific transitions in the life-cycle appear to influence leisure behaviour. These are marriage and parenthood. Hantrais (1983) disclosed that the arrival of (the first) child(ren) has a specific influence on leisure behaviour. After marriage and/or parenthood most leisure activities (of the parents) move to the home environment and are restricted to social intercourse with relatives, especially for the mother. Furthermore, she stated that the effect on leisure after the arrival of the first child is greater than the effect of marriage on leisure. With parenthood, intrinsic activities change into role-related activities. This means that before the birth of children, parents do certain activities simply because they like doing them. After the birth of children they do certain activities in their capacity of father or mother (e.g. playing games). First the spouse is the principal leisure partner, then when children arrive the family becomes the most important leisure context (Kelly, 1978). Moreover, the stage in the family life-cycle appears to influence the sort of activities a family chooses.

In research on family camping in the Netherlands, Van der Heiden (1966, 1968, 1972) and Hout (1993) found that changes in the family stage led to changes in the camping style too. For example, families with young children look for a different sort of camp site than families with teenagers: the difference between playgrounds or disco's and bars. According to De Hoog and Van Ophem (1994b) a large number of children leads to fewer expenses on eating away from home, and more shopping. An analysis of recreative behaviour makes clear households with children living at home show, generally spoken, a bourgeois lifestyle compared with households without children living at home: they are going out less and are spending less money on holidays, and they prefer more home tied hobbies.

Weeda (1984) found that married couples are ill-informed about the partner's leisure preferences, while the question how far spending leisure is experienced as a problem depends on several factors: the consciousness of choice, the extent of togetherness, the extent of harmony, the extent of communication and situational factors such as time and money.

Although many changes and developments in leisure behaviour and ways of spending leisure seem to be explained by the family life-cycle, this approach also has some drawbacks. The family life-cycle is built on an ideal from the fifties: a "normal" family (husband working outside, housewife and child(ren)), passing "normally" through the successive stages of the life-cycle. Because of the great increase in divorces and other cohabitation patterns, many lifestyles in contemporary society do not resemble this "traditional family", which was dominant in the Netherlands between the beginning of this century and the mid 1960s (De Hoog, 1989). Thus it is no longer possible to talk about one particular life-cycle that everyone passes through in the same way. It would be better to talk about life courses or biographies of people.

By life course or biography is understood an individual-specific and periodically situated path of life (Beckers and Van der Poel, 1990). By means of Giddens' theory of structuration, it is possible to analyze just how people give direction to their daily path and life. The theory of Hägerstrand (1970) (time-space geography) can be used to picture the different life situations of people and the daily paths belonging to them (Karsten, 1992). Giddens and Hägerstrand see a connection between daily paths and life paths. Changes on the life path do not remain without consequences for the daily activities.

Research has shown that biographical changes of women can lead to radical changes in the field of leisure. The birth of a child, mentioned above (Hantrais, 1983) or losing a partner are examples of such biographical changes.

Andersson and De Jong (1987) used the concept of biography as one of the four constituent elements of the recreation styles which arose from their empirical data (the other three were recreational profile, caring position and social context). These researchers were able to construct meaningful recreation styles embedded in the primary life domains of the actors (families, couples, singles, one parent families). The concept of biography in these recreation styles makes clear that former experiences are still 'working' at a latter stage. The stylecalled "We can manage", for example, described the present, frugal lifestyle of elderly working class couples, people who look twice at their money, educated before the Second World War to live economically.

How people interpret, value and digest the events that emerge on their daily path, largely depends on the experiences that they have already had in their course of life until that time, and their future perspective on their life's path. But, the use of daily paths has its limitations too. They give a simple picture of daily activity patterns, but do not provide insights into questions about the whys and wherefores of actions. More qualitative research might be necessary to find out what motivates people.

Issue 3: The family as a social context of leisure practices; individuality versus togetherness

Several social factors are influencing family life. As mentioned already, certain critical stages in the family cycle, like marriage and parenthood, influence the leisure of both parents. In these critical stages, leisure is strongly family and home-oriented. National surveys at the end of the sixties and the beginning of the eighties show that the vast majority of married couples prefer jointly spending leisure, although that majority is decreasing in the eighties (Te Kloeze, 1985c).

Te Kloeze *et al.* (1995) found that housewives think very subtly about aspects of togetherness. Most of them (60%) agree with the traditional (modern Western) statement that it is right that a family spends as much as possible free time together, because of the chance the family would disintegrate otherwise. A 'transitional' or 'associative' statement — "It is right a family is doing some things together and others things not together during free time, because you have the ability to lead your own life" — is more popular: 92% agreed. A more 'hyper-individualistic' statement received more agreement than the traditional one: 66% agreed with the statement "It is right that family members can do their own things during free time, because everybody must very clearly be able to live his or her own life". It seems that the 'togetherness bastion' is fragmenting: togetherness is OK, not because it ought to be so, but because it is a matter of free and conscious choice.

According to some authors, the effect of social class on leisure is less significant than the effect of gender (Roberts, 1978). Komter (1985) adds that in the lower social classes the majority of men and women are in need of joint social contacts. With regard to the effect of gender on the kind of social contacts, the following can be said: for women (especially housewives), family members and relatives are the most important social contacts; for men, work is a majore source of social relationships. For a long time women have been excluded from paid work and social contacts outside the home. Emancipation has brought about a change, but for some women it is still an underestimated phenomenon. The fact that men are more able to maintain contacts outside the home, is indirectly caused by the "ethic of care", which ties women down to their homes (Henderson and Allen, 1991). The results of studies on the out of the home orientation of men and the home orientation of women are disputable. The study by Rubin (1976) on working-class families shows that men see the home as a haven of refuge. The full-time housewife in particular, sees the home as a prison. In other words: the increasing importance of family and home activities can become a more important dimension in the life of men, whereas women get more and more entangled in domestic life (Allan, 1985).

Recently, De Hoog and Van Ophem (1992, 1994a) studied the differences in leisure behaviour of the poor and the rich in the Netherlands from a household approach. They concluded that the leisure of the poor is devoted to time consuming but cheap activities, mainly in or around the home. The relatively well-to-do show their high standard of living also in their leisure activities and behaviour. Leisure is an important part of their cultural capital, but differentiations occur within this income category. The traditional socio-economic and socio-demographic variables are more important than a hedonistic lifestyle variable. Some of their conclusions fit with those of Andersson and De Jong (1987) regarding the recreation style of the poor (e.g. "We can manage" by elderly working class couples) and the rich (e.g. "Enjoying old age" bythe well-to-do, retired couples).

Te Kloeze (1990b) reported on family recreation activities and constructed four factors which were regarded as family recreation styles:

1. family activities outside the home (going out: theatre, concert; going out: pub, eating out; going into the countryside; visiting relatives);
2. lively family activities inside the home (reading, handicrafts/hobbies, making music);

3. entertaining family activities inside the home (games, watching TV); and
4. sport.

Looking at the influence of the professional status and education (as indicators for economic and cultural capital), the author concluded that economic and cultural capital variance is substantially connected to the variance in three of the four family recreation styles. Neither economic nor cultural capital contribute to a differentiation of the preference for family activities outside the home. Cultural capital, however, is considered to be more important than economic capital for active and entertaining family pursuits within the home. The only difference is that the activity mentioned first is preferred by the cultural elite and the last mentioned by lower cultural strata. The preference for sport is especially strong among the economic elite. Within the framework of the family recreation styles, cultural capital would appear to carry out more weight than economic capital. As a matter of fact, in this study a family recreation *typology* has been developed rather than family recreation *styles*.

Issue 4: The family functions of leisure or the leisure functions of the family: a reciprocal relationship

In the 1960s some sociologists were dealing with research on family and leisure. As stated before, these studies were mainly focused on the family functions of leisure. In those terms it was concluded that spending Sundays outdoors was considered as an integrative climax of weekly leisure (Van der Heiden, 1968). Families choose aloofness, but reject isolation. Interaction between family members is influenced by the family life-cycle, the child orientation and the correspondence between family goals (Van der Heiden and Smeding, 1967).

In terms of the functional and institutional approaches besides family interaction and family integration, the function of leisure is, according to Carisse (1975), using privileged time to socialise children towards common values. By common values is meant common *cultural* values and norms. It appears that children by imitating adults in their play, are role-playing (preparing for real life). This could be socialisation into a particular lifestyle/ family style or even, a family recreation style (Te Kloeze, 1990b). Socialisation into leisure happens during childhood. A study among males and their mothers showed that father's behaviour is more important for the son's leisure behaviour than that of the mother (Kamphorst and Spruijt, 1983). Although everybody will subscribe the big influence of education and socialisation, the former study provides little to explain the still often dynamic changes of recreative behaviour in this century (Te Kloeze, 1994b). Furthermore, socialisation into leisure in more than 52% of the families in rural areas of the Netherlands is gender-specific (agreement with statements such as "knitting is for girls, and rugby is for boys") (Te Kloeze *et al.*, 1995).

The same study clearly shows that parents employ a differentiated pattern of allowing freedom of decision about leisure affairs to their children. The child's autonomy depends on the leisure domain and on the child's age. Two partial patterns of parental behaviour concerning children's independence were discovered and characterised: parents discriminate between 'influence on leisure as activity' (e.g. the choice of a sport) versus 'influence on leisure as time' (e.g. bedtime, or the question as to whether or not the child should accompany the parents on holiday). It could be that the variation in parental control over 'leisure as activities' is related to what parents want their children to do in their free time, whereas it seems that 'influence on leisure as time' has more to do with the parental problem of order and control, specifically in the sense of orderly time structure. The importance parents attach to this aspect of influence grows according to their concern over parental control and orderly time structure in general. Family life is indeed substantially structured by means of an orderly time schedule, by which mother's, father's and children's timetables have to run synchronously (Te Kloeze, 1994b).

Next to functions of leisure for the family, there are family functions of leisure too: the recreation function and the socialisation function. From the literature it is not clear whether the recreation function has increased or decreased in the course of time. There is also a different note about the growing role of commerce, taking over the recreation function of the family (Gunter and Moore, 1975). Although commerce is likely to take over some recreational tasks of the family, families with small children in particular will continue to spend most of their leisure within the family context.

The family functions as a socialisation setting in which attitudes of children regarding important institutions including recreation and leisure will be developed. Socialisation as a family function can be considered as socialisation of leisure styles. A new theoretical insight into socialisation and upbringing by Du Bois-Reymond (1993) states that "modern parents no longer wish to be the ideal educators of their children" (Zinnecker, in: Du Bois-Reymond, 1993). "As modern parents want to advance the educational goal of independence, unfolding of the individuality of their children, they take distance from their role as an 'ideal parent'" (Du Bois-Reymond, 1993: p. 130). This means that the upbringing of the modern parent is no longer focused on making the children look like them (i.e. the parents), or do as they do (following same religion, having the same or higher education, etc.), but on independence and the individuality of the children. Therefore, the peer group life of modern children and adolescents will become more and more important.

But values imparted by the commercial sector and the media, can be contradictory to those of the parents. The question is, how much do parents let their values and norms be influenced? The autonomy of adolescents is still increasing, including in the field of leisure and recreation. Adolescents are rich relative to their parents, and that is what the commercial sector is aiming at. The youth are confronted every day with values and norms contradictory to that of their parents. The question is, how far do the values of commerce and media influence the socialisation of adolescents? Socialisation takes place in the younger years. As they grow older, adolescents withdraw from parental authority. Still, the literature illustrates that the family, even when children grow older, remains the most important leisure context (Horna, 1989). This is confirmed by Philipsen (1963), who stated that 90% of leisure is spent within the family context. However, this was in the 1960s and in a more multiform society figures are lower: Te Kloeze (1989) estimates that two thirds of leisure time is spent within the family context.

Issue 5: Power and control, decision-making, rules, organisation and task-sharing within families with regard to leisure, and the conflicts that arise

One of the aims ofemancipation is to achieve a more equal division of domestic role- and task-sharing. Young and Willmott (1973) conceived of the "symmetrical family". They stated that the relationships within the family had become more symmetrical, with more interchanging roles of men and women than before.

Similarly, in 1972 Douma (1975) saw the contours of what he calls the "plastic family" in the Netherlands. The question is how far this has been carried out in practice. In reality, not far. Research by Tavecchio and Van IJzendoorn (1982) in the Netherlands showed that a complete symmetrical division of tasks was hardly pursued or realised. Women are still responsible for fulfiling of main specific household tasks (washing, cooking and cleaning), as **Table 1** shows.

Looking at these figures, some conclusions can be drawn. Men still enjoy the largest amount of free time, although this is decreasing, and working women are the most under-privileged, although to a decreasing extent. At first glance, housewives are the most privileged category. However, further analysis of data from the Social and Cultural Planning Bureau (Knulst and Schoonderwoerd, 1983) showed the poor quality of housewives' free time, which is very fragmented, less diversified and less gadabout compared with other categories. Relatively considered, working men are spending 33% more

Table 1: Time spent on daily activities, 1975 and 1990
(Dutch population aged over 11 years; 1 week in October)

(hours a week)	Household chores + Family tasks		Free time	
	1975	1990	1975	1990
Men	8.6	10.4	49.6	48.2
Women	29.5	26.5	46.2	46.2
Working men	6.3	8.4	43.5	41.1
Working women	13.5	16.4	37.2	38.5
Housewives	37.4	35.7	48.2	49.8

Source: Sociaal en Cultureel Planbureau, 1992

time on household chores and family tasks (working women 21% more; housewives 5% less). From the emancipation point of view, these developments are very slow indeed. Results of opinion polls by the Social and Cultural Planning Bureau indicate that the desire for a symmetrical relationship between men and women in households had increased between 1981 and 1991 (equal distribution of paid work from 57 to 61%; equal distribution of household chores from 61 to 73%; household tasks as a responsibility of both man and woman from 78 to 85%; child care as a responsibility of both man and woman from 78 to 85%) (Sociaal en Cultureel Planbureau, 1992).

Te Kloeze *et al.* (1995) studied both task-sharing in the household in general and in the leisure context. As reported by housewives in two villages, in 96% of the cases household chores are women's tasks, and in 4% shared by husband and wife. For child care these figures are 75% and 25%. The husbands are doing the 'pleasant' tasks such as playing, walking and reading with the children. According to these women, the ideal task-sharing is different from the actual (as reported by them); for household chores 77% for the housewife only, 23% shared, 1% for the husband only; for child care 50% for the housewife, 50% shared. Regarding task-sharing in the leisure domain, the same study showed gender specificity. Keeping contact with the wife's relatives, organising birthday parties, reading to children and serving coffee are housewives' tasks, keeping contact with the husband's relatives and playing with children are done by both, and serving a drink is a male task. The ideal task-sharing shows much less role differentiation, except serving a drink which remains a male task in more than 40% of the cases. So, again a remarkable difference between reality and ideal was found. It would appear the "symmetrical", "plastic" or "postmodern" family exists theoretically but is still not a fact in all cases: the "ethic of care" is still dominant.

Ideas about the division of tasks in the family seem to be class-related (Young and Willmott, 1973). Research by Andersson and De Jong (1987) in the Netherlands showed also that people from the lower classes are more family-oriented with frequent visiting of family (relatives) as a leisure activity. Social class and role (obligations) influence the access to resources (time, money, space, education, labour and facilities) and so influence leisure patterns. Like Young and Willmott, Komter's study (1985) in the Netherlands showed that women are more in need of social contacts and friendships than men. Women of both social classes stresses the importance of friendship with members of the same sex. The responsibility of keeping up social contacts in both social classes lay mainly with the women. The measure of social contact depended on how far people were home-oriented, and how far people used their homes to receive guests. The lower social classes were more home-oriented than the higher social classes. The former were more oriented to the "ethic of domesticity". Social contacts and leisure varied therefore per social class and gender. I agree, by the way, that privatisation, individualisation and home-centredness should not be interchanged conceptually (Allan and Crow, 1991).

Many women are not satisfied with the situation in which they find themselves. Komter (1985) revealed that 75% of women and 58% of men have other wishes for their leisure. In the lower classes about one third of the couples had occasional conflicts with social contacts or leisure; in the higher classes it was about half. A possible explanation may be that higher class women "fight for their rights", whereas lower class women adapt themselves to the family situation.

Time, space and money limit leisure participation, and obligations can hinder the leisure experience. Because leisure time is scarce and interchangeable, and because both men and women consider leisure an important aspect in life, conflicts often arise. Among family members conflicts arise not only about who is doing what, when and where, but also during leisure time. Discord over watching TV occurs in 47% of families in Dutch rural communities. In some families these problems are solved by having than one TV set and/or video (Te Kloeze *et al.*, 1995). As mentioned before, Weeda (1983a, 1983b, 1984) also reports on conflicts between 'family and leisure'.

More recently the identity of women with regard to leisure has been studied. Karsten (1992) believed that women should have the power to create their own leisure time within their daily activities, with the help of material and immaterial resources. There are obvious differences between the sexes in how far leisure gets a place in daily life and the form in which free time is available. Karsten (1992) divided time into three (overlapping) time domains: caring, work and leisure. For women leisure time is often fragmented and mostly takes place in "free-caring time" (e.g. knitting). On the contrary, the leisure activities of men take place in the "free-working time" (e.g. going to receptions, taking courses). As already stated, fragmentation of leisure time is greatest among housewives, less among working women and lowest among working men. But, changes are taking place both among and between the sexes (Te Kloeze, 1994a).

From the point of view of control over leisure, another aspect is important: the extent of freedom allowed to the partner (e.g. going on holiday separately from the intimate partner). Most housewives interviewed in two villages did not agree the freedom meant is good for a marriage. Moreover, this aspect in that study is one of the most traditionally defined by the housewives. This could be interpreted in this way that this sort of freedom has a possibly threatening meaning (no control over the husband's or wife's doings and goings) which could destabilise marriage (Te Kloeze *et al.*, 1995).

Issue 6: Caring position

According to Mommaas (1984) insight in the meaning of leisure and of leisure practices can be enlarged be using the concept of the "caring position" in order to be able to understand leisure of people in different positions. "The caring position" can be defined as the totality of rights and duties linked with looking after people (Mommaas and Van der Poel, 1985; Beckers and Van der Poel, 1990; Van der Poel, 1993). In that case, leisure has to be defined as the time about which actors do not need to give account in terms of the legitimate order belonging to the caring position in question.

Te Kloeze (1990a) studied housewives' and "househusbands"' leisure practices and experiences, thus of one and the same caring position, but of different sex and gender. Gender organises and reproduces the social relationship between women and men in society (Giddens, 1993). Gender-specific power relationships underlie social relationships in time and space and, as a result, men set bounds to the activities of women, and *vice versa*. Sex and caring position are jointly and individually able to explain some aspects relating to the differences in people's leisure. The caring position determines the day's structure and hence the feasibility of certain recreational activities. Sex, in the sense of gender roles, also determines how leisure is spent and perceived. The comparison between housewives and househusbands suggested that gender influenced how leisure was spent and perceived more than the caring position: the latter provides more structural influences.

Earlier, Withagen (1971) theorised about the functional and relational aspects of family roles in the leisure setting. He stated that, for example, the camping culture can conflict with family roles, which are characterised by their stress on privacy. Blok-Van der Voort (1977) aimed to explain the relationship between role performance and rhythmicising everyday life. Leisure, defined as exemption from work like household chores is an 'objectively centrally functional role'. People can pass from one functional role into another. Going on holiday is an example of such a transition. Holidays are, both quantitatively and qualitatively, different experiences than weekends. In a comment Van der Poel (1993) is of the opinion that from the structuration perspective the concept of 'leisure position' should be superseded by 'caring position' (see above).

As mentioned before, Andersson and De Jong (1987) used the concept of the caring position as well. These authors integrated the concept of the caring role in that of the eight recreation styles which emerged from their interview data: e.g., "Living with the diary" (young working, successful people), "Living without perspective" (young unemployed people) and "Alone but not lonely" (elderly, single women). A nice example of a study in which leisure of different caring positions is analyzed, is Karsten's study on women's control over leisure and leisure activities (Karsten, 1992). Leisure of five different groups of women was studied — housewives, both married and unmarried, working women (mothers out of two career households, single working mothers and single women) — which could be transformed into a typology: the classic, the family-oriented, and the individualistic type.

Towards a new approach to family and leisure

One of our aims was to arrive at family recreation styles by linking family styles to recreation styles. In the literature examined we were not able to find much literature and empirical data about this aspect. As mentioned before, Andersson and De Jong (1985, 1987) constructed a typology of recreation styles. They provided a theoretical framework for an integrated approach of the theory of structuration (Giddens) and time-space geography (Hägerstrand), although they were not able to link these theoretical insights with their empirical findings, unfortunately. Karsten (1992) paid more attention to this integrated approach and was inspired by the theory of structuration and the time-space geography as well. It is necessary to integrate these (new) theoretical insights applied to leisure studies, with new approaches in the sociology on marriage and the family. A first step to this integration can be found in a proposal for a new study on family and leisure (Te Kloeze, 1994a). Finally I will briefly elaborate on that new challenge.

Weeda (1992) theorises about man-woman relationships, lifestyles and social structures under the name of "gender culture theory". "Ideology and individual acting are related to socio-cultural and socio-economic structures and changes, while fundamental shifts in the points of view about the relationships between the sexes serve as a guideline" (Weeda, 1992: p. 20.1). Weeda referred to the ideological points of view about the relationships between men and women as sex paradigms (e.g. a closed (towards society) nuclear family in an industrial society in the 20th century: a complementary identity of husband and wife and a preponderant meaning of a partner-relationship; and an open (towards society) family life at the end of the 20th century: a preponderant meaning of a partner-relationship, linked to the ideology of self-fulfilment). Probably Giddens meant such an open family life when he states "marriage – for many, but by no means all groups in the population – has veered increasingly towards the form of a pure relationship, with many ensuing consequences" (Giddens, 1992: p. 58). With this in mind, my new study on family and leisure is focused on the question as to how relationships between family and leisure vary between sex paradigms, the power relationships connected with these paradigms, and the extent of individualisation of and within the family.

"Leisure and spending of leisure exist through the handling of people and handling with them. Therefore, the basis for a conceptualisation of leisure has preferably to be found in a general or social action theory" (Beckers and Van der Poel, 1990: p. 83). Beckers and Van der Poel link up with Giddens's theory of structuration in order to design a contextual approach to leisure. It concerns five main points (see also Karsten, 1992):

1. According to Giddens, people are knowledgeable agents. People do not act arbitrarily; on the contrary, they are governed by motives and preferences, although the majority happens unconsciously or very obviously anyway (everyday routines).
2. People are not (totally) free during everyday actions but are tied to social structures shown in three dimensions: meanings, standards and power. The meanings given by people, to leisure for example, are not detached from the rules that exist at the structural level.
3. Differences in accessibility to resources exist. These differences are concerned with different social positions or identities (e.g. woman and man) and caring positions (e.g. housewives and employees).
4. Acting is contextualised acting, whereby the context consists of the spatial environment, the interaction between actors, and the consciousness of both. Space and time are part of the context of acting. Thus, the socio-spatial and the institutional context will be reviewed. The institutional context exists of a time-spatially specific constellation of social, political, economic and cultural relationships. The last mentioned refers to (changes of) value orientations (*cf.* Te Kloeze, 1989).

5. Normative rules are continuously applied; this happens in three 'time strata': *durée* (here and now, a daily path), *Dasein* (life course) and *longue durée* (long term development of institutions).

The study will try to answer to how far the difference in control – as a consequence of differences of power between women/wives and men/husbands –influences the leisure activities undertaken by various members of the family and the relationship between the partners as indicated by the sex paradigms (Weeda, 1992) or ideologies of relationship (Hochschild, 1989) supported.

Power, control and gender seem to be central notions in both approaches (gender culture theory and contextual approach of leisure) and in my study which subsequently deals with the following concepts:

- meaning of leisure;
- daily path and life course;
- gender paradigm;
- social position and caring position;
- family recreation styles;
- the institutional and socio-spatial context.

There is a mutual relationship between the social position and the "caring position" on the one hand and the gender paradigm on the other hand; this means a mutual relationship between a specific set of rights and duties on the one hand and the relationships between husband and wife within the family on the other hand. These mutual relationships are also of importance with regard to control and meaning. How far people trespass on other people's leisure time and the meaning people give to leisure, are connected with the rights, duties and ideals and the relationships between husband and wife in the field of role- and task-sharing. All these factors debouch into a certain daily path. Therefore, certain family recreation styles can be constructed from the above concepts (the daily paths of family members, the gender paradigm, the meaning of leisure and the control over leisure).

References

Author's note: A more extended bibliography can be found in Betuw, A. and van Dijk, S. (1993) *Familia ludens: An integrated study. A Literature study on family and leisure, focused on the Netherlands.* Unpublished thesis. Wageningen: Centre for Recreation and Tourism Studies, Wageningen Agricultural University.

Allan, G. (1985) *Family life*. Avon: The Bath Press.

Allan, G. and G. Crow (1991) 'Privatization, home-centredness and leisure', *Leisure Studies* Vol. 10, No. 1: pp. 19-32.

Baumann, Z. (1993) *Postmodern ethics*. Oxford: Blackwell.

Carisse, C. B. (1975) 'Family and leisure: a set of contradictions', *The Family Coordinator*, April: pp. 191-197

Giddens, A. (1981) *A contemporary critique of historical materialism*. London: MacMillan.

——— (1984) The consti*tution of society*. Cambridge: Polity Press.

——— (1992) *The transformation of intimacy. Sexuality, love and eroticism in modern societies*. Cambridge: Polity Press.

——— (1993) *Sociology*. Cambridge: Polity Press.

Gunter, B. G. and H. A. Moore (1975) 'Youth, leisure, and the post-industrial society: implications for the family', *The Family Coordinator*, April: pp. 199-207.

Hägerstrand, T. (1970) 'What about people in regional science?'. Paper presented at the 9th European Political Science Congress of Regional Science Associations, Vol. 24: pp. 7-21.

Hantrais, L. (1983) *Leisure and the family in contemporary France: A research report based on an empirical study of the family leisure interface in a small French town in the Paris Basin*. London: Polytechnic of North London.

Henderson, K. A. and K. A. Allen (1991) 'The ethic of care: Leisure possibilities and constraints for women', *Loisir et Société*, Vol.14, No. 1: pp. 97-113.

Hochschild, A. (1989) *The second shift*. New York: Avon Books.

Holman, T. B. and A. Epperson (1984) 'Family and leisure: A review of the literature with research recommendations', *Journal of Leisure Research*, Vol. 16, No. 4: pp. 277-294'

Horna, J. L. (1989) 'The leisure component of the parental role', *Journal of Leisure Research*, Vol. 21, No. 3: pp. 228-241

Kelly, J. R. (1978) 'Family leisure in three communities', *Journal of Leisure Research*, Vol. 10, No. 1: pp. 47-60.

——— (1983) *Leisure identities and interactions*. London: Allen & Unwin.

Orthner, D. K. (1975) 'Leisure activity patterns and marital satisfaction over the marital career', *The Family Coordinator*, February: pp. 91-102

Parker, S. (1983) *Leisure and work*. London: Allen & Unwin.

Postman, N. (1985) *Amusing ourselves to death: Public discourse in the age of show business*. New York: Penguin Books.

——— (1993) *Technopoly. The surrender of culture to technology*. New York: Alfred A. Knopf.

Rapoport, R. and R. N. Rapoport (1975) *Leisure and the family life cycle*. London: Routledge & Kegan Paul.

Ritzer, G. (1993) *The McDonaldization of society*. Thousand Oaks, CA: Pine Forge Press.

Roberts, K. (1978) *Contemporary society and the growth of leisure*. London: Longman.

——— (1981) *Leisure*. London: Longman.

Rojek, C. (1985) *Capitalism and leisure theory*. London: Tavistock.

Rubin, L. B. (1976) *Worlds of pain: Life in the working class family*. New York: Basic Books.

Yankelovich, D. (1981) *New rules*. New York: Random House.

Young, M. and P. Willmott (1973) The symmetrical family: A study of work and leisure in the London region. London: s. n..

Dutch Bibliography

Andersson, E. A. and H. de Jong (1985) *Recreatie in een veranderende maatschappij. Deel 1: een literatuurstudie* [Recreation in a changing society. Part 1: a literature study]. Wageningen: Werkgroep Recreatie, Landbouwhogeschool.

Andersson, E. A. and H. de Jong (1987) *Recreatie in een veranderende maatschappij. Deel 2: een case-studie [*Recreation in a changing society. Part 2: a case study]. Wageningen: Werkgroep Recreatie, Landbouwhogeschool.

Beckers, Th. A. M. (1981) 'Vrije tijd en recreatie', L. Rademaker (ed) *Sociale kaart van Nederland* [Social Map of the Netherlands]. Utrecht: Het Spectrum, 338-354.

Beckers, Th., D. Aldershoff, M. ter Veer-Bos, en A. Van 't Eind (1980) *Huisvrouwen, uit of thuis. De rekreatie van huisvrouwen in de woonomgeving. Deel 1* [Housewives, out or at home. The recreation of housewives in the residential area. Part 1]. Wageningen: Vakgroep Sociologie van de westerse gebieden, Landbouwhogeschool.

Beckers, Th. and H. van der Poel (1990) *Vrijetijd tussen vorming en vermaak: een inleiding tot de studie van de vrijetijd* [Leisure between cultivation and pleasure: an introduction to the study of leisure]. Leiden: Stenfert Kroese.

Beckers, Th. and H. Mommaas (1991) *Het vraagstuk van den vrijen tijd. 60 jaar onderzoek naar vrijetijd* [The Problem of Leisure. 60 Years of Research into Leisure]. Leiden: Stenfert Kroese.

Betuw, A. van & S. van Dijk (1993) *Familia ludens: An integrated study. A literature study on family and leisure, focused on the Netherlands.* Unpublished thesis. Wageningen: Centre for Recreation and Tourism Studies, Wageningen Agricultural University.

Betuw, A. van, S. van Dijk and J. W. te Kloeze (1993) Familia ludens: A literature study focused on the Netherlands', *World Leisure and Recreation*, Fall 1993, Vol. 35, Nr. 3: 10-14.

Blok-Van der Voort, E. M. (1977) *Vakantie nader bekeken; een roltheoretische exploratie* [The holiday closer examined; a role theoretical exploration]. Leiden: Rijksuniversiteit Leiden.

Bogt, T. ter (1987) *Opgroeien in Groenlo* [Growing up in Groenlo. Amersfoort: Acco.

Bois-Reymond, M. du (1993) 'Pluraliseringstendensen en onderhandelingsculturen in het gezin' [Pluralisation tendencies and negotiation cultures in the family]', *Amsterdams Sociologisch Tijdschrift* Vol. 19, Nr. 3: 113-144.

Centraal Bureau voor de Statistiek (1994) *Jaarboek Toerisme en vrijetijdsbesteding* [Yearbook Tou rism and Spending Leisure Time] 's-Gravenhage: SDU-uitgeverij.

Dietvorst, A. G. J. (1989) *Complexen en netwerken: hun betekenis voor de toeristisch-recreatieve sector* [Complexes and Networks; Their Meaning for the Tourist-recreative Sector]. Wageningen: Landbouwuniversiteit.

——— (1994) 'Dutch research on leisure, recreation and tourism: A review', C. P. Cooper and A. Lockwood (eds) *Progress in tourism, recreation and hospitality management*. Chicester: John Wiley and Sons.

Dietvorst, A. G. J. and R. J. A. P. Spee (1991) *Wat weten we van recreatie en toerisme? Een beschouwing over kennis en kennishiaten. Met een bibliografie voor de periode 1986-1991* [What do we know about recreation and tourism? A reflection about knowledge and knowledge gaps. With a bibliography for the period 1986-1991]. 's-Gravenhage: Nationale Raad voor Landbouwkundig Onderzoek.

Dom, C. G. (1971) *Het gezin en de camping* [Family and the campsite] Scriptie. Breda: Nederlands Wetenschappelijk Instituut voor Toerisme en Rekreatie.

Douma, W. H. (1975) *Het gezin tussen verleden en toekomst* [The family between past and present]. Wageningen: Veenman & Zonen B. V. .

Duin, J. van (1983) *Verkering In Warmenhuizen: over gedrag, gevoel en moraal van meisjes en jongens in Warmenhuizen omtrent uitgaan, verkering krijgen en trouwen* [Courtship in Warmenhuizen: about behaviour, feelings and morals of girls and boys in Warmenhuizen about going out, courting and getting married] (Amsterdam: Universiteit van Amsterdam.

Dussen-Van Dongen, B. van and A. M. van der Heiden (1965) *Ouders over hun oudere kinderen; een onderzoek naar opvattingen en zienswijzen van ouders van Instuifleden, met betrekking tot dansen, en enkele andere vormen van vrijetijdsbesteding van hun kinderen* [Parents about their elder children; a study into attitudes and opinions of parents of members of open youth centres, with regard to dancing, and some other forms of their children's use of leisure]. Utrecht: Sociologisch Instituut, Rijksuniversiteit Utrecht.

Eind, A., van 't, M. ter Veer-Bos and Beckers, Th. (1981) *Huisvrouwen, uit of thuis. De rekreatie van huisvrouwen in de woonomgeving. Deel 2.* [Housewives, out or at home. The recreation of housewives in the residential area. Part 2]. Wageningen: Vakgroep Sociologie van de westerse gebieden, Landbouwhogeschool.

Hazekamp, J. (1985) *Rondhangen als tijdverdrijf* [Hanging around to pass the time]. Amsterdam: VU-Uitgeverij.

Heiden, A. M. van der (1966) *Gezinsrekreatie; observaties op campings* [Family recreation; observations on camp sites]. Utrecht: SISWO.

——— (1968) *Gezin en vrije tijd* [Family and leisure]. Utrecht: SISWO.

——— (1972) *Gezinskamperen; Deel I: algemene gegevens* [Family camping; Part I: common data]. Utrecht: SISWO.

Heiden, A. M. van der and R. Smeding (1967) *Dagrekreatie en het gezin* [Day recreation and the family]. Utrecht: SISWO.

Hofstee, E. W. (1980) *Vrijheid, gelijkheid en eenzaamheid* [Liberty, Equality and Loneliness]. Wageningen: Landbouwhogeschool.

Hoog, C. de (1982) *Partnerselectie bij huwelijkssluiting in Nederland* [Mate selection in the Netherlands]. Wageningen: Landbouwuniversiteit.

——— (1989) 'Het gezin: ontwikkeling en actualiteit' [The Family: Development and Actuality], *Gezin*, Vol. 1 (1989) Nr. 3, 128-148.

Hoog, C. de and J. A. C. van Ophem (1992) '*Poor families in the Netherlands*', in G. Kiely (ed) *In and out of marriage. Irish and European experiences.* Dublin.

——— (1994a) 'Differences in leisure behaviour of the poor and the rich in the Netherlands', in Henry, I. (ed) (1994) *Modernity, postmodernity and lifestyles* (LSA Publication Nr.48). Eastbourne: Leisure Studies Association, 291-305.

——— (1994b) 'Monetarisering, voeding en voedsel', in Y. K. van Dam, C. de Hoog and J. A. C. van Ophem (eds) (1994) *Eten in de jaren negentig. Reflecties op gemaksvoeding* [Eating in the nineties. Reflections on easy food] (Delft: Eburon).

Hout, F. A. G. (1993) *Kampeergroepen en kampeerlijnen; de achtergronden van verandering en stabiliteit in het kampeergedrag in de loop van de tijd van ANWB-leden* [Camping groups and camping lines; the background of change and stability in camping behaviour of ANWB-members in the course of time]. Wageningen: Werkgroep Recreatie, Landbouwuniversiteit.

Kamphorst, T. J. (1988) *Op weg naar buiten* [On the Way outdoors. Amersfoort: Giordano Bruno.

Kamphorst, T. J. and A. P. Spruijt (1983) *Vrijetijdsgedrag in het perspectief van socialisatie: een empirisch onderzoek naar samenhang tussen aspecten van socialisatieprocessen op de leeftijd van 5 t/m 10 jaar en op vrijetijdsgedrag op de leeftijd van 25 t/m 30 jaar* [Leisure and socialisation: an empirical study on the relation of aspects of childhood socialisation and leisure activities in later life]. Utrecht: Rijksuniversiteit Utrecht.

Karsten, L. (1992) *Speelruimte van vrouwen* [Room for women to play]. Amsterdam: SUA.

Kloeze, J. W. te (1985a) 'Recreatie en vrijetijd in verschillende leefvormen' [Recreation and leisure in different lifestyles]', *Vrijetijd en Samenleving* Vol. 3, Nr.2: 187-212.

——— (1985b) *Gezin en vrije tijd: een literatuurstudie ten dienste van het deelproject 'Gezin en vrije tijd in twee plattelandsgemeenten'* [Family and leisure: a literature study for the use of the project 'Family and leisure in two rural communities']. Wageningen: Vakgroep Sociologie van de westerse gebieden, Landbouwuniversiteit).

——— (1985c) 'Recreatie in een relatie', in C. de Hoog et al. (eds) *Tussen empirie en reflectie; verzamelde opstellen voor G. A. Kooy* [Between empiricism and reflection: collected essays for G. A. Kooy]. Wageningen: Ponsen & Looijen, 83-93.

——— (1985d) 'Recreatie en primaire leefvormen (2)', in H. van Leeuwen et al. (eds) *Nieuwe inventarisatie toegepaste huishoudwetenschappen, onderzoek en onderwijs Deel D. Algemene maatschappelijke vraagstukken* [Stock-taking applied home economics, research and education. Part D. General social problems] ('s-Gravenhage: VUGA) 27-32.

——— (1985e) 'Recreatie en primaire leefvormen (3)', in H. van Leeuwen *et al.* (eds) *Nieuwe inventarisatie toegepaste huishoudwetenschapppen, onderzoek en onderwijs. Deel D. Algemene maatschappelijke vraagstukken* [Stock-taking applied home economics, research and education. Part D. General social problems] ('s-Gravenhage: VUGA, 33-38.

——— (1985f) Recreatie en primaire leefvormen (4) in H. van Leeuwen *et al.* (eds) *Nieuwe inventarisatie toegepaste huishoudwetenschapppen, onderzoek en onderwijs. Deel D. Algemene maatschappelijke vraagstukken* [Stock-taking applied home economics, research and education. Part D. General social problems] ('s-Gravenhage: VUGA, 39-45.

——— (1988) Kind en vrije tijd in 1988', in T. Peek *et al.* (eds) *Jantje op weg naar 2008* [Jantje on the Way to 2008]. Utrecht: Nationaal Jeugdfonds, 57-73.

——— (1989) 'Gezin als vrijetijdsverband: een kwestie van maatschappelijke

verandering' [The family as a spare-time unit: a matter of social change]', *Recreatie en Toerisme* Vol. 21, Nr. 5: xxxii-xxv.

——— (1990a) 'Housewives and Househusbands' Leisure: A Study of the Experience and Perception of Leisure Among Women and Men Who Stay Home to Run the House'. Paper presented to The XII World Congress of Sociology of the International Sociological Association on "Sociology for one world: unity and diversity". Madrid, Spain. July 9-13, 1990. Wageningen: Department of Sociology/Centre for Recreation Studies, Wageningen Agricultural University) 10 .

——— (1990b) 'Changing Economic Conditions in Relation to Recreation Styles in the Netherlands'. Paper presented at the Polish Leisure and Recreation Association 7th Conference 'Leisure and Recreation of Different Social Circles. Leisure and the Future', November 29 – December 2, 1990, Zajaczkowo, Poland. Wageningen: Department of Sociology/Centre for Recreation Studies, Wageningen Agricultural University), 22 .

——— (1994a) 'Control over Leisure in Dutch Families'. Paper presented at the International Sociological Association XIIIth World Congress of Sociology "Contested Boundaries and Shifting Solidarities", July 18-23, 1994, Bielefeld, Germany. Wageningen: Department of Sociology/ Centre for Recreation and Tourism Studies, Wageningen Agricultural University), 18.

——— (1994b) 'Socialisation, the Family and Leisure'. Plenary Lecture Held at the Polish Leisure and Recreation Association 8th Scientific Conference "Leisure and Recreation of Different Social Groups" on "Leisure Education in the Family, School and Local Community" September 20-23, 1994 Wagrowiec, Poland. Wageningen: Department of Sociology/ Centre for Recreation and Tourism Studies, Wageningen Agricultural University), 10.

——— (1995) [Forthcoming]. *Children about their weekend. A Content Analysis of Essays.* Wageningen: Department of Sociology/Centre for Recreation and Tourism Studies, Wageningen Agricultural University).

Kloeze, J. W. te, van Bergen, M., Duivenvoorden, M. and de Hoog, C. (1995) [Forthcoming]. *Tussen vrijheid en gebondenheid. Gezins- en vrijetijds-domeinen getypeerd [Between Freedom and Commitment.* Family Domains and Leisure Domains typified]. Wageningen: Vakgroep Sociologie van de westerse gebieden, Landbouwuniversiteit) (wordt gepubliceerd)

Knulst, W. and L. Schoonderwoerd (1983) *Waar blijft de tijd: onderzoek naar de tijdsbesteding van Nederlanders* [Where's the time gone: a study into the spending of time by the Dutch] ('s-Gravenhage: Staatsuitgeverij.

Komter, A. E. (1985) *De macht van de vanzelfsprekendheid: relaties tussen mannen en vrouwen* [The power of the obvious: relationships between women and men] ('s-Gravenhage: VUGA.

Kooy, G. A. (1967) *Revolutie der gezinsfuncties* [Revolution of family functions].

——— (1977) *Het modern-westers gezin; een inleidende gezinssociologische beschouwing* [The modern Western family; an introductory sociological dissertation on the family]. Deventer: Van Loghum Slaterus.

Leeuwen, L. Th. van (1976) *Het gezin als sociologisch studie-object* [The family as sociological study-object]. Wageningen: Landbouwhogeschool.

Lengkeek, J. (1994) *De andere werkelijkheden van recreatie en toerisme. Een sociologisch-filosofisch essay over de grondslagen voor een collectief belang in recreatie en toerisme* (Other Realities of Recreation and Tourism. A Sociological-Philosophical Essay on a Collective Interest in Recreation and Tourism. Wageningen: Agricultural University.

Litjens, H. P. M. (1953) *Onmaatschappelijke gezinnen; sociologisch onderzoek naar de onmaatschappelijkheid te Maastricht* [Antisocial families; sociological research into antisociality in Maastricht]. Assen: Van Gorcum.

Mommaas, H. (1984) *Arbeid, vrijetijd en legitieme orde: een sociaal-theoretische verkenning* [Work, leisure and legitimate order: a social-theoretical reconnoitring]]. Breda: Centrum voor Vrijetijdskunde.

——— (1993) *Moderniteit, vrijetijd en de stad* [Modernity, Leisure and the City]. Utrecht: Jan van Arkel.

Mommaas, H., and Poel, H. van der (1984) 'Naar een sociologie van de vrije tijd? Deel I: De omschrijving van het probleem; een evaluatie' [Towards a sociology of leisure? Part 1: Definition of the problem; an evaluation], *Vrijetijd en samenleving* Vol. 2, Nr. 4: 475-505.

——— (1985) 'Naar een sociologie van de vrije tijd? Deel II: Vrije tijd en tijdsbesteding als product van sociaal handelen' [Towards a sociology of leisure? Part 2: Leisure and use of time as product of social acting]', *Vrijetijd en samenleving* Vol. 3, Nr. 1: 9-44.

Naber, P. (1985) *Vriendinnen* [Girl Friends]. Amsterdam: VU-Uitgeverij.

Poel, H. van der (1993) *De modularisering van het dagelijkse leven. Vrijetijd in structuratietheoretisch perspectief* [Modularisation of Daily Life. Leisure in the Perspective of the Theory of Structuration] (Amsterdam: Unpublished Thesis.

Philipsen, H. (1963) 'Gezin en vrijetijdsbesteding in het sociaal-wetenschappelijk onderzoek [Family and leisure spending in social-scientific research]', *Sociologische Gids* Vol. 10: 306-321.

Smelik, E. L. a. o. (1962) *Gezinsweekcommissie* [Family Week Committee]. 's-Gravenhage: Gezinsweekcommissie.

Sociaal en Cultureel Planbureau (1992) *Sociaal en Cultureel Rapport 1992* [Social and Cultural Report 1992] (Rijswijk: Sociaal en Cultureel Planbureau.

Sternheim, A. (1939) 'Het probleem van den vrijen tijd in den totalitairen staat' [The Problem of Leisure in the Totalitarian State]. *Mensch en Maatschappij* Vol. 15: 25-39.

Tavecchio, L. W. C. and M. H. van IJzendoorn (1982) 'Taakverdeling bij ouders van jonge kinderen: een onderzoek naar man-vrouw verschillen in het hedendaagse gezin [Task-sharing of parents with young children: a study on husband-wife differences in the modern family]', *Bevolking en Gezin* Vol. 1: 19-48.

Versteegh, T. F. (unknown) *Vrije tijd en gezin* [Leisure and the family] Scriptie. Utrecht: Sociologisch Instituut, Rijksuniversiteit Utrecht.

Vries-Bastiaans, W. de (1966) *Het gezin met zijn vrije tijd op weg naar een nieuwe einder* [The family and its leisure towards a new horizon] Scriptie. Utrecht: Sociologisch Instituut, Rijksuniversiteit Utrecht.

Waal, M. S. de (1989) *Meisjes: een wereld apart: een etnografie van meisjes op de middelbare school* [Girls: a world apart: an ethnography of girls at secondary school] Meppel: Boom.

Weeda, I. (1982) *Ideaalbeelden rond leefvormen* [Ideal images around life-styles] Deventer: Van Loghum Slaterus.

——— *Van huwelijk tot echtscheiding: een regenboog van ervaringen* [From marriage to divorce: a rainbow of experiences]. Wageningen: Vakgroep Sociologie van de westerse gebieden, Landbouwhogeschool.

——— *Voor en na de echtscheiding* [Before and after the divorce]. Utrecht: Het Spectrum.

——— *Huwelijksleven: ideaal en praktijk* [Married life: the ideal and in practice]. Utrecht: Het Spectrum.

——— *Vrouwen Verlangen MANNEN* [Women long for men]. Utrecht: Het Spectrum.

Wildenbeest, G. (1982) 'Boeren, bruiloften en scholtenbals' [Farmers, weddings and 'scholtenbals'], *Sociologisch Tijdschrift* Vol. 9, Nr. 3: 383-407.

Withagen, J. C. M. (1971) *Kampeerdersrollen en gezinsrollen; toepassing van het rolbegrip op de kampeersituatie* [Campers' roles and family roles; an application of the role concept at the camping situation] Scriptie. Utrecht: Sociologisch Instituut, Rijksuniversiteit Utrecht.

The Impact of a Federal Government Funding Programme on the Autonomy of Canadian National Sport Organizations

Lisa M. Kikulis
University of Saskatchewan, Saskatoon, Canada
and
Trevor Slack and C.R. Hinings
University of Alberta, Edmonton, Canada

Introduction

Researchers have shown a great deal of interest in the Canadian amateur sport delivery system. The focus of much of this research has been on the response of national sport organizations (NSOs) to external pressures, in particular, federal government policy initiatives and financial contributions (Harvey and Proulx, 1988; Kidd, 1988; Kikulis *et al.*, 1992; Macintosh *et al.*, 1987; Macintosh and Whitson, 1990; Slack and Hinings, 1992). Arguments presented in this literature suggest that since the early 1970s there has been increased intervention of the Canadian state in amateur sport and as a result, the once private and independent NSOs are now called upon to respond to public interests. Implicitly, these arguments suggest that it is the financial dependence of NSOs on federal government funding that has reduced their strategic and administrative autonomy.

Competing on the world stage has become the benchmark of success in many areas of social, political, and economic life, and amateur sport is no exception. Over the last 25 years the continued effort of the government of the day to uncover symbols of national unity and pride together with the increased media coverage and the growing consumer interest (Harvey and Proulx, 1988; Macintosh *et al.*, 1987) have all contributed to the "philosophy of excellence" that has come to define the appropriate goals, objectives, and policies of the Canadian amateur sport delivery system (Kidd, 1988). For NSOs, the result has been substantial pressure to focus their programme strategies on high performance sport. High performance sport refers to activities that have an objective of attaining the highest possible level of achievement in international competitions. In particular, those sports on the Olympic Games programme and those with regular world championships are designated as high performance sports in Canada (Fitness and Amateur Sport, 1988).

Macintosh and Whitson (1990) and Slack and Hinings (1992) have further shown how the federal government's financial contributions have been tied to the adoption of an "appropriate" structural design by NSOs. The freedom of NSOs to decide on the type of administrative structure they should adopt has been reduced by the pressure to become more "business-like" in their operations. More specifically, the structural design felt most suitable for the delivery of high performance sport is what Mintzberg (1979) calls a professional bureaucracy.

It is suggested that by focusing on high performance sport and linking its success to structural design, federal government agencies have set the standards to which NSOs must adapt. The argument developed is that the environment imposes such a high degree of constraint on organizational members that they have little choice in how they react to these pressures. The prescribed strategy and structure that are to ensure the viability of NSOs is in fact the only choice, and the organization's role has been characterized as having little influence in the relationship.

While we agree with the literature that suggests the state has intervened in the development and delivery of amateur sport and the impact has been a loss of autonomy for NSOs, the prevailing arguments that portray NSOs as passive receptors of government policy, programmes, and funding provide an incomplete picture of the relationship between the state and these organizations. What is presented is an overly deterministic view of NSOs absorbing the institutional beliefs of their environment as a sponge absorbs water. As Schreyögg (1980: p. 307) noted about organizational change in general, "...it is obvious that these transformation processes are not affected by mysterious undefined mechanisms but by people—the organizational members." Change in NSOs represents not only the external pressures on key people in NSOs, but the interpretation of these pressures by these individuals.

Although the pressures external to organizations may initiate the need for change, the process of change reflects the values, power, and interests of organizational members (Child, 1972; Ranson *et al.*, 1980; Walsh *et al.*, 1981). While NSOs have experienced forces for change from their external environment, primarily government agencies, the impact of these forces on the various systems and processes in these organizations may differ according to how organizational members interpret and enact these forces. We must, therefore, consider the other social pressures, the internal power structure, and the aspirations of key actors to understand how organizations respond to pressures for change. A consideration of the role of agency and choice would help us reconceptualize these organizations as reflecting both broader external pressures, such as those presented by federal government agencies, and also the vying interests of organizational members as they seek to advance and sustain their claim on the valued and scarce resources of their NSO.

In light of these arguments, this paper attempts to build on previous literature that has documented the substantial increase in state intervention in the Canadian amateur sport delivery system and the subsequent decrease in the autonomy of NSOs. The emphasis here, however, will be less on how NSOs have become isomorphic with their institutional environment (Slack and Hinings, 1992) and more on the strategic response of NSOs to these external pressures. In the following section arguments for including strategic choice and agency as critical elements for understanding the relationship between the federal government and NSOs is presented. This is followed by an overview of the setting for the empirical analysis of the impact of a federal government funding programme on the autonomy of NSOs. In the third section the research methods are outlined. This is followed by a presentation of results and a discussion on their implications in providing a more accurate reflection of the response of NSOs to their environment.

Conceptual framework: scope of autonomy for NSOs in response to institutionalpressures

Understanding change has been a central research focus in the study of organizations for a number of years. Institutional theorists have argued that organizations converge with their environment and conform to prescribed structures and practices to legitimate their existence and ensure access to a valued resources. Exerted by regulatory agencies such as the state, professions, or interest groups, these institutional pressures come to define the appropriate and necessary ways to organize (DiMaggio and Powell, 1983; Meyer and Rowan, 1977; Scott, 1987; Zucker, 1987).

While it is correct to imply that organizations change their structure to maintain a fit with their environment, it is important to consider the capacity of individuals and groups to influence outcomes, because as Zucker (1983: p. 12) suggests, "organizations are not simply constrained by the institutional environment: they often define their own position in it." It is this perspective that is emphasized by a number of organizational theorists that have developed an understanding of the strategic response of organizations to their institutional environment (DiMaggio, 1988; Oliver, 1991; Powell and Friedkin, 1986).

An understanding of "strategic responses to institutional processes" refers to "the behavior of organizations in institutional contexts and the conditions under which organizations will resist institutionalization" (Oliver, 1991: p. 145). That is, organizational members are faced with a choice on how to respond to institutional pressures for change. These choices, of course, are influenced by past decisions, values, and interests that may constrain or enable organizational change. The variety of responses has typically been ignored, in part because of the tendency to explain Canada's amateur sport delivery system solely as a creation of the state.

Oliver (1991: p. 152) has suggested five types of strategic responses that vary in how far organizational members enact their environment: acquiescence, compromise, avoidance, defiance, and manipulation. In applying these ideas to the relationship between the federal government and NSOs, we can see how the autonomy of organizational members varies according to how the pressures for focusing on high performance sport and reproducing professional-bureaucratic structures were interpreted.

It has been argued that the acquiescence of NSOs has enabled the federal government to promote the type of organizational design felt most suitable for delivering high performance sport, the professional bureaucracy (Kidd, 1988; Kikulis *et al.*, 1992; Macintosh, 1988; Slack and Hinings, 1992). In examining the diffusion and institutionalization of structural change, Tolbert and Zucker (1983) found that prescribed change was adopted quickly when it was mandated by the state, came from a single source, and was tied to valued resources. Similarly, Macintosh *et al.* (1987) have documented the growth of the federal government's involvement in amateur sport throughout the 1970s and 1980s from a "no strings attached" granting agency to a funding, policy making, programming, and evaluating bureaucracy. Increasingly, government funding was tied to specific policy and programme objectives. As Tolbert (1985: p. 1) points out, "...dependency relationships can, over time, become socially defined as appropriate and legitimate." Like other areas of social policy, amateur sport's reliance on government funding has become widely accepted and expected by NSO members. Having developed such a reliance on government funding, NSOs have conformed to many of the pressures and prescribed practices.

The most basic method by which the federal government, through its agent, Sport Canada, has influenced NSOs in adopting more sophisticated administrative structures was by contributing funding for the salaries of full-time staff such as Executive Directors and Technical Directors. Funding for these positions was conditional upon relocating the national offices of NSOs to the National Sport and Recreation Centre. Many NSOs chose to comply with these conditions, giving priority to self-serving benefits of administrative effectiveness over the risk of losing their autonomy. This active compliance was not the only response made by organizational members. Initially, many NSOs actively resisted these pressures for change (Macintosh *et al.*, 1987).

Today, however, the value of administrative rationalization is widely diffused and is unquestionably accepted as the way to organize. Professional staff and centralized offices are now taken-for-granted aspects of NSOs. Over 70 NSOs, multi-sport organizations, and administrative services are now housed in the Canadian Sport and Fitness Administrative Centre. It is not necessary to convince these organizations of the benefits of developing more "business-like" structures. The administrative hierarchy of NSOs is itself institutionalized, for example, all NSOs identify, at minimum, the roles of the president, vice president, past president, treasurer, secretary, executive director, and technical director.

These new patterns of authority (i.e., increasing specialization and centralized national offices) and of resource allocation (e.g., to high performance sport) are supported by a whole network of organizations (e.g., Coaching Association of Canada, Athlete's Information Bureau, Sport Marketing Council) that all employ a growing number of sport management professionals. Most professional staff and many volunteers, coaches, and athletes have welcomed these changes, viewing them as consistent with their own aspirations and as providing an opportunity to enhance their own career prospects.

The institutional pressure for a professional-bureaucratic form is consistent with the values of organizational members (Slack and Thibault, 1988) to the point that even organizations whose size does not necessarily require such sophisticated operations, mimic the structures of organizations that are successful (DiMaggio and Powell, 1983; Galaskiewicz and Wasserman, 1989) or ranked favourably by Sport Canada (Slack and Hinings, 1992). "[This] illustrates how the exercise of strategic choice may be preempted when organizations are unconscious of, blind to, or otherwise take for granted the institutional processes to which they adhere" (Oliver, 1991: p. 148).

NSOs, however, are not merely passive receptors of the values and beliefs promoted by Sport Canada, organizations negotiate and enact their own environments (Pfeffer and Salancik, 1978). Dominant coalitions and interest groups within NSOs (e.g., volunteers and professionals), in concert with Sport Canada, have helped create and recreate the values and beliefs that underpin Canada's amateur sport delivery system and the structures that characterize its organizations.

As Scott (1983) and DiMaggio and Powell (1983) have shown, professionals in pursuit of their own interests often influence the structuring of organizational systems and contribute to the process of institutionalzation. Similarly, Meyer and Scott (1983) suggest dominant coalitions attempt to use the power of institutions to meet their own objectives. Meyer (1983) and Meyer and Rowan (1977) have also shown how actors within organizations use institutionalized rules for their own purposes. We are suggesting that these activities take place in NSOs. Individual and collective actors in these organizations have embraced values that support high performance sport and the professional-bureaucratic form, and have encouraged NSOs to focus on these for their own ends.

The similarity of the socio-economic status, educational background, and training (Macintosh and Beamish, 1988), the internal labour market in the Canadian amateur sport delivery system (Slack and Hinings, 1992; Slack and Thibault, 1988), and the recruitment of volunteers from the professional and managerial classes (Macintosh and Whitson, 1990) have all facilitated the creation, diffusion, and persistence of these institutional pressures. Although there has been some challenge by organizational members to these pressures (Macintosh and Whitson, 1990; Slack and Thibault, 1988), Macintosh and Whitson have shown that in support of these national perspectives, key actors have pressed to manipulate NSO board composition to ensure those in opposition are marginalized from influential positions.

The direction and content of resistance in organizations operating in institutional environments with established value structures is limited (Zucker, 1987). The opportunity for dominant coalitions to preserve their positions of power, the fact that the costs associated with resistance (e.g., reduced funding or loss of legitimacy) may be seen as too great a price to pay by NSOs (Scott *et al.*, 1987), and the unquestioned acceptance of prevailing beliefs within the environment all mitigate against resistance to institutional pressures (Hinings and Greenwood, 1988).

While we agree that the creation of an institutional environment by the state and the requirements to receive funding that they have requested have promoted the types of changes we have seen in NSOs, we can not think of the relationship between the state and NSOs as one that is solely characterized by the aspirations of government bureaucrats. Whether NSOs have "bought into" or "sold out to" the institutionally prescribed amateur sport delivery system (Scott *et al.*, 1987), the strategic response of organizational members has ranged from "passive conformity" to "active resistance" depending on their awareness of the institutional pressures and how they were interpreted (Oliver, 1991).

The research setting

The arguments made in the preceding sections provide a strong rationale for understanding the relationship between the state and amateur sport according to the responses of NSOs to the institutional pressures for change. A central premise of this research is that investigations of organizational change require a consideration of the unique organizational interactions and the context in which they have developed. Building on past studies that have emphasized the domination of the state (Harvey and Proulx, 1988; Kidd, 1988; Macintosh *et al.*, 1987), the deterministic response of NSOs (Kikulis *et al.*, 1992; Macintosh, 1988; Slack and Hinings, 1992), and the widespread acceptance of the values for high performance sport and the professional-bureaucratic form espoused by the state (Macintosh and Whitson, 1990; Slack and Thibault, 1988), this research focuses on the variety in organizational responses to these institutional pressures in an attempt to provide a more complete explanation of the government-NSO relationship.

Recognition of the scope of organizational autonomy is stressed by Oliver (1991: p. 159) when she states, "organizational responses to institutional pressures toward conformity will depend on why these pressures are being exerted, who is exerting them, what these pressures are, how or by what means they are exerted, and where they occur." Application of these considerations to the relationship between the federal government and amateur sport provides a foundation for the empirical examination of a period when the institutional pressures for high performance sport and a professional-bureaucratic form were most intense.

Nowhere was the influence of the federal government seen more dramatically than in the period between 1984 and 1988 when Sport Canada provided in excess of $50 million to those NSOs that send athletes to the Summer and Winter Olympic Games. This funding programme, known as the Quadrennial Planning Programme (QPP), was a comprehensive and systematic federal government quest for international success. Specifically, the QPP focused the task of NSOs solely on the development of administrative and technical practices to enhance the performance of elite athletes at international competitions.

Tied to this funding programme was the requirement that each NSO develop a four year (quadrennial) plan to systematize their high performance sport objectives and the means by which these objectives were to be achieved. Sport Canada evaluated these plans and based on their evaluation, funds were allocated to assist NSOs with their plan implementation. The substantial funding attached to this programme gave the federal government considerable leverage in directing the structure and strategic initiatives of these organizations. In effect, this programme gave a strong push to what had been an ongoing process in the development of NSOs for the past two decades.

In large part, the aim of the federal government was to have NSOs adopt more professionally controlled administrative structures, as this was seen most conducive to meeting their political goals of the production of elite athletic performances at major games. Such a shift in control, however, challenged the power and autonomy of those volunteers who have traditionally been the mainstay of these organizations.

With a planning system in place for the development of high performance sport together with the values for more "rational" organizational forms, the scene was set for substantial change in NSOs. There were, however, many objections to the planning programme, least of which was its singular focus on high performance sport (Macintosh and Whitson, 1990; Slack and Hinings, 1992; Slack and Thibault, 1988). Nevertheless, the economic circumstances of NSOs made it difficult for them to defy the federal government's request for implementing the QPP.

Most NSO members saw themselves faced with the choice of either resisting the programme and risking funding cutbacks or conforming to the programme and reaping the financial benefits. It is not difficult to understand the preferred alternative! Tied to this choice was the need for NSOs to make substantial structural changes in order to implement the plans they developed. It is here where the outcomes of the QPP can be assessed in terms of the strategic response of NSOs. Considering these forces together it is possible to suggest a number of hypotheses regarding the impact of federal government funding on the structure of NSOs:

1. Pressures to adopt standardized high performance sport technical and administrative programmes will occur because these are the areas directly related to the federal government funding initiative.
2. Pressure to hire paid staff will occur because personnel are needed to implement the new programme.
3. The push to professionalize will be felt in the decision making structures where the focus on high performance demands more professional involvement.

Methods

Sample and data collection

The purpose of this paper is to examine the structural changes that took place in NSOs during the 1984-1988 period and the dynamics of this change. The organizations that were the basis of this study were the 36 NSOs that developed a quadrennial plan for the 1984-88 period (Fitness and Amateur Sport, 1988). This actually represents a population and these 36 NSOs were maintained throughout the project. The research was based on data collected during the change period. Repeated assessments of the structural and systemic elements in these organizations were recorded in 1984, 1986, and 1988.

Data was collected from two sources. The first was an analysis of documents such as high performance sport reviews, minutes of meetings, policies and procedure manuals, and organizational charts. The second source was interviews with key professional staff involved in QPP implementation. These individuals were interviewed using a standard schedule to record the presence and change of specific organizational characteristics. To determine the dynamics of the change process, interviews were conducted at least twice in each organization, with the individual responsible for the implementation of the NSO's plan.

Operational procedures

The first objective of this study was to identify the organizational structure of these organizations for the starting point (1984), the implementation period (1986), and the end point (1988) of the change period. This involved developing operational measures for organizational structure. To do this, three general measures of structural design were used:

a) specialization: how far roles are differentiated according to a particular task or purpose.

b) standardization: the existence of rules and regulations which guide the operations of organization.

c) centralization: the level at which decisions are made and the degree of involvement in decision making.

These dimensions of organizational structure have been theoretically and empirically established in the literature on organizational studies (Child, 1972; Hage and Aiken, 1967; Miller and Dröge, 1986; Pugh *et al.*, 1968, 1969). They have also been adopted for the analysis of amateur sport organizations (Frisby, 1986; Hinings and Slack, 1987; Kikulis *et al.*, 1989, 1992; Slack and Hinings, 1987, 1992; Thibault *et al.*, 1991).

Thirteen measures were developed to determine the organizational design changes that occurred over the four year period. **Table 1** lists the 13 measures of organizational structure specific to NSOs developed for this study. The number of items and the reliability coefficients, where applicable, are also listed in Table 1. In 10 of the 11 multi-item scales, the reliability coefficients were greater than.60 and thus were considered adequate measures of the constructs. The scale for specialization of volunteer roles was below the.60 level, however, following the suggestion of Kikulis et *al.* (1989), that volunteer roles in amateur sport are important yet not necessarily correlated, the items in the scale were retained in further analysis as a summed scale.

Table 1: Reliability coefficients for structural measurement

Scale	No. of Items	Reliability Coefficient
Specialization		
Professional Staff	13	.70
Support Personnel	10	.77
Volunteer Roles	15	.49
Number of Committees	1	NA
Standardization		
Administrative Systems	6	.74
Athlete Programmes	10	.70
Athlete Support Systems	7	.75
Evaluation Procedures	4	.67
Decision Making	6	.70
Centralization		
Locus of Decisions	6	.79
Participation in Decisions	6	.64
Concentration of Decisions with Volunteers	1	NA
Involvement of Volunteers in Decisions	1	NA

Note: NA = not applicable

Results and discussion

To determine the structural response of NSOs to the federal government's funding programme, t-tests were performed for each measure for the 1984-1986 and the 1986-1988 change periods. **Table 2** lists the mean scores for each of the 13 measurements for the three time periods (1984, 1986, 1988). The results of the t-tests show statistically significant changes in all aspects of standardization during the first 2 years and all except evaluation procedures in the later 2 years. We also found that changes in specialization were

Table 2: Scale means for Canadian Sport Organisations (NSOs)

Scale	1984 (N=36)	1986 (N=36)	1988 (N=36)
Specialization			
Professional Staff	4.75	6.22[1]	6.47
Support Personnel	2.47	3.22	4.08[4]
Volunteer Roles	8.17	8.56	8.22
Number of Committees	8.58	10.14	10.28
Standardization			
Administrative Systems	5.58	7.78[1]	9.19[3]
Athlete Programmes	10.00	13.86[1]	14.61[4]
Athlete Support Systems	5.58	8.33[1]	9.44[3]
Evaluation Procedures	2.42	3.92[1]	4.11
Decision Making	2.03	2.28[1]	2.43[4]
Centralization			
Locus of Decisions	4.07	4.03	3.93
Participation in Decisions	1.74	1.77	1.88
Concentration of Decisions with Volunteers	4.22	4.33	4.19
Involvement of Volunteers in Decisions	4.72	5.28[2]	5.06

1 Change from 1984 to 1986 significant at the 0.01 level
2 Change from 1984 to 1986 significant at the 0.05 level
3 Change from 1986 to 1988 significant at the 0.01 level
4 Change from 1986 to 1988 significant at the 0.05 level

significant for professional staff during the 1984-1986 change period and for support staff in the 1986-1988 change period. By contrast, the changes in centralization were less dramatic. The only significant change was an increase in volunteer involvement in decision making during the first 2 years of the QPP. The changes that have taken place in the structure of NSOs indicate that the response of NSOs to the institutional pressures for high performance sport and a professional-bureaucratic form were characterized by both compliance and resistance.

As we have stated, the main objective of the QPP was to improve the chances of NSOs in fielding their "Best Ever" teams for the 1988 Summer and Winter Olympic Games. The results support the hypothesis that changes in the standardization of technical and administrative programmes would occur in NSOs as they responded to this pressure for high performance sport. The reasons for this response can be explained by looking at the dynamics of this change process.

Oliver (1991) states that organizations evaluate the advantage of compliance in terms of economic and social rewards. For NSOs compliance with the pressure to systematize their high performance sport programmes was self-serving. Each NSO that developed a high performance quadrennial plan was provided with a substantial increase in funding. For example, the Canadian Volleyball Association's budget jumped from $397,070 in 1984 to $1,040,000 in 1988. Similarly, the budget of the Canadian Rhythmic Sportive Gymnastics Federation increased from $199,280 to $570,240. Such increases were the norm during this period.

The pressure to improve high performance sport resulted in the quick adoption of the technical programmes such as performance criteria for athlete selection, training camp schedules, and talent identification programmes to name a few. In addition, the introduction of more sophisticated administrative programmes were implemented to coordinate this increase in activities. Acknowledging the technical basis of the federally initiated funding programme, it seems logical to expect that these changes would be implemented. These planned changes were supported by financial resources and satisfied the interests of many organizational members in providing the best high performance programmes and services possible.

Although the financial reward was attractive, NSO members voiced considerable disenchantment with the singular focus on high performance sport. One Executive Director stated that he defied the request for developing a QPP and maintained this position until the threat for financial sanctions was made explicit. His response was what Oliver (1991) calls "pacifying activity" in that he redesigned his organization's long term plan to fit the requirements of the prescribed QPP criteria. As was made clear to this

Executive Director and others, the cost of active resistance to pressures for high performance sport was high for NSOs. Consequently, even when these pressures were in conflict with organizational interests, NSOs complied or compromised to the requests to plan and implement changes that were prescribed by the state. In essence, there was a conscious intent by members in these organizations to conform to the pressures for high performance sport during the 1984-1988 period.

Requiring a substantial commitment of time and expertise, it was hypothesized that the QPP and the pressure for high performance sport would be coupled with the pressure to hire more administrative and technical experts to manage this demand. As we have seen, adopting more "business-like" structures has become a natural response of NSOs when faced with increased programming demands. Professional staff have a legitimate role in NSOs to manage the day-to-day functioning and programming needs.

The desire for more professional expertise was supported by the existing professional staff of NSOs and by the NSO's "professional-volunteers", those individuals who were recruited to the executive board because of their corporate and political skills (Macintosh and Whitson, 1990). Generally, there was little resistance to hiring more staff. For those that were in agreement with the objectives of the QPP, more professional staff was a natural step for successful implementation. And for those that disagreed with the aims of the QPP, compliance to the pressure for hiring more professional staff was based on the need to manage the new demands. During this time frame then, a strong emphasis for increased "professional" staff in NSOs was a result of both an external push by the state and an internal pull by some NSO members.

With the responsibility for implementing the QPP falling squarely on the shoulders of professional staff, it was hypothesized that this would translate into more professionally controlled organizations. The results in Table 2 suggest there was resistance in NSOs to this aspect of "professionalization". Decision making remained at the volunteer committee level and volunteers made four out of the six decisions assessed in this study. In addition, volunteer involvement increased over the time period of the QPP. These results suggest NSOs were able to dismiss and even attack this institutional pressure for change. This active resistance can be explained by examining some of the factors that influenced the strategic choice of organizational members.

First, the pressure to move toward more professional control was not overtly stated by Sport Canada and thus, was not made concrete in the quadrennial planning programme. With little enforcement attached to this institutional pressure, NSOs perceived that there was little to lose by resisting such a change. Second, change in the decision making structure of these organizations involves changing values that have influenced their functioning since their formation, that is, values about volunteer control. Tushman *et al.* (1986: p. 35) state, "organizational history is a source of tradition, precedent, and pride which are in turn anchors to the past ... and may be a source of resistance to change." In this vein, researchers have reported strong commitment to traditional values of volunteer board control (Macintosh and Whitson, 1990; Slack and Thibault, 1988; Thibault *et al.*, 1991; Whitson and Macintosh, 1988). This conflict with internal values and the lack of external enforcement have enabled NSOs to dismiss or ignore pressures for change in their decision making structures toward more professional control.

In their analysis of change in NSOs, Slack and Hinings (1992) have identified the resistance to change toward professional control as a "hindrance" to "successful" change. The view is that this resistance must be "managed" in order for prescribed change to occur. Implicitly, then, success for these authors is measured by conforming to the pressures for professionalization espoused by the state and certain interest groups within NSOs. Resistance to professional control, however, has many viewing points, one of which may suggest that by not changing their decision making structure, NSOs have been able to maintain autonomy from the state in an area that is deeply rooted in these organizations.

It could be argued, however, that the "tradition" of volunteer control has itself been institutionalized as the appropriate control structure for these organizations and has not been "deinstitutionalized" by the state pressures facing NSOs. This raises the issue of whether these organizations were in fact, proactive in their response to these pressures by resisting change in decision making, or was it a "non choice" due to the ingrained nature of voluntary control? It is here where the awareness of organizational members of the dual institutional pressures from the state and the legal requirements of the nonprofit sector needs to be recognized.

As is the case in most nonprofit organizations, their legal status depends on the election of volunteer board members that are given the legitimate decision making authority to make policy and strategic decisions. The legitimacy of volunteer control in nonprofit organizations can be viewed as a force that maintains the tradition in NSOs. Comments from organizational members suggest that voluntary control is the norm and under normal circumstances is taken-for-granted. However, for most of these NSOs, the period between 1984 and 1988 were not "normal" circumstances, organizational members were aware of the pressures for change and the outcomes these changes may have on their decision making structure.

While funding programmes such as the QPP can strongly influence the autonomy of sport organizations, systems such as decision making are more difficult to change and it is here that volunteers are less likely to compromise the independence of their organization. The results of this study suggest there was resistance to new institutional pressures for change and commitment to old institutional pressures for stability. Specifically, the strong ties to volunteer led decision making that is embedded in the history of nonprofit organizations in general and NSOs in particular, made change in this area more difficult and enabled these organizations to maintain autonomy over this aspect of their organization.

The results of this study support the claim that the time period of 1984-1988 saw substantial changes in the organizational design of NSOs involved in the federal government's funding programme. This finding is in agreement with Kidd (1988), Macintosh *et al.*, (1987), Macintosh and Whitson (1990), and Slack and Hinings (1992) who claim that the involvement of the federal government in the delivery of amateur sport has had a tremendous impact on the strategic direction and structural design of NSOs during the 1984-1988 period.

Clearly, the substantial funding attached to the development and the implementation of the QPP had a significant role in this change. However, the structural response of NSOs to these requirements was more complex than has been previously suggested. The relationship between NSOs and the state is influenced by historical, political, and economic elements. The complexity of the relationship and the variety in structural responses leads to the issue of organizational choices. Specifically, for NSOs in this study, the priority attached to planning for high performance success and the weak institutional pressures for professional control resulted in a variety of strategic responses from NSOs. The willingness of NSOs to conform to institutional pressures for change was, therefore, influenced by their interpretation of the legitimacy of these pressures, interests in maintaining the status quo, and the economic or social benefits of compliance.

Summary and conclusions

Sport systems and sport organizations are not monolithic in their value systems. Within any system or organization there are competing values. The introduction of planning programmes such as the QPP force organizational members to confront their value differences. The values we see reflected in the nature of the Canadian amateur sport system and the structure of NSOs are those of the dominant coalitions. That is, those groups and individuals who are powerful are able to structure and restructure the sport system and sport organizations according to their own value preferences. These actors are often helped in their quest by the institutional pressures from agencies in the environment such as the state. Congruency with institutional values can help certain groups create structures that reflect their values and confer legitimacy upon the organization. So while we agree that NSOs have been heavily influenced by the goals, motives, and ambitions of the Canadian state, the network of relations involves much more than the compliance of NSO members to externally prescribed demands, issues of choice and agency also play a pre-eminent role.

Clearly, it is true that the institutional environment has had a substantial impact on the changing nature of NSOs. One the one hand, government involvement has assisted NSOs in "growing up" structurally, but on the other hand, this involvement has retarded their strategic thought processes by pressuring for a narrow focus on high performance sport programmes. When organizations lose autonomy they are less responsive and less flexible to changes in their environment. In comparison, when organizations are autonomous they have more discretion on how to respond and are more innovative in their responses. In light of these ideas, the Canadian amateur sport delivery system's focus on high performance sport, that was once described as the envy of the western world (Macintosh *et al.*, 1987), may become the ultimate seed of its own failure. One outcome of the QPP that is apparent, however, is the increased awareness of organizational members of the degree to which economic and political forces have come to influence their goals, objectives, structures, and systems.

Looking beyond the 1984-1988 strategic change period, there is a different set of pressures acting on the Canadian sport delivery system that have important implications for future research on the strategic change in NSOs. Since the 1984-1988 quadrennial, numerous concerns have been raised about the autonomy of NSOs and the amount of control the government exerted on them in pursuit of its political objectives.

As a result of the positive doping test of Ben Johnson at the Seoul Olympics, the Dubin Report (1990), the Sport Commission (1990), and the Minister's Task Force on Federal Sport Policy (1992), have all stressed the need for a reassessment and restructuring of the high performance sport emphasis, NSO autonomy, and NSO-federal government relations. As stated in the Dubin Report (1990: *p.* 529), "the day-to-day administration of sport in Canada has become a function of government to a degree that was never intended nor, indeed, is either healthy or appropriate for sport." The 1990s, therefore, have witnessed increasing challenges to these institutional pressures. In particular, there has been a long term forecast for a government relationship that is less of a coercive force on the programme development of NSOs.

It is important to note, however, that preliminary data collected on changes in the 1988-1992 quadrennial suggest that these NSOs have accepted a more professionally controlled management system and many view high performance sport as a primary aspect of the national organization. Thus implying that, although the federal government exerted less influence over NSOs during the 1988-1992 period, the strong institutional pressures of the previous quadrennial have carried through so that past initiatives may continue to have long term effects on the structure and operations of these organizations. As Kimberly (1984: p. 125) points out, much of the explanation for the way an organization looks the way it does today lies in its past. Therefore, to understand its current design it is necessary to develop an appreciation for the constellation of forces which, over time, together moved it on its developmental trajectory. More important, the possibilities of redesign the future are constrained by the past and present.

References

Child, J. (1972) 'Organizational structure, environment and performance: The role of strategic choice', *Sociology*, Vol. 6: pp. 1-22.

DiMaggio, P. (1988) 'Interest and agency in institutional theory', in L. G. Zucker (ed) *Institutional patterns and organizations: Culture and environment*. Cambridge, MA: Ballinger, pp. 3-21.

DiMaggio, P. and Powell, W. W. (1983) 'The iron cage revisited: Institutional isomorphism and collective rationality in organizational fields', *American Sociological Review*, No. 48: pp. 47-160.

Dubin, C. L. (1990) *Report of the Dubin inquiry into the use of drugs and banned practices intended to increase athletic performance*. Ottawa: Ministry of Supply and Services Canada.

Fitness and Amateur Sport. (1988) *Quadrennial planning and evaluation guide 1988-92*. Ottawa: Ministry of State, Fitness and Amateur Sport.

Frisby, W. (1986) 'The organizational structure and effectiveness of voluntary organizations: The case of Canadian national sport governing bodies', *Journal of Park and Recreation Administration*, Vol. 4: pp. 61-74.

Galaskiewicz, J. and Wasserman, S. (1989) 'Mimetic processes within an interorganizational field: An empirical test', *Administrative Science Quarterly*, Vol. 34: pp. 454-479.

Hage, J. and Aiken, M. (1967) 'Relationship of centralization to other structural properties', *Administrative Science Quarterly*, Vol. 12: pp. 72-92.

Harvey, J. and Proulx, R. (1988) 'Sport and the Canadian state, in J. Harvey and H. Cantelon (eds) *Not just a game*. Ottawa: University of Ottawa Press, pp. 93-119.

Hinings, B. and Greenwood, R. (1988) 'The normative prescription of organizations', in L. G. Zucker (ed) *Institutional patterns and organizations: Culture and environment*. Cambridge, MA: Ballinger, pp. 53-70.

Hinings, B. and Slack, T. (1987) 'The dynamics of quadrennial plan implementation in national sport organizations', in T. Slack and B. Hinings (eds) *The organization and administration of sport*. London, Ontario: Sports Dynamics,, pp. 127-151.

Kidd, B. (1988) 'The philosophy of excellence: Olympic performances, class, power, and the Canadian state', in P. J. Galasso (ed)*Philosophy of sport and physical activity: Issues and concepts*. Toronto: Canadian Scholars' Press, pp. 11-31.

Kikulis, L. M., Slack, T., and Hinings, B. (1992) 'Institutionally specific design archetypes: A Framework for understanding change in National Sport Organizations', *International Review for the Sociology of Sport*, Vol. 27: pp. 343-370.

Kikuis, L. M., Slack, T., Hinings, B., and Zimmermann, A. (1989) 'A structural taxonomy of amateur sport organizations', *Journal of Sport Management*, Vol. 3: pp. 129-150.

Kimberly, J. R. (1984) 'The anatomy of organizational design. *Journal of Management*, Vol. 10: pp. 109-126.

Macintosh, D. (1988) 'The federal government and voluntary sport associations', in J. Harvey and H. Cantelon (eds) *Not just a game*. Ottawa: University of Ottawa Press, pp. 121-140.

Macintosh, D. and Beamish, R. (1988) 'Socio-economic and demographic characteristics of national sport administrators', *Canadian Journal of Applied Sport* Sciences, Vol. 13: pp. 66-72.

Macintosh, D., Bedecki, T. and Franks, C. E. S. (1987) *Sport and politics in Canada: Federal government involvement since 1961*. Montreal and Kingston: McGill-Queen's University Press.

Macintosh, D. and Whitson, D. (1990) *The game planners: Transforming Canada's sport system*. Montreal and Kingston: McGill-Queen's University Press.

Meyer, J. (1983) 'Institutionalization and the rationality of formal organizational structure', in J. Meyer and W. R. Scott (eds) *Organizational environments: Ritual and rationality*. Beverly Hills, CA: Sage, pp. 261-282.

Meyer, J. and Rowan, B. (1977) 'Institutional organizations: Formal structure as myth and ceremony', *American Journal of Sociology*, Vol. 80: pp. 340-363.

Meyer, J. and Scott, W. R. (1983) 'Centralization and the legitimacy problems of local government', in J. Meyer and W. R. Scott (eds)*Organizational environments: Ritual and rationality*. Beverly Hills, CA: Sage, pp. 199-215.

Miller, D. and Dröge, C. (1986) 'Psychological and traditional determinants of structure', *Administrative Science Quarterly*, Vol. 31: pp. 539-560.

Minister's Task Force on Federal Sport Policy. (1992) *Sport: The way ahead.* Ottawa: The Minister of State, Fitness and Amateur Sport.

Mintzberg, H. (1979) *The structuring of organizations*. Englewood Cliffs, New Jersey: Prentice-Hall.

Oliver, C. (1991) 'Strategic responses to institutional processes', *Academy of Management Review*, Vol. 16, 145-179.

Pfeffer, J. and Salancik, G. R. (1978) *The external control of organizations.* New York: Harper and Row.

Powell, W. W. and Freidkin, R. (1986) 'Politics and programs: Organizational factors in public television decision making', in P. DiMaggio (ed) *Nonprofit enterprise in the arts*. New York: Oxford University Press, pp. 245-269.

Pugh, D. S., Hickson, D. J. and Hinings, B. (1969) 'An empirical taxonomy of structures of work organizations', *Administrative Science Quarterly*, Vol. 14: 115- 126.

Pugh, D. S., Hickson, D. J., Hinings, B. and Turner, C. (1968) 'Dimensions of organizational structure', *Administrative Science Quarterly*, Vol. 13: pp. 65-105.

Ranson, S., Hinings, B., Greenwood, R. and Walsh, K. (1980) 'Value preferences and tensions in the organization of local government', in D. Dunkerley and G. Salaman (eds) *The international yearbook of organizational studies*. London: Routledge and Kegan Paul, pp. 197-221.

Schreyögg, G. (1980) 'Contingency and choice in organization theory', *Organization Studies*, Vol. 1: pp. 305-326.

Scott, H., Paraschak, V. and McNaught, A. (1987) 'Canada's "other" Olympic legacy', Paper presented at the North American Society for Sport Sociology Conference. Edmonton, Alberta, November 7.

Scott, W. R. (1983) 'Health care organizations in the 1980s: The convergence of public and professional control systems', in J. Meyer and W. R. Scott (eds) *Organizational environments: Ritual and rationality*. Beverly Hills, CA: Sage, pp. 99-113.

——— (1987) 'The adolescence of institutional theory', *Administrative Science Quarterly*, Vol. 32: pp. 493-511.

Slack, T. and Hinings, B. (1987) 'Planning and organizational change: A conceptual framework for the analysis of amateur sport organizations', *Canadian Journal of Applied Sport Sciences*, Vol. 12: pp. 185-193.

——— (1992) 'Understanding change in national sport organizations: An integration of theoretical perspectives', *Journal of Sport Management*, Vol. 6: pp. 114-132.

Slack, T. and Thibault, L. (1988) 'Values and beliefs: Their role in the structuring of national sport organizations', *Arena Review*, Vol. 12: pp. 140-155.

Sport Commisstion (1990) 'The background to change: Discussion paper I', A discussion paper of the Sport Commission conducted at the Sport Forum meeting, Toronto, April 1991.

Thibault, L., Slack, T. and Hinings, B. (1991) Professionalism, structures and systems: The impact of professional staff on voluntary sport organizations', *International Review for the Sociology of Sport*, Vol. 26: pp. 83-99.

Tolbert, P. S. (1985) 'Resource dependence and institutional environments: Sources of administrative structure in institutions of higher education', *Administrative Science Quarterly*, Vol. 20: pp. 229-249.

Tolbert, P. S. and Zucker, L. G. (1983) 'Institutional sources of change in the formal structure of organizations: The diffusion of civil service reform, 1880-1935', *Administrative Science Quarterly*, Vol. 28: pp. 22-39.

Tushman, M. L., Newman, W. H. and Romanelli, E. (1986) 'Convergence and upheaval: Managing the unsteady pace of organizational evolution', *California Management Review*, Vol. 29: pp. 29-44.

Walsh, K., Hinings, B., Greenwood, R. and Ranson, S. (1981) 'Power and advantage in organizations', *Organization Studies*, Vol. 2, 131-152.

Whitson, D. and Macintosh, D. (1988) 'The professionalization of Canadian amateur sport: Questions of power and purpose', *Arena Review*, Vol. 12: pp. 81-96.

Zucker, L. G. (1983) 'Organizations as institutions, in S. B. Bacharach (ed) *Research in the sociology of organizations* (vol. 2). Greenwich, CT : JAI Press, pp. 1-47.

——— (1987) 'Institutional theories of organization', *Annual Review of Sociology*, No. 13: pp. 443-464.

Comparing Leisure in Different Worlds: Uses and Abuses of Comparative Analysis in Leisure and Tourism

Cara Aitchison

University of North London, UK

Introduction

The scope of recent leisure and tourism research has broadened to incorporate a wide range of comparative studies across all areas of leisure and tourism. However, this breadth of research has not always been accompanied by depth of research. There is now a need to promote a comprehensive rationale for comparative studies within leisure and tourism and to develop an underpinning theoretical and conceptual framework upon which future comparative research can build.

This paper examines the potential of comparative analysis in international leisure research and advocates a wide-ranging comparative perspective as a priority for future research. Comparative studies has been a neglected field within leisure studies and most leisure research which does claim to be comparative is based on single-nation studies and is not therefore genuinely comparative. The role of comparative studies and its problematic nature are examined and a review of the historical background to comparative analysis is undertaken by assessing both quantitative and qualitative methodological approaches. This includes an analysis of the comparative method from the positivist tradition and an evaluation of the contribution from the more humanistic school of comparative studies.

The paper looks at the background to, and trends in, international leisure research. To date, research methodology has tended to employ a few discrete techniques and studies undertaken have concentrated on individual countries or cultures rather than cross-cultural studies. Academic cross-cultural analysis has therefore had to rely on the extrapolation of relevant findings from largely quantitative research. The paper examines a range of previous research and identifies short-comings in their aims and methodologies. The tradition of comparative studies in sport and physical education is critically examined and more contemporary debate including areas of leisure policy and international tourism are assessed. Recommendations are then put forward for a possible framework for future comparative research in leisure studies.

The role of comparative studies and its problematic nature

In an article entitled 'Uses and abuses of comparative education', Harold Noah stated:

> Comparative analysis can help us understand better our own past, locate ourselves more exactly in the present, and discern a little more clearly what our future may be. These contributions can be made via work that is primarily descriptive as well as through work that seeks to be analytic or explanatory; through work that is limited to just one, or a very few nations, as well as through work that embraces a wider scope; through work that relies on non-quantitative as well as quantitative data and methods; and through work that proceeds with explicitly formulated social science paradigms in mind as well as in a less formalised manner. (Noah, 1984: p. 551)

However, the majority of leisure research claiming to be "comparative" has been "primarily descriptive" rather than "analytic or explanatory". Research has tended to be "limited to just one, or a very few nations" rather then "work that embraces a wider scope". Methodology has emphasised "quantitative data and methods" rather than "non-quantitative" work, and methodological and theoretical perspectives and paradigms have not been "explicitly formulated". Therefore, the role and potential of comparative analysis is a relatively untapped resource and this is perhaps more so in leisure studies than in other disciplines where there is a longer tradition of comparative studies.

Comparative analysis has to be viewed as a wide-ranging methodological approach, the aim of which is to provide information, understanding and appreciation within a diversity of theoretical and practical contexts. The ultimate objective of comparative analysis has to be the development of critical consciousness and understanding in an enlightened cross-national and cross-cultural context which addresses issues of theory, policy and practice. The value of comparative analysis goes beyond merely translating theory into practice. In terms of theory, comparative analysis can result in improved theoretical models by enlarging the framework within which theories are developed and increasing the credibility of a theory by providing comparative evidence. When translating theory into practice, comparative analysis provides knowledge of other situations and careful analysis can allow solutions to be adopted to meet a diversity of needs. However, as Noah (1984) states:

> The authentic use of comparative study resides not only in the wholesale appropriation of foreign practices but in careful analysis of the conditions under which certain foreign practices deliver desirable results, followed by consideration of ways to adapt those practices to conditions found at home. (p. 558)

A wide-ranging view of leisure policy or practices requires an equally wide-ranging theoretical perspective and methodological approach. As comparative analysis is a method of study which seeks to broaden horizons it is imperative that it utilises broad, open-minded methodologies. Comparative analysis goes beyond the objectivity involved in experiment and positivist methodology in general, as it involves the formation of concepts rather than just the collection and collation of information. The fundamental assertion of comparative analysis is that we can only understand our own culture within the context of other cultures, that is, there can be no understanding without comparison. Comparative knowledge has the potential to prevent over-generalisations and to highlight the ethnocentric nature of many currently accepted generalisations. Ultimately, knowledge and understanding are prerequisites to cultural co-operation, and, in an increasingly complex world of multi-polar international relationships, comparative knowledge can act to prevent supranational elitism and sub-state national parochialisms.

Historical background of comparative studies

Comparative analysis is by no means a recent methodology and has its roots in traditional geography and sociology. The aim of traditional Geography was to explain the differentiation and integration of places and people throughout the world but, rather than making genuine international or cross-cultural comparison, traditional geography tended to concentrate on regional differentiation through the study of regional geography which was often descriptive and deterministic rather than genuinely engaged in comparative analysis or synthesis. However, the discipline of geography has now developed to encompass wide-ranging examinations of intricate and dynamic interdependencies and comparisons between regions, nations and cultures across both the natural and social environment.

The early sociologists made extensive use of the comparative method as a means of investigating patterns of social change, particularly of a major historical nature. Thus Auguste Comte (1798-1857) explained the rise of industrial society as the logical conclusion of his "law of three stages" in which all societies move from antiquity based on the theological to the middle ages founded on the metaphysical to the industrial age based on the positive. Comte's work can be compared to the work of the geographer Malthus who again used comparative analysis to provide a rather prescriptive account of the developmental nature of society. Marx, too, used comparative analysis to support his theory that societies would inevitably move through a number of stages — although his theory moves on a stage from Comte's, to state that societies must pass through primitive communism to feudalism and capitalism to post-revolutionary communism.

Similarly, Weber, in his investigation of the rise of capitalism in Western Europe, and Durkheim in "Suicide" (1897, which represents his most frequently quoted example of a comparative study) both tried to isolate causal variables through comparative study to produce explanations of certain phenomena. Indeed it was Durkheim who claimed in 1895 that "Comparative sociology is not a branch of sociology. It is sociology itself". However, such studies relied on the positivist tradition and, as with geography, more recent sociological studies have drawn on a wider range of methodologies to provide a broader comparative perspective. Thus, whilst leisure studies is a fairly young discipline, and the use of comparative methodology within leisure studies is still a developing area, we can look to other areas of academic study to determine the relevance of comparative analysis within future developments in leisure studies. Of particular interest are the more developed areas of comparative study within geography, international sociology, social anthropology, and comparative education.

Theoretical perspectives in comparative analysis

1. Methodological debate

There is a long and healthy tradition of methodological debate within most academic disciplines. Such debate is necessary in a rapidly changing world where academic approaches must reflect the dynamic nature of society. Methodological debate underwent a polarisation during the 1960s with positivism, in the form of the scientific method, being contrasted against humanistic methods. The increasing respectability of science over social science led to an emphasis on the scientific methods of objectivity and deduction, the use of experiments, quantifiable data, verification procedures and the formation of scientific laws. The methods of the social sciences, many of which were still relatively young disciplines, were criticised for their subjectivity and many of the social sciences attempted to gain credibility by adopting and adapting methods from the sciences.

Perhaps such polarisation was a necessary stage in the development of a more liberal methodology, and by identifying the stultifying nature of such polarisation we can attempt to move beyond the dichotomy of science-social science and objectivity-subjectivity to a more holistic approach. Comparative analysis, within any discipline, provides an ideal framework within which the methodologies of positivism and humanism can contribute to a greater understanding of the human environment and experiences within that environment. To meet the need for a liberal methodology in comparative studies a combination of positivist, humanist and structuralist methodologies is appropriate. The importance of such a wide-ranging approach is reiterated when we look at the variety of uses of comparative analysis. It is an applied field of study, being instrumental in the practicalities of management, administration and policy making, as well as an academic field of study where increased knowledge, understanding and appreciation of other people's cultural values can be achieved. In this respect, comparative analysis can be seen as a potentially progressive and enlightening series of methods which transcend the traditional rigidly defined academic disciplines. It is therefore an appropriate approach to use within the field of leisure studies which itself seeks to cross many cultural and academic boundaries. In order to establish such a methodology it is necessary to identify the weaknesses and merits of each approach and see how these can be integrated.

2. The positivist approach

Positivism is central to the methodology of the natural sciences and has its roots in many of the scientific developments from the 15th Century. However, the approach was largely developed by the nineteenth century French philosopher August Comte and the approach investigates phenomena through the testing of hypotheses (the scientific method). These hypotheses are made from empirical generalisations by accepted procedures about observable phenomena. Comte believed that his method could be used as successfully in the social sciences. Although he admitted that not all questions could be answered using positivism, he emphasised that if a question could not be answered using the positivist approach then it could not be answered at all, and therefore there was no point in asking it.

Although we should have progressed beyond the positivist paradigm, our attitudes have been shaped to such an extent by positivist acceptance of the *status quo* that any radical or revolutionary approach to leisure studies has the odds weighted very highly against it. One significant means of maintaining positivism's influence in leisure theory has been the increased use of computer technology and advanced data-handling techniques, largely based on quantitative analysis and positivist methods. Positivism's reliance on models demonstrates quite clearly the superficiality of the approach as models are, by their very nature, abstractions and simplifications of reality in that they separate system (model) from environment. Models and positivism in general give a purely passive role to the individual, and it is this undermining of the individual's active and creative capacity which renders positivist theory inadequate as a full explanation. Positivist theory generalises to such an extent that it accepts given universals, often denying cultural specificity and therefore the positivist method has proved a slow route to progress in comparative analysis. Too often researchers have used positivist techniques as a means of alleviating their own consciences. By producing vast quantities of statistics relating to a problem they seem to think they are contributing to a solution, when, in reality, they are merely reinforcing the *status quo* and making the possibility of change even more remote.

The unrealistic nature of positivism is further influenced by its reductionist approach which sees parts of systems as unrelated elements, uninfluenced by external societal and environmental factors and this promotes the reification of individuals. Within comparative analysis, positivism has relied too heavily upon description and classification. Raivola argues that an essential condition of comparison is to establish a point of reference:

> ... so that all the units to be compared can be examined in the light of a common variable, the meaning of which is constant for all units under comparison. (Raivola, 1985: p. 363)

This assumes that objective information on leisure or cultural relations does actually exist and can be gathered and analysed in an objective manner. There are many areas of leisure and culture where objective data is limited, primarily because leisure, recreation, tourism and culture involve relationships among people which cannot always be measured objectively. Lack of objective data has meant that those areas of recreation which can be quantified, such as sports participation figures, numbers of countryside visits and distance travelled have been studied obsessively and at the expense of more meaningful relations and concepts. Marxist and socialist feminist critiques of the use of positivist approaches in leisure studies have focused on the inadequacy of relying on statistical information to present a picture of gender relations which are underpinned by deeper structural constraints within society. Even when objective data does exist it cannot be investigated in a truly objective manner as all research is imprinted, to some degree, by the researcher's assumptions, values and prejudices.

Therefore, positivism can never provide a complete methodology in comparative analysis. At most, it can be incorporated into more subjective methodologies by providing another research tool and a means towards greater understanding rather than an end in itself.

3. The humanistic approach

Humanistic epistemology states that knowledge is obtained subjectively in a world of meanings created by individuals. Humanism's ontology, or theory of reality, states that what exists is that which is perceived to exist and its methodology emphasises individuality and subjectivity. This can be achieved through unique case studies involving hermeneutic (interpretive) analysis and intuitive and empathetic understanding (*verstehen*). Thus, humanistic approaches focus on people as thinking individuals, emphasising the subjectivity of both observer and observed. The aim is not necessarily to increase explanation or predictive power but to improve understanding. There are a number of differing humanistic methodologies including idealism, existentialism and phenomenology. For the purpose of comparative studies, phenomenology is the most important although it is also worth considering some of the issues which arise from an existentialist approach.

The common factors of phenomenological approaches are "intentionality" — that the world exists as a series of mental constructions created in intentional acts; "*verstehen*" which emphasises interpretive and empathetic understanding rather than explanation; "hermeneutics" which attempts to explicate meaning behind action through interpretation; and "bracketing" which emphasises that individual situations should be studied free of preconceived ideas. Participant observation incorporates many elements of the above and can be used successfully as a means of comparative analysis. Participant observation studies in sociology and human geography are well documented, but there are fewer in leisure studies where research expanded at a time when funding for resource intensive projects was diminishing.

As phenomenological investigation is dependent upon communication and intersubjectivity, the importance of language is paramount. Language always introduces a subjective element into research as language and labels for concepts may not always be understood identically by people speaking the same language, and are frequently understood in different ways following translation. This problem has been emphasised by recent projects focusing on cultural aspects of leisure and tourism including the whole concept of "heritage" which does not translate readily across language or cultural boundaries. This point emphasises the importance of international co-operation in aspects of comparative studies rather than relying on the work of one researcher or a team of researchers from only one country.

Phenomenology is also the parent body of ethnomethodology which has contributed to cross-cultural studies. Such studies attempt to present a view of the world as it is perceived by the subjects and not as it is structured *a priori* by the observers. Two of the most useful methodological approaches within ethnomethodology are the interview and participant observation which, although still subject to interpretation by the researcher, provides an insight into the "life-world" of those being interviewed or observed. There has been relatively little use of interviews or participant observation in wider comparative studies of leisure. Such techniques tend to be limited to smaller local studies and it is certainly worth evaluating their potential and usefulness in comparative studies.

Existentialism is rooted in the individual even more than phenomenology. Much of existentialist theory has become known through the work of Jean Paul Sartre and Søren Kierkegaard and it is through artistic expression, especially in the form of literature, rather than formal methodology, that attitudes and characteristics are explored. Existentialism emphasises the need for individuals to be autonomous moral agents where personal authenticity can only be achieved through individual freedom, decision-making and responsibility and if choice is hampered, individuals become inauthentic. Existentialism could prove a valuable methodology in comparative analysis of leisure, tourism, recreation and culture due to its already well-formed cultural associations and its emphasis on the individual. However, it could be argued that comparative analysis cannot exist in the existentialist mind where all meaning is created intrinsically by the individual and not determined by comparison. Therefore, is comparison a means of simplifying and bringing order to observations which the existentialist sees no need to order, classify and categorise? Or, is comparative analysis a means of widening our horizons in an effort to move away from categorisation and generalisation?

An evaluation of humanistic methods is not easy as there are no explicit or tangible criteria against which they can be assessed and the work is not necessarily cumulative in the sense that much scientific work is. Humanistic approaches can allow appreciation of ambiguities and inherent contradictions in cultures without making generalisations and simplifications. Such ambiguities should not be distorted by quantitative techniques which may act to hinder understanding and can be used as a basis for social engineering. As Coenen-Huther states:

> There are too many research reports which confront the reader

> with a mass of unstructured facts. The attempt to provide over-comprehensive results ends in interesting information being drowned in a welter of data of lesser interest. (Coenen-Huther, 1978: p. 85)

Research findings may also be distorted by the nature of the organisation which commissions the research. Coenen-Huther points to the "bureaucratisation of research" which has come about as a result of the involvement of international organisations in research programmes. Similarly, the source of finance may affect the chosen methodology or actual results. Comparative methodology is relatively costly simply because of its wide-ranging nature and the "cost-effectiveness" obsession since the early 1980s has crept into research programmes, with increasing emphasis on speed and results (which usually means quantitative results) at the expense of qualitative insight.

Humanistic methods have been criticised by positivists for being subjective and non-scientific in that theories cannot be verified by testing hypotheses. However, it should be recognised that there can be no such thing as definitive qualitative or quantitative social science research as neither can be replicated exactly or verified completely. Therefore, comparative studies seeks to add to existing knowledge through methods which are more akin to Lakatos' "research programme" philosophy of an agreed core and disputed periphery. Such a view would state that theoretical revolutions are accomplished slowly through simultaneous competing research programmes rather than through full scale overthrow of theoretical paradigms as advanced by Kuhn or by conjecture and refutation advanced by Popper.

Structuralists have also criticised humanist methods for their failure to recognise societal constraints. It is therefore worth examining these criticisms by looking at structuralism and by debating ways in which structuralism and humanism can be integrated in a comparative approach.

4. The structuralist approach

Structuralism seeks explanations for observed phenomena in general structures which underpin all phenomena but are not identifiable within them. With the "structure as construct" theory, observed phenomena are seen as representations of deep structures genetically imprinted on human consciousness, e.g. the linguistic theories of de Saussure and Chomsky, the social anthropological theories of Levi Strauss, and the psychological theories of Piaget. However, structuralism can also be seen as "structure as process" and here phenomena are seen as representations of underlying social structures whose base lies in the transformation of structure at societal rather than neural level and this structure itself is continually being transformed.

Such theory has formed the basis of Marx's work, of the Marxian humanism of the Frankfurt School, the critical theory of Habermas and Giddens' theory of structuration.

Whereas traditional structuralist theory emphasises the importance of societal structure and constraint, and humanist theory emphasises the importance of human agency; theorists such as Giddens and Berger point to the mutual dependency of both structure and agency so that a dialectic is formed between individuals and society with each influencing the other in a continuous process. Thus the individual both shapes and is shaped by society. So although culture can be created through the interaction of subjective meanings shared by individuals and communities, this subjectivity can be studied in a more objective manner as cultural meanings are often built into the institutions, symbols and cultural artefacts of society. Just as political polarisation is often accused of preventing real change or progress, so too is methodological polarisation. By moving towards a more integrated comparative methodology it may be possible to achieve a more comprehensive understanding of the meaning and value of leisure and tourism within society. Giddens' work has recently come under wider scrutiny and it would be worthwhile considering the merits of the contribution of both structuration theory and dialectic materialism to comparative studies.

A critique of previous comparative studies in leisure and tourism

The methodologies employed in comparative analysis within leisure and tourism have stemmed largely from the positivist tradition and have tended to focus on description rather than analysis and synthesis. Those areas of leisure which claim to have undertaken comparative studies are dominated by fairly formal recreational activities and here again these areas may have been chosen for the relative ease with which quantifiable research may be undertaken. There have, however, been a number of significant studies which incorporate an element of comparative research of less formalised leisure pursuits or cultural activities although most of this research comes from cultural studies or social anthropology rather than leisure studies.

Within the field of leisure studies, the three areas of sport and physical education, leisure policy, and international tourism provide examples of research which claims to be comparative. However, a critique of previous research demonstrates that there is still a long way to go before research in leisure studies can claim to be genuinely comparative.

1. Sports studies and physical education

In sports studies there is now a twenty year tradition of comparative sports studies although here, perhaps more so than in any other area, the extent to which such studies are genuinely comparative is questionable. Whilst there are two texts titled *Comparative physical education and sport* (Bennet *et al.*, 1975; Simri, 1979) and there have been a number of international seminars on this subject, genuinely comparative material is limited. The numerous sports studies and leisure studies courses which include teaching of comparative aspects of sport and/or leisure tend to draw on single nation studies and rely on the extrapolation of relevant findings from largely descriptive and quantitative research. Many of the library stocks in European institutions teaching sports studies and leisure studies contain a plethora of texts which focus on sport in "East Germany", the "USSR" and other former Soviet satellite states. Whilst these texts are now of great historical value they offer little to contemporary debates on comparative sports studies and physical education.

However, there are a number of more positive developments currently taking place in leisure/sports studies and the work of Bunuel, Fasting, Pfister and Scraton provides an ongoing example of a more genuine comparative study of women and sport across Europe. Their research project, "Experiences of Sport in the Lives of Women in Different European Countries", is underpinned by feminist theory and the adoption of more explicit theoretical and conceptual frameworks could provide a stronger methodological underpinning to other future projects, although not necessarily of a feminist nature. Other comparative sports research fails to acknowledge the influence of wider international trends and pays insufficient attention to the development of leisure policy and its implications for sport.

2. Leisure policy

The issue of comparative leisure policy is addressed in *Leisure and Urban Processes: Critical studies of leisure policy in Western European cities*, edited by Bramham *et al.* (1989), in which the editors acknowledge that the field of comparative leisure policy has been seriously neglected. However, *Leisure and urban processes* also falls short of providing genuinely comparative research as the book comprises a series of mostly individually authored, discrete case studies which fail to relate to one another. However, the editors do state that:

> The aim of this collection is to contribute to comparative analysis in the leisure studies field, and, more precisely, to the topic of

> urban leisure policy. As such it represents the first stage, the raw materials for such analysis since each of the studies deals predominantly with aspects of policy development in a single nation state, and indeed focus on specific urban localities. (Bramham *et al.*, 1989: p. 4)

The priority now, for comparative leisure research, is surely the analysis of the "raw materials" of research rather than the continual collection of further data and case studies; or at the very least, the analysis should keep pace with the collecting and classification. Bramham *et al.* state that:

> ...the state of the art in the field of leisure policy research does not yet allow the more systematic approach which might provide such knowledge. (p. 5)

But surely it is our responsibility, as leisure researchers claiming to be interested in comparative studies, to formulate such an approach or series of approaches. Fortunately, Bramham *et al.*

> ...do not expect this collection to be the last word on this topic, but rather the beginning of an ongoing and vital debate. (p. 12)

Current research by Bramham *et al.* (1993) and Henry (1993a/b) does move the comparative policy debate on in a more positive way. However, there is undoubtedly still scope to improve the theoretical underpinning of comparative policy analysis and there is a strong case for institutional collaboration across different comparative projects in order to strengthen comparative theoretical and conceptual frameworks.

3. International tourism

Pearce and Butler (1993) recognise that the development of tourism theory, concepts and methods has not been given sufficient priority and that much recent tourism research lacks an adequate conceptual underpinning. In *Comparative Studies in Tourism Research* Pearce emphasises that "the comparative approach has yet to emerge as a distinctive readily recognisable methodology in tourism research." Pearce then goes on to discuss a range of previous research which he classifies under the three headings of "comparative case studies", "element by element comparisons" and "quantitative and graphical analysis". However, many of the research examples given can be criticised for some or all of the reasons outlined previously in this paper. In broad terms, many comparative case studies are not designed as such and lack an underpinning conceptual framework from comparative studies or, where comparative analysis is part of the initial research remit, the comparative element is limited to a discrete section of the research report. Element by element comparison provides a detailed if somewhat rigid framework for comparative analysis but quantitative and graphical analyses can fall foul of many of the criticisms levelled at the positivist approach in general.

Tourism and Economic Development: Western European Experiences, edited by Williams and Shaw (1991), utilises comparative national case studies, follows a similar format to leisure and urban processes and can be criticised for all the same reasons. But perhaps even more so with *Tourism and Economic Development* there is a case for accusing the authors and editors of failing to utilise the full potential of the case studies discussed. The raw materials for in-depth comparative analysis are all there and it would have been excellent to bring the authors together to work on the comparative aspects of the research. Again it is possible for the reader to extrapolate comparative findings but such conclusions would be more genuinely comparative if the authors, many of whom have researched and written about Tourism in their native country, had worked together to draw out the comparisons.

Similarly, there is now a wealth of raw materials analysing the development, nature and potential of tourism in a range of countries. Much of the information produced in *Tourism Analyst* by the Economic Intelligence Unit could be reworked into a more comparative and analytic form to produce a more complete and comparative understanding of the role of tourism. Research produced by the World Tourism Organisation (e.g., WTO, 1992) tends to take the form of quantitative and graphical analysis and, although accompanied by broad-based analysis of tourism trends, there is little discussion of underpinning methodology for conducting global comparative analysis.

The European Community has recently commissioned the Association for Education in Tourism, Leisure and the Arts (ATLAS) to research Cultural Tourism in Europe. This research highlights many of the difficulties of conducting comparative analysis, particularly when there is a political and economic agenda which assumes that there are more comparisons than contrasts to be made. The research design incorporated both quantitative and qualitative elements in the form of a user survey conducted in nine E.C. nations and qualitative analysis of behaviour patterns of cultural tourists. Whilst Richards acknowledges that many of the basic technical problems can be resolved, the research has highlighted the difficulty of conducting genuinely transnational research:

> The assumption is that adding nations together creates a transnational perspective. However, the experience of the cultural tourism research has demonstrated that rather more than a

> simple addition exercise is required. (Richards and Bonink, 1992: p. 8)

The research also demonstrates the artificiality of assuming cultural coherence within given geographical boundaries. It is difficult to identify a single British culture and it would seem impossible to identify a European culture. We can, perhaps, point to similarities in some aspects of culture in different areas of Europe e.g. the Celtic culture of Scotland, Wales, the Basque region of Spain and Brittany in France. But this coherence is partially identified as a result of differentiation from the dominant culture within each of the countries mentioned thereby highlighting the lack of a European culture.

A framework for future comparative analysis

Any framework for future analysis must address the need for a strengthened academic underpinning to the study of comparative leisure and tourism. In order to undertake genuinely comparative studies, a wide range of research methodologies must be employed and such methodologies should be derived from good practice in both quantitative and qualitative methodology.

It should also be appreciated that there may not be immediate returns on such research and therefore it should not be resource driven. Initial descriptive or quantitative research has to be expanded to derive genuine comparison as it is insufficient to collate a series of single-nation studies and label them comparative. As Bramham *et al.* state:

> ...the contributions to this text are largely single nation studies, and there is a need therefore to generate genuinely cross-national studies to build on this initiative, which represents merely the first stages in a programme promoting comparative studies. (Bramham *et al.*, 1989: preface)

At a time when leisure studies is still struggling to be recognised as a legitimate academic field and discrete area of research by academic institutions, research funding bodies and leisure and tourism organisations it is vital that leisure studies promotes critical academic debate concerning the theoretical and methodological underpinning to these studies.

Therefore, a more comprehensive framework for future comparative research in leisure and tourism might address issues of theory and method in the following six areas:

a) Theoretical perspectives

Future research should involve greater attempts to integrate a range of theoretical perspectives from all underpinning disciplines and should include positivist, humanistic and structuralist philosophy. Organisations such as the leisure studies Association and ATLAS could provide appropriate forums for such discussion.

b) Research methodologies

There is a need for less emphasis on the logical-positivist method of comparative studies and an appreciation of the need to research previously neglected areas of leisure and tourism which are not easily quantified.

c) Geographical relations

More emphasis should be placed on contemporary geographical relations of uniqueness-interdependence between places, internationalisation, globalisation, and uneven development. Less emphasis should be placed on traditional spatial relationships and on nation-state boundaries as causes of external differentiation and internal homogenisation.

d) Social relations

There is a need for greater emphasis on contemporary social relationships of work-leisure patterns and expectations, social class, gender, age and ethnicity; and an appreciation of the ways in which social relations inform both social policy and leisure policy.

e) Economic relations

More emphasis needs to be placed on contemporary economic relations of internationalisation of capital and the increasing hold of the multinational corporations, combined with an analysis of the ways in which economic policy shapes social and leisure policy.

f) Political relations

More emphasis is required concerning changing political relations of supra-state nationalism and sub-state nationalism, and an appreciation of the importance of political ideology in shaping leisure and tourism policy.

This framework could be developed to provide a conceptual model for comparative analysis but, as always with models, there is a danger that this would become prescriptive and may act as a strait-jacket to future research rather than a foundation or checklist upon which research should build. All six recommendations reiterate the multidisciplinary nature of leisure studies and emphasise the need for debate, discussion and paradigmatic development within the discipline. Bramham *et al.* were right to refer to comparative analysis within leisure studies as an "ongoing and vital debate" and it is now the responsibility of academics and practitioners within leisure and tourism to ensure that it remains so.

References

Bennett, B. *et al.* (1975) *Comparative physical education and sport.* Philadelphia, PA: Lea and Febiger.

Billinge, M., Gregory, D. and Martin, R. L. (Eds) (1982) *Reflections on a revolution.* London: Macmillan.

Bramham, P., Henry, I., Mommaas, H., and van der Poel, H. (1989) *Leisure and urban processes: Critical studies of leisure policy in Western European cities.* London: Routledge.

Bunuel, A., Fasting, K., Pfister, G. and Scraton, S. (forthcoming) *Experiences of sport in the lives of women in different European countries.*

Coenen-Huther, J. (1978) 'International Research and Cultural Policy', in *Explorations in cultural policy and research.* Strasbourg: Council of Europe.

Henry, I. (1993a) 'Leisure policies in unified Europe', Paper presented at 4th European Leisure Studies Winter University, Wageningen University, April.

——— (1993b) *The politics of leisure policy.* London: Macmillan.

Noah, H. (1984) 'Uses and abuses of comparative education', in *Comparative Education Review,* Vol. 28, No. 4.

Pearce, D. and Butler, R. (1993) *Tourism research: Critiques and challlenges.* London: Routledge.

Raivola, R. (1985) 'What is comparison? Methodological and philosophical Considerations', in *Comparative Education Review,* Vol. 29, No. 3.

Richards, G. and Bonink, C. (1992) 'Problems of transnational research: Cultural tourism', Paper presented at LSA/VVS International Conference, Tilburg University, December.

Simri, U. (1979) *Comparative physical education and Sport.* Israel: Wingate.

Williams, A. and Shaw, G. (1991) *Tourism and economic development: Western European experiences* (second edition). London: Belhaven Press.

World Tourism Organisation (1992) 'Tourism Trends to the Year 2000 and Beyond', presentation by R. Cleverdon at EXPO '92, World Trade Centre, Seville, Spain.

Wynne, D. (1990) 'Leisure, lifestyle and the construction of social position', in *Leisure Studies, Vol.* 9, No. 1: pp. 21-34.

Leisure in Different Worlds: the Survey Evidence

A. J. Veal
University of Technology, Sydney, Australia
and
Grant Cushman
Lincoln University, New Zealand

Introduction

This paper examines the range of insights which national leisure participation surveys have to offer in research on "Leisure in Different Worlds". It draws particularly on experience in the UK, Australia and New Zealand.

Participation surveys in leisure studies

In the early days of the modern era of leisure research large-scale, national or regional, questionnaire-based community leisure participation surveys vied with site (usually outdoor recreation) or user surveys as the main research vehicle. While academics were involved with these surveys as advisers and as primary and secondary analysts, the initiative and resources for the work tended to come from government and quasi-government agencies, driven by policy concerns. Thus the early US surveys arose from the work of the Outdoor Recreation Resources Review Commission (1962); the initial surveys in Britain were sponsored by the British Travel Association (BTA, 1968) and the Government Social Survey (Sillitoe, 1969); in Australia the sponsoring body was the government Cities Commission (1975) and in New Zealand it was the Council for Recreation and Sport (Robb and Howorth, 1977).

These early surveys were generally purely descriptive — that was their purpose. But they laid the groundwork for the development of a variety of traditions in leisure studies. US researchers developed a quantitative/modelling/prediction tradition which, together with quantitative methods at the individual/psychological level, has tended to dominate leisure research in America ever since. In the UK the quantitative/modelling approach was soon abandoned in favour of a more direct use of such data in policy formation and monitoring. For example, the low levels of participation in sport revealed by the surveys — particularly among young people — spurred the 'Sport for All' campaign and the extensive programme of community sport/leisure facility provision in the 1970s and 1980s. Continuing inequalities in participation revealed by the surveys, in terms of social class, age and gender, can be seen as contributing to the development of targeted policies by such organisations as the Sports Council. In Australia and New Zealand large-scale surveys conducted in the 1970s challenged the direction of earlier views on leisure participation in which sport and physical recreation were assumed to be central to the leisure phenomenon and to government policy. National surveys informed policy-makers for the first time of the diversity of leisure pursuits. These surveys provided grounds for questioning certain values, experiences, preferences and priorities in policy: those of male, white, middle class groups whose leisure was perceived as being exemplified by a certain range of sporting and physical recreation activities (Laidler and Cushman, 1993). The early surveys were part of a general concern for social policy issues which was a feature of social democratic governments in Britain in the 1960s and in Australia in the early 1970s (Hamilton-Smith and Robertson, 1977).

Leisure participation surveys have continued to be conducted as part of a recognised responsibility of central governments to monitor social conditions and the impact of policies. For example, in 1985 an Australian government policy document stated:

> It is now widely accepted that the development and implementation of effective government policies and programs must be based on accurate information about current conditions in the community. [...] the Department of Sport, Recreation and Tourism is already working to establish a data base which will provide a national perspective on recreation behaviour. (Brown, 1985, p. 15)

In Australia, a national Recreation Participation Survey (NRPS) was conducted in 1985 and repeated four times in 1985/86 and in 1987 and 1991 (Veal, 1993). In Britain the General Household Survey (GHS) is now well established as the main vehicle for leisure participation data collection (Office of Population Censuses and Surveys, Annual). In New Zealand the 1980-81 Social Indicator Survey (Dept. of Statistics, 1984) has been followed by the 1991 Life in New Zealand (LINZ) project (Cushman *et al.*, 1991).

Uses of surveys in theoretical/critical research

Theoretical and critical researchers in the leisure area, while generally eschewing the survey method, have often drawn on the evidence of survey data as a starting point, particularly in relation to social class differences in participation levels, and particularly in relation to publicly subsidised areas of leisure such as elite sport, the arts and outdoor recreation. Theoretical and critical research on leisure tends to be conducted by academics rather than government agencies. Academics in the social sciences — and in leisure studies in particular — do not themselves generally have access to resources to conduct large-scale empirical research and so have been reliant on government sponsored surveys when discussing general patterns of leisure behaviour in relation to such aspects as social class or gender, particularly in relation to publicly subsidised areas of leisure such as sport and the arts (see, for example, McKay, 1990; Parker and Paddick, 1990).

Recently surveys have had a 'bad press' from academics, particularly in light of the growing popularity — and indeed orthodoxy — of qualitative research methods in the field. In order to establish the case for undertaking or placing more emphasis on qualitative empirical research and non-empirical theoretical research, commentators often outline the shortcomings of survey methods, while tending to ignore their merits and exaggerating the claims made by their proponents. The following comment by Rojek is an example:

> Empiricism is a philosophy of knowledge that assigns a privileged status to quantitative material in understanding. In leisure and recreation studies, its principal research methods are questionnaires, surveys, and statistical analysis. Empiricists claim to start with observable facts and to build analytical statements upon the accumulation of facts. They assume that subjective experience is the only basis for knowledge. The questions of what experience is, and what the historical and social context of subjective experience consists of, are dismissed as second-order issues. (Rojek, 1989: p. 70).

Rojek does not give examples or references in relation to these remarks and it is possible that he is referring only to particularly quantitative research in the 'scientific' mode, as seen typically in, for example, the But any such subtlety is lost in claims that appear to refer to all quantitative, questionnaire-based research. Our views do not accord with those of empiricists as outlined by Rojek: we certainly do *not* dismiss as second order the sorts of questions he raises.

Karla Henderson's (1991) work on qualitative research methods is more balanced in its approach and she argues that research methods should be selected which are appropriate for the job in hand but, in contrasting qualitative and quantitative methods, she appears to have in mind only one type of 'scientific' quantitative methodology and she therefore misrepresents survey methods in stating:

These characteristics of the quantitative and qualitative approaches, respectively, include:

(a) preordinant (structural) design compared to emergent (processual) design,

(b) measurement using only numbers compared to meaning using only words,

(c) controlled (manipulated, impersonal) settings compared to natural (interactive, personal) settings,

(d) confirming theory by analysing variables compared to developing theory by examining patterns,

(e) rational procedures compared to intuitive processes. (1991:p. 26)

The impression is left that the researcher who wishes to be involved with process and meaning, natural, interactive and personal settings, and development of theory and intuition, will opt for qualitative methods, while the quantitative researcher is concerned with preordinant structures, numerical measurement, control and manipulation, analysing variables and rational procedures. Qualitative research is painted as very human compared with the cold, rational quantitative process. In fact, much survey research is the result of a long process of piloting, focus groups, and consultation and the analysis is often extremely *inductive* rather than deductive and, if well done, involves as much intuition as any other type of research. It could also be argued that the typical questionnaire-based survey interview can be as interactive and personal as many qualitative-style interviews — the charge of 'manipulation" certainly seems inappropriate.

The cumulative effect of repeated detailing of their failings has been to put surveys in bad odour with some of the leisure research community. This seems particularly unnecessary since qualitative and quantitative methods are, in fact, widely viewed as complementary. The limitations of surveys are sometimes listed as irredeemable defects when clearly all research methods have limitations and none should be promoted as seeking to achieve what they are incapable of achieving. This is not to say that users of any method will not attempt to push data to their limits. This temptation arises in all forms of research. For example, for the survey method, making definitive descriptive statements about the community as a whole is routine, but *explanation* of observed behaviour is often speculative — but this does not prevent the researcher from speculating ! Conversely qualitative methods are often strong on explanation but on weak ground when it comes to generalisation to the community — but this rarely stops researchers, despite qualifications at the beginning of their papers, generalising extensively to the whole community and beyond by the time they get to the end of their paper!

Some of the implied criticism of surveys is that they consume extensive resources which are therefore being denied to (and would go much further in) qualitative projects. Roberts, for example, in 1978, stated: "sociologists are entitled to protest at this rampant and excessive fact gathering" (Roberts, 1978: p. 28). But, insofar as large-scale surveys tend to be conducted for policy rather than theoretical purposes, it is not realistically the case that surveys and qualitative research compete for the same resources — the *money* comes out of different 'pockets'. The considerable resources devoted to the conduct of policy-orientated leisure participation surveys would not be available for purely academic research purposes. Virtually all academic use of such survey data is secondary and is often undertaken with little or no specific *funding*. Of course qualitative methods also have a place in policy research and this is being increasingly recognised by policy agencies; but such research tends to be conducted *in addition to*, rather than instead of, survey work. The need for governments to base policy development and evaluation on quantitative statements about the whole community is likely to remain and the prospect of their diverting substantial resources into qualitative research is remote.

The implication is that leisure participation surveys are, in a number of countries, here to stay — not primarily because of leisure research needs but because of government policy needs. It would seem wise therefore for the leisure research community to make use of this resource and, where possible, to seek to influence the design of the surveys to maximise their utility for research purposes. In arguing that surveys have a role to play in leisure studies we are not claiming that they should have any pre-eminence, merely that they should take their place alongside other research methods.

This paper now outlines examples of the ways in which leisure participation surveys can continue to play a role in leisure research and how, with the passage of time, such surveys are becoming even more useful in this regard.

The generation of surveys

Participation surveys continue to be conducted for and on behalf of governments and their agencies. The 'new generation' of leisure participation surveys, conducted in the late 1980s and early 1990s, are an improvement on their 1960s and 1970s forebears in at least three respects. Firstly, more faith can now be placed in their validity and reliability. Secondly, because of the cumulation of survey data over time, the new surveys are beginning to be able to address the question of trends and social change. Thirdly, the design and scope of the questions asked in the surveys has improved, involving the inclusion of attitude questions and the coverage of a wider range of leisure activities. These aspects are discussed in turn below.

An important aspect of surveys which is beginning to be addressed is the question of validity and reliability. Some research, for example by Chase and Godbey (1983), has suggested that survey data lacks validity because respondents simply do not tell the truth about their patterns of leisure behaviour. In particular they are likely to exaggerate participation in socially approved activities — for example physical exercise and the arts — and under-report participation in activities which are not socially approved — for example drinking and gambling. This concern cannot be fully addressed without considerable resources, which are unlikely ever to be available. The concern therefore remains. However, two features of surveys to some extent ameliorate these concerns.

Firstly, unlike early American surveys, which collected information on people's reported participation over the full year prior to interview, surveys in Britain, Australia and New Zealand have concentrated on shorter 'reference periods'. A period as long as twelve months offers a great deal of scope for respondents, either intentionally or unintentionally, to 'massage' their responses. In the UK, the reporting period of the General Household Survey is one month, and in Australia the period for the National Recreation Participation Survey is one week only. Such time periods, while not eliminating inaccurate reporting, are nevertheless likely to reduce it.

Secondly, the comparison of survey results over a period of time has shown considerable consistency: reported participation rates have not fluctuated wildly or inexplicably. This relates to reliability rather than validity — that is it may merely indicate that people are *consistent* in their inaccurate reporting! But, bearing in mind that consecutive surveys involve samples of different people, the finding that what is being reported is consistent is a valuable one.

The rest of this paper gives examples of some of the output from the 'new generation' of participation surveys in Britain, Australia and New Zealand. Three areas are focused upon. Firstly the question of social change: what can participation surveys tell us about changing leisure behaviour patterns? Secondly we address the question of attitudes — early surveys included only participation data, but later surveys have attempted to tap into attitudes and motivations. Thirdly we consider the range of activities covered; early surveys were often very restricted in this respect — recent surveys have 'branched out' to give a fuller picture of leisure. Fourthly we address the question of leisure and social inequality.

Social change

The early surveys were either conducted on a 'one-off' basis or were irregular. One of the advantages of more recent surveys is that, in addition to providing a 'snap shot' picture of leisure at a single point in time, they can be used to monitor change over time by means of comparison with previous surveys. This possibility is only beginning to emerge because it takes time and policy commitment to establish a *series* of comparable surveys.

In Australia, the work of Bittmann in analysing government-sponsored time-budget surveys, while subject to a number of qualifications because of problems of comparability between surveys conducted 13 years apart, throws some intriguing light on the changing patterns of time use of men as compared with women. Table 1 shows that, between 1974 and 1987, Australian women, on average, appeared to have swapped unpaid work for paid work and experienced a decline in overall leisure time. But while men reduced their paid work time they only took up part of the unpaid work no longer done by women, but increased the time they spent on personal needs and voluntary, community and religious activities. The result was a move from *equality* in leisure time in 1974 to *inequality* in 1987. Whereas in 1974 women, on average had the same quantity of leisure time as men, in 1987 they had two hours a week less leisure time than men. Similar analysis, with similar findings, has been carried out by Gershuny and Jones using British data (Gershuny and Jones, 1993).

As we have seen, Rojek claims that 'empiricists' see quantified data as the only source of knowledge and questions concerning social and historical explanation as secondary. Table 1 illustrates the idea that survey research is merely *one* contribution to knowledge: no exaggerated claims need be made to justify its use. The findings in Table 1 are neither the beginning nor the end of debate about gender and leisure, merely a contribution.

Table 1: Changing Time Use of Women and Men Australia 1974-1987

	Women (20-59)			**Men (20-59)**		
	1974	1987	Change	1974	1987	Change
	Minutes per Day					
Paid Work	148	187	+39	425	377	-48
Unpaid work	343	307	-36	104	124	+ 20
Personal needs	636	636	0	600	615	+15
Voluntary/ Community/ Religion	25	32	+7	21	38	+17
Leisure	289	276	-13	289	286	-3

Attitudes

Both the Australian National Recreation Participation Survey (NRPS) and the Life in New Zealand survey (LINZ) include attitudinal questions. The NRPS asked respondents to give reasons why they had not taken part in those activities which they would have liked to participate in, while the LINZ survey asked respondents for reasons for stopping leisure activities. The results from both surveys are brought together in Table 2. The range of reasons given differ, reflecting the difference in the question asked and the coding systems adopted as well as cultural differences, but the one feature which the two surveys have in common is that, reflecting the 'harried' thesis, lack of time is put forward as the major constraint on leisure activity. In-depth, qualitative work could be undertaken to investigate the validity of such a finding; it could explore, for example, the question of whether people are short of time, or whether they see 'lack of time' as a plausible excuse for not making the effort to engage in certain activities. But whether 'lack of time' is a 'genuine' constraint or a 'plausible excuse', it has implications for providers and marketeers in the public and private sectors. Whereas traditionally providers, particularly in the public sector, have been concerned with the supply and availability of facilities and with price, the surveys suggest that, for a substantial number of 'non participants' to be persuaded or enabled to participate, the activity offered must at least be *perceived* as being not excessively demanding of the potential participant's time.

The range of activities

Many early surveys were restricted in the range of activities covered which, in effect, saw leisure only in terms of sport and outdoor recreation. This is not surprising since, as discussed above, the initiative and resources for the work tended to come from government agencies with a primary involvement in policy problems concerned with these two forms of leisure. At the time these surveys were developed there was concern by policy agencies for the implications of increasing use of public lands for outdoor recreation, growing affluence and changes in discretionary time and income of an increasingly sedentary and expanding urban population, and a need to understand the leisure-time patterns of young people. Leisure was viewed by these agencies as being limited to 'constructive', 'socially responsible' and 'wholesome' activities concerned with physical fitness, community health and social reform, so the concern of surveys with a narrow rather than wide range of activities is understandable. Forms of leisure which were home-based and informal and concerned with entertainment and social engagement tended to be overlooked. A feature of second generation surveys is that the scan of leisure is

Table 2: Attitude Questions

	NEW ZEALAND	AUSTRALIA
	Reasons for stopping activities — Rank	Reasons for not doing desired activities — Rank
No time	1	1
Work	2	*
Family	3	*
Took up other activity	4	*
Lack of energy	5 =	*
Physically unable	5 =	*
Lost interest	7	*
No company	8	7
Cost of equipment	9	
Cost of facilities	10	3
Health/not well	*	2
Weather	*	5
Didn't get around to it	*	4
No facilities	*	6

Sources: Wilson (1990); DASETT (1991)

wide, normally including home-based leisure, social activities and entertainment, arts and cultural interests, recreational tourism and informal learning, as well as sport and outdoor pursuits.

In New Zealand, for example, the LINZ study examined a number of health-related factors in respondents' lifestyles and everyday life, including physical activity, nutrition, general health and leisure. Leisure patterns were, for this reason, considered in a similar research context to patterns of eating, drinking, exercising and smoking and thus the scan of human behaviour was wide: the aim was to view leisure in its wider social context. The survey covered a wide range of leisure to the extent of including explicit consideration of four of the Roberts (1978) 'big five' of leisure, namely drinking, television watching, smoking and gambling, with implicit attention to sexual activity. In addition the survey included activities as diverse as 'hanging around', 'Marae, iwi activities', and 'gathering food'. A characteristic of earlier surveys is that these popular lifestyle activities were either excluded deliberately or through oversight. For example, the New Zealand Recreation Survey (NZRS) omitted drinking and pub-going through oversight and excluded sexual activity and television-viewing by design (Tait, 1984). In Australia, the NRPS includes such activities as 'talking to friends on the telephone for more than 15 minutes" and 'relaxing/doing nothing'.

The LINZ survey and NRPS also include questions on the use of facilities. While the lists of facilities are dominated by such items as leisure centres, swimming pools and national parks, and a few commercial facilities, such as cinemas, video hire shops, restaurants and hotels/motels, an innovation of the LINZ survey was to include shopping centres as leisure facilities, while the NRPS included 'shopping for pleasure/window shopping' as a leisure activity. The significance of this is that the use of shopping centres for leisure emerges as the highest among the thirteen facilities listed in the LINZ survey and shopping for pleasure had the second highest out-of-home participation rate in the NRPS. Shopping as leisure is a topic which has received only limited attention in the leisure research literature (Jansen-Verbeke, 1987; DEHCD, 1978; Aronowitz, 1980: p. 10).

The future

A number of issues arise in relation to the future of large-scale leisure surveys. Firstly, while ongoing improvements in methodology are to be desired, the value of the surveys will increase markedly the longer the time series of comparable data which can be established. Secondly, while we believe that such surveys are here to stay "they nevertheless have continually to prove their worth to governments and their agencies. One way of enhancing their worth is to increase their use, by government at all levels and by academics, Participation survey data have often been under-analysed and under-utilised" (O'Leary, 1987), but modern computing technology makes secondary analysis of large data bases easier than in the past. Thirdly, efforts could be made to increase the international comparability of the survey data. To this end a project under the auspices of the World Leisure and Recreation Association Research Commission is aiming to establish the first step in such a process by bringing together the findings from surveys undertaken in a number of countries into a single publication, to be produced in 1994/95 (Cushman, Veal and Zuzanek, forthcoming).

Note: The UK General Household Survey is conducted annually, but leisure questions are not included every year.

References

Aronowitz, S. (1980) On *the theorisation of leisure* Vol. 4. University of Birmingham: CURS, pp. 3-10.

Bittman, M., (1991) *Juggling time: How Australian families use time.* Canberra: Office of the Status of Women, AGPS.

British Travel Association (1968) *Pilot National Recreation Survey*. Keele, Staffs: BTA/University of Keele.

Brown, J. (1985) *Towards the development of a Commonwealth policy on recreation*. Canberra: AGPS.

Chase, D. R. and Godbey, G. C. (1983) 'The accuracy of self-reported participation rates', *Leisure Studies*, Vol. 2, No. 2: pp. 231-236.

Cities Commission (1975) *Australians' use of time*. Melbourne: Cities Commission.

Cushman, G., and Laidler, A. *et al.* (1991) *Life in New Zealand Commission Report, Vol. IV: Leisure*. Dunedin: University of Otago.

Cushman, G., Veal, A. J., and Zuzanek, J. (eds) (forthcoming 1996) *Leisure participation in the global village*. Oxford: CAB International.

DASSETT (Department of Arts, Sport, the Environment, Tourism and Territories) (1971) *Recreation participation survey*. Canberra: DASSETT.

DEHCD (Department of Environment, Housing and Community Development) (1978) *The shopping cnetre as a community leisure resource*. Canberra: AGPS.

Department of Statistics (1984) *Report on the Social Indicators Survey: 1980-1981*. Wellington: Dept. of Statistics.

Gershuny, J. and Jones, S. (1993) 'The changing work/leisure balance in Britain 1961-1984', in J. Horne *et al.* (eds) *Sport, leisure and social relations*. Keele, Staffs: *The Sociological Review*, pp. 9-50.

Hamilton-Smith, E. and Robertson, R. W (1977) 'Recreation and government in Australia', in D. Mercer (ed) *Leisure and recreation in Australia*. Malvern, Vic.: Sorrett, pp. 175-186.

Henderson, K. (1991) *Dimensions of choice: A qualitative approach to recreation, parks and leisure research*. State College, PA: Venture.

Jansen-Verbeke, M. (1987) 'Women, shopping and leisure', *Leisure Studies* Vol. 6, No. 1: pp. 71-86.

Kelly, J. (1990) 'Leisure and common life in New Zealand'. Paper presented to the Life in New Zealand Survey data release conference, Wellington, August, 1990.

Laidler, A. and G. Cushman (1991) 'Life and leisure in Now Zealand'. Paper presented to the WLRA World Congress on Leisure and Tourism: Social and Environmental Change, Sydney, July, 1991.

——— (1993) 'Leisure participation in New Zealand', in H. C. Perkins and G. Cushman (eds) *Leisure, recreation and tourism*. Auckland: Longman Paul, pp. 1-14.

McKay, J. (1990) 'Sport, leisure and social inequality', in D. Rowe and G. Lawrence (eds) *Sport and leisure lrends in popular culture.* Sydney: Harcourt, Brace Jovanovich, pp. 125-160.

Mercer, D. (1977) 'The factors affecting recreation demand', in D. Mercer (ed) *Leisure and recreation in Australia.* Malvern, Vic.: Sorrett, pp. 59-68.

Office of Population Censuses and Surveys (Annual) *General Household Survey.* London: HMSO.

O'Leary, J. J., Maguire, F. A. and Dottarrio, F. D. (1987) 'Using National Survey data in developing recreation policy and planning options', *Policy Studies Review*, Vol. 7, No. 2: pp. 370-376.

Outdoor Recreation Resources Review Commission (1962) *Outdoor recreation for America.* Washington, DC.: ORRRC.

Parker, S. and Paddick, R. (1996) *Leisure in Australia.* Melbourne: Longman Cheshire.

Perkins, H. and Gidlow, R. (1991) 'Leisure research in New Zealand: patterns, problems and prospects', *Leisure Studies*, Vol. 10, No. 2, pp. 93-104.

Robb, M. and Howorth, H. (1977) *New Zealand Recreation Survey: Preliminary Report.* Wellington: wZealand Council for Recreation and Sport.

Roberts, K. (1970) *Leisure.* London: Longman.

——— (1978) *Contemporary society and growth of leisure.* London: Longman.

Rojek, C. (1989) Leisure and recreation theory', in E. L. Jackson and T. L. Burton (eds) *Understanding leisure and recreation.* State College, PA: Venture, pp. 69-88.

Scott, D. and Godbey, G. (1991) 'Reorienting leisure research: The case for qualitative methods', *Society and Leisure*, Vol. 13: pp. 189-205.

Sillitoe, K. (1969) *Planning for leisure.* London: HMSO.

Tait, D. (1984) *New Zealand Recreation Survey: 1974-75.* Wellington: N. Z. Council for Recreation and Sport.

Veal, A. J. (1993) 'Leisure participation in Australia 1985-91 — a note on the data', *Australian Journal of Leisure and Recreation*, Vol. 3, No. 1: pp. 37-43.

Wilson, N., Russell, D. and Paulin, J. (1990) *Life in New Zealand: Summary Report.* Wellington: Hillary Commission.

Other recent LSA volumes in Leisure Studies

For further information on Leisure Studies Association Membership, Conferences, Newsletter and Publications prices contact Leisure Studies Association (attn. M. McFee) Chelsea School, University of Brighton, Eastbourne BN20 7SP, UK

FAX: (0323) 644641
e-mail: 100722.2234@Compuserve.COM